INSIDE
100
GREAT CARS

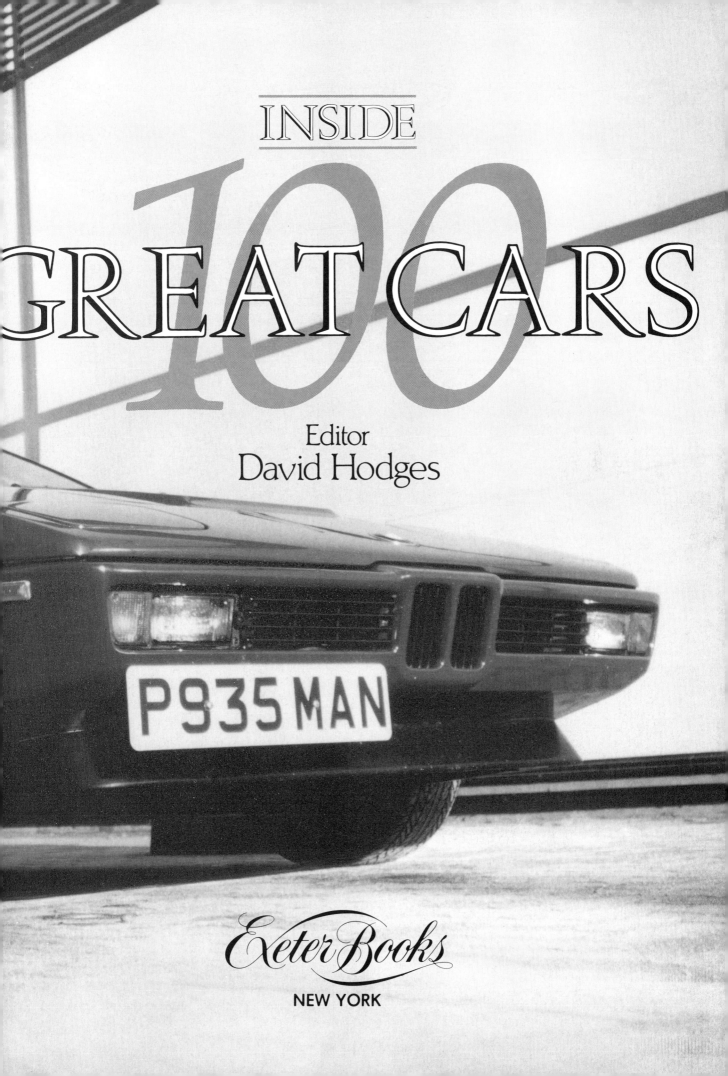

INSIDE

100 GREAT CARS

Editor
David Hodges

Exeter Books

NEW YORK

Contents

House Editor: Joey Chapter
Art Editor: Gordon Robertson
Production: Craig Chubb

Original partwork 'The Car' © Orbis Publishing
Limited 1984/1985
This edition: 1988 © Marshall Cavendish Limited

First published in USA by Exeter Books
Distributed by Bookthrift
Exeter is a trademark of Bookthrift Marketing, Inc.
Bookthrift is a registered trademark of
Bookthrift Marketing, Inc.
New York, New York

ISBN 0-671-08911-0

Printed in Spain

TITLE-PAGE the Giugiaro-designed BMW M1
BELOW the Prince Bira of Siam Delahaye 135 which was given the spurious title of 'Fastest Road Car in Britain'

Introduction

Admiration of outstanding cars is as old as the enlightened acceptance of the car itself – since the last years of the 19th century people have flocked to motor shows to admire cars they will almost certainly never own.

As a means of transport modern cars are more efficient in all respects than their counterparts of, say, half a century ago, but there are no more cars built today that a future generation will regard as 'great' than there were in any decade since the Edwardian period. In large part, this premiss defines the content of this book – a hundred great, or admirable, cars described in historical and technical detail and laid bare through an art form that is younger than the automobile, the cutaway drawing.

The cars illustrated run from the AC Cobra to the VW Beetle, and between those alphabetical and functional extremes there is a wide variety. Rarity as such of size, high cost or high performance has not been the main criterion: in any cross-section utility cannot be ignored and on that score the Ford Model T and the VW Beetle must be at the top of any list, for between them they account for around 38 million vehicles. That figure says more than the software in a statistics bank about the spread of motoring in the 20th century.

Be that as it may, high performance, particularly when it is hand in hand with efficiency, figures prominently in the selection. High cost does figure, but only when it relates to a car that is outstanding, because of originality in design or craftsmanship in building, comfort or the manner of its going. In that context, it may surprise some that so many genuinely high-class luxury cars were produced in the unhappy Depression period of the 1930s. Size, lavishness or vulgarity have not been taken into account, nor are 'replicars' included, however much traitorous thoughts that some of these are functionally better machines than the originals they attempt to duplicate might fight to the surface!

Modern racing cars have quite deliberately been excluded, although there are representative sports-racing cars. The racing cars of the 1920s and 1930s – the Bugatti T35 and the Alfa Romeo P3 are examples – were very closely related to the road machines of those generations, while the sports Lago Talbots of the late 1930s gave rise to a racing car. But broadly since the mid 1930s, racing cars, especially Grand Prix racing cars, have been highly specialized machines and are therefore outside the scope of this book.

All the cars included are classics, and most of them would feature in any enthusiast's top hundred choice. A book of another hundred could perhaps be compiled – after all, automobile tastes must be almost as wide-ranging as the models the industry has introduced – but it would lack the handful universally recognized as all-time greats, for they are here already. And it would certainly not include the cutaway drawings showing each car in such detail, which give this book a value beyond many hundreds of pages of conventional description.

BELOW The Mustang was America's first muscle car, and sales grew as rapidly as the options list and power output

AC Cobra

This was one of the great muscular sports cars, the outcome of a highly successful Anglo-American liaison in the early 1960s which seemed to have outlived its time by the end of that decade. Yet the appeal of the car was so strong that almost twenty years later nine 'replicars' were offered by British constructors, and one of these was approved as an extension of the original Cobra line.

AC had launched the Ace in 1954, with a tubular chassis designed by John Tojeiro, and using the company's venerable six-cylinder engine designed by John Weller in the early 1920s. In 1961 Carroll Shelby saw the chassis as an ideal basis for his sports car concept, and this was to go ahead.

The only modifications needed were moving the steering box, to make room for the broader V8, and the rear differential mounting to suit a Salisbury 4HA final drive and because Shelby wanted inboard rear disc brakes (all subsequent Cobras had conventional outboard, wheel-mounted, rear disc brakes). The Ace's front discs were retained. The original rearward position of the Ace engine was useful in preventing the extra mass of the 'substitute' V8 spoiling the balance too much.

Those early Cobras had 260 bhp under the driver's foot, and tuning up to 330 bhp was available, but in 1963 Ford's better-known 289 V8 was substituted. This gave around 11 extra bhp, with a useful increase in torque, and made the Cobra a 135 mph (220 kph) car, noisy and heavy to drive, but just what some enthusiasts wanted. Confusingly, the car was marketed as an AC in some countries, but as a Ford or a Shelby in the USA.

AC improved 'their' part of the car in 1962, notably with stronger front suspension and rack and pinion steering. This Mk II Cobra was originally built with the 4.7-litre V8, although the engine options list meant that engine capacity varied. All Mk II Cobras had left-hand drive, as did a handful of subsequent examples.

The final production redesign of the Cobra was the Mk III, which began to emerge in January 1965 from Thames Ditton and Shelby's shop in Venice, California (where most drive units were fitted). Here was the most brutal of all Cobras, powered by the Ford 6997 cc (427 cu in) or the less powerful but cheaper 7013 cc (428 cu in) V8s. The Mk III had the most significantly altered chassis, while the faithful transverse leaf springs which had acted as top suspension links were replaced with coil springs and full unequal-length double wishbones.

Cobras were raced in open and coupé forms, most successfully to win the 1965 GT championship in the name of Ford. Then Ford concentrated on the GT40 and its successors. AC built 80 Frua-styled, fixed-head coupés on a long wheelbase chassis, naming these AC 428 as Ford owned the Cobra name and had by then applied it to a badge-engineered Mustang.

Alfa Romeo 8C

The world was in the throes of the Depression in 1931, and many sports car manufacturers were having to retrench while some, like Bentley, were forced out of business. Yet that year Alfa Romeo launched the 8C 2300, apparently from a position of some strength as part of the combine that had existed since Nicola Romeo took over Alfa in 1915 and renamed the company Alfa Romeo.

Vittorio Jano had been brought in to design successors to the Merosi models of the early 1920s, brilliantly with the P2 Grand Prix car in 1924 and with straight-six sports cars. By the end of the decade another range was needed to complement these, and Jano came up with another winner, the 8C 2300 (eight cylinders, 2.3 litres).

The engine was the outstanding feature of this car, for it was a straight eight made up of two separate light-alloy cylinder blocks. Between the blocks, a train of gears drove the camshafts, supercharger, dynamo, and oil and water pumps. There was a single Roots-type supercharger.

The cars were used for several purposes – as road sports cars, competitions sports cars, and as Grand Prix cars – and had different power ratings. For the standard cars, 142 bhp at 5000 rpm was quoted, Le Mans models had 155 bhp (at 5200 rpm) engines, Spyder Corsa, Mille Miglia and early Monza GP cars had 165 bhp units, the 1933 Monza engine was rated at 178 bhp, and the 1934 Le Mans cars had 180 bhp engines.

In production terms the cars were sensible, with many parts carried over from the 6C models (which continued in production alongside the eights).

There were two chassis lengths, the 310 cm (122 in) Le Mans type taking drophead coupé or four-seater bodywork, the 274 cm (108 in) Mille Miglia type generally having two-seater spyder bodywork. The standard four-seaters were just capable of 100 mph (161 kph), the short-chassis cars had a top speed of 108 mph (174 kph), while the early Le Mans competition cars could eventually reach 130 mph (210 kph). By the standards of the day, they had a reputation for being light cars to drive, albeit with heavy steering at low speeds.

These sports cars had a remarkable racing record, with successive outright victories at Le Mans and in the Mille Miglia, and they are remarkable today for the sheer functional simplicity and elegance of their lines. The 8C 2300 models continued in production until 1934, when their immediate replacement was a milder 6C 2300 series.

Alfa Romeo P3

Alfa Romeo built many competition cars between the two world wars, and in each of the decades produced a classic Grand Prix car, the P2 in the 1920s

and the P3 in the 1930s, both designed by Vittorio Jano. The P2 was born out of despair, as the P1 was uncompetitive and involved in a fatal accident, so was never raced, while the P3's career ended with the Italians in despair, overwhelmed by a new generation of German Grand Prix cars. Both Alfas had supercharged overhead-camshaft straight-eight engines, neither was so totally specialized that it could not be used on the road – indeed, the P2's last races were sports car events, and an odd adapted P3 was also run as a sports car.

The P2 set new standards in Grand Prix racing in 1924-25, then became redundant as the regulations were changed, although it lived on in *formule libre* events in Italy.

For the early 1930s, Jano produced the dual-purpose sports and Grand Prix 2.3-litre Tipo 8C in 1931. This was particularly successful in sports car guise, winning four Le Mans 24-hour Races, from 1931-34. A version with higher supercharger boost followed, and this was to be named Monza after its first Grand Prix victory at that circuit, in May 1931.

However, the Monza was by no means unbeatable; Maserati and even Bugatti were able to challenge it, so Jano was given the go-ahead to design the new Grand Prix car. This emerged in 1932 as the Tipo B2600, which became unofficially known as the P3, and as the *Monoposto,* for it was the first true single-seat Grand Prix car.

The red cars provided an image of the Grand Prix car that outlasted their front-line life, for they were functional and purposeful from classic radiator to neatly-tapered tail, with a wide track and large wire wheels carrying large brakes in polished aluminium drums. The straight eight was in two blocks of four cylinders, with a central drive for the camshafts and the twin Roots-type superchargers, and it produced its initial 215 bhp without undue stress. It drove through a four-speed gearbox, immediately behind which was a differential and the unconventional bifurcated drive, with two angled propellor shafts to the rear wheels (the driver's seat was not dropped between them, so Jano did not introduce them to save height).

The car was a winner in 1932, but was set aside as Alfa Romeo was restructured in 1933, until Enzo Ferrari persuaded the management to release them. With Scuderia Ferrari, the P3s immediately started winning again, and they won in 1934 – until the new German GP teams got into their stride and put an end to the P3's supremacy.

The P3s were uprated with 2905 cc (177 cu in) 255 bhp engines and three-speed gearboxes, then in 1935 with 3165 cc (193 cu in) 265 bhp engines, Dubonnet independent front suspension and hydraulic brakes. There was one last glorious victory, when Nuvolari humbled the Germans in their home Grand Prix, as a climax to the outstanding racing career of Jano's Alfa Romeos.

Alfa Romeo 2900

The sales figures for the brilliant Alfa Romeo 8Cs of the first half of the 1930s were disastrous, and had the company's fate been determined by economic factors alone it would have gone to the wall. But in Mussolini's Italy a healthy industry had high priority, and so did prestige, so the Government agency set up to rescue lame-duck companies, IRI, kept Alfa afloat. Although priorities were changed to concentrate on aero engines, some effort was spared to develop prestige cars for the late 1930s.

The result was the most brilliant of Alfa Romeos – fast and sleek thoroughbreds which embodied all the company stood for in the world of performance cars. Only a handful were built, and in competitions their performance was matched, or eclipsed, by some less ambitious cars, in part because times were changing.

As a basis, Jano took the chassis of the 8C 35 racing car and its independent front suspension, and for a power unit looked to the proven straight eight he had used in the P3 Grand Prix cars. This was mildly detuned, and in its 2905 cc (177 cu in) form it delivered a useful 220 bhp at 5300 rpm.

It drove through a normal single propellor shaft – Jano did not repeat his angled twin shafts idea from the P3 – with a straightforward differential and half shafts arrangement. The car's dimensions were exactly the same as the GP single-seater, and in the two-seater the driver was on the right, as was customary for competition sports cars (and, indeed, for high-quality cars of the period). In this form, the 2900 was capable of 140 mph (225 kph).

The other priority, building cars that would enhance Italian prestige, was first met as Alfa Romeo built five 2900As, with sweeping sports bodywork fitted in the company's coachworks. In 1937 a longer series of 2900Bs was introduced, in two forms: the Corto (short wheelbase) version and the more spacious Lungo. The engine was detuned again for the production car and power dropped to 180 bhp at 5200 rpm. This reduced the top speed to 115 mph

(185 kph), still highly creditable for a road-going sports car of the 1930s. The Lungo version had a chassis which was 20 cm (8 in) longer and weighed another 100 kg (220 lb) in road trim, but thanks to Jano's magnificent engine and the twin blowers dating back to the P3, it could still manage a top speed of almost 110 mph (177 kph) and carry a variety of sumptuously styled bodies.

The 2900 was born at the wrong time, and made for the wrong reasons – but it summed up the unmatchable Alfa blend of performance and style, perhaps better than any other car they ever made.

Alfa Romeo Giulietta and GTV

This family of stylish coupés was very important to Alfa Romeo from the mid-1950s through to the mid-1970s, and that long life was one testimony to the strength of the original design. The first Giulietta coupé was introduced in 1954, but built in very limited numbers, and the range made its true debut at the 1955 Turin Motor Show.

These were small cars, designed to serve as popular saloons but with versatility built in so that they could be a basis for elegant coupés and even competition cars. The Giulietta's heart was a twin-cam engine, slightly undersquare (74 mm × 75 mm/ 2.9 in × 2.95 in) with a significant contribution to its 80 bhp rating made by the top-end design, which featured two chain-driven overhead camshafts operating two valves per cylinder and hemispherical combustion chambers.

The suspension was strong and simple, with double wishbones and coil springs at the front and a live rear axle, located very securely. The standard saloon bodies may have appeared dull, but the coupé styled by Bertone was a light, compact and graceful two-door 2+2.

Bertone improved on it dramatically in 1957 with

the lower and flamboyant Giulietta Sprint Speciale. Its looks were reflected in its aerodynamic qualities, and on 100 bhp it could achieve 125 mph (200 kph). It was not built in large numbers, but lived on until 1965 as the Giulia SS with the 1570 cc (96 cu in) engine of the later cars.

Constantly changing Alfa line-ups could be confusing, and in that tradition the first Giulia coupés used the old Giulietta body. The Giulia Sprint with Bertone's definitive coupé body came in 1963, and was to last through to the 1970s.

By 1962 the twin-cam had been enlarged to a displacement of 1570 cc/96 cu in to give 92 bhp, then soon to give 106 bhp at 6000 rpm for the Sprint. The suspension was developed in parallel, and in particular the weight of the live rear axle was reduced as an alloy differential casing was used.

The Giulia Sprint became the Sprint Veloce, or GTV, in 1966 with the free-revving and flexible engine slightly uprated, to 109 bhp. In the mid 1960s changed race regulations spelled the end for specialized racers like Alfa's TZ (*Tubolare Zagato*), while the racing career of the coupé really took off. The weight problem was largely overcome as an alloy body was created for the standard floorpan; in the designation GTA, A stood for *allegerito* (lightened), and to meet homologation requirements, 500 GTAs were built for sale.

With the GTA, Alfa Romeo took the European Touring Car Championship 1966-68. The approach was widened as the GTA Junior appeared with a fuel-injected short-stroke 1270 cc (78 cu in) engine, and there was even a twin-supercharged GTAS. The next derivative was the 1750 GTAm, and that won the ETC title in 1970-71.

The 1750 GTV came in 1967, with a 1779 cc (109 cu in) engine, but this was not a sales success and so Alfa stretched the twin-cam for the last time, to 1962 cc (120 cu in) for the 2000 GTV in 1971. That ran through to 1976, and the end of a classic line.

Alpine A110

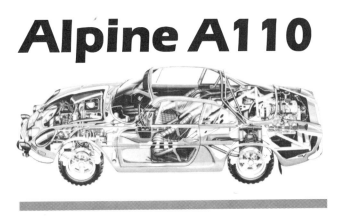

There were few more stirring sights in the rallies in the late 1960s and early 1970s than that of a works Alpine A110 in full cry. The little blue cars looked fast, and were fast, and they were tough enough to come

first in major rallies in all the international series.

For years these Alpines were France's nearest approach to true production sports cars, for at the end of the 1960s annual A110 production was into four figures, and the car was licence-built in small numbers in Brazil, Mexico, Spain and even Bulgaria. Yet it had been virtually ignored for years while Alpine founder and managing director Jean Rédélé concentrated on racing cars, and it became established at a time when its mechanical make-up – rear engine, simple suspension and maximum use of standard parts – was already outmoded.

Rédélé's first complete independent design was the A108, with distinctive bodywork designed by Marcel Hubert that was carried on a steel-tube frame. It did not become a serious proposition until Rédélé designed a replacement chassis in the form of a steel platform with a central backbone. With more powerful engines came the 1963 change of designation, to A110. Most of the components, such as suspension, were Renault production items, and the rather flimsy bodywork at least kept out most of the weather!

The engine was mounted aft of the transaxle, and in line, which meant that there were few problems in installing alternative units (good traction and braking balance, as well as the clean nose lines made possible, were felt to outweigh problems brought on by the rearward weight bias). At the end of the 1960s the then-new Renault 16 unit was brought into use.

In the early 1970s Alpine had a range of 1300 and 1600 models under the general name Berlinette. These ranged from the base 85 Tour de France, through the 1300G and 1300S (a competitions model) to the 1600 and 1600S. This had a 138 bhp engine, and was used by the works rally team, which was supported by Renault. In 1971 Alpine won the International Rally Championship with these cars, in large part due to Ove Andersson's victories.

Into the 1970s the A100 1600 was increasingly outclassed by its more powerful rivals; to combat this the Renault engine's capacity was taken to 1796 cc (110 cu in), and in 1973 the works cars had 170 bhp engines. As the production 1600's weight was only 635 kg (1400 lb) that gave a formidable power/weight ratio.

The final attempt to keep the Alpine a front-runner came with the 1974 Berlinette A110 Prototype. The 1.8-litre engine was retained, but with Lucas fuel injection the power output was increased to 187 bhp, at 7200 rpm. This was the only A110 to have double wishbone rear suspension, with the drive shafts playing no part in wheel location. Its body was substantially modified, with wide wheel arches and spoilers front and rear. But it lost its competitive edge to cars like the Lancia Stratos, after serving Renault well.

Amilcar

These pretty little sports cars typify a breed familiar in the 1920s and 1930s, expressing a small sports car theme that was to flourish in England, and with a competitions background that was so important in the 1920s.

The origins of Amilcar are to be found in another small French company, Le Zèbre, whose designer, Jules Salomon, left to join Citroën. Two Le Zèbre engineers, Edmond Moyet and André Morel, then found backing for a small sports car project in the erstwhile owners of Le Zèbre, Fernand Lamy and Emile Akar. They arranged finance for a company that was eventually named Amilcar in an anagram of Lamy and Akar.

The first little car had a version of a Salomon-designed side valve engine, and Morel drove one to win the first Bol d'Or 24-hour Race, beating two Salmsons and initiating a rivalry that was to last through the 1920s. There was no real development potential in the first 904 cc (55 cu in) Amilcar engine, and the backers agreed that a 'proper' engine with racing potential should be laid down.

The new engine was inspired by contemporary racing units and had a basic layout very similar to the 1923/4 Sunbeam engine. Bore and stroke ratio was almost identical, 55 mm × 77 mm (2.2 in × 3 in) for the Amilcar and 67 mm × 94 mm (2.6 in × 3.7 in) on the Sunbeam. The twin overhead camshafts were gear-driven from the rear of the crankshaft. Amilcar chose to develop their own Roots-type supercharger, trying many configurations. Eventually 75 bhp was claimed for the normal unit, 83 bhp for the super-charged version.

Whatever the origins of the engine, the chassis was pure Amilcar, with an undertray contributing the stiffness, and generally neat (if not too well finished) 'one-and-a-half seat' bodywork was fitted.

Once teething problems were sorted out Morel

gave the car, designated Type CO, its competition debut in a hill climb, and early in 1926 a pair was raced to a first-time victory at Miramas. In the following year a true single-seater (Type MCO – 'M' for monoplace) was tried, but the Amilcar management was more interested in running cars at Le Mans, and that called for a production run of 50.

For this the Type C6 was laid down on the same general lines as the CO, with a modified version of the engine for which 62 bhp at 5000 rpm was claimed, enough to give a top speed of 105 mph (169 kph) on a typical rear axle ratio of 4.5:1.

As the world moved into recession, works participation ended, and as Lamy and Akar wanted their money back a new company was incorporated as the Société Anonyme Français d'Automobiles.

Aston Martin DB2

Aston Martin's survival in the immediate post-war period was by no means certain, and it was to depend heavily on David Brown. He also bought Lagonda, planned to operate the two as the sporting and luxury marques of his car-building operation and moved both companies into adjacent premises at Feltham. By then it must have been obvious that the classic 2.6-litre twin-cam engine designed by W.O. Bentley for post-war Lagondas would make a much better sports car engine than Aston's Claude Hill-designed pushrod ohv 'six'.

The Aston Martin that was to be retrospectively dubbed DB1 was half-heartedly advanced towards production. Two cars had the 2.6-litre straight six, in a shortened chassis with striking body lines by Frank Feeley. One of these was the direct forerunner of the production DB2.

It was conventional, with a chassis welded up from square-section tubes of various sizes, deriving much of its stiffness from its high ladder-frame sill sections. Claude Hill's trailing-arm ifs was used, and the live rear axle, coil sprung and located by trailing arms and a Panhard, was also a well-tried feature from earlier Astons. The body styling was individual, and would now be described as fastback.

Bentley's engine was straightforward, notable for its smoothness and in modern terms had an unremarkable power output of 105 bhp – but that was on the very low-octane fuel of that time.

The DB2 was a success, even though in roughly three years of production (mid-1950 to mid-1953) only just over 400 were made, of which 50 were the rare drophead version. Three cars a week was a start, but to appeal to a wider audience the car was upgraded to an 'occasional' four-seater.

This was achieved by adding 17.8 cm (7 in) to the overall length, with one of the earliest hatchback arrangements. The longer tail also gave a near-perfect weight distribution. By the time this DB2-4 reached production premium-grade fuel was once more available, and with an 8.2:1 compression ratio power output was increased to 125 bhp at 5000 rpm – just about enough to offset the extra weight of the car and give a maximum speed of 111 mph (179 kph), adequate for a car of this class.

Inside a year the engine capacity was pushed up to 2922 cc (178 cu in), and power output to 140 bhp. With this engine the car was slightly restyled as the Mark II in 1955. Two years later the Mark III (which quickly and misleadingly became known as the DB Mark III) appeared with a restyled body and mechanical improvements which included a reworked engine, the standard (DBA) engine rated at 162 bhp and versions giving up to 195 bhp available, and front disc brakes.

However successful the Mark III, its days were numbered once the DB4 had been launched in 1958. In 1959 production came to an end.

Aston Martin DB3S

The Aston Martin company which David Brown took over in 1947 had a tradition of racing, and although the evidence that this 'improved the line' or helped

sell production cars was sometimes flimsy, the policy was pursued through the 1950s to an eventual triumphant conclusion in 1959, when after ten years of frustration an Aston Martin finally won at Le Mans, and the team won the world sports car championship.

As the Le Mans 24-hour Race was revived in 1949, Aston Martin entered three cars, two with 2-litre four-cylinder engines and one with the 2.6-litre straight six designed by W. O. Bentley, originally for Lagonda. Only one of the trio finished, in eighth place, but then the 2.6-litre car was third in the Spa 24-hour race in Belgium. Further encouragement came in 1950 as the coupés were well placed in major races in France, Italy and Britain, as a prelude to the introduction of the production DB2.

Their competitions successor was the open DB3. This was designed by Eberan von Eberhorst, best known for his late-1930s Grand Prix Auto Unions, around a new tubular frame, with torsion bar springing, a De Dion rear axle and a 140 bhp version of the straight six. Its lines were chunky, reflecting an ugly 'portcullis' radiator grille, and it proved to be overweight. Its race debut in the 1951 TT was promising, as it was second before retiring, but although it went on to win the Goodwood Nine Hours it was not a front-rank contender.

A refined version developed by Willie Watson was shorter, lower and lighter, with a modified chassis, a 2.9-litre version of the engine with an initial output of 160 bhp, a needle-roller bearing four-speed gearbox and an improved rear end. Its body, designed by Frank Feeley, was more attractive and more efficient. But the team cars were completed only just in time for the Le Mans race, and that meant that they went to it under-developed. The first successes came in the summer of 1953 in secondary British events, before late-season victories in the Goodwood Nine Hours and in the TT, when Peter Collins and Pat Griffith scored Aston's first win in a world sports car championship race.

In 1954 lack of development and a relative lack of power compared with rival cars let the DB3S down – the reputation for good handling was maintained, and disc brakes helped, but the essential speed was just not there. A coupé version looked handsome, but was no more effective.

For 1955 there was more power, and Peter Collins and Paul Frère placed a DB3S second at Le Mans, while there were outright wins in lesser races. Until the DBR1 was ready, the DB3S had to serve the team in 1956, when Collins again drove one into second place at Le Mans, this time sharing it with Stirling Moss.

The DB3S was still used as the team's second string car in 1957, when the emphasis shifted to the DBR1. In 1959 there was a 1-2 at Le Mans for the DBR1/300, as the jewel in Aston Martin's crown in the year the company was sports car champion.

Aston Martin DB4, DB5 and DB6

When the DB4 was announced in 1958 it appeared to be the finest British interpretation of the GT theme, and although it was to be plagued by unreliability in its early period it sold well and paved the way for the more successful DB5 and DB6.

In 1950 John Wyer and design-draughtsman Harold Beach started work on Project 114, which was to become the DB2 series replacement designated DB4. It took shape with a perimeter chassis frame, a sophisticated de Dion rear axle and a wishbone and coil spring front suspension in place of the DB2 trailing arm system. A 3-litre version of the twin-cam six was used, and Frank Feeley designed a body which carried through the DB2 lines.

Significant changes were made in 1956, when the purpose-designed Aston Martin twin-ohc straight six, then rated at 240 bhp, took the place of the Lagonda unit. Wyer also decided that a body should be styled by Touring in Milan, and their Superleggera construction called for a platform chassis. Beach designed one in six weeks flat in the summer of 1957!

More powerful variations on the DB4 theme soon appeared with the 260 bhp Vantage, then in 1969 a GT with lighter bodywork and 302 bhp, which made it a 150 mph (240 kph) car, and ultimately the Zagato, with a 314 bhp engine, which enjoyed some success in GT racing.

The DB5 which came in 1963 had a 3995 cc (244 cu in) 282 bhp version of the engine, a marginally better top speed and much better acceleration. Gearbox problems were resolved by replacing the David Brown unit with a five-speed ZF box. A drophead coupé was listed under the name Volante, and a steel hardtop was available; Harold Radford built 12 examples with an estate car body, and

although there was not a GT vesion as such, the Vantage 314 bhp engine was an option.

The DB6 of 1966 was in effect a response to demands for improved rear seat accommodation, and it had a longer wheelbase. A distinctive tail spoiler reflected the works team's experience of serious front end lift problems, and although the car was mechanically almost identical to the DB5, its superior aerodynamics made it 6 mph (8.6 kph) faster, with top speed close to 150 mph (240 kph).

In the Mk II of 1969 the Superleggera type of construction was abandoned, and arches flared to house larger wheels and tyres made the car look even more purposeful. From 1968 the DBS was produced alongside the DB6, succeeding it as DB6 production ended in 1970. By that time 1575 had been built (1330 Mk I, 245 Mk II) making the DB6 the most successful Aston Martin to that time.

Aston Martin V8

In the 'supercar' era Aston Martin was in danger of losing its pre-eminent position as a builder of high-performance cars, as Italian manufacturers offered increasingly powerful engines, so that for all its virtues the Aston Martin twin-ohc 3.7-litre six-cylinder unit began to look weak.

The designer of that engine, Tadek Marek, looked to a V8 as its successor, initially intending to use as much of the straight six as possible. But problems arose, both minor (the vee angle would have to be narrowed to 64 degrees to avoid the inlet cam covers sticking up too far) and major – high stresses and overheating encountered in an engine run at Le Mans had distorted the block.

Delays while urgent remedial work was put in hand meant that the DBS was introduced in an under-powered form with the old engine. The V8 was finally ready for production in 1969; the DBS V8 was launched that September, and was distinguishable by the 'power bulge' which was needed in order to clear the V8 cam covers.

The cars were renamed Aston Martin V8, or just AM V8, for marketing reasons in 1972. Meanwhile, the company had been hit by the collapse of its American market, and David Brown relinquished control. In 1975 Aston Martin actually ceased trading, and the rescue by Alan Curtis and his American partners came almost too late, for Rolls-Royce had recruited many of the company's skilled panel beaters. Curtis directed energy into three avenues with the V8 range: to recoup 'lost' engine performance, to create a genuine high-performance model (the Vantage), and to develop a convertible.

The Vantage and the Volante came in 1977, the former with a 360 bhp engine, the latter after some problems with scuttle shake had been overcome. The engine was reworked again for 1980, with a gain of around 10 per cent in the standard unit. Then in 1986 came a return to fuel injection, when Aston Martin announced a power output of 305 bhp in standard form (much more was to come for the limited-production Zagato model).

Two other changes ensured continuity. In 1981 the Curtis-led consortium sold out to another headed by Victor Gauntlett, and then late in 1987 Ford took over. By then the V8s were ageing supercars, but still with the appeal of exclusivity.

Auburn Speedster

The Speedsters were visually impressive, uniquely American cars, and the Auburn 851 Speedster of 1935 is a particularly fine tribute to its stylist Gordon Buehrig, who might otherwise be known only for the revolutionary Cord 810.

In 1924 Auburn output was down to six cars a day; Errett Lobban Cord, a master car salesman, took over the lacklustre company, and brought in James Crawford to design a new range.

The first Auburn eight was launched in 1925, and renamed the 8-88 in 1926 with a 4.8-litre

side-valve 68 bhp Lycoming engine. That remained in use until 1930, when it developed 115 bhp, hence the Speedster 115 model name.

The rest of the car was straightforward. Suspension was by semi-elliptic springs all round, and after experiments with hydraulic brakes Auburn opted for mechanical brakes. The three-speed gearbox was in unit with the engine. The impressive open two-seater body styled by Count Alexis de Sakhnoffsky featured a boat-tail and a vee screen.

The 115 became the 125 in 1930, with a Cabin Speedster among the models, advertised as a 'racing car with the comfort of a closed car', with a 125 bhp vesion of the Lycoming eight giving it a claimed top speed of over 100 mph (161 kph).

A V12 range, using a 6.4-litre (390 cu in) engine designed by George Kublin and built by Lycoming, was a failure, and 1934 marked its demise. Yet Auburn was to enjoy a memorable final fling with the 851 Speedster. This was introduced in 1931 with masterly bodywork by Gordon Buehrig that was ingeniously and cheaply built. The car was simple enough. The alloy flat-head eight was strong and reliable and it was not stressed too much. Those sweeping lines concealed some interesting technical features such as the Columbia dual-ratio rear axle. That was achieved by interposing an epicyclic gear train between the axle and the crown wheel. When it was engaged the final drive ratio became a 'fast' 4.5:1. It was disengaged by moving a steering-wheel mounted lever and dipping the clutch, whereupon the ratio became a more leisurely 3:1. The three-speed synchromesh gearbox along with that dual-ratio axle gave a six-speed transmission.

In 1936 came the 852, identical to the earlier models with the exception of the 852 on its radiator grille! The end, however, was not far off and Auburn ceased car production in 1937.

Audi quattro

Audi revealed their high-performance four-wheel drive coupé at the Geneva Show in 1980, a new design clothed in two-door bodywork that would be the basis for a multiple winner of the World Rally

Championship during the 1980s, and would contribute to Audi becoming the most prolific builder of permanent four-wheel drive saloons in the world.

Audi technicians used existing parts and experience with military vehicles to short-cut development as they reintroduced four-wheel drive to utilize fully the output of turbo engines, and package speed and safety in a practical car.

In the 1970s Audi began to blossom under VW ownership, and some of the elements of the quattro started to appear. The 80, for example, provided the floorpan, which was used in stretched form, and the engine was a version of the unique in-line five-cylinder unit from the 100 and 200. Other key items in the transmission and suspension were production components from the military Iltis.

Hans Nedvidek's team was given the task of designing the transmission. They decided on a straight 50/50 split, achieved with bevel gearing, but the cleverest feature was to incorporate a hollow shaft within the largely standard Audi 100/200 five-speed gearbox.

Within a length of just over 25 cm (10 in), this shaft within a shaft fed power from the central differential to the forward diff. Power to the rear was taken simply by a propshaft from the rear of the gearbox. The standard front-drive layout, a simple longitudinal one, made the conversion comparatively easy once the team had come up with the hollow transmission idea for the lower gearbox shaft.

Deliveries of the first quattro commenced in September 1980. The quattro is assured of a place in motoring history for its sporting successes, and above all as the car that influenced a wave of similar high-performance cars all over the world.

Austin Seven

Sir Herbert Austin gambled when he backed the Seven, personally financing the venture in the face of opposition from his fellow directors. It was to be an

outstanding success, enjoying a 17-year production run, and becoming the best-selling Austin from 1926 until 1932.

Sir Herbert can be credited with the idea of a very small Austin, but the diminutive four-cylinder engine which was crucial to its success must be credited to an 18-year-old draughtsman, Stanley Howard Edge. When he returned from his summer holiday in 1921, he was asked to go and work on it at Sir Herbert's home, in the billiard room, and every evening Austin would return home to discuss progress.

The 668 cc (41 cu in) Peugeot Quadrilette provided the inspiration for the baby Austin while in detail design Edge was impressed by the four-cylinder Belgian FN motorcycle engine and the lower half of the Seven's engine, with its two roller-bearing splash-lubricated crankshaft, followed this. The rest followed traditional Austin practice, with a side-valve cylinder block, with detachable head, bolted directly on an aluminium crankcase. As designed by Edge, the Seven had a capacity of 696 cc/43 cu in (55 mm × 77 mm/2.2 in × 3 in).

The chassis, steering box, brakes and coachwork designs were Austin's contribution to the Seven. He adopted an A-frame chassis and it seems likely that the transverse leaf front and quarter-elliptic rear suspension were borrowed from the Peugeot. The Seven boasted four-wheel brakes, a revolutionary feature for a small car even though they were not particularly efficient.

The public saw the Seven at the 1922 London Motor Show, but only 1936 were built in 1923, the first year of production. Late that year the first significant change was made when the engine capacity was increased to 748 cc (46 cu in).

In 1926 Sir Herbert's faith was really justified, for 14,000 Sevens left the Longbridge plant. That year a saloon had been introduced, and in 1927 a fashionable fabric version appeared (the metal saloon proved more enduring). In 1928 the wide-door 'Top Hat' came, and the painted radiator gave way to a nickel-finished one.

The best production year was 1935, when 27,280 were built, the engine was revised in 1936 (output rising from 12 bhp to 17 bhp), and Girling brakes replaced the questionable cable-operated drums. For 1937 the 900 cc (55 cu in) Big Seven was in production, although the last Seven was not built until January 1939.

Sevens had been raced successfully since 1923, with many class successes. In 1924 Austin had introduced the Sports, Gordon England built Brooklands Super Sports, and in 1929 Austin brought out the lowered Ulster Seven, with an optional supercharger. Well into the 1930s Austin continued to do battle with MG for small-class honours in races and records which were held at venues such as the Brooklands Motor Course.

Austin Healey 3000

New marques are seldom conceived in exhibition centres, but at the 1952 London Motor Show a stylish open two-seater entered Earls Court as a Healey 100 and left it as an Austin Healey. The

EVOLUTION — AUSTIN HEALEY 3000

1952 Introduced as the Healey 100 at London Motor Show

1953 Production began at Jensen's plant in West Bromwich and Austin's Longbridge plant. Headlights raised to conform to US regulations and 11 in drums replaced the prototype's 10 in variety

1955 Three-speed gearbox with overdrive replaced by four-speed, with overdrive on third and fourth gears. Morris-based rear axle introduced. 100M model introduced with 110 bhp and modified suspension

1957 100/6 introduced with 2.6-litre six-cylinder 102 bhp engine. Chassis lengthened 4.2 cm (1.66 in), horizontal-bar radiator grille, fixed windscreen and 2+2 body. Production transferred to MG in Abingdon. Later in 1957 six-port cylinder head introduced, raising power output to 117 bhp

1958 Strict two-seater version reintroduced on longer wheelbase of 100/6

1959 3000 introduced with 2.9-litre six-cylinder 124 bhp engine. Front disc brakes introduced

1961 3000 Mark II introduced with vertical slatted radiator grille and 132 bhp engine

1962 Wind-up windows added and hood improved. 2+2 discontinued

1964 3000 Mark III introduced with 148 bhp. Wooden dashboard standard equipment

1967 Production ceased after 72,022 cars built with 100/4s accounting for 14,662, 100/6s for 14,436 and the 3000s (Marks I, II and III) for 42,924

marque would win laurels for the newly-formed British Motor Corporation, especially when the four-cylinder engine of the 100 was replaced by a six. The resulting 'Big Healey' with its rally record, its rugged mechanical make-up and 120 mph (193 kph) top speed, was for many the epitome of the traditional British sports car.

Donald Healey set up a company to build high-performance saloons in limited numbers in 1945, at Warwick, then because steel was allocated according to export performances the company concentrated for a while on the Nash Healey for the US market.

The Healey Silverstone of 1949 gained an excellent club racing record and is much prized today, but it was hardly a mass-market sports car. For that Donald Healey and his son Geoffrey turned to a new design, using the 2.6-litre Austin Atlantic engine, gearbox, front suspension and other parts. The body was built by Tickford to a design by Gerry Croker, and the prototype was complete for that 1952 Show.

There Leonard Lord, who was looking for a BMC sports car, decided the Healey would be ideal, and Donald Healey agreed to his proposal that BMC should produce it as an Austin Healey.

Publicity was gained from record runs and a class clean sweep in the Sebring 12-hour Race and, in a major modification, the BMC C-series six-cylinder engine was brought in for the 1957 100/6. Production was transferred to the MG plant at Abingdon that year, and that move also saw the introduction of a new cylinder head which resulted in the power output rising from 102 bhp to 117 bhp.

The 100/6 became the 3000 when the in-line six was stretched from 2.6 to 2.9 litres and the transmission was strengthened to cope with the increased power. Output rose to 124 bhp and top speed was raised to around 114 mph (183 kph).

The Mark II came in 1961, with a 132 bhp engine, and in the following year the two-seater was discontinued and wind-up windows specified for the BJ7 2+2 version.

Meanwhile, a competitions record was being built up, and with the arrival of the 3000 in 1959 Austin Healey really began to make an impact. In its first competitive year Pat Moss came second in the German Rally and managed the same result in the Alpine Rally the following year. Then she won the Liège-Rome-Liège rally in 1960. From then until 1965 when the 3000 was officially withdrawn by BMC, the cars scored 40 class wins in major rallies.

Competition work saw some chassis improvements in the Mark III and a power rise to 148 bhp, giving a 120 mph (193 kph) top speed. Mark IV prototypes came to nothing, nor did a Rolls-Royce-engined model, and the end officially came in December 1967, although the final 3000 chassis was actually completed in March 1968.

Bentley

Bentley was probably the most outstanding marque of the 45 that were launched in Britain immediately after World War 1. Formed by W.O. Bentley in 1919, Bentley Motors Ltd lasted only 12 years, suffering severe financial problems for most of them. Despite this, 3034 top quality cars were built – more than a third of them survive – ten major races fell to Bentleys, and the marque became legendary.

The Bentley was a car of its time – rugged because the roads of the 1920s demanded strength, sporting because owners sought sport, aesthetically pleasing with well-balanced proportions.

The first 3-litre Bentley car was running in October 1919, with a four-cylinder single overhead camshaft engine. There was a four-speed gearbox, a very sturdy chassis with semi-elliptic springing all round with friction shock absorbers, and rear wheel braking only.

A racing programme was soon started, a stripped 3-litre winning its first race at Brooklands in 1921, driven by Frank Clement. With Clement, London motor trader John Duff ran a car in the first Le Mans 24-hour Race in 1923, finishing only fifth but impressing W.O. Bentley. He entered the car in 1924, when Duff and Clement covered the greatest distance. Meanwhile, Bentley had created a 4½-litre engine, by adding two cylinders and shortening the stroke. Then he enlarged this to 6½ litres, to give an unstressed 147 bhp and a car that was quite capable of carrying heavy saloon bodies.

Bentley's announcement of a withdrawal from racing in 1926 brought capital in from Woolf Barnato, and Bentley embarked on a successor to the 3-litre. However, one of these older cars ran in a legendary Le Mans race. Driven by S.C.H. ('Sammy') Davis, it was involved in a multiple crash with the other team cars. Davis got it back to the pits and, co-driven by Benjafield, it won.

By then the new 4½ was reaching customers, and one won at Le Mans in 1928, but it was hard pressed. Bentley began development of the model that became known as the Speed Six, following his

usual course of prescribing a larger engine. This produced a reliable 180 bhp, and a Speed Six led three 4½s to Bentley's greatest Le Mans triumph.

For 1930 three more Le Mans Speed Sixes were built, while the first car, dubbed Old No 1, headed a Bentley 1-2 win in the Brooklands Double 12 and did the same at Le Mans after a dramatic struggle with a 7-litre Mercedes-Benz.

Bentley started on the 8-litre, which was to be announced in September 1930. With a 220 bhp 7982 cc (487 cu in) engine it was a challenge to Rolls-Royce and Hispano-Suiza, but as the Depression bit hard, sales of all luxury cars tailed off. Bentley Motors' mortgages could not be met, and in July 1931 a receiver was appointed. Brokers representing Rolls-Royce acquired the company.

Bentley Continental

After 1931 many Bentleys through to the 1970s were Rolls-Royce models with a Flying B badge, but distinctive cars did appear. The Continental had origins that could be traced back to 1938-39, to a car commissioned with a streamlined four-seater body developed through wind-tunnel tests. Built under Rolls-Royce supervision, it was intended that it should be the prototype of a new limited-production Bentley.

The 1939 car was run at Le Mans in 1949, Hay and Wisdom placing it a creditable sixth. At that time the dream of a streamlined sports Bentley was very much alive, in part encouraged by Pininfarina's 1948 Bentley Cresta; Facel-Metallon then built Crestas II and III in 1951, the latter a low car that did not please all the critics. At about that time, Rolls-Royce people were talking to coachbuilder H.J. Mulliner about a 'performance model' on the Bentley Mk VI chassis. All these strands were to lead to the Continental. This was to have the 4566 cc (274 cu in) engine, with modifications that increased its power to around 150 bhp, perhaps 20 bhp more than the standard unit.

Development began in 1951 and by using alloy panelling and other weight-saving devices, Mulliner kept the coachwork below 340 kg/750 lb and the entire car weighed 1696 kg (3739 lb), compared with 1850 kg (4078 lb) for the standard Mark VI saloon.

It was still a massive car, but the increased power and better aerodynamics of its fastback two-door coachwork, allied to a higher final drive ratio, gave the new Continental impressive performance characteristics – the Bentley was probably the world's fastest production four/five seat saloon car, capable of 120 mph (193 kph) when the production version was announced in 1952.

Each Continental was built to bespoke order, though of the 207 Continental chassis actually built (in five consecutive series) between 1952 and 1955, all but 16 were fitted with the well-known Mulliner coachwork. The principal modifications were the adoption of a 7.2:1 compression ratio in 1953 on the third series cars from chassis BC4C, and of a big-bore (95.25 mm/3.75 in) engine displacing 4887 cc (293 cu in) 7.25:1 compression on the fourth series of Continentals in 1954.

The Continental designation was continued on the SI Bentley introduced during 1955, but the S Type Continentals were less sleek vehicles than the original, more akin to the normal production model.

BMW 328

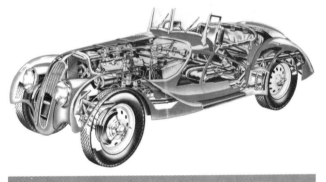

The BMW 328 was a rare design that set new standards; indeed, of all pre-war cars it was perhaps the most significant in the development of modern sports cars. In the 1930s German sports cars were generally uninspired and lacking in performance, so when the 328 made its first appearance in a race and won it convincingly there was an almost immediate awareness that a car head and shoulders above the rest had arrived. Its lines would not date for many years, and they inspired later designers, while its engine was to enjoy a long second life as a Bristol power unit.

In 1933 Fritz Fiedler had joined BMW from Horch to develop the six-cylinder range, and for the 328 he designed valve gear that led to a massive power increase, to 80 bhp at 5000 rpm. The chain-driven camshaft was still low down on the left of the engine, from where it had previously operated

in-line valves through pushrods and rockers. Now there were hemispherical combustion chambers in the new alloy head, with inclined valves. The inlets were opened by pushrods and rockers, but the exhaust valves had two sets of pushrods and rockers, one set of pushrods being placed horizontally so that the valves could be located on the other side of the combustion chambers. This arrangement worked well despite its apparent complexity, and provided most of the advantages of overhead camshafts without the need to redesign the whole engine; indeed, with its twin rocker boxes the Type 328 engine looked like a dohc unit.

At a time when most sports cars still had separate wings and lights, the 328 showed the way to a transition to all-enveloping bodywork. In aspects such as suspension, though, it was conventional.

Road-equipped 328s became available in 1937, and these needed little attention to achieve 100 mph (161 kph), and up to 120 mph (193 kph) was possible with more extensive tuning. To take full advantage of this performance – which was remarkable for an unsupercharged 2-litre car with full road equipment – BMW listed a wide range of special equipment. The cars were extensively used in competitions, and the factory ran some as coupés in major events. That phase ended after the 1940 Mille Miglia, which BMW won.

BMW only built 461 328s; a few were later assembled from parts, by the Aldingtons in England, and the engine developed for the early Bristol cars.

BMW M1

In the late 1970s BMW needed a new competition car to fly the company flag, as the winged CSL coupé showed its age. The need was identified as a senior-league supercar, and the car that emerged was the M1, but the story of BMW's dream car reads in its early stages more like a nightmare.

Competitions manager Jochen Neerspach made the right moves. Because main-line production could not be disrupted the M1 was to be styled in Italy by Italdesign and built by Lamborghini, while BMW's own 3.5-litre straight six was to power the car. BMW and Lamborghini worked well on the chassis, while Dallara developed the suspension. Prototypes were built, then suddenly Lamborghini was in very real financial trouble, appearing near collapse. The project was too far advanced to be stopped, but at least suppliers could still deliver and final assembly was undertaken in Germany by Baur.

The M1 that went on sale in 1979 – a year late – was impressive, with a strong square-section steel space frame and mid-mounted 277 bhp engine for the road version, and around 470 bhp in the Procars. These were built for a series of one-model races, set up by Neerspach who realized the overweight car would never be competitive in main-line racing.

This made the M1 famous. Procar was a sort of Race of Champions, matching 15 private owners against the five fastest Friday afternoon qualifiers at each Grand Prix. The Procar racers were essentially in Group 4 spec, with rose-jointed suspension, no brake servo but circuits with adjustable front-rear distribution, wider wheels and tyres, quicker steering and a deeper front air dam.

Not that the standard car was any slouch. Independent tests confirmed that it could attain 160 mph (258 kph) and hit 60 mph (96 kph) from a standstill in 5.4 seconds. So the M1 ranked with the very quickest of contemporary supercars, and delivered its mighty performance with an admirable lack of temperament or fuss.

A total of 450 M1s was built. The M1 never really had the impact on the track its specification suggested although its very existence was a potent statement of BMW's yearning to succeed in the toughest arena of all — endurance motor racing. Conceived and developed as a pure racer, the M1 could easily have made it but for the many and seemingly interminable problems that dogged it.

Bristol Sixes

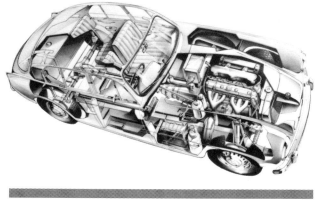

Before the end of World War 2 the directors of the Bristol Aeroplane Company began to consider diversifying into car manufacture, and once committed to

this the need to get into the market quickly was recognized. That came about, too, as Bristol director H.J. Aldington was instrumental in obtaining not only the pre-war BMW designs but BMW's pre-war designer, Dr Fritz Fiedler.

Bristol brought together the best features of the 326 (chassis), 327 (styling) and 328 (engine). Dimensional changes made to the BMW engine were slight, but metallurgical improvements were considerable, and gears and bearings were to aircraft-specification quality.

The public first saw the Bristol 400 at the 1947 Geneva Motor Show, although a prototype had run in 1946. The 400 set a pattern, with its efficient long-stroke six-cylinder engine and handsome low-drag body. The first engine produced 85 bhp, but sports engines giving as much as 140 bhp could be factory fitted.

Mechanically the 401 of 1949 was similar to the 400, but it was clad in a beautiful new body, ultra-smooth and aerodynamically refined yet very roomy and practical. Nothing protruded from its smooth skin – the doors had flush buttons with aircraft locks, and all other hatches were opened from inside, making it burglar-proof – and the skin itself was varied in the thickness, hardness and ductility of its aluminium alloy according to the loads it might have to support.

Italian and other bodybuilders tried their hands on Bristols, but the results were always inferior in quality and usually in looks. Bristol made two dozen 402 dropheads. The 403 looked almost identical to the 401, but there were bigger brakes. It was a faster car, the standard engine giving 100 bhp in 1953.

The 404 was the only short-wheelbase two-seater production car. The exterior styling was quite new, with vestigial tailfins echoing the Type 450 sports-racing cars. Clearly related to the 404, the 405 was the only four-door body Bristol ever built.

Only two further refinements were needed, and both appeared in the 406 of 1958 (though a handful of 405s were also given the treatment). One was the use of a Watt linkage to locate the rear axle laterally and the other was disc brakes.

A lot has happened to Bristols since those days of the six-cylinder engines which ended when the 2.2-litre 406 gave way to the V8 407 in 1961 as Bristol Cars came to be a private company without facilities for making its own engines.

Bugatti Type 35

Ettore Bugatti took the 1924 French Grand Prix very seriously. The six new Bugatti racing cars were the real centre of attraction, for this race saw the public debut of the Type 35, now regarded by many people as the quintessential Bugatti. The purity of its lines was the more remarkable because the previous Bugatti racing car, the T32, had been a technical and aesthetic dog. Since the T35 turned out to be much better engineered than the T32, it must be assumed that Bugatti had an assistant who could turn his scribbled ideas into engineering drawings.

There was artistry in the styling of the T35. In plan, the body was an elegant streamline, tapering forward from the cockpit (the widest point) to the radiator in the traditional horse-shoe shape, and back to the neat tail.

The cast aluminium wheels were distinctive (and also cheaper to make than wire wheels) and were a weak point in the Type 35. In the engine,

Bugatti used roller bearings to support the crankshaft, which was pressure-lubricated. The wet-sump system was affected by oil surge, however, and this called for diligent riding mechanics, while Bugatti also made less than adequate cooling arrangements.

The valves were restrictive, and the engine in its first form was far from competitive, so the adoption of a supercharger on the Type 35B of 1926 was inevitable. In unblown form, the 2-litre Type 35 engine developed some 90 bhp and around 120 bhp supercharged: the 2.3-litre 35T also produced about 120 bhp, the blown 2.3-litre derivatives probably 135–140 bhp. In their day, Bugatti engines turned at speeds of up to 5500 rpm, astoundingly fast for the period.

That the Type 35 was an effective motor car was proved not by those myriad victories in Bugatti-only races for 'les boys et girls' but by its brilliant run of success against all-comers in the Targa Florio in Sicily between 1925-29.

By 1929, even Ettore Bugatti was forced to admit that his single-overhead-cam engines had reached the end of their development life and he turned for inspiration to an American Miller straight eight for a twin-overhead-camshaft design. But among his racing cars, the Type 35 represented the peak of Ettore Bugatti's genius.

Bugatti Royale

The Bugatti Type 41 was a whim, and a very substantial whim, with a bonnet of such length that a Mini could be parked upon it. Ettore Bugatti called it Royale because it was to sell mainly to crowned heads, and it carried a lifetime guarantee.

During the early 1920s le Patron designed the Type 41, and the prototype was built and tested very thoroughly. It had an open tourer body (said to have come from a Packard) and was typical of Bugattis in all but size, yet so well proportioned that its size did not impress in photographs.

The chassis which carried that first open tourer was slightly larger in engine and wheelbase than the six 'production' chassis which followed, which had an engine capacity of a mere 12,763 cc (779 cu in). The straight eight weighed 349 kg (770 lb), of which 108 kg (238 lb) came from the cast-iron block and integral head, which was 140 cm (55 in) long. The whole engine was lightly stressed, which was just as well because to change a valve meant removing that crankshaft. There was a cavernous three-speed gearbox in unit with the back axle.

Each of the Royales had individual bodywork. The prototype was rebodied with a tiny closed Coupé Napoleon body in 1928 and then with a more spacious saloon in 1929, and it saw service as a demonstrator. For Bugatti family use a Weymann close-coupled coupé body was fitted, then a 'double berline' body, and finally Jean Bugatti transformed it again as a coupé de ville (town carriage).

In 1932 a customer came forward, one Armand Esders, who was apparently impressed by the coupé de ville version and commissioned a two-seater sporting body. Then Joseph Fuchs bought a chassis, a Kellner-bodied saloon did not sell, and one chassis found an English buyer, and was given a limousine body by Park Ward. This is one of two Royales that were acquired by the Schlumpf brothers for their museum at Mulhouse.

The Royales were a magnificent folly but they brought wonderful publicity and Bugatti eventually found a new market for his great lazy 14.75-litre engine, as power units for fast *autorails*, or railcars.

The cars are not quite beyond price. In 1987 Christie's sold the Kellner-bodied car at auction in London for £5,500,000, or $9,867,000, far and away a record price for a car.

Bugatti Type 57

The Type 57 was in all respects the most civilized and refined model produced by Bugatti. It should have marked an easy transition between the intuitive

brilliance of Ettore Bugatti and the more polished brilliance of his son Jean, who started work with Meo Costatini on a chassis for a replacement for the Type 49. Some of their ideas, for example for independent front suspension, were overruled by Ettore Bugatti (he did go so far as to allow a split axle which was a total failure and replaced by a rigid axle). Ettore also insisted on a fixed cylinder head, but Jean had his way with the transmission, the gearbox being the first to be built in unit with the engine.

The first engine was tested in 1933, giving some 120 bhp, but as Ettore Bugatti thought this 2866 cc (175 cu in) unit too small the stroke was lengthened to give a swept volume of 3257 cc (199 cu in).

Most catalogue Bugatti bodies were constructed by Gangloff of Colmar, and as far as the Type 57 was concerned the most common was the Atalante faux-cabriolet; then there were the Ventoux coach (a two-door saloon), the Stelvio coupé, the Galibier saloon, the Aravis convertible coupé (only built in 1939) and, most extraordinary of all, the Atlantic coupé (originally known as the Aerolithe), with a gloriously flowing body form, distinguished by riveted spines down the centre line of body and

EVOLUTION — CADILLAC V16

1930 Series 452 V16 introduced in January. High-speed axle dropped 1 June. Annual production: 1826 cars

1931 Series 452A introduced. Annual production: 1424 cars

1932 Series 452B introduced in January with restyled bodies, triple-silent gearbox, detail mechanical improvements, modified chassis, ride control and choice of 363 cm (143 in) and 378 cm (149 in) wheelbases. Annual production: 296 cars

1933 Series 452C introduced in January. Annual production: 125 cars

1934 Series 452D introduced in January with 185 bhp power output, dual X-braced chassis and independent front suspension. Annual production: 56 cars

1935 Series 60 452D introduced in January. Annual production: 50 cars

1936 Series 90 with modifications to bodywork. Annual production: 52 cars

1937 Series 90 with hydraulic brakes added. Last season for overhead valve V16. Annual production: 49 cars

1938 Series 90 with 135 degree side-valve 7023 cc (428 cu in) V16 engine introduced. Annual production: 311 cars

1939 Series 90 continued. Annual production: 136 cars

1940 Series 90 production ended. Annual production: 61 cars. Total V16 production amounted to 4386 cars

wings. Of course, bare chassis were also supplied to the cream of Europe's coachbuilders.

The T57 was steadily refined, with a modified chassis in 1936, a power increase in the same year, and shock absorber changes in 1936 and 1938, the year when Jean at last got permission to fit hydraulic brakes. The supercharged Type 57C came in 1936, with a 160 bhp engine that lifted top speed to around 105 mph (170 kph); later that year a sports version, the T57S, appeared, and that was soon available as the T57SC with a supercharger.

The archetypal racing T57 with enveloping bodywork came in 1936, and was referred to as the 57G. At Le Mans in 1937 Wimille and Robert Benoist broke the British and Italian domination of the 24-hour race in a 57G.

A few weeks later Jean Bugatti was testing this car on a public highway when a drunken cyclist wobbled into his path; Bugatti swerved to avoid him, crashed into the ditch, and was killed instantly.

The Type 57 series was Jean Bugatti's greatest achievement, a remarkable evidence of maturity.

Cadillac V16

This was a grand gesture, the car that was to re-establish Cadillac at the top of the luxury-car league as the 1920s ended, the world's first and most successful production V16. Under Alfred P. Sloan General Motors was a growing force, with products for every market sector. But in the luxury class Packard outsold Cadillac, and as a legacy of its Twin Six had a well-established image as the company that could provide ultimate automobiles.

So plans for a Cadillac to steal the crown were laid, as early as 1926. A V8 was ruled out, partly because it would need a new drive line, and a V12 as it would invite comparison with Packard's Twin Six. So Ernest Seaholm and Owen Nacker, chief engineer and designer respectively, turned to a V16, and in 1930 the series 452 V16 was unveiled.

In broad terms the V16 was a conventional pushrod ohv engine, with great care taken in valve

gear operating methods. Live axles were used, but during the early 1930s Maurice Olley, who had been with the American Rolls-Royce company, worked on developing this, and in 1934 his SLA front suspension of unequal-length wishbones and coil springs was adopted for the V16.

By the standards of the time braking was also praiseworthy, despite the problems inherent in overcoming the interia of a moving machine weighing some two and three-quarter tons.

Sales started well, and in the first seven months 2000 V16s were completed. Then the Depression bit, and in 1931 sales totalled 750, with the aid of heavy dealer discounting. Sales were down again in 1932; Cadillac announced that only 400 would be built in 1933, but in the event a mere 126 were made, and until 1937 average annual production was 50 cars.

To some extent Cadillac had undermined their own position when a V12 was announced in 1930, with an engine that was a derivative of the V16 (the chassis of the contemporary V8 was used). By 1937 ten V12s were being sold for every V16.

In 1936-37 these Series 90 V16s were offered in 12 forms, and of the 49 completed in 1937 only the normal seven-seat limousine reached double-figure production. That year the division announced, not unexpectedly, that the V16 was to cease production. Quite unexpected, however, was the announcement that its replacement was to be another V16.

1938's V16 engine was square (83 mm × 83 mm/ 3.25 in × 3.25 in, giving 7.1 litres compared with the earlier unit's 7.4 litres), lighter and similarly rated at 185 bhp. But progress in engine design, materials and installation had made the whole concept of a super-smooth V16 an anachronism. The annual sales rate picked up, but in the three-year production life just 508 were sold.

Chevrolet Corvette

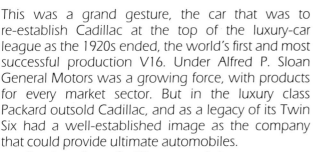

The Corvette was a remarkable car to come out of General Motors in the 1950s, and while the slogan 'America's Only Sports Car' was perhaps never really justified – and in any case is now many years in the past – later Corvettes were true high-performance machines. For GM this was never a high-volume line, but it generated a lot of publicity and prestige.

In the early 1950s Harley Earl, in charge of GM's Art and Color Studio, and Chevrolet Chief Engineer Ed Cole shared an ambition to build a car that had a sporting image, well removed from Chevrolet's normal staid and boring image. Whims could not justify a radically different car, but a low-production car would be undertaken as a means to evaluate glassfibre bodies. The Corvette was to continue its test-bed role throughout its life, for example in the 1980s being used to pioneer the use of lightweight mono-filament leaf springs.

The first car was an amalgam of production parts, such as Chevrolet's stolid 3.8-litre (235 cu in) straight six, modified to produce 150 bhp and driving through the least sporting of transmissions, the two-speed Powerglide automatic. A solid box-section frame and conventional suspension completed the specification. The open body was homely rather than sleek – certainly it did not match up to the XK120 that had been Earl's inspiration – but public reception was enthusiastic when the car was shown at Motorama extravaganzas in 1953. So it was put into limited production.

It was transformed for 1956, with sleek lines and Chevrolet's latest and lightest V8, coupled with a manual gearbox, and sales soared. The Corvette epitomized the open sports car, and while it was not sophisticated it looked good and was very fast. By 1959 the V8 had been bored out to displace 4.6 litres, (283 cu in) and in its high-tune form with the troublesome GM fuel injection, 283 bhp (SAE gross) was claimed for it. As the end neared for these second-generation models, a 5.3-litre (327 cu in) V8 producing 360 bhp was available, to give a top speed of almost 150 mph (241 kph).

The starkly different Sting Ray came in 1963, and when the horsepower battles of the 1960s were fought, Chevrolet had a 7-litre (427 cu in) V8 at the top of the Corvette options line. A new, sharper, body based on the 1965 Mako Shark show car was introduced in 1968, and at the end of the decade a short-lived top model, the ZL-1, had over 400 bhp under its hood.

In the 1970s emission and safety regulations, and fuel crises, took their toll (although IMSA 'silhouette' racing Corvettes were formidable 7-litre 650 bhp cars). The 1980s opened with only the L-81 5.7-litre (350 cu in) V8 catalogued. The new Corvette was a significantly smaller and lighter car, which from 1984 seemed to be aimed at a significantly richer clientele.

In the late 1980s Callaway Cars produced some turbo Corvettes with shattering performance, but in the area of realistic road cars the Corvette continued as mildly old-fashioned GT cars.

Chevrolet Camaro and Pontiac Firebird

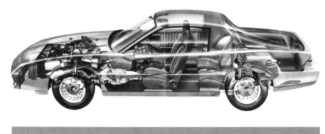

The Camaro and Firebird – the 'F-cars' - are often thought of as General Motors' response to the Ford Mustang, although the realities of lead times in the car business largely rules that out – GM engineers and stylists had been working on sporty cars for some time, and apart from the Corvette there had been the Monza coupé and roadster versions of the otherwise sad rear-engined Corvair.

But the success of the Mustang – sales of 418,000 in a year – could not be ignored, so a styling exercise that had been in GM's advanced project studio for some time was brought forward, primarily as a Chevrolet but with Pontiac boss John De Lorean given a share, to satisfy his ambitions to include a two-seater sports car in his line.

The Camaro that appeared in 1966 was based on the chassis of the Chevy II saloon and the live rear axle suspension came from the same source (for the Firebird that came a year later, Pontiac engineers added a pair of trailing links in an attempt to cure axle tramp). A range of engines was available, the base Camaro having a 3.8-litre (231 cu in) in-line six rated at 140 bhp, with the most powerful option being a 375 bhp 6.5-litre (397 cu in) V8, really too powerful for the car's simple suspension. Pontiac included an ohc 215 bhp version of the GM six, and V8s going up to a 335 bhp 6.6-litre (403 cu in) unit.

Partly to meet production racing class regulations, hybrid engines were listed, as were other modified components, in an effort to transform the Z28 Camaro into a worthwhile race car.

In 1969 Pontiac came up with the name TransAm for their high-performance model. With the 6.6-litre V8 and suspension modifications to make its power usable, Pontiac had a success.

In the 1970s the emphasis slanted towards comfort rather than performance, save for the TransAm which was continued with even more aggressive body details. But in the 1980s, as F-cars were increasingly standardized with Chevrolet hardware, Pontiac's final fling with a 4.9-litre (303 cu in) turbo V8 was a pale shadow of past cars.

1982 saw the introduction of the third-generation Camaro and Firebird. To some, these cars were relics, retaining the old-fashioned front-engine rear-drive configuration space, but no one could argue the brilliance of their styling.

General Motors still promoted a performance image, and the 1984 IROC Z28 Camaro model was based on the race-prepared cars used in the International Race of Champions. Then as inhibiting factors such as long-past fuel crises receded, GM worked back towards the original pony car concept, with cars that were almost as fast as their 1960s counterparts, had much better handling and, with discs all round, much better braking. In truth they were very different cars, with the same names.

Citroën DS

André Citroën's front-wheel drive car of 1934 was enshrined as *le Traction*, set remarkable new standards, and pushed his company towards such serious financial difficulties that within a year it had been sold to Michelin. Late in the decade the manager installed by Michelin, Pierre Boulanger, began to think about a car to exploit new technologies. However, the DS that eventually emerged in the mid-1950s was a compromise car, for example using the engine that had served in *le Traction* rather than a new flat-six engine.

But there was no compromise in the body lines by Faliminio Bertoni – stylistically original and refreshing, aerodynamically right. The basis of the structure was a floor pan and skeletal superstructure to which panels could be bolted, making for quick and cheap damage repairs. The roof was to be in translucent GRP, but in the interests of stiffness a steel roof panel had to be used.

In the suspension, Citroën's engineers came up with a system that offered a constant ride height, spring frequencies that made for a soft ride, stiffness that increased as the loading on a spring increased,

ride height adjustability, automated jacking and the advantages of independent suspension. In this steel springs were abandoned in favour of 'gas' springs. There was a self-levelling element in the suspension which called for a hydraulic system, with an engine-driven pump to force fluid into a 'pressure-accumulator'. This system was tapped to operate brakes and steering (which had priority, in case of a leak in the system), clutch and gear change. As well as the semi-automatic and 'unassisted' four-speed synchromesh gearboxes, there was a five-speed box for later models, or a Borg-Warner automatic.

The engine was uprated from time to time, and raised from 1911 cc (117 cu in) to 1985 cc (121 cu in), then for the DS21 to 2175 cc (133 cu in) and for the DS23 to 2347 cc (143 cu in). The last of these, with fuel injection, gave the DS23 a maximum speed of over 120 mph (193 kph) – a 30 mph (48 kph) improvement over the first DS.

That had been achieved on a mere 75 bhp, in part because of the clean aerodynamics of the car. Moreover, there was no call to slow down over rough pavé or the deformed roads that were still all too common in France through to the 1960s. This Citroën family transformed its class of motoring.

Citroën SM

This car was introduced to a chorus of praise; it was strong, fast and stylish, with outstanding aerodynamic properties, superb steering and lights. Yet it was not a success, and only 12,854 were sold.

Citroën bought Maserati, quite cheaply, in 1968, in an expansionist period. Maserati fitted well into Citroën's overall plan, for with its thoroughbred engines it could provide the one thing that Citroën lacked. France did not have a high-performance, high-class car, and Citroën could see a beckoning opportunity. The DS could provide running gear, suspension, brakes – anything except an engine. Citroën briefed Maserati to provide it quickly, specifying a light and short unit to deliver 150 bhp. As it happened, Maserati could produce an engine more quickly than Citroën imagined possible, for they had recently created a 4168 cc (255 cu in) V8, and a V6 derivative with slightly reduced bore and stroke (to avoid a punitive French taxation class) giving a swept volume of 2670 cc (163 cu in). In that form it was normally rated at 178 bhp.

Citroën's five-speed manual gearbox was appropriate (it was later to be used by Lotus in the Esprit), and Citroën sought Borg-Warner collaboration in confecting an automatic transmission, which came later, with an increase in engine displacement to augment the torque. When the engine was enlarged in 1973 (by reversion to the original bore, giving 2965 cc/180 cu in), European customers continued to enjoy the Bosch fuel-injection system which had increased the power output. Top speed and acceleration were both excellent without being incredible. About 136 mph (219 kph) was the limit for the former.

The DS provided the self-levelling progressive-rate suspension, a braking system of outstanding power, and the basis of a remarkable steering system, with progressive power assistance.

Citroën took no chances in the construction of the bodyshell which was very strongly integrated with the floorpan to create an immensely strong chassis-hull, with little but the doors, lids and front wings removable.

The SM was beautiful, and it was sophisticated. But in 1973 this last of the French grand tourers was doomed. Michelin had given way to a management of hard-headed businessmen, and as sales dropped dangerously low they very soon ended production.

Cord 810

When the Auburn-Cord-Duesenberg Corporation defined its new model requirement in 1933, Gordon Miller Buehrig, chief body designer for Duesenberg, saw an opportunity to turn into production reality a design concept that had been shelved while he created the classic Auburn Models 851 and 852. It was picked up as a Cord, a spiritual successor to the grandiose front-wheel drive car L-29 of 1929-32. Its lines were original, having horizontal louvres around the nose and retractable main lights.

The project was given a go-ahead, with the stipulation that the car should be ready for the 1935

New York Show, then only four months away. And to be eligible for that as a production car, a minimum of 100 had to be built. To meet this almost impossible deadline within the group's tight financial constraints, short cuts were taken: the doors were symmetrical apart from wheel cut-outs, so dies were made for only right-front and left-rear doors, some handles were bought at a bankruptcy sale, instruments were acquired cheaply, and those retractable lights were actually aircraft landing lights.

The 4.7-litre (287 cu in) V8 was carefully designed, but had a weakness in its restricted water passages in the aluminium cylinder heads, which frequently cracked. And the front-drive transmission, with its electric pre-selection, proved to be clever but over-ambitious and failed to live up its promise. The novel front suspension used trailing arms sprung by a transverse semi-elliptic leaf spring, while a light 'dead' axle saved weight at the rear.

Mechanical failings meant production lagged, and as E.L. Cord lost interest in cars, the management turned to the tactics used to boost Auburn sales: fit a supercharger. The result was the Cord 812, introduced for 1937 with an improved Lycoming FC engine and a Schwitzer-Cummins centrifugal supercharger. The faster, more flamboyant 812 could be distinguished by twin flexible exhaust pipes protruding from either side before they merged into a single tail-pipe.

It was in vain. Cord 810/812 production reached just 2320 cars before the receiver was called in. The dies eventually went to Nissan, where they were kept into the 1960s. By then attempts had been made to revive the marque, but Cord lingers as no more than a revered name in automotive history.

Daimler Double-Six

For many years Daimler was the chosen make of car for the British royal family, and for a period in the 1920s and 1930s no state occasion was complete without its line of Daimler Double-Sixes, with the appropriate flag or shield mounted above each lofty windscreen. The company had been wedded to the unorthodox 'Silent Knight' double-sleeve-valve engine since Edwardian years, but when Laurence Pomeroy became chief engineer he set about changing its approach.

He was contemptuous of low-powered engines, however refined, and in 1926 introduced the Double-Six engine, which has been described as the most complex power unit ever made for a private car. Pomeroy took two of the 25-85 Daimler six-cylinder blocks and mounted them at 60 degrees to each other. There was a massive aluminium crankcase, each block was split into two groups of three cylinders, so there were in effect four cylinder heads, and as the cylinder banks were not offset, all the right-side connecting rods had forked big ends, and shared their crankpins with the left-side rods.

The sheer size of the 7-litre engine made for problems and the chassis to carry it had a wheelbase of no less than 414 cm (163 in) and a track of 152 cm (60 in). The chassis weighed in the region of 2268 kg (5000 lb).

King George V never did buy a full 50 hp Double-Six, initially having two earlier Daimlers converted for the V12 engine; two of the smaller 30 hp (3744 cc/223 cu in) models were added to the Royal fleet late in the 1920s, while three 40-50 limousines and two 30-40s were acquired in a part-exchange deal in 1930.

At the end of the 1920s Daimler catalogues listed seven different Double-Six chassis, and with Daimler coachwork 15 variations were possible, while specialist coachbuilders could fit bespoke bodies. In complete contrast there was a small number of sporting Double-Sixes, including a very handsome Corsica cabriolet and the cars developed by record machine designer Reid Railton. These models had tuned engines, and light bodywork on a short chassis.

Pomeroy improved the Daimler range for 1931 by combining a fluid flywheel with an epicyclic pre-selector gearbox to provide something approaching an automatic transmission system. This was listed as an option for the Double-Six 30 and for two new V12s, a 6511 cc (397 cu in) 40-50 and 5296 cc (323 cu in) 30-40.

The engines were revised in detail, using more aluminium to reduce chassis weight. By 1933 the 30-40 and 40-50 Double-Sixes had been redesignated '40' and '50' respectively, and all other Daimler models had poppet-valve engines. The new poppet-valve straight eight that was introduced in 1934 did not immediaely supersede the Double-Six, as a few V12s were built with poppet valves, including the last ceremonial 50 hp limousine built by Daimler, expressly for the 1935 Silver Jubilee celebrations.

Datsun 240Z

Very, very few Japanese cars have achieved the indefinable blend of 'character' and 'status' to mark them out for future collectors, and most have been quite unmemorable. One of the exceptions was the Datsun 240Z, launched in 1969 and soon accepted as a sports car throughout the world.

The Nissan Motor Company had established a US presence with Datsun in 1960, and recognized the market in that country for sports cars. Its own first step towards becoming a sports car manufacturer could be seen in the SP310 Fairlady in 1961, and that name was used at the end of the decade, for the Nissan Fairlady Z that was shown at the 1969 Tokyo Motor Show.

This was a fixed head coupé, styled by Albrecht Goertz, a German-born American consultant who had made his name with the BMW 503 and 507 coupés, and Nissan had gone for this style out of a conviction that their main sales target, the American customer, was no longer partial to wind-in-the-hair motoring.

As many standard parts as possible were used. The Bluebird 510 four-cylinder engine was the basis of the straight six, with two cylinders added, and a new crankshaft, block and head. The major parts exclusive to the Z included the rack and pinion steering and the independent rear suspension.

As the 240Z it had the appeal of power, although at first outputs tended to be quoted in gross SAE terms. Later a DIN output figure of 130 bhp was claimed, and with the reasonable car weight of 1034 kg (2280 lb) this gave it a competitive performance. It would reach 100 mph (161 kph) from a standing start in under 30 seconds and had a maximum speed of 125 mph (317 kph).

The 240Z was by no means perfection in roadholding, ride or handling (amongst other things it had heavy steering), but its very eccentricities struck a chord, particularly in some British hearts, in the way one had to fight the beast to get the best out of it, as with the old Austin Healeys. The strengths of the original 240Z in the export markets were its quite lusty power-to-weight ratio and consequent performance, and, in the American market for which it was specifically designed, its value for money.

The sturdy 240Z was the first sports car to win the demanding Safari Rally, and while it was familiar in rallies elsewhere the next-best result in a main-line event was third in the Monte Carlo Rally. It was raced most frequently in SCCA production classes.

The successors to the 240Z, the 260Z in 1974 with a 2565 cc (156 cu in) engine, and the 280Z which followed only a year later with a 2573 cc (157 cu in) fuel-injected engine, were less sporting.

De Dion Bouton Voiturette

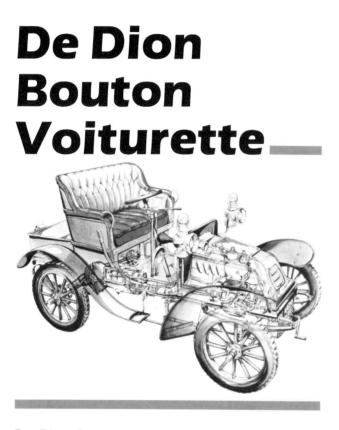

De Dion Bouton became firmly established as a manufacturer of horseless carriages with a variety of steam vehicles in the 1880s and 1890s, ranging from feathery two seaters to very substantial tractors, and it was for these that engineer Trépardoux designed the De Dion axle arrangement that keeps the company's name alive today. In this, the final drive gears are fixed to the chassis with half shafts running to the wheels, and these are linked by a rigid beam (the De Dion tube). Patented in 1893, this system gives many of the advantages of independent suspension at little cost in complication, weight or space. Ironically, within two years the De Dion internal combustion engines designed by Georges Bouton, Trépardoux' brother-in-law, had become advanced enough to persuade the Comte Albert de Dion to turn to this form of power unit, and steam disciple Trépardoux quit.

Those first single-cylinder petrol engines ran up to the prodigious speed of 3500 rpm on test, and the 1800 rpm limit of the first production versions was still very fast by contemporary standards, achieved in large part by the pioneering use of a mechanical contact breaker. These little engines were sold to other constructors (some 20,000 by 1900), while De Dion used them in sporting tricycles, and in a light four-wheel derivative that came in 1899.

That was quickly followed by the rear-engined 402cc (24.5 cu in) Model D voiturette, which was produced in quantity (in 1900-01 De Dion was probably the largest car-manufacturing company in the world), and others followed through to 1904 in an expanding range. By then De Dion was giving way to 'market forces' (a term that would have been meaningless to Edwardians) and turned to the 'conventional' front engine rear drive format, in the K and subsequent models.

These little front-engined cars gained the appellation 'Populaire', actually used by the company for the N, Q, R and Y, and were indeed the true replacement for the everyday pony and trap. They quickly became familiar in '6 hp' and '8 hp' forms and continued in production well after the single-cylinder vehicle concept was outmoded, until 1912 in vans. The cars usually had open bodies.

The engine took up little space under the alligator bonnet, and like every part of the car was beautifully made. Simplicity in the engine compartment was offset by complication facing the driver: on the floor were pedals to engage reverse gear and to operate a decelerator (this operated an exhaust-valve lifter, which slowed the engine, and the transmission brake), and the handle of the engine lubrication system pump; hand controls included a combined gear lever and clutch (a foot clutch came in 1906), ignition, throttle and exhaust-valve levers, and the brake lever. To a modern driver the little 'ding-dong' would be a test of dexterity.

These cars marked a significant step towards mass production and standardization, and towards popular motoring. And the survivors are delightful.

Delage D8

Louis Delage was a man of style, and the long, low and fast D8 reflected the man. It was a natural *concours d'elegance* winner at fashionable resorts; it inspired the best French coachbuilders; it was a glamorous car which also had a racing pedigree.

In his engine design for the D8, Maurice Gaultier sought to eliminate noise, with an arrangement of pushrods and valve springs for the two valves per cylinder. The crankshaft was machined from a solid billet, and as the detachable block and cylinder head were in cast iron the engine was assured of longevity. In standard form, it gave 102 bhp.

Drive, four-speed gearbox, worm and nut steering and vacuum-servo-assisted cable-operated brakes were straightforward, as was the cruciform-braced pressed-steel chassis. Suspension was by very flat semi-elliptic springs, initially with friction shock absorbers, later with more sophisticated dampers. Three wheelbase lengths were offered, from 330 cm (130 in) to 361 cm (142 in).

To prove the performance of the D8, a light two-seater was used to break records at Montlhéry. Meanwhile, Gaultier modified the front suspension to overcome steering shortcomings, and performance rapidly improved, turning what had been an elegant clothes-horse into a formidable sporting machine, raising an original top speed of 80 mph (129 kph) to a guaranteed 100 mph (161 kph), a rare performance for the period. Power rose to 118 bhp at 3800 rpm on the D8S and on the D8SS the permissible revs rose to 4500, and the output to 145 bhp.

The big straight-eight Delage had some smart coachwork, a trifle flashy, but not so vulgar as much French coachwork during the later 1930s. Louis Delage was forced to sell out to Delahaye. One feels that in Gaultier's D8, D8S, D8SS and D8SS 100, Louis Delage had created a car in his own image.

Delahaye 135

Emile Delahaye started making cars in 1894, and for four decades his factory produced a succession of generally uninspired vehicles, heavy touring cars not unrelated to the firm's trucks. The Super Luxe therefore came as a surprise at the 1933 Paris Motor Show, for it had a lively and robust straight-six engine and suspension and chassis that were thoroughly modern by mid-1930s standards. In 1934 Delahayes did well in major rallies, and in 1935 a lighter and livelier version won sports car races at the highest level. Meanwhile, in 1934 a streamlined single-seater had broken 18 duration and distance records at Montlhéry, to prove 135 potential.

The top of the range 3.2-litre, 110 bhp model was designated 135 in 1935, and this was very much a dual-purpose car – it was much favoured by coachbuilders, thus a rival to the Delage D8s in their hands and at concours d'élégance (the two firms amalgamated in 1935, but for a while their models continued), and it built up an excellent competitions record.

At first this was achieved with standard cars in rallies and hill climbs, but with the 135 Compétition in 1936, and the limited-production Compétition Spéciale, the name Delahaye began to feature prominently on the results lists of major events.

These had 3558 cc (217 cu in) engines, rated at 160 bhp in the Spéciale, and Delahaye's claimed top speed of over 125 mph (201 kph) was verified when one lapped Brooklands at 126.09 mph (203 kph). The four seaters, incidentally, were good for 105 mph (169 kph) with 120 bhp engines.

The potential of the Compétition cars was more than demonstrated in 1936, when they were second in events as varied as the Monte Carlo Rally and the French Grand Prix (run as a sports car race that year, as the French disliked the idea of staging another German triumph!). There was a second place at Le Mans in 1937, and victory in the 24-hour race that every French manufacturer cherishes came in 1938. That win by Chaboud and Trémoulet (at 82.35 mph/ 132.67 kph for the 24 hours) was a reward for reliability rather than speed, as earlier in the race the big new Delahaye V12s, Alfa Romeos and Talbots had led, but a victory is a victory.

The Delahayes seemed outclassed in 1939, save in rallies, but they were brought out again after the war and raced with some success in the late 1940s – there were fifth, ninth and tenth placings at Le Mans in 1949.

At that time the 135 was back in production, with a new full-width body that had been styled by Philippe Charbonneaux, was made only by Delahaye and first shown in 1947. The 3.6-litre engine was continued during the recovery period, then superseded by a 4½-litre derivative in the 175. This found few buyers, and Delahaye increasingly turned back to commercial and military vehicles. The last car to be listed was the 235, in most respects a 135 with modern bodywork, which lasted until 1954 when the company was taken over by Hotchkiss and the Delahaye line ceased.

Delaunay-Belleville Sixes

In the decade before World War 2, Delaunay-Belleville produced a series of imposing six-cylinder cars which were the equals of any quality machines of the period. In this they echoed the high reputation the company had for marine and locomotive steam boilers, which was quite deliberately reflected in the shape of their cars' bonnets.

Automobiles Delaunay-Belleville was formed in 1903, and the first cars were introduced in the following year. Designed by Marius Barbarou, who had worked with Benz and Lorraine-Dietrich, the first range comprised three big four-cylinder models. The first sixes followed in 1907, the 15 hp Type H and the larger 40 hp Type C.

The H had a 4-litre six-cylinder engine cast in two blocks of three cylinders, with only three main bearings but with full-pressure lubrication. Transmission was through a four-speed gearbox and a live axle was fitted. The 8.1-litre Type C was a big chain-driven car (shaft drive was to be used on all models from 1910). Although both of these early sixes were renowned for their smoothness and flexibility – the quality of pulling from very slow speed in top gear was a merit sought in all big Edwardian cars – still larger engines were to come.

In 1908 the CA had a 9.3-litre six, and the SMT had a capacity of 11,846 cc (723 cu in). The SMT was a rare car, and three were built to the most exacting standards – 'SMT' signified *Sa majesté le Tsar*. It had a compressed-air starter, so that the SMT could be started and run in top gear from a standstill without emitting explosive noises. The engine ran on compressed air for the first few yards, when the fuel supply was turned on and it fired normally.

One of the SMT cars was fitted with a vast limousine body by Kellner of Paris, who within its 244 cm (8 ft) overall height had to allow for a passenger to stand upright. At the chauffeur's feet were nine pedals – left and right differential brakes, engine brake, sprag, clutch, accelerator, engine oil pump, carburettor agitator and whistle.

Only a little lower down the scale, the Type F was a 5.9-litre model which found customers among Europe's royal families while the Type I was the smallest of the early Delaunay-Bellevilles, with a 2.5-litre straight six. Derivatives continued to be built into the mid-1920s, and the company survived as a minor manufacturer through to 1950.

De Tomaso Pantera

Alejandro de Tomaso was an all-round motoring entrepreneur in the 1960s – once a racing driver, he built racing cars, which were generally unsuccessful, and high-performance road cars in small numbers. Two of his cars, the GT Vallelunga of 1965 and the open Pampero of 1966, led to the elegant Mangusta which was the direct forerunner of the Pantera.

The car followed the contemporary mid-engined layout proved in circuit cars and increasingly favoured for road-going supercars. For his Mangusta engine, de Tomaso had turned to the known Ford 289 V8 – cheap, reliable and powerful. It made the car attractive to Ford, who were still cultivating a 'performance image' in the USA and wanted to distribute a GT car that could be produced in reasonable numbers.

As the alliance with Ford became firm, de Tomaso's design team, headed by Gianpaolo Dallara, laid down a new monocoque design, with a shell of fabricated sheet steel and subframes to support the engine and rear suspension. Wishbone and coil spring independent suspension was used all round, and the sleek lines were the work of Ghia.

A new Ford V8, the 5.7-litre (351 cu in) unit introduced in 1969, took the place of the 289 V8. In the base L model this was rated at 330 bhp in 'European' form and 310 bhp when US emissions ancillaries were added. It drove through a ZF five-speed gearbox. Respectively, the two versions of the engine gave claimed top speeds of 170 mph (274 kph) and 162 mph (212 kph), although in fact all-out performance fell a little short of those figures.

The Pantera was officially launched in 1970, and although it was well received sales never remotely justified the original 4000 per annum production target. Certainly from 1974 de Tomaso did not even claim a four-figure annual production.

For 1971 de Tomaso announced an ambitious racing programme, backed by Ford, and competition engines were prepared by Bud Moore to produce around 400 bhp. However, this made no impact – the best showing came in the Monza 1000 km race, where one Pantera was fifth.

As a road super car it survived, practical in its mechanical parts, not so practical in its accommodation. It was occasionally uprated, and in its GT5 form sprouted bulges and a prominent rear wing, unnecessary as the car's handling was always good.

The Ford association ended in 1974, and when production of the US-sourced V8 ceased de Tomaso turned to Ford of Australia for a 300 bhp alternative. Production was moved across Modena to a modest factory, where a few cars were built each year.

Duesenberg Model J

When Frederick and August Duesenberg built their first production car, the Model A, in 1921 they already had a formidable reputation for their racing engines, as well as powerplants for other uses. Through the 1920s that reputation grew, with a victory in the French Grand Prix in 1921 and three in the Indianapolis 500 during the decade. In 1926 Errett Loban Cord bought the factory and, recognizing Fred Duesenberg's talents, set him to designing an outstanding road car.

That design took shape as the Model J, which was launched at the 1928 New York Motor Show. It was a very substantial car, with deep pressed-steel chassis side members 216 mm (8½ in) deep at their centres and six cross members – the chassis weighed

more than 2000 kg (4409 lb), before coachbuilders added their bodywork. Semi-elliptic leaf spring suspension was used front and rear; contemporary reports praised ride and handling. Hydraulic 15 in drum brakes took care of stopping.

The straight-eight engine was built by Lycoming to Duesenberg's designs. It was a twin overhead camshaft unit, with aluminium connecting rods and pistons and a massive fully-balanced five-bearing crankshaft. The publicity claims for its output were 265 bhp, and the reality was not far short of that, at 250 bhp at 4250 rpm. That gave the open four-seater J, with a road weight of some 2500 kg (5512 lb), a top speed of 115 mph (185 kph).

Initially all bodies were built by outside specialists, but in 1929 a factory body styling department was set up under the redoubtable Gordon Buehrig.

That car carried the company through the worst years of the Depression, then in 1932 a supercharged version, the SJ, was announced. This did bring the car into the sporting category where all Js have sometimes been placed, for the addition of the centrifugal supercharger increased the maximum power to 320 bhp, and speed to 130 mph (210 kph). Outwardly chromed exhausts distinguished the SJ – but dummies could always be added to a J.

August Duesenberg took over as chief engineer when Fred died after an accident in an SJ in 1932, but there were few more developments. The most spectacular were two short-wheelbase SS SJ roadsters built in 1936 and sold to Clark Gable and Gary Cooper. The marque survived until 1937, when the plant was sold. Production petered out, the last car being completed in 1940, to bring the total to 472.

Facel Vega

Facel Vega was the brainchild of Jean Daninos, whose Facel company (Forges et Ateliers de Construction d'Eure et de Loire) had undertaken some body manufacture for companies such as Panhard and Simca. At a time when the last of the great French luxury and specialist car marques were fading away, victims of taxation, he aspired to recreate the *grands routiers,* the grand touring cars of the not-so-distant French past. He also chose to approach the project realistically, in that he appreciated that one way to achieve high performance without high engine development costs was to buy in ready-made American V8 power units. When Facel backs were turned on that premiss the company got into real trouble.

Power was the essence of the Facel Vega line, from the 4.5-litre (275 cu in) 180 bhp Chrysler V8 in the first car to be shown (in 1954) and put into production, through the 360 bhp of the 1960 6.3-litre (384 cu in) version to as much as 390 bhp by the same V8 in the 1962 Facel II.

The physical make-up of these big cars was straightforward, with strong tubular chassis and well-made and well-proportioned 2+2 bodies. The suspension was conventional, with a live rear axle; it was generally 'soft', but the cars had a good ride and good roadholding, and they were quiet. Transmission was through a four-speed manual gearbox or a three-speed Torqueflite. Stopping – and there was a lot of car to stop – was initially by massive alloy drum brakes, but discs were to come in 1960.

The Excellence four-door pillarless saloon was introduced in 1956, to be produced in very small numbers through to 1960 (156 were built in all).

The first major redesign of the 2+2 produced the best-known Facel Vega, the HK500 with a 5.9-litre (360 cu in) engine, in 1958. This was a 145 mph 235 kph) car, and for the first years it still had drum brakes.

These cars had a real place in the French and wider European car markets, but the company faced a classic dilemma: it could continue as a successful low-volume specialist, or it could expand. The choice was to branch out with smaller models, and ultimately that proved fatal.

The Facellia was offered from 1960 as a 2+2 coupé or convertible, with a mechanical specification that was closely similar to the big cars' (save that disc brakes were specified from the launch) and it retained the balanced lines of the HK500, at the size of an MGB. However, Facel chose to develop its own twin-ohc power unit for these cars, and while it was rated at 115 bhp to give a 110 mph (177 kph) top speed, it was notoriously unreliable. Warranty claims became common, causing the company grave embarrassment.

A 1.8-litre Volvo engine was offered in a version designated Facel III (Facel II had been a restyled big car), while a more promising line was initiated with a new model powered by the 2.8-litre 150 bhp BMC C-series engine. It also had long overdue revisions to the chassis. But it was too late, the company failed, and the last cars were built in September 1964. Surviving Facel Vegas are relatively scarce, and are much prized by their owners.

Ferrari 250GTO

A '250GT' designation recurs through more than a decade of Ferrari history, and even among the red cars from Maranello the 250GTO stands out. More than half of the cars produced were brought together for a reunion in France in 1987 to mark the 25th anniversary of the first 250GTO, and that defines the model's status and magic more emphatically than pages of words or statistics.

The first 250s had been open sports cars built around the Colombo-designed and Lampredi-developed 60-degree V12 engine in 1952, when Bracco won the Mille Miglia in a 250 Sport, and that led to the 250MM appellation. Most of those 250s were open cars with bodies built by Vignale, but Pininfarina built some with attractive coupé bodies, and these could be regarded as forerunners of the GT range.

Ferrari had begun to take GT racing seriously in the mid-1950s, and built numerous *berlinetta* 250GTs, then at the end of the decade a full international GT championship was announced. As the main-line Ferraris retired at Le Mans in 1959, a 250GT came through to finish third, heading two more coupés in fourth and sixth places.

They had a new body shape that was carried through to short-wheelbase cars announced later that year, and this 250GT was homologated as a GT car in mid-1960. It had a tubular chassis – not then a space frame as such – and retained a live rear axle. Disc brakes were fitted all round. The *Lusso* was on paper the road car version, with trim in the cockpit and a steel body; the Competition version had alloy bodywork and a 270 bhp V12. The first success for these cars after homologation (ie, acceptance that sufficient had been built to a specification to comply with requirements in the international regulations) came at Le Mans, where they placed 4-5-6 in 1960.

Meanwhile Ferrari was working on the 250GTO development, where one objective was high-speed stability, and in this engineer Bizzarini made use of a wind tunnel – an application not very common in the middle-years Ferrari history! A dry-sump engine allowed the nose to be lower, while an elegant spoiler was added at the tail. That set a seal on the elegant body. For this car, the V12 was initially rated at 295 bhp at 7500 rpm, and it drove through a five-speed gearbox (the 250GTs had been effective with a mundane four-speed box). It was a car with a potential maximum speed of 180 mph (290 kph), although as that called for seldom-used gearing, a more realistic figure was probably around 165 mph (265 kph).

The 'O' in the designation stood for *omologato*, a statement that production exceeded 100; this claim was accepted, although the real production was 39 cars. Next time Ferrari presented a car for homologation, the authorities looked much harder!

Be that as it may, the cars dominated the GT championship for three seasons, and slightly modified versions of the GTO known as GTO 64 were run in the third of them. Then Ferrari turned away from GT racing, and soon collectors sought his beautiful and successful 250GTOs.

Ferrari 275

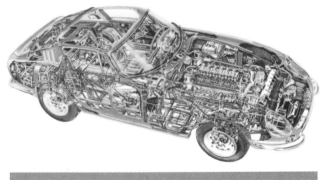

This was an important Ferrari, in itself and as the first of a line of classic two-seater Gran Turismo Berlinetta models, and a very significant move towards the marque's later supercars. It was the first road-going Ferrari with all-independent suspension and a five-speed gearbox, and during its production run it was to become the first to have a twin-ohv V12. In both coupé and convertible forms it had svelte and balanced lines by Pininfarina.

The 275 was unveiled at the 1964 Paris Motor Show, fitted with the ultimate enlargement of the Colombo-originated 60-degree V12 engine, with the bore taken out to 77 mm (3 in) to give a capacity of 3285.7 cc (200.5 cu in). The 'normal' version breathed through three Weber twin-choke carburettors and produced 280 bhp at 7600 rpm; buyers could specify six twin-choke Webers, and that raised the output to 300 bhp at 7500 rpm.

There was much beyond the engine to attract attention in Paris, for example in the five-speed gearbox which was mounted in unit with the final drive in the interests of overall balance as the engine was positioned well forward to give adequate foot wells. The independent suspension was by double wishbones and coil springs front and rear. Beside this the chassis was very traditional, consisting of two substantial tubular members with ladder cross bracing, sub assemblies to mount the suspension and outrigged members to carry the body.

Although both bodies were styled by Pininfarina, that house built only the 275GTB coupés, while Scaglietti continued his long association with Ferrari and made the 275GTS convertibles. These were rather let down by the chassis which relied for some of its stiffness on the steel bodywork of the coupé – the convertibles and the GTB/C competition cars with alloy bodies were unsatisfactory in this respect.

There were other problems – propellor shaft flexing which induced vibrations (a torque tube with a centre bearing to house the shaft cured this), severe brake fade with the small discs, and front-end lift at high speeds (wind tunnel work resulting in a slightly extended nose cured that).

The major change to the specification came in 1966 when a four-cam version of the V12, rated at 300 bhp, was introduced in the 275GTB/4. Wider wheels came, a ZF limited-slip differential replaced the Ferrari unit, and there were detail improvements. Better brakes were not among these, which seems a little odd with a 160-plus mph (260 kph) car, and nor was a higher standard of cockpit trim and fittings. That was to come with the Daytona, in some ways the successor to the 275.

Ferrari Daytona

This was the ultimate front-engined Ferrari for the road – not the last, as the 400 went on into the 1980s, but the last of a classic line. It was supremely elegant and, in its day, the fastest road car in the world, capable of speed matched by few later supercars.

The Daytona picked up where Ferrari had to leave off with the 275. The basic layout followed that car, with the engine positioned well forward and the rear-mounted gearbox combined with the differential. The 275 had used the original V12 stretched to its limit, and tuned beyond the point acceptable in some emissions-conscious regions. To achieve similar performance, a larger engine was called for, and that existed in the 'big-block' 60-degree V12 that had been designed by Lampredi in 1951. A twin-ohc version was developed for the Daytona, and in this form and with a capacity of 4.4 litres it was rated at 352 bhp at 7500 rpm, with massive torque, 318 lb/ft at 5500 rpm, which spelled Acceleration.

Maximum speed was helped by effective aerodynamics – here was an outstanding case of 'what looks right, is right'. Once again Pininfarina was responsible for the styling, and Scaglietti for building the production bodies. The lines were smoother than those of the 275GTB, and were sensible from the headlight treatment to the practical luggage accommodation at the rear.

Suspension was again all-independent, using unequal length wishbones and coil springs, with anti-roll bars, and coupled with a high degree of chassis stiffness this gave it largely neutral handling. The masses at the extremities – engine at the front, transaxle at the rear – could result in embarrassing oversteer, but this was a supercar that any sensible driver could handle. And sense was obviously called for, as even if Ferrari's claimed 180 mph (290 kph) top speed seemed just a little beyond actual achievement, an *Autocar* road test proved a 174 mph (280 kph) capability. In this Ferrari, the disc brakes (11 in ventilated Girlings) were quite adequate.

Although the glass area appears limited, visibility from the cockpit was good. And, unlike the 275GTB, the interior was by no means sparse. Just over 100 of the 1500 Daytonas were convertibles, which are now so sought after that coupés have been converted and 'replicar' companies such as PLIA, RAM and Robin Hood have specialized in lookalikes in the second half of the 1980s, most using Jaguar components, once the supply of parts from crashed coupés ran out ('repairs' to spyder form were most common in the USA).

Although this was a highly refined grand touring car, independent entrants did race Daytonas, with top-six placings at Le Mans in 1971-73, while a Daytona was second in the Daytona 24-hour race in 1973 and 1979, the latter placing gained by a NART car when the model had been out of production for some years!

Sadly the Daytona had to give way to mid-engined cars, and production ended in 1974. But the Daytona stands out as one of the all-time Ferrari classics.

Ferrari Dino

Ferrari stories often start with an engine, and the story of the very pretty little Dino road cars follows that tradition. The Dino V6 engines were named for Ferrari's son, who died in 1956, for he had played a part in the development of Vittorio Jano's original design for this power unit. It was used in various competition cars, and in various forms, for ten years before thought was given to using it in a road car.

That was spurred by a perceived need to broaden Ferrari's market, and a smaller car to compete with Porsche was attractive in that respect. Then there was the realization that a race-bred V6 would be ideal for the Formula 2 racing category that was to come into effect in 1967, which had regulations calling for production-based engines.

To that end, the V6 was reworked to make it suitable for production, as a twin-ohc 65-degree unit, substantially over-square with bore and stroke dimensions of 85 mm × 57 mm (3.4 in × 2.2 in), to give a capactiy of 1987 cc (121 cu in). It was rated at 180 bhp at 8000 rpm.

The first prototype car was shown by Pininfarina in 1965, and the second, tidied and rationalized for possible production, was shown a year later. In its first form, the car had the engine installed longitudinally, but in the definitive version it was mounted transversely ahead of the rear axle line. Double wishbone and coil spring suspension was used, relatively large disc brakes were fitted, and this was the first road Ferrari to have rack and pinion steering.

It was put into production hesitantly, for there were misgivings about a 'poor man's Ferrari', and Fiat also introduced a Bertone-styled Dino coupé and a Pininfarina-styled Dino convertible. That ensured that the V6 was produced in quantity, if in modified form. Primarily, the Fiat cylinder blocks were cast in iron rather than in light alloy, and both bore and stroke were opened out to give a capacity of 2418 cc (148 cu in). In this form, maximum power of 195 bhp was achieved at a slightly lower engine speed of 7600 rpm.

Ferrari production of the Dino 206GT was low, but quickened when the Fiat engine was adopted for 1969 and sheet steel bodywork substituted for the hand-shaped aluminium panels of the 206GT. Other changes increased the overall dimensions slightly, but to all outward appearances the models were identical. The only substantial change before production ended in 1974 was the introduction of a Targa-top 246GTS in 1972. The 246 was never developed for competition as the 206 had been.

In part it was heavy, at 1090 kg (2403 lb), and this meant that in maximum speed terms it was no quicker than its rivals, with a 148 mph (238 kph) top. In many other respects – overall handling qualities, braking, traction and cockpit habitability – it excelled. Production in six years totalled 3900 cars, almost a third of them GTS cabriolets.

Ferrari 308

Ferrari had to look to a successor to the Dino 246 for the mid-1970s, as the market for cars in this category was then at best static and rival manufacturers were fighting for a larger share of it, particularly Porsche with the developing 911 and, nearer home, Lamborghini with the Urraco and Maserati with the Merak. To combat these a new Ferrari had to be larger, and thus heavier, so a new power unit was necessary.

The 308GT4 made its debut at the 1973 Paris Motor Show, and caused something of a stir. For the first time since 1953 Ferrari had a production model styled by a house other than Pininfarina, and the engine was a V8, a very rare type in the Ferrari repertoire. Bertone undertook to clothe the tubular chassis frame, and met the daunting requirement to produce a 2+2 within relatively tight dimensional restrictions, while not aping the curves of the earlier Dinos. In overall terms the specification was similar.

The new engine was a 90-degree V8 (81 mm × 71 mm/3.2 in × 2.8 in, 2926 cc/179 cu in) with a light-alloy block, cylinders fairly close as transverse mounting meant that engine length had to be watched carefully, and four overhead camshafts. It was rated at 255 bhp at 7700 rpm.

In terms of performance it matched the Dino 246, with a marginally higher maximum speed. But the first 308GT4 2+2 was not an outstanding success, and in 1975 the Autumn motor shows featured the Pininfarina-styled 308GTB. This was closer to the original Dinos and, indeed, it had a family resemblance to the 512B Boxer. Its dimensions

were similar to the smaller car's, it was a two-seater, and it was the first production Ferrari to have a glassfibre body (by Scaglietti). A steel body was to come in 1977, with the GTS Targa version.

Through the late 1970s, and into the 1980s, there was a constant struggle to maintain the power outputs of the V8 and meet emission regulations – for some time, the 308s were the only Ferraris that were street-legal in the USA. In 1981 fuel injection took the place of the four Weber carburettors, and peak power dropped from 255 bhp to 214 bhp, but tighter emission requirements were met while another version was developed.

This appeared in 1982 as the Quattrovalvole (QV), as the cylinder heads were modified to accommodate four valves per cylinder. Power output went up again, to 240 bhp at 7000 rpm, and the 308GTBi had a maximum speed of over 150 mph (240 kph) again. Meanwhile the 308GT4 had a replacement in the form of the Mondiale and in 1985 the capacity of the V8 shared by these models (was increased to give 3185 cc/194.4 cu in (83 mm × 73.6 mm/3.3 in × 2.9 in) to keep them ahead.

Ferrari Boxer

This was perhaps the outstanding supercar of the 1970s, the first large mid-engined Ferrari intended for road use, with purposeful and elegant Pininfarina styling which echoed a 1968 show car. Even then it seemed Ferrari was lagging behind Lamborghini, but Ferrari was not to be hurried — when the Berlinetta Boxer did appear it stole Lamborghini's thunder, and was a usable street car rather than near-racer with a civilized veneer.

Ferrari had used 'boxer' (horizontally-opposed) 12-cylinder engines in its racing models from 1964, and a 4390 cc (268 cu in) unit on these lines was chosen for the road car in preference to a V12. This type of engine allowed Ferrari's designers to install the transmission under the engine and thus avoid an unacceptably long engine/transmission, or a transverse engine installation.

The engine itself used many components from

the Daytona's V12, and had the same capacity. The chassis was conventional, with a square-tube frame and central sheet monocoque, steel-panelled save for glassfibre nose and tail sections. Front and rear suspension was naturally independent (with four shock absorbers at the rear) and ventilated disc brakes were fitted all round. The car was strictly a two-seater, with a functional cockpit; coupé bodies were the norm, the spyder, or Targa-bodied, version being rare. There were no concessions to US emissions requirements, or to safety regulations, so the engine was not strangled and nor were ponderous impact fenders added to ruin its lines.

Daytona sales held up well, so early BB production was not high, and in its initial form fewer than 400 were built before it was superseded by the 5-litre 512BB in 1976. Bore and stroke were increased, from 81 mm × 71 mm/3.1 in × 2.8 in up to 82 mm × 78 mm/3.2 in × 3 in; dry sump lubrication replaced the wet sump. At first a power output of 360 bhp was specified, the same as the 4.4-litre engine, but this was later amended to 340 bhp. However, there was a useful improvement in torque. Both cars had a maximum speed of almost 170 mph (275 kph), and that remained so when fuel injection replaced the four-Weber set-up in 1981.

With the larger engine came slight body changes, with wider wheels and a nose spoiler to eliminate some 'wander' at high speeds. Unsightly aerofoils were added to 512BBs that were raced. These cars enjoyed little success, 10th at Le Mans in 1980 being a highlight.

The Boxer was not perfect, but it was an outstanding supercar and more than 2500 were built before it was superseded by the Testa Rossa in 1984.

Ford Model T

The Model T was known by many nicknames, 'Tin Lizzie' perhaps being the most familiar and 'The Universal Car' the most appropriate. For Henry Ford's greatest creation really was that – unlike any car before or since, the Model T bestrode the roads of the world in its heyday to the exclusion of almost anything else. As the 1920s opened, half the cars in the world were Model Ts, and although its production record was eventually to be exceeded, that only happened in a very different age when car ownership was infinitely more widespread.

During the winter of 1906–07, Ford set up a tight little group to design a car to succeed the Model N. There was engineer Joseph Galamb, metallurgist Childe Harold Wills, machinist Jimmy Smith and pattern maker Charles Sorensen. And, according to Ford lore, there was Henry himself, feeding them ideas that came to him as he sat in his mother's rocking chair. The prototypes were run for a year before the Model T was announced to Ford managers in September 1908, and most of the first dozen were then sent to Europe to be shown at the London and Paris motor shows.

The Model T was a minimal car. The chassis frame had just two cross members, which also served to mount the transverse-leaf suspension front and rear, and a three-point mounting for the engine. That was advanced in some respects, in large part due to up-to-the-minute foundry work – its cylinders were cast in unit with the upper part of the crankcase and, uniquely among low-price cars of the period, it had a detachable cylinder head. It was also lightly stressed and very flexible, and that meant Ford was able to get away with a two-speed epicyclic transmisson with very wide gaps between bottom and top gears. There were brakes of a sort on the back wheels, a rather ineffectual transmission brake, and, to a modern driver, there was a profusion of controls.

No matter – it was to put the world on wheels (another Ford-inspired slogan). And, more than that, it showed the way into mass production as the modern industry might recognize it, for Henry Ford exploited economies of scale with parts standardization and coupled this with the moving production line at the Highland Park factory, introduced in 1913. Therein, too, is the reason why between 1914 and 1925 (with odd exceptions at branch factories) all Model Ts were black – coach paints dried too slowly, and the only suitable coating was a substance known as Black Japan. That was even used to coat the radiator from 1916.

There were revisions. Electric lights came in 1915, an electric horn in 1917, a battery starter for the saloon models in 1918, there was a choice of colours again in 1925, and so on. By 1925 the T was obsolete, and soon even Henry Ford had to accept that. Its successor, the Model A, was ready to go into production in the late Spring of 1927, and that was when Model T production ended. Even dedicated Ford historians cannot decide precisely how many were made. Their close estimate is 16 million.

Ford Thunderbird

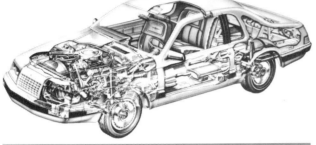

Some of the early Thunderbirds were classics, and only later was the name applied to mundane sedans. To enthusiasts in the mid-1950s it was an American sports car, however wide of the mark that might have been in European terms, and however much Ford might have insisted that it was a 'personal car'. It evolved in parallel with Chevrolet's Corvette, and its final design phase was hurried as that car was launched – indeed, the T-bird was announced before dealers had any cars. A then-unnamed prototype was shown in Detroit early in 1954, and the car was a key element in Ford's 1955 model range, announced in September 1954.

In Ford terms those early two-seaters were small cars, with a 259 cm (102 in) wheelbase and 142 cm (56 in) track, and apart from the 'personal car' theme there was nothing novel in them. Indeed, Ford simply drew most components from the corporate parts bin. The engines were V8s, the first being a Mercury 4785 cc (292 cu in) 198 bhp unit, followed by a 5112 cc (312 cu in) 225 bhp version in 1956, and the next year there were four V8 options, the largest at 5768 cc (352 cu in) offering more than 300 bhp. These were mounted well back in the substantially-braced chassis to give a 49/51 weight distribution. That promised good handling, but the promise was undermined by stock sedan suspension.

The first face-lift came in 1956, when the spare wheel was mounted almost horizontally under a metal cover at the rear, and a detachable hard-top (with portholes) was available. A year later there were tail fins, albeit modest ones in that period of 'rocket' styling. In 1958 the main-line T-bird was a four-seater, with a short-lived roadster two-seat option. Cynics dubbed it 'Squarebird'; the sales increased.

There had been a brief flirtation with power in 1957 when in response to the fuel-injected Corvette Ford built 100 cars with Paxton-McCulloch super-charged V8s rated at 325 bhp. But that passed, and the emphasis was increasingly on luxury. Varying styles were offered and engine size reached 6997 cc

(427 cu in) with 425 bhp in the mid-1960s – too much, really, for the sedan suspension. Through another styling change in 1967, when there was also a reversion to a separate body and chassis, the car continued as a large model until the mid-1970s.

The first small Thunderbird came in 1977, in a badge-engineered clone of the Mercury Cougar. An ugly version came in 1980, again with unitary construction, and for the first time with in-line six-cylinder engines. In one of the options offered for the sleeker 1983 range there was a four, an ohc unit with Brazilian origins and a turbocharger. At that time the 2.3-litre (141 cu in) unit was over-stressed, but when uprated to 190 bhp for 1987 the Thunderbird had real performance again, with a 130 mph (210 kph) top speed to match its swoopy good looks.

Ford Mustang

This was the first of the 'pony cars', conceived and introduced at precisely the right time to capture a vast new buying public in America, the people of the post-War baby boom, many of whom were enthusiasts for sporting cars. As the Thunderbird had been allowed to grow fat and soft, Ford had entered the 1960s without a sporting car in their range and Lee Iacocca, a Ford vice-president and intuitive marketing man, saw the sales potential. The Mustang was laid down to fit his projections, and proved the demand for a fairly small personal car beyond any doubt – a million were sold in two years, and the rest of the industry would follow Ford's example.

Mechanically, there was nothing novel about the Mustang range that was launched in 1964, and the wide variety of engine and transmission options was 'borrowed' from the Falcon, Fairlane and Galaxy lines. Initially, a 2.8-litre (171 cu in) 101 bhp straight six, a 4.2-litre (257 cu in) 164 bhp V8 and a 4.7-litre (287 cu in) 210 bhp V8 were listed, with three- or four-speed manual gearboxes or the Cruise-O-Matic three-speed automatic. A platform chassis with body panels welded to it was in effect a unitary structure. Options included 'special handling suspension', Kelsey-Hayes disc brakes in place of the inadequate Ford drums and engine tuning.

Late in 1964 Carroll Shelby started to rework the Mustang around the basis of that very stiff chassis, concentrating on the engines and enjoying great success in SCCA production class racing. Best-known

EVOLUTION — FORD MUSTANG

1962 Mustang shown to test public reaction to a small sporty Ford

1964 Mustang production car introduced as a 1965 model with a 2.8-litre (170 cu in) in-line six-cylinder engine as a standard, while options included 3.3-litre (202 cu in) six and 4.3- and 4.7-litre (262 and 286 cu in) V8s. Three body styles were available – hardtop convertible and coupé

1965 Shelby Mustang GT-350 introduced with 4.7-litre (289 cu in) V8

1966 Base engine became the 3.3-litre six

1967 Optional 6.4-litre (390 cu in) V8 with 320 bhp introduced. Shelby GT-500 introduced with 400 bhp 7-litre Cobra Jet V8 became available.

1968 5-litre (302 cu in) with 230 bhp and 390 bhp big-block 7-litre (427 cu in) V8 introduced as options. Later in the year the 7-litre Cobra Jet V8 became available

1969 Mustang Grande introduced as luxury version. Mach I introduced as high-performance variant. Styling revised. Mach I available with either the 250 bhp 5762 cc (351 cu in) or the 355 bhp 428 Cobra Jet V8 and two ultra high-performance models introduced – the Boss 302 and Boss 429

1970 GT suspension package discontinued exept on Boss and Mach 1 models. The big-block 6.4-litre (390 cu in) V8 discontinued.

1971 Range restyled. Boss 302 and 429 dropped and replaced by the limited-production Boss 351

1974 Mustang II introduced. Base engine was the overhead-cam 2.3-litre (140 cu in) four while the Mach I was powered by a 2.8-litre (170 cu in) V6

1979 Third generation Mustang introduced with completely new styling and MacPherson strut front suspension. Base engine was still the 2.3-litre four with the 2.8-litre V6 and 5-litre (305 cu in) V8 as options. A turbocharged 2.3 was optional equipment and standard on the Mustang Cobra

1982 Mustang GT reintroduced with 5-litre V8

1983 Mustang Convertible reintroduced with 3.8-litre (232 cu in) V6 or in GT form with the 5-litre V8. Five-speed manual gearbox standard on GT.

1984 SVO Mustang introduced with turbocharged 2.3-litre four with intercooler

1986 1987 GT/LX 5.0 had uprated running gear and 225 bhp 4950 cc (302 cu in) V8

Shelby variants were the GT-350 two-seater, and the GT 500 KR (King of the Road) with a 7-litre (428 cu in) V8 producing over 400 bhp. Having created a great performance image for the Mustang, Shelby then tired of the association and sold out to Ford. Meanwhile, in Europe, Mustangs run as four-seater saloons enjoyed a parallel period of racing successes, with teams such as Alan Mann's.

The Boss Mustang was the dominant TransAm car of 1970, notably the Bud Moore-prepared cars with 460 bhp engines, refined suspension and brakes, and aerofoils. Inevitably, the Mustang was then 'down-sized' towards the mid-1970s, starting with the Pinto-based Mustang II (which had 2.3-litre/ 141 cu in and 2.6-litre/159 cu in V6 engines), then the 5-litre (305 cu in) V8 from late 1974, strangled by emissions controls. Those three engines were featured in the third-generation Mustang announced for 1979, which had notchback or fastback bodies.

Through the early 1980s Ford carefully felt its way back towards high-performance Mustangs, via an unhappy first experience with turbocharging the 2.3-litre six. By 1984 there was even a convertible again.

That year Ford got it right with turbocharging, too, with the sophisticated SVO Mustang. By 1987, the model bearing the name was once again in the 'performance car' league, in the form of the LX. Outwardly this was a restrained car, using the uprated transmission, steering, suspension and brakes from the GT, with a 225 bhp (SAE) fuel-injected ohv V8. That 4949 cc (302 cu in) unit gave it acceleration that almost matched the early-1970s 302 in Boss Mustangs.

Frazer Nash

A mere 323 chain-driven Frazer Nash sports cars were built, between 1924 and 1939, but their reputation and the affection in which some of their idiosyncracies are held far outweighs the modest production numbers.

Archibald Frazer Nash and Henry Ronald Godfrey started to produce GN cyclecars in 1910, initially fairly crude devices typical of the breed, but powered by a twin-cylinder air-cooled vee twin engine designed by Godfrey in 1911. In 1916 a single car was built with chain drive in place of the belt, and this was followed through in post-war GNs. By 1921-22 the boom years for cyclecars were over, and after a receiver was appointed to look after GN's affairs for a second time Godfrey and Nash left.

Nash set up a company in Kingston, Frazer Nash, to build sports cars and these were unique as he adapted a GN-type transmission. This had a solid rear axle and separate drive chains, with sprockets and dog clutches for each of the three forward speeds and reverse, which made for a light quick-change system, accessible for ratio changes.

To distance the cars from a cyclecar image, Nash used conventional proprietary engines, initially Plus-Power ohv four-cylinder 1.5-litre units in three stages of tune, for the 38 bhp Tourer, the 52 bhp Sports and the 60 bhp Super Sports. They were installed in a light simple frame, with quarter-elliptic suspension front and rear. Two- or three-seater bodies were fitted, and as bodywork was light to complement the rest of the car, performance was good.

But the Plus-Power company failed when 16 cars had been built, and Nash turned to Anzani side-valve engines for the first well-known Frazer Nash, the Boulogne of 1925. That year 50 cars were produced, the best-ever for Frazer Nash, and there was an important racing success when Clive Gallop won the Boulogne Grand Prix.

But the company was not healthy, and the Aldington brothers took over at the end of 1928. They introduced a Meadows 1.5-litre engine, then for 1930 brought out a new generation of cars, most notably the TT Replica, an 80 mph (130 kph) car. AFN developed the Meadows engine to produce 55 bhp, then offered a six-cylinder Blackburne engine in both 1499 cc (91 cu in) and 1660 cc (101 cu in) forms, and Frazer Nash's own Gough-designed single-ohc four-cylinder unit (made for EFN by Bean).

Through the mid-1930s the cars performed well in races and rallies, but by 1934 the 'chain-gang' cars were increasingly pushed to one side, for AFN had an agreement to market BMWs in Britain. The last chain-drive car was delivered in 1939, but production had not reached double figures in any one of the preceding three years.

Hispano-Suiza Alfonso

The Hispano Alfonso was one of the first great sporting cars, in concept perhaps owing something to the American raceabouts, and outlining the 'flexible four-cylinder' pattern to be followed in later sports cars. Its creator was a Swiss engineer, Marc Birkigt, who had become involved in early Spanish car ventures. Its name was bestowed after the Queen of Spain gave her husband a 15-45 hp two-seater Hispano-Suiza knowing that he already appreciated the marque's virtues of performance and flexibility. Royal permission was duly granted to name the 15T the Alfonso XIII.

Birkigt had been involved with the company that

built Castro cars, and out of the wreckage of that the second firm to include Hispano-Suiza in its title was created, with Birkigt as engineering director. The basis of the 15T was a 2.6-litre four-cylinder car that won two important voiturette races in France in 1910 and was successful in Catalan Cup events run under the patronage of Alfonso XIII.

The racing engine had a very long stroke (65 mm × 200 mm/2.6 in × 7.9 in) but for the road car Birkigt changed the ratio in the interests of flexibility, to 80 mm × 180 mm (3.1 in × 7.1 in), to give a swept volume of 3619 cc (221 cu in). It was a side-valve T-head four, in which the inlet and exhaust valves were on opposite sides of the cylinders. The engine was built in unit with the gearbox, initially a three-speed box, although four speeds were to be offered later.

However, the familiar image is of rakish two-seaters or three-seaters, and their sporting character-istics meant that Alfonsos were raced at venues such as Brooklands. It seems most Alfonsos were built in the Hispano-Suiza Paris factory, rather than in Spain.

By the time production was under way Birkigt was working on other projects. The Alfonso con-tinued until 1914 and the car's popularity ran on into the 1920s, particularly in Britain where its long-stoke engine was suited to a peculiar road tax system based on cylinder bore.

Hispano-Suiza Type 68

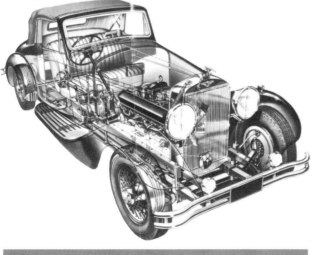

The supreme Hispano-Suiza came from the com-pany's French factory at an inauspicious time, and one mark of its quality is to be found in the simple

fact that more than a hundred were sold in a most severe economic period, and in competition with several other *voitures de grande luxe*. Soon after the Type 68 was announced, the company's efforts were to be redirected 'down-market', with little success, and to armaments. So this was a last grand gesture, and it was to remain in very limited production until the French arm of the company with the Spanish-Swiss name turned its back on cars in 1938.

The first 'French' Hispano-Suiza had been the H6B of 1919, and the straight-six theme introduced with that car was to be followed through to the end. But for the Type 68 Birkigt laid down a V12, and in the interests of quiet running he turned away from overhead camshafts to pushrod-operated overhead valves. The aluminium block of the 60-degree unit was cast in two sections, each bank of cylinders had its own water pump, there were twin ignition sets with two plugs per cylinder, and the two Hispano-Suiza carburettors were between the banks. A bore and stroke of 100 mm × 100 mm (3.94 in × 3.94 in) gave the generous capacity of 9425 cc (574.9 cu in), and the power output was of the order of 220 bhp. A Type 68-*bis* was to appear with a 120 mm (4.7 in) stroke (capacity 11,310 cc/690 cu in), and rated at 250 bhp. Both were to be used in French railcars, which increased the production run and helped offset development costs.

A conventional ladder-type chassis was pro-vided for coachbuilders, and apart from town cars and limousines, they responded with some of the most elegant coupés and two-seater convertibles created in the 1930s. The Paris factory did not build any complete cars.

The transmission was conventional, with a three-speed gearbox and a choice of four alternative axle ratios, while the drive shaft was in two parts, with a mid-point uj in a rigid housing, whence it was carried in a casing to the live rear axle. Suspension comprised semi-elliptic springs, with Duplex friction dampers that could be adjusted from the driver's seat. The brake servo system which Hispano-Suiza had introduced to the world of motoring in 1919 was naturally incorporated.

Cars with most bodies were capable of 100 mph (161 kph), and the few with more ponderous bodywork must have had a top speed approaching that magic figure.

Apart from odd cars assembled in Spain, V12 production was concentrated in France, where 110 Type 68s were built before the company became more and more committed to armament and aero-engine work. Limited Hispano-Suiza production was resumed at the Barcelona plant after the Civil War and continued until 1944, but after World War 2 the Paris factory turned out only a single prototype car. Perfectionist Marc Birkigt kept one of the V12 cars for personal use through his retirement in Switzerland, where he died in 1953.

Horch V12

Horch was one of Germany's oldest car manufacturers, dating from 1900, which built a wide range of models through to the 1920s. During that decade its production dwindled, to the point where just a few prestige straight eights were being built under the direction of Paul Daimler, son of the great pioneer Gottlieb Daimler. He left in 1929, to be replaced by Fritz Fiedler, who persuaded the directors that the salvation of Horch as a car manufacturer lay in direct competition with the top models in the Mercedes-Benz range.

That was ambitious, but credible when defined as offering a luxury car with a V12 to compete with a similarly priced car with a straight eight. And the car that emerged in 1931 was impressive, massive and thoroughly Teutonic in character.

Its 6-litre engine was an unadventurous side-valve 60-degree unit, rated at 120 bhp. This drove through a four-speed ZF gearbox. The heavy ladder-type chassis with box-section side members was underslung and beam axles were used front and rear. It was available in two wheelbase lengths, and the shorter of these was common to straight-eight models that were run in parallel, and often had closely similar bodies.

The 600 chassis was used for pullman body-work, usually large four-door cars, while the two-door cabriolets which are more familiar today (perhaps simply because all the Horch V12s to survive are this type) were 670s on a short 345 cm/136 in chassis. However, some sedans were built on this chassis, and from 1932 a longer (375 cm/148 in) wheelbase was available for a Pullman Sedan, and also bodied from the next year as a 'Pullman Cabriolet', which in its open form remains familiar from newsreels as a parade car.

Without a payload, the lightest of the 670 cabriolets weighed in at around 2200 kg (4850 lb), and with no more than 120 bhp available the cars were not exciting in outright speed terms – 87 mph (140 kph) was the manufacturer's claimed top speed.

By that time, the management that had commissioned the V12s had gone, for Horch became part of the Auto Union combine in 1932, joining Audi, DKW and Wanderer. Production did not last long, with the last V12s being completed in 1935. Some of the tooling and other production equipment was useful for the eight-cylinder models which continued through to the end of the 1930s, while the machine-tool department also made a contribution to the Auto Union Grand Prix cars.

A V12 in itself would not have saved Horch – the formation of Auto Union and a change of regime did that – but the car stands out as a soundly-conceived and craftsman-built example of a breed of luxury cars that came out of the Depression.

Isotta Fraschini Type 8

Cesare Isotta and Vincenzo Fraschini founded the company that bore their names in 1899 to import Mors and Renault cars into Italy, soon took the obvious step towards manufacturing by importing French engines to use in their own chassis, and produced their own car in 1903. This was the work of Giuseppe Stefanini, and in 1905 he was joined by the brilliant Giustino Cattaneo.

Isotta Fraschini survived an economic crisis, was taken over by the French De Dietrich company for two years, and was independent again from 1909. A sound range of cars was developed, together with an aero-engine business that was to become significant during World War 1, and a military truck line. During the war an eight-cylinder engine was developed, and a prototype car with this power unit was reported.

Straight eights were not new, for they had been seen in racing in 1907, but a true production straight eight was new when Isotta Fraschini announced theirs in 1919. The announcement was premature, but nonetheless it was soon in production and it was to be exported in some numbers, particularly to the United States.

The massive chassis and the running gear of the Type 8 were unremarkable, and bodies tended to be stately and well proportioned. The engine was in effect two four-cylinder units end to end on a light alloy block and with two cylinder heads, one for each 'set' of four cylinders. In spite of long experience with overhead camshaft engines, Cattaneo chose to specify pushrod overhead valves for this unit. The power output of the first engines was a modest 80 bhp, underlining an emphasis on smoothness and reliability rather than speed, and indeed the car was to be criticized for its sluggish performance. A top speed of 70 mph (113 kph) was quoted, possibly sufficient for the chauffeur-driven cars bought by personalities of the day.

To meet critics, the 8A was introduced in 1924 with a 7372 cc (450 cu in) engine rated at 120 bhp at 2400 rpm. This gave a top speed approaching 90 mph (144 kph); consequently larger brakes were fitted. A higher compression ratio engine producing 135 bhp was developed for a sports version, the 100 mph (161 kph) 8ASS of 1926.

A final redesign of engine and chassis produced the 8B in 1931. Larger side members and additional cross members made the chassis more rigid, higher revs made the engine more lively and a Wilson four-speed pre-selector gearbox was optional.

In the following year a new management team headed by Giovanni Caproni took over and, save for the short-lived Monterosa of the late 1940s, Isotta Fraschini abandoned car production.

Itala Grand Prix cars

In the earliest days of racing the way to achieve higher speeds was almost invariably through larger and larger engines, and this was seldom discour-

aged by the regulations for major races. Among the companies which sought prestige, and sales, through racing was Itala, relatively young (it was founded by Matteo Ceirano in 1903) and small.

In 1905 technical director Alberto Balloco started work on the first of a series of 'giant' racing cars, and that year a 14.7-litre Itala started in the Circuit des Ardennes. It retired, but a month later a team was run in the Coppa Florio at Brescia, when Giovanni Raggio drove one of them to win the 500 km race, averaging 65 mph (105 kph). The racing programme was continued in 1906, when 7.4-litre Italas finished first, second, fourth and fifth in the first Targa Florio in Sicily.

A three-car team was entered for the first French Grand Prix in 1906, the first national Grand Prix as such, when the cars were described as '120 hp' Italas. They featured only as early retirements – one was rolled on the first lap, another was involved in a crash on the second, and the last of the team fell out on the third lap when its radiator was holed by a stone. Two of the cars were run in the Vanderbilt Cup Race, with no more luck.

Itala prepared 14.4-litre cars for the 1907 Grand Prix, but these were run only once that year, in the Coppa della Velocita at Brescia, where Itala lead driver Alessandro Cagno stopped to put on 'non-skid' tyres as rain started to fall, and while others slid off the roads he motored on to win by more than three minutes.

That car was bought by a British enthusiast, Edgar Thornton, who fitted lights and mudguards. It was run in the 1908 St Petersburg (Leningrad) to Moscow race — the only event with top-line pretensions ever run in Russia — when H.R. Pope placed it third, and it was then used by Thornton as a road car until 1931. It has since been preserved in the form it was in when Cagno drove it to victory at Brescia in 1907.

Its 1908 successor in the Grand Prix was a 12-litre car – a maximum engine size was in effect imposed for this race, by a 155 mm (6.1 in) limit for the cylinder bore of four-cylinder engines (the Itala engine measurements were 154.8 mm × 160 mm 6.1 in × 6.3 in). Despite continuing to use '120 hp' these engines produced 100 bhp, at 1800 rpm. They followed Itala practice in having a single camshaft operating side exhaust valves and overhead inlet valves. At least the Italas had shaft drive (most cars in the 1908 GP had chain drive), but chassis and suspension were rudimentary, and being 1400 kg (3086 lb) the Italas were the heaviest cars in the race, despite their 'stripped' appearance.

In France the three-car team achieved 11th and 20th places, and in the American Grand Prize later that year Fournier placed one 8th while two retired. That was the end of their front-line career, although one was later raced at Brooklands, and is preserved in 1908 Grand Prix form.

Jaguar SS90 and SS100

Bill Lyons – later Sir William Lyons – was a shrewd businessman, the driving force and the stylist of the SS company. During the life of SS and his time with Jaguar he was adept at providing what the public wanted, and his cars usually combined striking lines with a good performance and value for money.

In partnership with William Walmsley, he developed the Swallow Sidecar and Coachbuilding Company in the 1920s, and from 1927 began to build bodies which transformed otherwise mundane cars – the Austin Swallow, based on the Seven, Fiat, Wolseley, Swift and Standard Swallows. The company's first full car, the SS1 coupé, made a sensational debut at the 1931 London Motor Show; albeit with a 2054 cc (125.3 cu in) side-valve Standard engine its performance hardly lived up to the promise of its long engine compartment and coupé body.

The SS name was never fully explained, and it could be applied to several combinations of Lyons' company and car initials; late in the 1930s it came to have unhappy connotations and was discarded.

September 1935 saw the announcement of Jaguar models with a 2.6-litre pushrod ohv engine, developed from the old side-valve Standard unit by Weslake (head and ports) and by Jaguar's first chief engineer, William Heynes. In place of the 70 bhp of the old engine, maximum power went up to 104 bhp at 4500 rpm.

Meanwhile, earlier in 1935 the exciting SS90 had been launched. Sports car traditionalists tried to dismiss it, but this model with its low sweeping lines, open cockpit with cutaway doors and short tail, which on all cars save the prototype carried an exposed spare wheel, really caught attention. Production was limited, and the car was obviously tailor-made for the new engine.

With that it became the SS100, which was not quite a 100 mph (161 kph) car in its first form. That speed came in 1937 when in common with the

saloons the sports car began to offer a 3845 cc (212.6 cu in) engine. Also common to both ranges was the basic chassis of box-section side members, under-slung at the rear, semi-elliptic springs suspension and effective drum brakes. A 1.5-litre ohv engine was an option. Apart from a one-off fixed-head coupé shown in 1938, all the 90s and 100s were open two-seaters.

Through the second half of the 1930s the cars were successful in rallies, in Europe as well as in Britain (they were raced but the factory preferred competitions that enhanced the image of a fast road car). Most impressively, perhaps, was Ian Appleyard's running of a 100 that was not registered until 1947 in two post-war Alpine Rallies, placing third in class in 1947 and winning a Coupe des Alpes in 1948.

Jaguar XK ━━

Few cars remain instantly recognizable more than a quarter of a century after the last in the range was built, and few designs influenced the changing shape of the sports car as much as the XK series. Yet the XKs came about almost incidentally, to publicize a new engine for Jaguar's saloons. These had been conceived during the War by William Lyons, chief engineer William Heynes and his assistant Walter Hassan, and draughtsman Claude Baily, their target being a 100 mph (161 kph) luxury saloon.

The engine design that took shape during fire-watching sessions that were later to become well publicized was for the XJ 2-litre four and XJ and XK straight sixes (3.2 and 3.4 litres). The XK was to emerge as the first mass-production twin-cam engine, which developed its target power of 160 bhp from the start and through over-engineering had considerable development potential.

The engine was ready for production in 1948. The saloon was two years off. So a limited run of sports cars was laid down, and came into being very quickly. The chassis of the Mk V saloon was pressed into use, in a slightly shortened form. Under Lyons' instinctive eye a series of mock-ups led to a graceful body with lines that flowed from nose to tail. It was a two-seater, not very spacious, and with a bench seat. Torsion bar front suspension and a live rear axle gave a ride which seemed less than 'sporting', although it had good handling qualities.

At the 1948 London Motor Show the one-off XK120 was a knockout. Jaguar's plans for a run of 200, built in a traditional manner with alloy panels over an ash frame, looked silly. Dies for steel bodywork production were prepared and some 12,000 XK120s were to be sold. Straight-line speed was proved on a Belgian autoroute, and sporting potential in events such as the Tourist Trophy and the Alpine Rally, while a private venture entry at Le Mans focussed Jaguar attention on that race and led to a splendid series of sports-racing cars.

The XK120 was succeeded by the XK140 in 1954. The new car had similar lines, a more spacious cockpit, minor suspension and weight distribution modifications which improved the handling quite considerably, and the straight six uprated to give 190 bhp, with an optional 210 bhp version that gave a 129 mph (207 kph) top speed.

The XK140 was replaced by the XK150 in 1957. This looked heavier than the XK120, but its cockpit was more comfortable (and there were wind-up windows) and, more important than comfort, it had Dunlop disc brakes front and rear. They complemented an increase in power and performance. The 210 bhp Blue Top engine was standard, then in 1958 a 250 bhp 'S' version was offered, and in 1959 a 265 bhp 3.8-litre engine was available.

Jaguar D-type

The svelte D-type was the most handsome sports-racing car of the mid-1950s, tailor-made to win the Le Mans 24-hour Race – Jaguar's own team achieved this in 1955, and the Ecurie Ecosse team won the French classic for Jaguar in the next two years. The cars were driven to win races all over the world and a road-equipped derivative, the XKSS, is now one of the most sought-after sports cars.

The D-type was to carry on the racing tradition so firmly based on the successful C-type, or XK120C, and some components were carried over, notably the suspension and the disc brake set-up that had been pioneered on the earlier cars, with triple-pad front brakes and double-pad rear brakes, plus a handbrake pad in the rear brakes.

The chassis, however, was completely new, built around an elliptical magnesium-alloy centre section monocoque, with substantial bulkheads front and rear. At the front a tubular subframe carried the engine and front suspension, while the rear axle was attached to the bulkhead by trailing links and a subframe carried the fuel tank and spare wheel. The aerodynamic body was the work of Malcolm Sayer, who picked up the cross-section of the monocoque, and this was also reflected in the neat oval radiator air intake. Outwardly there were several detail changes through the car's career, most notably as the first faired-in headrest behind the driver's seat was usually fitted with a fin, contributing to high-speed stability, longer noses were developed for 1955, and wrap-round screens replaced the early aero screens. A de Dion rear suspension was also tried in 1955.

The engine was the familiar straight six, with 3442 cc (210 cu in). Dry-sump lubrication, which halved the sump depth, and installation at eight degrees to the vertical, together with a cooling system which had the header tank positioned behind the radiator, helped to keep down the overall height of the nose. For the first D-types the engine was developed to give 245 bhp, and the 1955 team cars had 270 bhp units.

Dirty fuel which blocked filters almost certainly cost Jaguar a debut victory at Le Mans in 1954, when one of the D-types was beaten by a Ferrari by a mere 105 seconds, or roughly 2½ miles (4 km). But the team dominated its next race, at Reims, and won at Le Mans in 1955.

That year 'production' D-types appeared, and an Ecurie Ecosse car saved the day for Jaguar at Le Mans in 1956, as the works cars were put out in accidents or in one case delayed with a fuel supply defect. That was the works team's last race (although a successor was to come in the mid-1980s), but the D-types were still raced, some with 3781 cc (230.6 cu in) engines then, when race rules changed to a 3-litre limit in 1958, some with short-stroke 2986 cc (182 cu in) power units. An Ecurie Ecosse D won at Le Mans in 1957.

Early in 1957 a batch of 16 XKSS were built, with a passenger door and other 'civilized' touches, but before that theme could be extended the designated production area of the works was destroyed by fire.

Jaguar E-type

This was the supercar of the early 1960s, successor to Jaguar's XK ranges, with sleek lines and a competition background, which offered real high performance at a surprisingly low price. There were detail shortcomings in the early cars, and towards the end of its life the E-type lines were to appear a little dated. Faults there may have been, but this was another landmark car.

The Jaguar sports car line had seemed to wither as the XK150 put on weight and its heavy cart-sprung rear axle became a relic of another age, but in 1958, when that model was only a year old, the first prototype of the E was running. A definitive prototype, E2A, was raced at Le Mans by Briggs Cunningham in 1960. The significance of that car was its independent rear suspension, although it had other novelties such as a fuel-injected engine.

The E-type was first offered with open and fastback bodies, both strictly two-seaters. It followed the sports-racing D-type, having a steel monocoque centre section with front and rear subframes. Two major points disappointed enthusiasts who expected an 'all-new' car – the straight six was carried over from the XK150, in its 265 bhp form, and so for a while was the heavy gearbox (apologists pointed out that the engine torque meant little use need be made of the gearbox once the car was running).

It was a well-balanced grand touring car in most respects, and for a while it seemed that Jaguar also thought of it as a full-blooded sports car. A batch of lightweight competition cars was released in 1963, with modified suspension, engines rated at up to 344 bhp, and some with ZF five-speed gearboxes. The cars were no match for the dominant GT Ferraris, and apart from a few minor successes when the E was introduced, its outstanding competitions results came near the end of its life, when Group 44 campaigned late E-types very successfully in US racing.

By that time the car had changed a lot. A 4.2-litre

engine came in 1964; in 1966 the wheelbase was stretched by 23 cm (9.1 in) and some of the balanced elegance was lost in a 2+2 coupé. This longer wheelbase anticipated the 1971 Series 3 cars.

Not for the first time in Jaguar history, an engine was ready before the cars it was to power. So the big alloy overhead-cam V12 for the XJ and XJS was used to extend the life of the E. The front subframe had to be redesigned, and there were detail changes, for example in wheel widths and in the introduction of ventilated disc brakes at the front. The car weighed some 1500 kg (3300 lb) in S3 form.

The V12 was rated at 272 bhp, and so top speed dropped slightly to 145 mph (233 kph), but the engine delivered its power very smoothly. And the only other GT cars on the market offering 12-cylinder motoring were by Ferrari and Lamborghini, at several times the price of an E-type.

Jaguar XJS

Jaguar went through a difficult period in the early 1970s, as part of the troubled British Leyland group – Jaguar management could clearly see the need for a high-performance replacement for the E-type, but corporate minds wanted to funnel development funds into a Mini replacement programme. Fortunately Sir William Lyons was still a powerful figure, and the XJS programme that had been initiated in 1969 (as project XJ27) went ahead, as did the V12 engine that had also been in jeopardy.

The XJS ran late, finally appearing at the 1975 British Motor Show, when there was some disappointment among enthusiasts who had been expecting an E-type replacement. It had not been designed as a sports car, and was modelled to meet the increasingly stringent US safety regulations, which meant for example that there were substantial bumpers, and that a soft-top option was not offered. The overall shape also came in for criticism, although it had a lower drag coefficient than the E.

There was a conventional unitary-construction two-door coupé body, with front and rear subframes, wishbone front suspension and the Jaguar rear arrangement with drive shafts acting as upper links, with two coil spring/damper units per side. The fuel injection V12 was initially rated at 285 bhp, and when the car was announced it was fitted with a Borg-Warner automatic transmission (to be replaced by a GM unit in 1976, when a four-speed manual gearbox was also specified).

With the manual gearbox an early XJS could top 150 mph (241 kph), but an automatic car had a maximum speed of 142 mph (229 kph), and its fuel consumption proved unacceptably high through the 1978-79 energy crisis. That led to the HE range, with engines featuring the 'Fireball' combustion chamber. This improved fuel consumption, raised peak power and gave a speed of 153 mph (246 kph).

It also led to the adoption of the new twin-cam 3.6-litre AJ6 straight-six engine, rated at 225 bhp. This XJS was offered with a Getrag five-speed manual gearbox, and was available in convertible form which, while not transforming it into a sports car, made it acceptable to sports-car minded buyers. In coupé form it had a 136 mph (219 kph) top speed. In 1987, when the AJ6 engine became smoother as the XJ6's management system was adopted for it, maximum power dropped slightly (to 221 bhp) and top speed was down to 134 mph (215 kph).

Earlier in the 1980s the big Jaguar coupés had been raced in European Touring Car events by Tom Walkinshaw Racing, with mixed results – TWR and Jaguar achieved much more with the XJR-8s that won the world endurance championships in 1987.

By that time Jaguar was an extremely successful company again, with splendid GT and semi-sporting models in the straight six and V12 coupé and convertibles in the XJS range.

Jensen Interceptor

The last Interceptors were in a direct line of evolution from Jensens of the 1950s, each a 'businessman's express' with handsome lines, using the unstressed lazy power of large engines, most notably American eight-cylinder units. In 1950 the name Interceptor was used for a cabriolet with the 4-litre Austin A135 engine; that model was replaced by the 541 in 1954, which gave way to the glassfibre-bodied CV8 in 1963. This was a 132 mph (212 kph) car powered by a Chrysler 5.9-litre (360 cu in) V8 and one of the earliest cars to have disc brakes all round.

The bodywork let it down, so Jensen looked to a steel body to mount on their existing robust chassis, accepting an inevitable weight penalty, which in any case was offset as a 6276 cc (328 cu in) V8 was to be used, rated at an optimistic 325 bhp compared with the 305 bhp produced by the 5.9-litre engine. The suspension was conservative, but the weight distribution was 50:50 and the car could be cornered briskly, with little roll.

The lines of Vignale's fastback body lasted well, for the Interceptor was stylish when it was introduced at the 1966 London Motor Show, and were quite acceptable a decade later. As far as the conventional Interceptor was concerned, the first 'sub-model' was the Director in 1969, equipped with a radio telephone, dictating machine, built-in typewriter, and so on. Only four were built.

Interceptor Mk II with minor changes came in 1970; Interceptor SP with a 7.2-litre (440 cu in) Chrysler V8 and the power steering the car had always needed came in 1971. Those models lasted until 1972 and 1973 respectively. A detuned version of the 7.2-litre engine was fitted to normal Interceptors, identified by a 'J' as the engine was Chrysler's J Series V8, and in an effort to broaden the car's appeal a handsome convertible version of the Vignale body was introduced. A coupé with a fixed and partly transparent hard top followed.

However, those were minor diversions compared with the FF. This most famous of Jensens had come in 1968, in effect a stretched Interceptor with Ferguson Formula four-wheel drive. The additional chassis length was called for to accommodate the system's torque-splitting centre differential – otherwise the car was little changed – and for balanced handling the split was 37 per cent to the front wheels, 63 per cent to the rear. The confidence the FF engendered in widely-varying conditions, especially as four-wheel drive was complemented by the Dunlop Maxaret anti-lock braking system, attracted much praise. Unhappily, in the late 1960s it seems there was little call for a luxury car with such sophisticated refinements, and sales of the FF totalled a mere 320.

By 1976 the Jensen company was in deep trouble, as the Jensen-Healey sports car programme faltered and failed. After the crash, a few personnel set up a repair and restoration business and acquired a stock of parts. This enabled them to restart very limited Interceptor production in 1984, and the British Motor Show that year saw a new S4 Jensen Interceptor, with a 5.9-litre (360 cu in) Chrysler V8 and offered in saloon and convertible forms.

Lagonda 4½ Litre

The company founded by Wilbur Gunn, and given the Indian name for a creek near his home town in Ohio, had a wide model range in the early 1930s. Most of the cars had good reputations for build quality and handling, but not for sparkling performance. And in company terms the management constantly fought to stave off disaster – that came the day after a Lagonda won the Le Mans 24-hour Race, as the company was declared bankrupt.

In 1933 Lagonda introduced the modest 1.1-litre Rapier and the 4.5-litre M45 towards the other end of the scale. The basis of the large car was a 3-litre chassis, which could carry more powerful engines. That was the proposition a group of drivers put to Lagonda, and the company started work. The agreement fell through, but another company's misfortune meant that a ready-made engine became available (the Meadows six-cylinder ohv unit in hand for Invicta when that company failed) and so Lagonda went ahead.

The chassis was sound, brakes and Lagonda's gearbox were both good, and the handsome if substantial open M45 was good for over 90 mph (145 kph). Fox and Nicholl, which had prepared Lagondas for racing since the 1920s, reworked the engines for a team of cars, which in those days naturally had 'stripped' bodies. These cars showed well, particularly in the 1934 TT. Lagonda incorporated some of this work in the M45R, the Rapide, in the Autumn of 1934. It had a short chassis, new brakes, and a 3.5-litre engine option.

Fox and Nicholl ran a pair at Le Mans in 1935, and John Hindmarsh and Luis Fontes drove one steadily through bad weather and a minor collision, disregarding flashes of speed from the Italian and French opposition, to win the event. That happened too late to save the existing Lagonda company, but as it was restructured by Alan Good (and kept out of the hands of Rolls-Royce) it was a factor in W.O.

Bentley's decision to join them as chief designer.

He came up with the LG45 for 1936, in effect a reworked Rapide with a mildly revised Meadows gearbox and engine and features such as built-in hydraulic jacks under a smooth body styled by Frank Feeley. The next phase was the LG45 Rapide, with a more extensively modified engine good for 108 mph (174 kph). The ultimate version of the straight six came for 1937, its head developed by Weslake, but that was a stage towards its replacement.

That was the LG6, with a new chassis that would accept the straight six but was really intended for a Bentley-designed V12. Although a mock-up was shown in 1936, it was not ready for real production when it was announced for 1938. A demonstration car completed a one-hour run at Brooklands, covering 101 miles (163 km), and then two were run at Le Mans in 1939, finishing third and fourth. Development was progressing well towards definitive cars in 1940, but events that year abruptly halted the careers of these Lagondas.

Lamborghini Miura

Ferruccio Lamborghini entered the motor industry in the early 1960s, supposedly as a challenge to Ferrari in reaction to a personal slight by Ferrari, and on his own admission because he wanted to make perfect GT cars. His entry was certainly timely, and his name would become synonymous with 'supercar'.

The first Lamborghinis were front-engined, the 3½-litre 350GT of 1963 and the 1966 4-litre 400GT. The engine used was a 60-degree four-cam V12 based on a design which Giotto Bizzarini already had in hand. Then at the 1965 Turin Motor Show a chassis was exhibited with this engine transversely mounted between the cockpit and the centre line of the rear wheels, and with wishbone and coil spring independent suspension all round. At the Show orders were taken – for a car that was a year away, for which a body had yet to be designed.

Chassis designer Gianpaolo Dallara had broadly followed Ford's GT40 layout – save in the significant aspect of the transverse engine position – and it had to be modified only slightly for production. Styling was entrusted to Bertone, and one of his bright young men, Marcello Gandini, took on the project.

The first car came together for the 1966 Geneva Motor Show, where this low sleek machine was the dominant exhibit (and where it was actually named Miura). Its steel centre section with aluminium front and rear body sections lifted to give excellent access. The main lights were raised electrically, the large screen was steeply raked (and had a greenhouse effect in hot weather) and a distinctive slatted rear window cover was an aid to hot air extraction.

The Show sensation was developed into a practical road machine and deliveries started in 1967, when 108 cars were completed. The P400S came in the following year with larger tyres, which made handling more predictable, and claimed power output increased to 370 bhp, and a roadster version was shown in 1968. During the 2½-year life of the S ventilated disc brakes were to be introduced.

The SV came in 1971, with revised styling, interior modifications, beefed-up suspension and chassis, another power increase (up to an asserted 385 bhp), and a ZF limited-slip differential. It was the last of the 'regular' Miuras, and due to wider tyres probably no faster in 'flat-out' terms than the earlier cars capable of 172 mph (277 kph).

A derivative on competition car lines, the Jota, was completed as a one-off in 1971. In this some purity of line was sacrificed for downforce, many of the components were racing car ware, and the engine was rated at 440 bhp. It was never raced, but some replicas were completed, as Miura SVJs.

Ferruccio Lamborghini rated the Miura highest among his supercars.

Lamborghini Urraco

The timing of the Miura had been fortunate; the Urraco could hardly have arrived at a less fortunate time. This was to be the Lamborghini to make an impact on the market sector where the Porsche 911 and the Ferrari 308 had been so successful, to give the company greater volume production than the Miura or the Countach, but it absorbed a great deal of design and development time, was introduced when a fuel crisis was raging, and never generated worthwhile orders. Indeed, it almost brought the company down, and Ferruccio Lamborghini was to leave his company as its bankruptcy loomed.

Yet the Urraco was an attractive proposition, and cleverly engineered. Execution was entrusted to Paolo Stanzani, who had little option but to stay with the mid-engined concept. A straight six had appeared in a Lamborghini show car (the Marzal), but Stanzani elected to develop a new V8, and this took shape as an oversquare (86 mm × 53 mm/3.4 in × 2.1 in) 90-degree unit which in its first 2.5-litre form produced 220 bhp at 7500 rpm. The five-speed gearbox was at the right of the engine.

The body was in sheet steel, and Stanzani rejected wishbone suspension in favour of the simpler MacPherson strut arrangement, front and rear. The body was the work of Bertone's Gandini, and is generally looked upon as a compromise between the Bertone 1968 Carabo show car (on an Alfa Romeo base) and the Fiat X1/9. In the way of compromises it did not quite come off.

The Urraco was introduced at the Turin Show, when a top speed of 149 mph (240 kph) was claimed, and orders were taken. But there were long delays before the car got into even limited production. Lamborghini had elected to built it on a computer-controlled automated line. That had to be scrapped as cash ran short (and Lamborghini had to sell his controlling share) and Urraco production undertaken on traditional lines, which in turn made nonsense of the costings.

Production was sluggish as two more versions came. A 2-litre P200 was a 'natural' for the Italian market, for it fitted a tax category, and an up-market S with better trim was offered. Neither was a success.

Finally, late in 1974, came the 3-litre P300, with a 250 bhp twin-cam 2996 cc (183 cu in) version of the V8. This was probably what the Urraco should have been, but it came at a time when the market for high-performance cars was worse than stagnant. The Targa-top Silhouette derivative was tried, and failed.

As Lamborghini 'fell under the control of the Italian government' (ie, went bankrupt), Giulio Alfieri was brought in as a consultant, and one of his first recommendations was that the Urraco be scrapped.

The Mimram family who took over Lamborghini encouraged development of the Jalpa, based on the Urraco and Silhouette, with a 255 bhp 3.5-litre engine based on the Urraco V8. It was not a large volume car, nor was it a 'small Lamborghini', but it earned its place in the range.

Lamborghini Countach

This extraordinary machine was the outstanding supercar for a dozen years, unchallenged until 1987 when Ferrari revealed the F40 and Porsche undertook limited production of the 959. To that time it was probably the fastest of all road cars, for Lamborghini guaranteed that all Countach Quattrovalvoles would achieve a top speed of 183 mph, or 295 kph. But as transport the Countach was probably the least practical of all supercars.

It was first seen as a show car at Geneva in 1971, on the Bertone stand, and at that stage it was an ideas car. But it was to reappear towards the end of 1973 in production form.

Aerodynamically it needed to be better than the Miura, which had tended to lift at high speeds. The sheet steel semi-monocoque of the Geneva show car gave way to a complex space frame and wishbone and coil spring suspension was used all round. The show car had a 5-litre engine, but for the first production cars the 4-litre V12 was used. On the Countach this was mounted longitudinally (hence the LP designation – *Longitudinal e Posteriore*) and in the interests of a near-even weight distribution the gearbox was ahead of the engine, with a drive shaft running back through the magnesium sump casting to the rear wheels (that incidentally avoided long linkages).

Twin radiators were positioned horizontally in the rear wings, with 'shoulder' intakes and warm air expelled over the flat deck above the engine. Larger intakes were to be called for, but generally Bertone's original ultra-smooth lines had to be disturbed only in detail. Doors were hinged at the front, opening upwards to give good access to a functional cockpit.

The production version made its appearance at Geneva in 1974, although the build rate was slow – it was a labour-intensive car, and Italy had a lot of labour troubles at that time.

The LP400S version came in 1978, with new lower-profile Pirellis calling for suspension modifications, but the first major changes were announced in 1981, the LP500S which had a V12 with bore and stroke increased, to give a 4754 cc (290 cu in) capacity.

Four years later the Countach Quattrovalvole arrived with a four-valves-per-cylinder 5167 cc (316 cu in) version of the V12, rated at 455 bhp. At the same time a prominent rear aerofoil was added.

In 1987 the prospects of Lamborghini matching Ferrari in production and in the performance of models in the range were enhanced as Chrysler bought the company. That year, too, a 'Super Countach' mobile laboratory gave some clues to the make-up of a possible successor for the 1990s.

Lancia Lambda

The Lambda was a great car, ahead of its time, a rare car in that it was designed from first principles. When it was launched in 1923 many cars on the market

---

EVOLUTION — LANCIA LAMBDA

1922 Introduced at London and Paris motor shows, as a four-seater torpedo-bodied touring car with monocoque body and chassis. It also had independent front suspension and an overhead-cam V4 engine which produced 50 bhp. First, Second and Third Series were mechanically identical

1925 Fourth Series fitted with a four-speed gearbox. Fifth Series cars were fitted with low-pressure balloon tyres and Marelli electrics instead of Bosch

1926 Sixth Series wider and roomier, with a new and stronger stressed skin construction

1927 Seventh Series introduced, with a separate chassis offered as an option. This model was fitted with the new 2370 cc (144.5 cu in) Tipo 78 engine, which produced 59 bhp

1929 Eighth Series introduced, with platform chassis as standard, and long-wheelbase version available as an option. The new 2570 cc (156.7 cu in) Tipo 79 engine was fitted, producing 69 bhp

1930 Series Lambdas introduced, identical to Eighth Series cars except for coil instead of magneto ignition

1931 Production ended. Total sales: 13,000

were Edwardian in concept and design; the Lambda had a steel body-cum-chassis, an overhead camshaft V4 engine, and independent front suspension in its advanced specification.

Vincenzo Lancia was granted a patent for a load-bearing metal hull in 1919, and incorporated a propellor-shaft tunnel which formed a backbone. As passengers in the Lambda sat alongside it, rather than above the propellor shaft, a lower car became possible. The chassis was built up of steel stampings for the sides, the scuttle bulkhead and the integral transverse seat backs which made for great rigidity, reinforced by the seat pans and engine bearers. The stressed structure was skinned in aluminium.

The independent front suspension was a sliding pillar type, rigidly cross-braced by tubes and not unlike the system pioneered on Morgan three-wheelers, except that Lancia also incorporated telescopic hydraulic dampers.

The engine was unorthodox – a short V4 with staggered cylinders in an aluminium block with inserted steel liners. The vertical overhead valves were operated by a single overhead camshaft. From fan to flywheel it was 55.8 cm (22 in) long, so that there was room in the engine compartment for the three-speed gearbox – or, indeed, for a larger engine; one experimental car was in fact fitted with a V8, but this was not taken up.

Effective four-wheel brakes were fitted, and although the Lambda was not fast in straight-line terms, those brakes combined with the exceptional road-holding and cornering imparted by the independent front suspension meant that it could cover ground at close to its maximum speed. In the early cars that was 71 mph (114 kph), in the late models 78 mph (125 kph). That reflected an increase in the power from 49 bhp at 3250 rpm to 69 bhp at 3500 rpm, and also the provision of a four-speed gearbox from 1925.

Outwardly the Lambdas were never elegant cars, and from a practical point of view the unitary chassis-body meant door apertures were shallow. So for the saloon versions a Lambda with a platform chassis was introduced in 1927, with the Sixth Series cars. This was really a new design, and the structure changed again for the Seventh Series, when the cross bracing behind the front seats was dispensed with. This at least gave coachbuilders full rein in their traditional ways.

It was also a heavier car, so engine capacity was increased to 2370 cc (145 cu in), and it went up again in 1929 for the Eigth Series cars, to 2570 cc (157 cu in). And that was needed, as some of the long-chassis cars were loaded with formidable saloon bodies.

Production continued until 1931, when the Lambda was succeeded by three models, all of which had narrow vee engines and independent front suspension.

Lancia Aurelia

In one of its forms, the Aurelia has a claim to be the forerunner of modern GT cars, and in overall terms it was the world's first production car with a V6 engine – Lancia has always had a reputation for original and distinctive cars, and the Aurelias enhanced this.

After World War 2, Lancia continued with the Aprilia and the smaller Ardua while a successor to the Aprilia was laid down. In this work, the company had the priceless assets of the brilliant Vittorio Jano and his young assistant Francesco de Virgilio. He proposed a V6, in the face of tradition which held that there was an inherent difficulty of balancing primary and secondary masses (the Lancia museum included an experimental V6 from 1924 as an object lesson). But de Virgilio persisted, as the only way to provide the power and torque the Aurelia would need.

The independent rear suspension set-up from the Aprilia was refined, while in the interests of balance Jano combined gearbox and final drive in a transaxle arrangement and positioned the rear brakes inboard. A less than happy innovation was a steering column gearchange. The standard body was a pillarless design by Pininfarina which, despite the saving of some aluminium panelling, was heavy.

As the B10, the car was announced at the 1950 Turin Motor Show, with a claimed top speed only slightly higher than the Aprilia which it replaced (on poor petrol, the engine gave only 56 bhp), but soon shown to have vastly superior handling when then-new Michelin radial tyres were fitted – another first.

As petrol quality improved, so engine output went up, for example to 75 bhp for the short wheelbase B20 2+2 coupé in 1951. That version became familiar in races and rallies, outstanding results being Bracco's second place in the 1951 Mille Miglia and Claes' win in the gruelling Liège-Rome-Liège Rally. Supercharged versions of the third-series 2451 cc (150 cu in) engine were run in 1952, and this engine was used as the basis of the power units for the later D20, D24 and D25 sports-racing cars.

Meanwhile the 2500GT had appeared, with a performance that persuaded Lancia to opt for a transverse-leaf spring de Dion rear axle. This car could hit 115 mph (185 kph). In 1954 Louis Chrion drove one to win the Monte Carlo Rally.

In 1955 the B24 Spyder was introduced on a short wheelbase, and remains the most attractive of Aurelias for many enthusiasts.

Lancia Stratos

This was an Italian sports car, evolved as an 'homologation special' to win rallies – it would be difficult to find a practical use for it. It was dominant in rallying, taking the International championship three times before changing parent company policies sidelined it. Its electrics were unreliable, like so many Italian cars; it was difficult to see out of, like so many Italian stylists' creations; its production was exaggerated for homologation purposes: the Stratos was very Italian.

The origins of the Stratos were in a tiny, frail-looking Bertone styling exercise at the 1970 Turin Motor Show. Lancia competitions manager Cesare Fiorio needed a special car to maintain the Fiat group's rallying position, and with Fiat backing he could create a car. In the Bertone machine he saw a prototype. The Stratos that emerged a year later, when it was run in the Tour de Corse, was a very different car. A Ferrari Dino 246 V6 took the place of the Fulvia V4 in the show car, but it was still mounted ahead of the rear wheels in a machine that was in the mainstream of competition car design, having a very strong chassis/body with a central monocoque and tubular subframes front and rear.

The Ferrari drive train was used, with its five-speed gearbox and transaxle. Wishbone and coil spring suspension was used all round on the first cars, but most had strut-type rear suspension. Welded steel parts made up the load-bearing chassis, with glassfibre being used for simple covers.

The engine was normally rated at 190 bhp at 7000 rpm; for competition versions up to 270 bhp was claimed for two-valve types and up to 285 bhp for the four-valve version, the last two figures being perhaps a little optimistic. Then there was a 335 bhp 24-valve derivative used after the Stratos was ruled out of main-line rallies, and a target output of 400 bhp for a turbocharged version.

A first victory came in the car's fourth rally, when Sandro Munari drove it in the 1973 Rally of Spain. A string of outright victories followed, until 1978 when Fiorio's works team turned to the Fiat 131 Abarth, although private Stratos entrants would continue to campaign the car. Bernard Darniche, for example, took the fifth Monte Carlo win for a Stratos in 1979.

In major rallying, the Stratos failed only on the RAC (best placing third in 1974) and the Safari (best placing second in 1975). This amazing little car was without equal.

Lotus Elite

Colin Chapman's first Elite, the Lotus 14, marked a stride forward for his still-small company. It was a GT car, widely admired for its bold conception, its lines and its staggering performance with a small engine, mistrusted because of its fragility and unreliability. The Elite was daring; it was also unrealistic.

The Elite was a road car with racing car suspension. It had a double wishbone layout using coil springs enclosing telescopic dampers at the front, with an anti-roll bar considerably increasing roll stiffness. At the rear Chapman used a design first seen on the Lotus 12 Formula 2 racing car, with 'Chapman struts' incorporating coil spring/damper units; lateral location was taken care of by fixed-length universally-jointed drive shafts; longitudinal location was provided by a single radius arm on each side, although this was to prove inefficient as severe suspension movement induced rear-end steering, and on later cars triangulated wishbones replaced the radius arms. This set-up gave controllability to an unusual degree, and a comfortable ride.

It also spread loads, and that helped make the unique glassfibre hull practicable. This was made of three major pieces, the principal mouldings being a 'floor' (up to the wheel arches), an inner layer which through the transmission tunnel and torsion boxes contributed stiffness, and the upper part. Metal was used in a hoop running up from the jacking points through the front of the door spaces (for the hinges) and over the screen, thereby avoiding bulky pillars, and in the nose to mount suspension and steering. The mechanical parts and running gear were mounted directly to the hull, which varied in thickness according to loadings, and in places could be very thin in pursuit of lightness. Flexing was inherent, and the shell would have broken if an attempt had been made to build a rigid construction.

The basic lines were the work of Peter Kirwan-Taylor, and were beautiful, while aerodynamic refinement was contributed by Mike Costin. To this day, very very few cars match the Elite's Cd of 0.29. That was marginally improved on in a Le Mans car, which with a 1216 cc (74 cu in) engine was timed at 141 mph (227 kph). The normal engine was the Coventry Climax FWE 1216 cc sohc four, in single-carburettor form, which gave 75 bhp and 110 mph (180 kph), and in twin-carb form for the Elite SE that came in 1962 85 bhp and 120 mph (195 kph). BMC or ZF gearboxes were used.

The commercial career of this outstanding little car was unhappy. Quality control was a problem, some redesign (eg, in the rear suspension) was needed after the launch, apparently trivial breakages could be costly to rectify (and still are, for preservation enthusiasts), and Lotus lost money on every one sold. Chapman gave up the struggle to produce this sophisticated Elite in 1963, when 998 had been built.

Lotus Elan

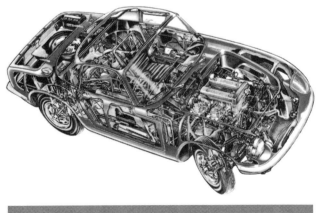

The Elan was a superbly balanced little sports car, in all respects. It combined sleek, handsome lines with light weight, ample power and excellent handling.

Like its predecessor, the Elite, the Elan had glassfibre bodywork, and the original intention was that it should be a monocoque. But for a hack to prove his suspension designs for the new car,

Chapman had a backbone chassis made up. This turned out to be extremely rigid, and an ideal base for an open glassfibre body, which could be unstressed and therefore less critical (crucial parts were reinforced in the final Elan body). The backbone was fabricated in steel, and forked at the front and the rear to the suspension mountings, with the engine and gearbox between the front 'prongs' and the transmission running along the boxed backbone. Cross members linked the 'prongs'.

The front suspension and steering components derived from the small Triumph sports cars, while the 'Chapman strut' rear arrangement was carried over from the Elite. The body had neat lines, with a clean nose achieved through the use of an integral bumper and retractable headlights. The cockpit was comfortable, and there was even adequate luggage space in the squared-off tail.

The basis of the Elan engine was the five-bearing Ford 116E Cortina unit, but as a pushrod ohv engine was felt to be out of character in such a car, Chapman commissioned Harry Mundy to design a light alloy twin overhead camshaft for it. In its first 1498 cc (91.4 cu in) form this developed 100 bhp, but after only 22 cars had been made a 1558 cc (95 cu in) version rated at 105 bhp was introduced, in large part because the 1.6-litre racing category had become more important. This engine produced a 110 mph (180 kph) top speed.

The Series 2 model of 1964 had revised trim and front brakes, and a coupé (Lotus 36) was introduced in 1965. There was a Special Equipment S2 in 1966, with a 115 bhp engine and revised gearing leading to a 125 mph (201 kph) top speed, and in the same year the 26R lightweight competitions version was listed. The Series 3 (Lotus 45) had suspension revisions and the 115 bhp engine, while the Series 4 cars that came in 1968 had stronger bodies and detail improvements.

By that time (it had actually been announced in mid-1967) the Elan Plus 2, 25.4 cm (10 in) wider and 58 cm (23 in) longer, was available. It was slightly larger in all dimensions, to accommodate two small rear seats, and was offered in fixed-head form, with a fractionally better drag coefficient than the Elan. It was to outlive that model.

The finest variant of the Elan came in 1970, in the form of the S4 Sprint. This was fitted with the 'Big Valve' 126 bhp engine developed by Tony Rudd, and while it was geared for acceleration rather than top speed, it was still a 120 mph (193 kph) car, and a very sophisticated sports car.

Lotus Esprit

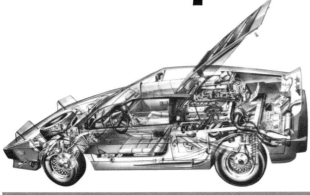

The introduction of the Esprit Turbo in 1980 rounded off Colin Chapman's programme to move the whole Lotus road-car range up-market. This had started in the 1970s, as the second Lotus to be named Elite and the Eclat took the place of the Elan in 1974 and the Esprit was introduced in 1975, effectively in place of the Europa. It became a true prestige car when the Turbo version appeared.

Its origins were in a 1970 project, M70, that began to take its outward shape when the Italian stylist Giugiaro worked with Lotus on a car exhibited at the 1972 Turin Motor Show. His lines were subject to considerable development, particularly in aerodynamic refinement, before the shape was finalized in 1973. It was to be built in glass-reinforced plastics, where Lotus had very considerable experience (the Elite became the first GRP car to gain a Don Safety Award, in 1976).

This body was made in two parts, bonded along the waist line and mounted on a backbone-cum-space frame chassis. The car was strictly a two-seater, with a cockpit that was comfortable but not spacious, and it suffered the all-round visibility problems common to the mid-engined high-performance cars of its generation.

The engine was Lotus' Type 907 dohc 16-valve straight-four, mounted at 45 degrees to horizontal. In this form it developed 155 bhp. Drive was through a five-speed gearbox supplied by Citroën, originally developed for their front-wheel drive Maserati-engined SM. The linkage was involved, but in service was trouble-free.

That could not be reported of the car as a whole, which suffered too many teething troubles for an entry into the 'Porsche class'. Most of the problems were overcome by the time a Series 2 Esprit was introduced in 1978, which also had a developed engine, and was also to be subjected to some garish 'limited edition' colour treatments quite out of place on a car in this category.

The Esprit Turbo was launched in 1980, in the flashy colours of that short-lived Grand Prix sponsor Essex (a turbocharged engine was preferred to the Lotus V8 originally projected for the car). Stroke was increased from 69.2 mm (2.7 in) to 76.2 mm (3 in), to give a capacity of 2174 cc (132.6 cu in); the engine was strengthened for the greater pressures, and a Garrett AiResearch T3 turbocharger was added, to increase power by 35 per cent, to 210 bhp. That lifted the top speed to 152 mph (245 kph) compared with the 135 mph (218 kph) achieved by the normally-aspirated model.

Importantly, the chassis and rear suspension were also strengthened, and a new front suspension introduced. In that form the Esprit ran on through the 1980s, with only minor refinements until 1987 when a new body with more rounded lines and designed entirely in house was introduced for both versions.

Marcos

Few British specialist car constructors departed so radically from established practices in the early 1960s as Marcos, with the 'wooden car'. And few car shapes have lasted so long as the model introduced in 1964, with lines by Dennis Adams which proved efficient and acceptable a quarter of a century after he had designed the car.

The first model dated from 1960, although Marcos was formed in 1962, by Jem Marsh and Frank Costin ('Mar' plus 'Cos'). The first odd-looking GT car was raced, and in large part its success persuaded sceptics that its composite chassis of marine plywood was an acceptable automotive structure. Among the drivers, in club level racing, was one Jackie Stewart.

The equally distinctive, but sleek, Adams-bodied car came in 1964. It was a big step forward, for it was a properly-equipped road-going GT car. Costin was an admirer of de Havilland's wooden monocoque aircraft fuselages, which lasted into the jet age, and he drew up a chassis which was lighter than a metal equivalent and as stiff. The body design imposed limitations, for example in the cockpit which had semi-reclining fixed seats and an adjustable pedal assembly, and in the rear suspension layout. The earlier cars had a live axle and hard ride qualities. A de Dion arrangement was tried on the early 1800 cars, but Marsh then reverted to a live axle, with radius rods for longitudinal location, a Panhard rod for lateral location and coil springs and dampers. Later in the car's life, extra weight actually seemed to help road-holding. At the front a sub-assembly took care of the wishbone and coil spring arrangement.

The first engine was a Volvo pushrod ohv 'four', which produced 114 bhp and propelled the Marcos to 118 mph (187 kph). Variants with Ford engines followed; the 1.5-litre (92 cu in) unit cut costs, but also cut maximum speed to 100 mph (161 kph), then a Lawrence-tuned and enlarged 1650 cc (101 cu in) version giving 120 bhp restored the top speed. Larger Ford engines followed, with the 3-litre (183 cu in) V6 introduced into the Marcos in 1969, which gave a 125 mph (200 kph) top speed.

In the following year the wooden chassis gave way to steel tubes, while Ford V4 and V6 engines and the Volvo B30 straight six were offered (the Swedish unit in part because its emission control was expected to make it acceptable in the USA). To a degree, ambition toward market expansion, which had led to a new factory, was the downfall of the original company which sold the designs for the Mini-Marcos and the ugly Mantis, but which still collapsed in 1975.

In 1981 Jem Marsh set up a new and realistically smaller company, to market the old design in 'kit' form. Three years later he introduced a version with the Rover 3528 cc (215 cu in) V8 which proved popular, and gave the Mantula, as it was by then named, a maximum speed of 137 mph (220 kph). Handling was good, but the ride was still sometimes too hard. A very attractive convertible model was introduced in 1986.

Maserati 3500GT

Well into the 1950s, Maserati existed for racing, although a handful of road cars was produced. The Orsi family, primarily Count Adolfo who had bought Maserati in 1947 and his son Omer, who ran the company, had begun to change this emphasis when a catastrophic racing season in 1957 meant that change had to come, fast. Retrenchment and rationalization were the order of the day, and the Modena factory was to concentrate on producing road cars to be sold at a profit, with the American market to be a prime target.

Maserati already had a suitable model, which had made its debut as the 3500GT at the 1957 Geneva Motor Show. This was built around a light-alloy twin-cam straight-six engine, which Alfieri had designed as a racing unit in 1956. Even in detuned form for road use it produced 236 bhp, and that was to go up to 270 bhp when Lucas fuel injection was introduced in 1963, although that figure reflected puny Italian horses, or optimism.

The 300S sports-racing car also contributed the origins of the welded tubular frame, although it was longer and wider for this GT car use, and this was ideal for Carrozzeria Touring's *superleggera* coupé bodywork (convertibles were to be built by Vignale and by Frua). The suspension was conventional, the use of a rigid rear axle with semi-elliptic leaf springs being hardly avant-garde, and disc brakes were to be fitted all round, after the early drums had proved much less than satisfactory.

A shorter wheelbase chassis came for a Vignale coupé in 1961, and that helped improve handling. But in an Italian tradition better performance in other respects was more important, hence the injected GTI in 1962, which had the option of a five-speed ZF gearbox and was a 137 mph (220 kph) car. This was the basis for Vignales's Sebring coupé and spyder models. In 1963 the engine was stretched to 3692 cc (226 cu in), for the Frua-styled Mistral, which was built on a shortened Sebring chassis (239 cm/94 in compared with 249 cm/98 in).

The last of the original 3500GTs was completed in 1966, but the Mistral was no more successful as a successor than it had been as a parallel model. To keep it in the new supercar league, the twin-cam engine was enlarged again, to 4012 cc (245 cu in) in 1968. The power output claim was more realistic, for its 255 bhp was lower than the 'official' figure for smaller versions of the engine. Claimed maximum speed for this late Mistral was 158 mph (254 kph).

These Maseratis never achieved the status of contemporary Ferrari and Lamborghini models, although they were handsome cars in their own rights and now enjoy 'classic' status.

Maserati Bora and Merak

These were mid-engined supercars in the fashion established by Lamborghini with the Miura, sensible in mechanical make-up, equipment and size, with fine lines by Giugiaro and lightly stressed engines.

The Bora came in 1971 with a V8 that had its origins in the mid-1950s, and had been developed as a production engine almost a decade later, when it had been used to power the Indy, Mexico and Ghibli GT cars as well as the ambitious four-dour Quattroporte. It was an oversquare four-cam 90-degree unit, rated at around 330 bhp at a fairly low 5500 rpm. Most were 4.7-litre units, but a few Boras had a 4.9-litre version.

The basis of the car was a square-tube frame, with lower panels welded to it to make a platform chassis, with body panels also welded so that the whole thing had the qualities of a monocoque, at a cost in weight. The suspension followed lines by then well established, with unequal-length wishbones, coil springs and dampers, and anti-roll bars front and rear, while ventilated disc brakes were used all round. The body was as efficient as it looked, in drag terms not matching the Lotus Elite of a dozen years earlier, but essentially complementing the car's performance.

However, the Bora did not perform too well in sales terms, and here the Citroën takeover created an opportunity to take this mid-engined GT design into

a lower price category, to compete with the 3-litre Ferrari and Porsche GT cars.

Introduced at the 1972 Paris Motor Show, the Merak had the same platform and suspension of the Bora, many of the body panels and doors, and the suspension. Whereas the Bora had a glassed-in fastback, the Merak had a flat engine cover flanked by 'buttresses' following through from the roof line.

Power was provided by a 3-litre version of the V6 developed for the Citroën SM, rated at 190 bhp in the first Meraks, offering a saving of weight in itself and in the fact that unlike the V8 it did not call for a separate subframe. It was also shorter, facilitating 2+2 accommodation, whereas the Bora was a two-seater. The transmission laid out for the Citroën SM was used, and so were elements of that car's hydraulic systems, with pump, plumbing and so on installed just to operate the retractable headlights and the over-sensitive brakes. Critics of the Merak's harsh suspension felt that was the area where Citroën sophistication should have been applied.

The Merak's top speed was 140 mph (225 kph), while the 220 bhp Merak SS that came in 1974 was not much faster. By then Citroën had backed away, and de Tomaso stepped in to save Maserati, continuing these models through to the end of the decade. Then the company moved away from the supercar image, with the Biturbo range of the 1980s.

Maybach Zeppelin

The name Maybach is as old as the motor industry, although the car-making company lasted only 20 years from 1921. Wilhelm Maybach was Gottlieb Daimler's first designer, and he was also responsible for the cars that took on the Mercedes name in 1901. He set up an aero-engine business with Count Zeppelin in 1907, with his son Karl looking after the design side. After World War 1, Karl turned the factory towards making automotive engines, initially with a 5.7-litre straight six, but as he found only one customer (Spyker) he made a virtue of necessity and started building cars for his Maybach engines.

This was never a high-volume operation, on average turning out less than 200 cars a year. Maybach's first V12 was a 7-litre unit in 1929, which was rated at 150 bhp in the DS7. That Maybach 12 was superseded a year later by the Zeppelin, with the engine enlarged from 6962 cc (425 cu in) to its definitive 7922 cc (483 cu in), and in this form it produced 200 bhp.

One of the engine's virtues was its flexibility, to the extent that a gearbox was hardly necessary, but one of the outstanding Maybach features was sophisticated transmission systems. The Zeppelin had an all-synchromesh four-speed box, in which gears could be pre-selected and changes made by lifting off the throttle and operating a small lever. A low ratio option in effect gave four more ratios.

A pressed-steel chassis with rigid axles front and rear was conventional, while like other cars in the class there was central chassis lubrication and built-in hydraulic jacks. An 'equalizing device' increased brake forces according to road speeds. These could be considerable, of the order of 110-115 mph (177-185 kph) depending on bodywork. That was always fitted by outside coachbuilders, the German Spohn company clothing most of the 300 Zeppelins that were produced. That was a significant total, matched by few luxury car makers of the period, and about one tenth of the V12 Maybach cars survive.

Maybach did not resume car production after World War 2, and the company was eventually absorbed by Daimler-Benz in 1960, six years after Karl Maybach died.

Mazda RX-7 ▬

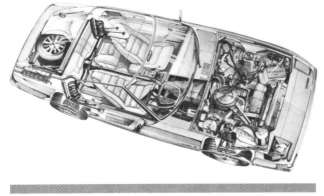

Outwardly the Mazda RX-7 was a sleek and functional coupé, with internationally-acceptable lines where some of its predecessors had verged upon the bizarre. The one thing that always made it stand out was its rotary engine, and the Japanese company remained faithful to that type of power

EVOLUTION — MAZDA RX-7

1978 RX-7 introduced at Tokyo Show with a twin rotor Wankel rotary engine

1979 Exports, of the 2+2 version only, began to the UK.

1981 Engine uprated, increasing top speed acceleration and top gear performance, and disc brakes introduced at the rear. Cosmetic improvements included front and rear air dams, new rear light treatment, and the addition of extra equipment

1983 Turbo version introduced but sold in Japan only. The combination of turbocharging and electronic fuel injection boosted power to 165 bhp at 6500 rpm and torque to 163 lb ft at 4000 rpm, giving a top speed of 143 mph (230 kph). Adjustable dampers fitted

1985 A totally new RX-7 introduced. It featured rack and pinion steering and independent rear suspension and the larger 13B rotary engine previously used in the RX-4. It was produced in both normally aspirated and turbocharged form, the first producing 150 bhp, the second 182 bhp

1988 Refined RX-7, outwardly distinguished by new tail spoiler, introduced with electronic speed-sensing power-assisted steering, electronic cruise control, and other innovations

unit long after other one-time protagonists such as Audi/NSU and General Motors had abandoned it. Togo Kogyo produced the millionth rotary-engined Mazda in 1979.

When the RX-7 appeared in 1978, Mazda had 17 years' experience with rotary engines, and had gradually overcome the problems that had doomed cars such as the NSU Ro80, particularly the short life expectancy and sealing, by changing seal areas and materials. Mazda worked towards the goals of adequate power and torque, longevity and an acceptable fuel consumption (in Mazda's main market, the USA, its lack of economy was not a significant factor), while an exhaust thermal reactor largely kept the emission problem in check.

The twin-rotor engine of the RX-7 was a refined version of the unit that powered the RX-3 saloon, and in the sports car its narrow effective power band was acceptable. Each of the co-axial rotors swept 573 cc (35 cu in), which gave an equivalent capacity of 2292 cc (140 cu in) once the FIA equivalency factor (2 × 2 × 573/35) was applied. It was rated at 105 bhp, just about comparable with contemporary 2-litre sohc engines. The rotary unit was light and compact, and this gave its designers a freedom which in some respects they failed to exploit. The chassis and suspension of the RX-7 was unadventurous but sound. The engine was set well back, giving a weight distribution of 51/49, and the drag coefficient with the main lights retracted was only 0.34. In Europe the RX-7 was regarded as a 2+2 coupé, but in the USA it was more realistically listed as a two-seater, with a flat luggage platform built in behind the seats.

The RX-7 followed a Japanese tradition in being light to drive, and it reached its 117 mph (188 kph) top speed smoothly and quietly, with no unnecessary fuss.

That 2+2 description meant that it raced as a saloon in Britain, where it was driven to win the RAC Saloon Car Championship in 1980. It was claimed the car's engines produced 200 bhp, and certainly 165 bhp was available in 'production' racing RX-7s. That figure was also achieved in turbocharged versions.

Cosmetic changes had been made to suit markets, then in 1985 a new RX-7 was introduced. It still had rotary power (rated at 148 bhp), and two chambers of 654 cc (40 cu in) gave a capacity of 2354 cc (144 cu in) under a new equivalency factor of 1.8. A complex new independent rear suspension was introduced. The body emphasized the car's less sporting role.

Mercedes-Benz S series

The big six-cylinder Mercedes-Benz sports cars designed by Ferdinand Porsche were to become as legendary as their Bentley contemporaries towards the end of the Vintage period. In motor sport, the German companies had not enjoyed much success earlier in the 1920s, and the S series cars were to set that right after the amalgamation of Mercedes and Benz in 1926. Both companies had an image of high quality and high technology, and a conscious effort was to be made to extend this tradition of prestige and desirability.

Like W.O. Bentley, Dr Porsche recognized that the best way to obtain reliable high performance was then to be found in large and lightly stressed engines. Since 1921 Mercedes had catalogued a

production car equipped with a supercharger, and had essayed supercharged engines in competitions cars, using Roots-type compressors that were not permanently engaged – that was automatic, though, depending on pressure from the foot which operated a clutch beyond the normal full-throttle position.

This was applied to the big straight-six engine Porsche laid out when he joined Mercedes from Austro-Daimler in 1922, first for the 24/100/140 touring car (that designation reflected, in sequence, the German fiscal rating, the normal power output of the engine and the output of the supercharged model).

The immediate antecedent of the S was the K, a 6.2-litre touring car. The single-ohc six had a light-alloy block and crankcase, and the Roots-type supercharger blew through twin carburettors rather than inhaling through them, as was normal. For the S, the swept volume was increased to 6789 cc (414 cu in), and the power output of the engine was rated at 180 bhp.

In the S ('Sport') it had to haul along a large four-seater body, which was carried on a chassis of substantial pressed-steel side members which swept up at the rear, with non-independent suspension and semi-elliptic springs and friction dampers (at the rear the springs were underslung). These cars won the 1927 German GP (for sports cars) and other races, and the progression to more sporting versions was natural.

The SS had a lower frame, the 7069 cc (432 cu in) engine producing 200 bhp, and it won the 1928 German GP and the 1929 Ulster TT. The SSK had a short chassis (K denoting *Kurz*, or short) – the wheelbase was 295 cm/116 in compared with the 337 cm/132½ in of the S and SS – lighter and more handsome two-seater bodywork, and 225 bhp. It was a powerful and more agile car than its predecessors, good for a maximum speed of around 125 mph (200 kph) and a winner in numerous races.

Finally, the SSKL (L denoting *Leicht*, or light) had the short chassis, drilled for lightness, and a larger 'Elephant' supercharger which pushed output up to 265 bhp. This was the car Rudolf Caracciola used to such good effect, from his astonishing drive to third place in the first Monaco Grand Prix (he actually led the race in this big and apparently quite unsuitable car), to his near-legendary victory in the Mille Miglia in 1931.

Caracciola was one of only a handful of drivers who could exploit these powerful cars to the full, and performances such as these two suggest that the roadholding and handling qualities were indeed as good as legend suggests, and that the brakes were better than legend insists they were. Then, as far as the racing circuit was concerned, these big cars disappeared, having to give way as a new age of efficiency dawned.

Mercedes-Benz 540K

The Mercedes-Benz supercharged cars of the 1920s and 1930s found their ultimate expression in the 540K sports-tourers, which were still heavy cars in the tradition of the S series and Grosser Mercedes that were their predecessors but were much more sophisticated designs. They would have outstandingly well-proportioned bodies – saloons, cabriolets and open sporting types.

The 170 was a significant forerunner, for it had independent suspension all round, with transverse-leaf springs at the front and swing-axle rear suspension. In the sporting 380 of 1933 a new coil spring and wishbones front suspension was introduced, with swing axles at the rear, and this layout was carried through to the 540K.

The 380 was a relatively short-lived sporting car, with a 3820 cc (233 cu in) straight-eight engine rated at 140 bhp, and it was just a 100 mph (161 kph) model. It was superseded by the 5-litre 500 saloon, and 500K open two-seater, in 1934. That in turn led to the 5.4-litre supercharged models designated 540 and 540K.

These inherited the 329 cm (129½ in) wheelbase chassis of the 500, together with the suspension arrangements first introduced on the 380. The pushrod ohv straight eight was rated at 115 bhp, or 180 bhp with the supercharger engaged. As on the S series cars, this came into operation automatically as the driver overrode a strong spring at normal full-throttle position. The four-seater cabriolet 540K had a claimed top speed of 106 mph (171 kph).

Three cabriolet versions were offered, a 2+2, a genuine four-seater, and a seven-seater designed for state occasions, available with armoured sides and inch-thick 'bullet-proof' glass. There was an open five-seater and, perhaps best-known of 540Ks, the Sport-Roadster and Sport-Coupé.

These cars were in production through to 1939, when one chassis was equipped with a 5.8-litre engine which anticipated the 580K successor that never reached production status. In all, 409 540Ks were built, the last three not completed until 1942.

Mercedes-Benz 300SL

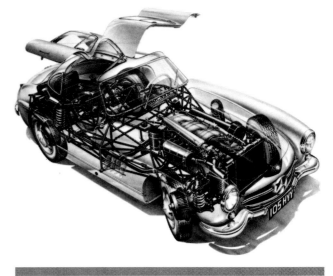

The 'Gullwing' was one of the memorable sports cars of the 1950s – marking a Mercedes-Benz return to racing, the first production car with a space frame, and the first with a fuel-injection engine. Its success was such that, under pressure from the US agent, the company had to set aside the original proposition to build ten to be raced by a works team and put the Gullwing into production.

The original batch of W194 sports-racing cars were designed with economy in mind, using the straight-six engine from the 300S saloon, together with that model's transmission, independent front suspension and swing-axle rear suspension. It pioneered the space frame, in parallel with Lotus, using square-section tubes in a structure that weighed no more than 82 kg (181 lb), relying on the distribution of loadings through its members rather than on a mass of metal. To maintain the integrity of this structure, the door sills were high and the doors were actually hinged in the roof.

The straight-six engine was canted at an angle to give a low nose line. In its first form, with three carburettors, it produced 175 bhp. In a reversal of normal practices, the production engine was to become more powerful than those first competition units as Bosch fuel injection was introduced.

The first race for the 300SL was the 1952 Mille Miglia, when the cars were 'only' second, third and fourth. That frightened their opponents at Le Mans, leading Jaguar to redesign the C-type body, its nose in particular, frantically, so that the Coventry cars overheated and the race was handed to Mercedes (because of the advantages of disc brakes, the Jaguars could well have matched the 300SLs through 24 hours). Mercedes were first and second at Le Mans, scored a similar result in the Carrera Panamericana, then the team's space-framed coupés were put away.

Pressure from America led to a 1000-car order for a production version, which came in 1954. The space frame was modified to allow slightly larger doors to be specified, the body lines were changed and large outlets introduced on each flank to relieve engine compartment air pressure, and direct fuel injection boosted engine power to 240 bhp. That gave a 140 mph (225 kph) top speed – theoretically it could exceed 165 mph (266 kph). Drawbacks were the drum brakes and the swing-axle rear suspension. The 300SL roadster that came in 1957 was to have low-pivot swing axles to give more predictable handling, and late cars had disc brakes.

Meanwhile production Gullwings enjoyed a successful rally career, but even the lightweight cars (which had alloy body panels instead of the normal steel) were not outstanding in racing.

MG T Series

These spindly little machines came to epitomize the small British sports car, in a classic series that lasted for 20 years spanning World War 2. Their introduction marked a fundamental change in MG policy, when company founder Cecil Kimber was shifted to a secondary management role by Lord Nuffield and his competitions programmes were abandoned – racing successes had not sold bread and butter cars.

One of the first two new models was the TA, replacing the sporting ohc-engined PB Midget in the range, though the name Midget was to be retained for some time. The TA was larger and heavier than previous Midgets, with a similar pressed-steel frame which had side members sweeping up over the front axle and running under the rear axle. There were semi-elliptic leaf springs and hydraulic dampers all round. Although the engine specification sounded unexciting, the long-stroke 1292 cc (79 cu in) pushrod ohv four-cylinder unit produced 52.4 bhp compared with the PB's 43.3 bhp, to give the TA a top speed of 80 mph (129 kph).

It ran until 1939, when the TB with the 1250 cc (76 cu in) engine of the Morris 12, a closer-ratio gearbox and a dry clutch was introduced. This engine had a shorter stroke and gave only a little more power, but it had much more potential for development.

The TB had a very short production life, although in most respects it was born again as the TC in 1945. That was a very significant little car, for although its performance was hardly exhilarating and it was soon out-moded, although every one had right-hand drive and none had a radio or a heater, it was an outstanding export success. Roughly one-fifth went to the USA, as fun cars which contrasted strongly with local products, and they played a major role in stimulating a new interest in sports cars and road racing.

In 1949 the Midget was modernized, to a degree, with the TD. This used the chassis of the Y-type saloon, shortened to give the same wheelbase as the TC, and the Y's independent front suspension and rack and pinion steering. It gave a better ride, good roadholding and adequate performance for club racing. Moreover, a left-hand drive version was available.

The TD Mk II had a mildly tuned engine, which produced an extra 3-4 bhp, and this engine, with its revised cylinder head, was then mildly 'de-tuned' for the TF. That apart, changes were cosmetic, to give the car a more modern look as a stop-gap while its successor was prepared. Finally it became the TF 1500, with a 63 bhp 1466 cc (89 cu in) engine. This model was not well received – today it is sought after – and it was discontinued in 1955, to be superseded the same year by the MGA.

MG MGA

This was a significant MG sports car – the first since Cecil Kimber was moved aside to be designed by an MG team as an MG, and the first in the fashion of the era of a mass following for sports cars, as it had to compete in a competitive market. The magic of the name was no longer enough in the consumer's market atmosphere of the 1950s.

The origins of the MGA can be traced back to TCs and TDs with less bluff bodywork, particularly a one-off by MG for George Phillips to run at Le Mans in 1951. With a TD engine it was almost 50 per cent faster than a TD, and it led to Project EX-175 with a similar body on a new and appropriately lower chassis. One of the two models built was used for the EX-179 record car, and its success was another factor in persuading BMC's hierarchy to give the go-ahead for an MG to replace the fading T-series cars.

The forerunners of the new cars were entered at Le Mans in 1955, where two of the three finished, one of them completing the 24-hour race in 12th place at an 86.17 mph (138.65 kph) average. Later in the summer the MGA was launched, with the BMC B-type engine used in the ZA/ZB Magnettes (BMC badge-engineered saloons which ran in parallel), and in this 1489 cc (91 cu in) form rated at 68 bhp in the first MGAs, this figure being increased to 72 bhp a year later.

There was nothing novel in the suspension, but the whole car was well balanced in the measurable fact of weight distribution (virtually 50/50) and the less tangible aspects of its proportions and lines. Maximum speed fell fractionally short of 100 mph (161 kph), handling and road-holding were predictable and safe, and it proved an acceptable MG sports car for new enthusiasts and diehard marque supporters.

The Twin Cam appeared in 1958, with disc brakes all round and the engine enlarged to 1.6 litres, with a twin-cam head. This variant had an output of 108 bhp which gave the car a 113 mph (180 kph) top speed, but it was also troublesome and a rash of service complaints contributed to the company's decision to drop the model early in 1960. It transpired that many of the problems dogging the Twin Cam could have been avoided if a lower compression ratio had been adopted.

Meanwhile the pushrod ohv engine had been enlarged in 1959, to 1588 cc (97 cu in) and to give a power output of 75 bhp, while disc brakes took the place of drums at the front. This version was not much faster, but had better acceleration than the previous model.

The Mk II MGA 1600 which came in 1960 had a substantially reworked engine with a capacity of 1622 cc (99 cu in). This was rated at 93 bhp, and in Mk II form the MGA was a genuine 100 mph (161 kph) car, certainly in hard-top form, as this version always had better aerodynamics than convertible models.

MGAs were modestly successful in major rallies, while in racing the independent or quasi-independent entries were increasingly overshadowed. But it was a good club car, and a coupé won the 2-litre class at Le Mans in 1960. There was competition in the area of production too, but the car lasted until the middle of 1962 and in the end over 100,000 had been sold.

Mini

This was the outstandingly innovative popular car of the 1950s, launched as that decade ended and gaining individual-make status in 1970. In the

EVOLUTION — MINI

1959 Introduced in August as the Austin Seven and Morris Mini Minor, a highly compact four-seat saloon of integral construction powered by the 848 cc (52 cu in) BMC A-series four-cylinder engine

1960 Mini Van, Countryman and Traveller introduced

1961 Mini Super saloon launched; also Mini Cooper fitted with front disc brakes and a 997 cc (60.8 cu in) version of the engine, later changed to 998 cc (61 cu in). Riley Elf and Wolseley Hornet variants introduced

1962 Austin model redesignated Austin Mini. Riley Elf and Wolseley Hornet fitted with the 998 cc engine

1963 Mini Cooper S launched, with 1071 cc (65 cu in) engine

1964 Mini Cooper S's 1071 cc engine replaced by the 1275 cc (78 cu in) and 970 cc (59 cu in) units. Improved gearboxes introduced to the range, along with diaphragm spring clutch and Hydrolastic suspension on the saloons. Mini Moke launched

1965 A four-speed automatic gearbox became optional (with uprated engine) on some models

1966 Mk III Elf and Hornets launched, with improved trim

1967 Mk II Mini Cooper, Standard and Super Deluxe saloons launched, with new trim. Cooper S fitted with an all-synchromesh gearbox. Mini 1000 Super Deluxe introduced, with 998 cc (61 cu in) engine

1968 Elf, Hornet and Mini Moke were discontinued. On other models the cable interior door-lock mechanism was replaced by handles. All-synchromesh gearboxes became standard. Mk II models replaced by saloons with wind-up windows, concealed hinges for the doors and dry-cone suspension

intervening decade it had profoundly influenced small-car design, been extraordinarily successful in races and in rallies at the highest level, and induced a widespread generic use of the word 'mini'.

It is associated with one man, Sir Alec Issigonis. He returned to BMC just before the Suez crisis, and the effects of that persuaded BMC management to set him to an economy car crash programme. He simply sought the smallest and lightest way to 'package' four seats, with an acceptable amount of space, and the mechanical elements. In this last respect there was the complication of the overriding requirement that the BMC A-series engine be used.

The cornerstone of his design was the combination of front-wheel drive and transverse engine mounting, with the refinement of the gearbox squeezed into the sump of the engine – one of the few innovations the car's many imitators have not used. Beyond that, there were very small wheels, a characteristic dumpy shape with a small engine compartment and no 'third box' boot, and a spartan interior with oddities such as a curiously upright steering wheel, sliding windows and wire door-catch pulls to complete the make-up.

It proved to be classless and versatile, initially troublesome (notoriously with water leaking in through floor and doors, drowning the distributor), and with a fairly modest performance. Its 37 bhp gave a top speed of just over 70 mph (113 kph) and acceleration that was not vivid; as it was light the little Lockheed drum brakes took care of stopping; there was a characteristic noise from a transfer-gear system necessitated by the gearbox position (and some uncertainty was caused by Rzeppa constant-velocity joints), and the ride on the Moulton rubber-cone suspension was a revelation.

'Badge-engineered' variants came and are listed in the Evolution Panel, but the car really cried out for performance. This came with the Mini-Cooper, with its 997 cc (61 cu in) engine giving 55 bhp (and 85 mph/137 kph) and disc brakes. Suddenly they were in rallies everywhere, and as opposition became more serious there was the Mini-Cooper S, usually with a 1275 cc (78 cu in) engine. These cars won the Monte Carlo Rally in 1964-65 and 1967, and were moral winners in 1966.

Those heady days passed; variants came and went as the vacillating management of the new British Leyland combine could not decide whether to develop the Mini. It was perhaps saved by fuel crises, its successor the Metro did not quite replace it, and it continued through to the second half of the 1980s.

1969 Mini Cooper Mk II discontinued. Mini 1275 GT saloon introduced, with disc brakes and Hydrolastic suspension, also Mini Clubman saloon, with 998 cc (61 cu in) engine and Hydrolastic suspension, and Clubman Estate, with dry-cone suspension, replacing the 1000 Countryman and Traveller models

1970 Mini Cooper S Mk III introduced, fitted with wind-up windows, concealed hinges and new trim and seats

1971 Dry-cone suspension fitted to the Mini Clubman. Cooper S discontinued

1973 Shorter-travel gearchange introduced

1974 Automatic gearbox only available on home market

1975 Mini Clubman's 998 cc engine replaced by the 1098 cc (67 cu in) engine, except on the automatic versions

1979 Mini City 850 launched, but then the 850 series was discontinued. Mini 1000 redesignated the Super. 1000 City introduced, with estate version, available in manual and automatic versions (numerous 'special edition' Mini variants were to be contrived through the 1980s). The 848 cc (52 cu in) pickup was discontinued

1980 Mini Clubman was discontinued

1982 Mini 1000 estate discontinued, the City was renamed the Mini E, the HL the HLE, the HLE the Mini Mayfair. All van and pick-up versions were discontinued

1984 Mini 25 commemorated a quarter of a century of Mini production

1986 The five-millionth Mini produced, celebrated with a special, limited-edition model

1988 City E and Mayfair 998 cc (61 cu in) engined range continued towards 30th anniversary of Mini introduction

Morgan Three Wheelers

The three wheeler was once common on Britain's roads, and in very small numbers such vehicles were still built in the 1980s, most for utilitarian purposes

EVOLUTION — MORGAN THREE WHEELER

1908-9 Prototype Morgan three wheeler built, powered by an air-cooled Peugeot vee twin motorcycle engine with two-speed gearbox, tiller steering and sliding-pillar front suspension

1916 Grand Prix model introduced, with 10 bhp MAG engine, disc wheels and longer chassis

1923 Front-wheel brake option introduced

1926 Electric starter introduced as option

1928 Super Sports Aero introduced with 10-40 hp water-cooled JAP vee-twin

1929 Front brakes made standard

1931 New chassis introduced with three forward gears. Electric starter standard

1933 First four-cylinder Morgan three wheeler introduced with Ford 933 cc (57 cu in) side-valve engine, the first model to have all three brakes connected to the brake pedal. Later the 1173 cc (71 cu in) Ford engine offered. It was longer and wider than the traditional three wheelers and provided the basis for the first four-wheeled Morgan

1952 Morgan three wheeler production ceased

but with just a handful of sporting types. They echoed the Morgans, particularly those of the inter-wars years that fell somewhere between motorcycles and cars – perhaps inclined towards the former, as in motor sport they fell under the wing of the Auto Cycle Union – and providing a particularly exhilarating form of transport.

H.F.S. Morgan built his first Morgan at the garage he owned in Malvern Link, establishing the stable layout of two front wheels and a single rear wheel that was to continue until Morgan built its last three-wheeled vehicle. A front-mounted engine was used (a Peugot vee twin on the first Morgan), and the drive was taken back to a rear-mounted two-speed gearbox through a tube which also formed part of the chassis. Steering was by tiller, soon to be replaced by a wheel.

The enduring feature of that first car was its independent front suspension, by coil springs and sliding pillars, extraordinarily advanced for the time and destined to outlive the three wheelers in its application to Morgan vehicles.

Within a year a two-seater had been built, and H.F.S. Morgan had laid the foundations of a sporting career with a penalty-free run in the 1910 Exeter Trial. In 1912 he had formed the Morgan Motor Company with his father, the Rev Prebendary H.G. Morgan, as its chairman. The two-seater became well established (and there were to be four-seater runabouts) and a variety of engines came to be used, some exposed, some cowled – 'standardization' did not feature in Morgan's working practices.

Production resumed and through the 1920s a

more identifiable model range evolved. There were front-wheel brakes (optional, from 1923) and self-starters from 1928. A four-seater 'Family' model continued – in Britain there was a tax advantage – but the ultra-light Super Sports Aero, with its little twin half-round aero screens, was the best-known Morgan, usually with a JAP twin that gave it an 80 mph (129 kph) top speed.

In 1933 the first Morgan to use a car engine appeared, with a Ford 933 cc (57 cu in) 'four' in a new pressed-steel chassis, on a longer track and wider wheelbase. Larger Ford engines became available, then a Coventry Climax engine, but through the 1930s sales declined. More people could afford 'real' light cars, and from 1936 a Morgan four-wheeled car was available, but production of Ford-engined three wheelers continued until 1952.

Morgan Four Wheelers

These highly individualistic sports cars changed little in make-up through half a century. A near-Vintage design, built by near-Vintage methods in a pre-Vintage factory, they have proved timeless. Yet because the constantly changing element has been the power units, Morgans have been high-performance sports cars throughout.

Morgan had flirted with a four-wheel project in the 1920s, but did not show a car until 1935. Put into production in 1936, this 4/4 (four wheels/four cylinders) amounted to a four-wheeled version of the contemporary F-type three wheeler. It had a rigid ladder-type chassis with Z-section side members, kept low as it was underslung at the rear. Morgan's coil spring and vertical pillar front suspension was used, while a rigid axle at the rear was sprung by semi-elliptics. That much of the specification stands to this day, and by chance the suspension is well suited to modern low-profile tyres.

The cockpit bodywork was on a wooden frame, and that too holds good with the 125 mph (201 kph) Morgans of the late 1980s (that sort of speed is achieved with a 3.5-litre Rover V8, in the Plus 8). While Meadows, Moss and Rover gearboxes have been used down the years, most changes have been in the engine department.

A Ford 993 cc (60.5 cu in) side-valve engine proved less than adequate in the first car, so when production got under way the 4/4s were powered by a 1122 cc (68 cu in) Coventry Climax engine, which drove through a separate gearbox (a box in unit with the engine came with the Rover power unit many years later). In 1939 the 36 bhp Climax engine gave way to an ohv 1172 cc (71.5 cu in) Standard engine, which produced 40 bhp. That continued until 1950, when the Plus 4 came with a wheelbase extended by 5 cm (2 in) to accommodate the 2.1-litre 68 bhp ohv Standard Vanguard engine, and that in turn was followed by Triumph TR engines – going from 1991 cc (121 cu in) and 90 bhp in TR3 guise, up to 2138 cc (130 cu in) and 105 bhp from the TR4, and that made the Plus 4 a 100 mph (161 kph) car.

Meanwhile, the 4/4, which had lapsed, was brought back in 1955 with a Ford engine, and continued with 105E and 109E engines from the same source. As far as styling was concerned little changed. Nose and tail were less angular and upright after 1955, to the car's advantage, while there was an odd lapse with the aerodynamic coupé body of the Plus 4 Plus in 1963; after that exploratory venture into glassfibre bodywork, Peter Morgan retreated back into the known world of tradition! Some lightweight cars with alloy panelling were also built, as Plus 4 Super Sports.

However, the ultimate in performance terms came with the adoption of the Rover engine in 1968. The Plus 8 is a quick car, to be treated with respect.

NSU Ro80

This was a car of great promise, which proved to be fatally flawed. It provided effortless, comfortable travel for four people, with a smooth engine and supple suspension; its lines were attractive and aerodynamically effective, and in many mechanical respects it was exemplary. But it is recalled for its Wankel rotary engine, and that was to prove the cause of its downfall.

NSU had started working towards this car with studies on rotary-engined front-wheel drive cars early in the 1960s. To gain experience a pilot production run with a small Wankel-engined car was undertaken in 1964. This Spider was based on the contemporary Sport Prinz, with an attractive roadster body by Bertone, and powered by a little single-rotor 500 cc (31 cu in) engine which produced 60 bhp – enough to give the Spider a brisk performance. Some 2000 were sold, but many engines had to be replaced under warranty, undermining profitability.

Despite this experience, NSU carried on with the major project, and when this was announced in 1967 as the Ro80 leading journalists unhesitatingly voted it Car of the Year. Apart from its engine it was an advanced saloon, with independent suspension and disc brakes all round, to give a good ride and good handling qualities. It had timeless lines, which had a drag factor (Cd) of 0.355, and this helped performance once this relatively heavy and unquestionably thirsty car was under way.

The twin-rotor Wankel engine displaced 994 cc (60.6 cu in), which gave it a capacity equivalent to a conventional engine of 1990 cc (121 cu in). Its power output of 113.5 bhp would have been acceptable in a 2-litre piston engine, and it was delivered smoothly and quietly. However, it drove through a three-speed semi-automatic gearbox, where a five-speed manual box might have been felt more appropriate. The choice of three widely-spaced ratios, allied to a torque converter, was to all intents and purposes imposed on NSU, in order to overcome some engine problems. It did not help the car's heavy fuel consumption.

At a steady speed of 50 mph (80 kph), the Ro80 returned a costly 28 mpg but genuine steady speeds are seldom achieved in everyday motoring. It is unlikely that the claimed 21 mpg was ever recorded in 'real' motoring conditions – where 50 per cent of that could actually have been returned – and by the time of the mid-1970s oil crises the Ro80 had an unfortunate but unavoidable reputation as a gas guzzler.

By that time some of the problems, for example with sealing, were nearing solution. But sales had fallen off dramatically, and so had production. A merger with Volkswagen had brought Audi expertise to bear, and efforts to improve the car continued until well after the takeover. Production ran until 1977, when 37,204 Ro80s had been built, some of them to suffer being re-engined with a Ford piston engine. This 107 mph (172 kph) luxury saloon deserved better.

Packard V12

Some of the finest cars of the 1930s were built in the USA, and the V12 Packards were supreme among these. The patrician Detroit company was the first to put a V12-engined car into production, in 1915, under the model name Twin Six. This was costly, and highly successful, for 35,046 were built before it gave way to a straight eight in 1922. In production terms the second-generation Packard V12s, those of the 1930s, seem less successful. But these rare cars were fully deserving of a 'classic' label.

The Twin Six was reborn in mid-1931, as a response to Cadillac's V16. The decision to go ahead had been taken in 1930, when two projects were developed. The option of front-wheel drive was rejected in favour of a wholly conventional rear-drive car, and this led to a short gestation period, less than a year from concept to launch.

The engine had its cylinder blocks set at the unusual included angle of 67 degrees, and in terms of valvegear was a quite conventional L-head. Each unit was carefully run in before being fitted into its chassis – turned over by an electric motor for an hour, run for six hours on a bench, then for 75 minutes on a dynamometer to check that it was developing the specified 160 bhp. The chassis was then run through a 250 mile (400 km) proving routine on the Packard test track. Packard claimed that these Ninth Series cars (these 'series' coincided with model years, running from 1923) were capable of 100 mph (161 kph), which for a stock car was an optimistic round-up.

Initially the bodies were similar to those on the top-of-the-range Eights, and despite carrying the prestigious Dietrich name they were slow movers. Custom bodies on the substantial X-braced chassis frame were more costly, but later in the 1930s some outstanding coachwork was to be married to the Twin Six. Whatever the body, the cars were heavy, and that perhaps helped riding qualities with non-independent suspension.

Twelfth Series cars (1934 onwards) had engines with increased stroke, to give a swept volume of 7755 cc (473 cu in) and a claimed 175 bhp. Independent front suspension and hydraulic brakes

in place of mechanical brakes came with the Fifteenth Series.

Sales had never been good; by 1937 the decision to phase out the V12 had been taken, and the last Packard V12 cars were built in 1939.

Pegaso

This was a marque created for the wrong reasons – a mix of personal frustration, a search for prestige and, to underpin these, the formation of a finishing school for technical craftsmen; the hard facts of commercial life, or many of the realities of gran turismo motoring, were not part of the equation.

A Spanish national commercial vehicle company, ENASA, was set up in the old Hispano-Suiza factory in Barcelona in 1946, and Wilfredo P. Ricart was appointed to run it. He had an extensive background, with a particular reputation as an engine designer, and his position at Alfa Romeo in the late 1930s had been central to Enzo Ferrari's split with that company. Once truck and bus build was under way at the Barcelona plant, the not-so-strange notion that apprentices might polish their crafts building sophisticated cars in small numbers was mooted, and put into effect.

The first Pegaso car was exhibited at the 1951 Paris Motor Show, where its generally advanced specification and its improbable background set the automotive world buzzing. As an overall concept it was not far removed from the Grand Prix cars of an age that was passing. The engine was a dry-sump twin-oc alloy V8, initially of 2474 cc (151 cu in), but to be enlarged to 2.8 or 3.2 litres in definitive Z102 cars, and with a supercharging option. Claimed power ranged from 165 bhp for the first engines to 225 bhp for a supercharged 3.2-litre V8, and with up to 260 bhp reckoned possible.

Power was needed as the cars were heavy, with a platform frame of pressings welded to square-section steel tubes. Torsion bar suspension was used at the front, with the de Dion arrangement at the back; located by radius rods running to the rear, the de Dion axle was ahead of the gearbox, which drove forward to a limited-slip differential. Generous drum brakes were fitted, inboard at the rear.

Most of the Z102s had bodies by Saoutchik, Pegaso's own coupé body was heavy, with deep flanks, the most attractive coupé and spyder bodies were by Touring, and inevitably with such a car there were odd styling exercises. Only a handful of Z103s with larger pushrod ohv engines were built – one for each capacity, 4.0, 4.5 and 4.7 litres.

Pegaso's competitions efforts were confined largely to minor Spanish events, with open Z102SS cars which were modestly successful. Attempts have been made to show that Pegaso could have been successful in top-class sports car racing, but this is based on the inadequate evidence of the performance of one car that crashed in the 1954 Carrera Panamericana (it had run as high as second). Two cars entered for Le Mans that year were withdrawn after a practice accident.

Sensibly, the company dropped this indulgence in 1958, when 125 cars had been built.

Pierce-Arrow V12

Too many luxury cars were built in the 1930s, and inevitably some of their manufacturers crashed. Unhappily, the makers of one of the best of the multi-cylinder big cars, Pierce-Arrow, was among them.

Pierce was one of the oldest companies in the American industry; its first Arrow appeared in 1902, and in 1909 it became Pierce-Arrow. In the late 1920s, and in common with many other companies, it was in trouble. But that year saw the introduction of a successful 6-litre straight eight, and an injection of cash from a merger with Studebaker which enabled development of a V12 reply to Cadillac's V16 to be put in hand.

It was put into production late in 1931, and the 1932 range comprised Models 51, 52 and 53, with three wheelbase options and 17 body styles catalogued. That was impressive, and sales of 447 V12s

in the first full year were reasonable, but not sufficient to justify Studebaker assertions that the cars would also be built in their Canadian plant.

The V12 was available with two displacements, 6524 cc (398 cu in) and 7035 cc (430 cu in). It had the unusually wide angle of 80 degrees, in order to make the central camshaft more accessible; a vibration damper took care of that wide-angle worry, and the cars were reported to be very smooth.

The chassis was conventional, upswept at each end, X-braced and with the scuttle and radiator designed to increase stiffness. It rode on non-independent suspension, with semi-elliptic leaf springs and Delco-Lovejoy hydraulic shock absorbers which could be adjusted to give a soft ('town') or firm ('highway') ride.

In an effort to boost flagging sales, David 'Ab' Jenkins undertook a 24-hour run on the Bonneville Salt Flats in a roadster with a 7566 cc (462 cu in) V12. He covered 2710 miles (4363 km) in the 24 hours, the fastest ever in the USA but not recognized as a record as it was not officially observed.

An engine of that capacity was added to the range for 1933 and the smaller V12 dropped, while Pierce-Arrow achieved another American 'first' by fitting hydraulic tappets. But 1933 was another troubled business year, and Studebaker went bankrupt. Pierce-Arrow regained independence of a sort, and recovery was planned under Chanter and Faulkner. One element was the dramatic fastback 7566 cc (462 cu in) Silver Arrow, which was given much attention at the Chicago Exposition of 1933; and Ab Jenkins officially broke records at Bonneville, in a stripped convertible.

Sales did not recover. They picked up early in 1936, when only the largest of the V12s was listed, in modified form producing 185 bhp, then fell again. In 1937 only 167 were sold; late that year production ended, with 17 nominal 1938 models assembled.

Porsche 356

This was the first car to be sold as a Porsche, with a designation indicating that it was the 356th project from the Porsche Büro – the 'new' marque had a

Porsche 911

pedigree. It was to establish the name on world markets, and lay the foundations for Porsche's eminence in sports car racing and rallying.

The design which Ferry Porsche and two of his father's associates, Karl Rabe and Erwin Komenda, worked on in 1947 had its origins in a VW-based sports car project designed by Professor Ferdinand Porsche before World War 2. The first car was completed early in 1948, using VW running gear and torsion bar suspension all round, with a modified VW 1131 cc (69 cu in) engine mounted ahead of the rear wheels in a tubular frame, with very smooth low-drag bodywork.

The definitive car took shape in 1948, when a pair of what might now be referred to as 'pre-production' cars were completed at Gmund in Austria (where the first 50 Porsches were to be built). These had pressed-steel chassis with aluminium bodywork, and the engine had been repositioned behind the rear axle line. The flat four was rated at 40 bhp, and it gave this light car an 85 mph (140 kph) top speed.

Owners soon started to use these cars in competitions, and the factory was to retain four of the aluminium-bodied early cars to use specifically for this purpose.

Serious production got under way at Stuttgart in 1950, when the adjacent Reutter company undertook the steel chassis/body unit build. In 1951 1.3- and 1.5-litre engines were introduced, a one-piece screen and synchromesh gearbox came in 1952, and development moved on quickly – there were to be many variations throughout the 17-year life of the 356.

The 356A came in 1955, with five engine options (1.3 to 1.6 litres in varying states of tune), the 356B in 1959 and the C in 1963. Best known of the 356As were the Speedster and the Carrera which superseded it in 1955. This had a twin-cam 1.5-litre engine, soon a 115 bhp 1.6-litre unit, and these Carreras were the first Porsches to have disc brakes. The name, deriving from the Panamericana road race, also caught on and was to be perpetuated by Porsche. Some of the 356Bs also became more familiar under designations which related to engine bhp – 60, 75, 90 and Super 90. By 1961 the top Carrera engine was a 1966 cc (120 cu in) 130 bhp unit which made this a 125 mph (200-plus kph) car.

The Carrera GTL of 1960 had lightweight Abarth bodies and 1.6-litre engines developed to give up to 135 bhp (one of these cars won its class at Le Mans in 1960).

As the Porsche 911 programme gathered momentum, 356 production started to tail off with the C. This differed from the 356B in detail, but the range was cut to two models, the 74 bhp 1600C and 95 bhp 1600SC. In 1965 the last 356s were built. Total production was 76,303 cars, and few marques have got off to a more solid and well-found start.

Porsche had to move on from the 356 with its VW origins, and in 1963 exhibited the forerunner of a model that would still be in production a quarter of a century later. That first car was shown as a 901, but because Peugeot had already registered all three-figure numbers with a 'zero' second figure Porsche changed the designation to 911 before production started in the Autumn of 1964.

The basis was an outstanding new flat-six light-alloy engine, still air cooled, in its first 1991 cc (121 cu in) form rated at 130 bhp. This had considerable 'stretch' potential. The engine was installed overhung at the back, and in an effort to overcome the inherent handling problems that led to, Porsche engineers discarded the swing axles of the 356 in favour of a semi-trailing arm system. It was still a tail-happy car, and indeed on through the 1980s was to have a reputation for challenging handling.

An integral steel body was fitted, initially only in coupé form (as a realistic two-seater, with niggardly 2+2 provision). The first significant variant was the Targa of 1965. The car was almost redesigned in 1969, with longer wheelbase and wider track, and a MacPherson strut front suspension, changes which paved the way for more powerful engines.

Power had already gone up to 170 bhp in the 911S of 1966, a 135 mph (220 kph) car; a 2.2-litre engine came in 1969 and in 1971 the capacity went up to 2.4 litres, with power ranging from 110 bhp in the 911T to 170 bhp in the 911S (those figures would have been higher if policy had not dictated a drop in compression ratios so that all Porsche engines were able to run on low-grade fuel).

The 2.4-litre (actually 2341 cc/143 cu in) engines lasted only until 1973, when the model range was changed to a base 911 (150 bhp), the 911S (175 bhp) and the RS Carrera with 210 bhp. These power outputs were produced by 2.7-litre engines with Bosch continuous fuel injection.

Throughout this period the 911 had built up a distinguished competitions record, rally successes coming to it in 1965 and being capped with Elford's Monte Carlo victory in 1968 and Waldegaard's wins in that event in 1969-70. Ten years after Elford's victory, Nicolas won the Monte in a private 911. On the circuits the 911 and its lightweight offshoot, the Carrera RSR, were prominent contenders well into the 1970s, when they became overshadowed by turbo cars.

In that context, the outstanding member of the 911 family to appear in the 1970s was the Turbo (works designation 930) which fitted neatly into the supercar category. The first version, in 1974, had a 3-litre engine, 260 bhp and 155 mph (250 kph), while a 3.3-litre Turbo came in 1978, with 300 bhp and 160 mph (260 kph). Spoilers front and rear, although providing stability and acceptable cornering behaviour, tended to emasculate the overall performance.

In 'normal' form the 911 continued towards its quarter century, although sales fell as its prices rose. However Porsche insisted that it would continue production of this model into the 1990s, as a new Zuffenhausen body plant would lead to flexibility and four-wheel drive 911s.

Porsche 928

This was a flagship model for Porsche, introducing the company to a sector of the market where the emphasis was as much on luxury as on performance. It was Car of the Year in 1978, but during the next decade there was some uncertainty about its supercar role, and a reaction against its high price, although its position as an outstanding GT car was never questioned.

It was a wide, bulky car, with a luxury interior quite unlike any other Porsche; the engine was a relatively large V8 in the interests of silence and unstressed power that would not be sapped as obligatory emissions control equipment was added, and the transmission was at the rear in the interests of neutral handling. Its curvaceous lines lacked the crispness associated with Porsches, with a curiously rounded tail and a poor drag factor of 0.39 (that was to be improved on Series 4 cars, to 0.34-0.35 depending on the position of the automatic engine cooling duct), while the early alloy wheels were far from attractive.

Under the skin of the part-alloy-panelled steel monocoque there was a conventional front suspension and a Porsche-Weissach rear suspension (named after the Porsche research centre). This used articulated lower semi-trailing arms, upper transverse link, coil springs and dampers, and anti-roll bar. A prime objective had been to avoid oversteer with 'anti toe-out geometry'.

When the 928 was announced in 1977 the engine was a light-alloy single-ohc V8 of 4474 cc (273 cu in), which produced 240 bhp quietly and smoothly, with abundant torque and on low-grade fuel. That first engine gave the 928 a top speed of 144 mph (232 kph), well within road-holding limitations. It was continued until 1982, but meanwhile the 928S had come in 1979 with a bored out 4.7-litre version rated at 300 bhp, and that made the 928S a 155 mph car, a figure that becomes more significant as 250 kph. There was another slight increase in power as Bosch Jetronic fuel injection was introduced in 1983. Series 2 cars were then fitted with low-profile tyres, and anti-lock braking had become standard equipment by 1985.

EVOLUTION — PORSCHE 911

1964 Introduced with 1991 cc (121 cu in) flat six, air-cooled, overhead-cam engine

1966 Carrera competition model introduced with twin-cam version of the 1991 cc six producing 210 bhp

1968 Semi-automatic transmission available

1969 Wheelbase and track increased significantly and front suspension changed from wishbones and torsion bars to MacPherson struts

1970 Fuel injection introduced to form the 911E (*Einspritz*) and displacement increased to 2195 cc (134 cu in). 911T basic carburettor version produced 110 bhp, then 911E (140 bhp) and 911S (170 bhp)

1972 911S engine displacement 2343 cc (143 cu in), producing 190 bhp

1973 Carrera RS introduced with 2.7-litre six-cylinder engine producing 210 bhp

1974 T/E/S line-up discontinued in favour of basic 911 (150 bhp), 911S (175 bhp) and RS Carrera (210 bhp)

1975 Turbo introduced with 3-litre engine

1978 Five-speed gearbox became standard equipment. Turbo engine increased to 3.33 litres and 300 bhp

1982 Carrera became the standard 911 with 3164 cc (193 cu in) displacement and 231 bhp

1983 Carrera Cabriolet introduced at Geneva Show

1986 Carrera SE introduced, in effect a Turbo with normally-aspirated 231 bhp engine

1987 250,000th 911 completed. Carrera Club Sport lightweight version of standard car with 231 bhp engine introduced

The increase in power that came with the Series 4 model's larger (4957 cc/302 cu in) 32-valve engine was not great – from 310 bhp to 320 bhp – but the increase in torque made for a useful improvement in acceleration, where the early 928s had been far from lively. The 928S4 had a maximum speed of 158 mph (255 kph). The car was not above criticism as its ride was harsh at some speeds, while road and suspension noise could be louder than the engine. Luggage space was minimal, and so was room in the foldable rear seats.

The 928 worked well for everyday drivers, unlike some 'traditional' Porsches that called for unusual driving skills, but for a car at such a high price it was slightly flawed.

Rolls-Royce Silver Ghost

The earliest Rolls-Royce cars were very good, but they were not the best cars in the world. That claim was based on the merits of the outstanding 40/50, which came in 1907 and with minor changes ran until 1925; nowadays one of the most familiar Edwardian car images in the world is that of the 13th car in the 40/50 series. This had a silver paint finish and silver-plated fittings, and its name, Silver Ghost, came to refer to 40/50s. From 1907 until 1922 it was the only Rolls-Royce, and many 40/50 chassis carried armoured car bodies after 1914.

Innovation was not the Royce way, but attention to mechanical detail and his relentless demand for craftsmanship to the point of perfection were evident on his cars. So the 40/50 was conservative, albeit with a new straight-six engine.

This comprised two cast-iron blocks on an alloy crankcase, with a very substantial and stiff seven-bearing crankshaft and, it followed, sturdy crankpins and so on through the engine. Each of the two monobloc units had an integral head. Side valves were preferred, for quietness and ease of tappet adjustment. Timing drive was by gears. Most of the electrical equipment was made by Rolls-Royce, and

a dynamo was not fitted to 40/50s until 1919.

The model owed its designation to horsepower ratings – 40 according to the RAC taxation rating which was determined by piston area, and 50 being the actual brake horsepower. The ladder-type steel chassis was well braced with six cross members, and the most famous of chassis, the 13th, carried dignified *Roi des Belges* bodywork by Barkers, a style that had first graced a Panhard built for that monarch in 1901. Rigid axles were of course used, with semi-elliptic leaf springs, while the earliest 40/50s also had a transverse leaf spring at the rear.

That car was used in officially observed trials of speed, flexibility, reliability and roadworthiness, all arranged by Rolls-Royce general managing director Claude Johnson for publicity. And, indeed, the company Silver Ghost fulfils that role today as it has run on most of the continents.

The RAC produced a very detailed report of the most famous of the early runs, when Johnson completed 14,731 miles (23,706 km) in the car in the Spring of 1907, with involuntary stops for tyre changes and once when a rough road vibrated the petrol tap shut. In the course of this run the Ghost took part in several competitions, such as the 747-mile (1202 km) Scottish Reliability Trial at one extreme and the Bexhill Speed Trials at the other (at Bexhill the car was timed over a flying quarter mile at 52.94 mph/85 kph, while it was driven from the South coast to Scotland in top gear).

Some revision was carried out when 40/50 production resumed in 1919, and although it was a dated design a few cars were built by Rolls-Royce America in the early 1920s. In May 1925 the Silver Ghost was replaced by the new Phantom.

Rolls-Royce Phantom III

The Phantom III had few equals in the luxury car class in the second half of the 1930s, and this car firmly brought Rolls-Royce up to date with its

Rolls-Royce Silver Shadow

contemporaries, laying to rest suggestions that the company was living in the past. It was the first Rolls-Royce V12, the first model with independent front suspension, and although it usually carried upright and stately coachwork it was no sluggard, with some examples capable of 100 mph (161 kph).

By the standards of the time, it came at the end of a long programme. Project work started in 1932, an experimental car was running two years later, and production started in 1936. It was announced well ahead of its introduction, in October 1935, eight months before production began.

The engine had little in common with the company's V12 aircraft power plants, having its cylinder banks cast *en bloc* in light alloy with cast-iron wet liners and set at an angle of 60 degrees. The crankcase and cylinder heads were also light alloy castings. There was a single camshaft in the centre of the vee, operating the valves throughout pushrods and rockers. At first hydraulic tappets were fitted, in a quest for mechanical silence, but solid tappets were adopted in 1938. There were two plugs per cylinder, with an infinitessimal time lag between firings, one of each pair being operated by separate ignition systems.

Power output estimates for the V12 ranged from 165 bhp for the early engines to 180 bhp in later cars.

The coil spring and wishbone front suspension was compared to a General Motors system that had been announced early in 1934, albeit that Rolls-Royce's ifs was more refined. It improved ride and handling compared with the Phantom II. A live axle was used at the rear, with semi-elliptics, a transverse torsion bar (acting as an anti-roll bar) and hydraulic shock absorbers that could be adjusted from the driver's seat. This suspension carried a pressed-steel box-section chassis, cross braced and very rigid. The cross-bracing separated engine and gearbox, which were kept apart in the interests of good weight distribution.

Coachbuilt bodies were of course the norm, and when the Phantom III was unveiled at the 1935 London Motor Show the display included limousines by Barker and Hooper and a sedanca de ville by Park Ward. Many of the bodies were ponderous, reflecting the stately touring uses to which they were put, but in the late 1930s some elegant versions were built. In an early road test, *The Autocar* recorded a maximum speed of 91.84 mph (147.77 kph) with a ponderous seven-seater Park Ward limousine, but much more importantly the car was very flexible, offering a 'remarkable combination of comfort and road holding', with firm accurate steering and very sure braking.

The car was to be criticised, largely on the grounds that overhauls were very expensive, the root cause of this often being less than meticulous maintenance. World War 2 ended Phantom III production, when some 710 cars had been built.

The Silver Shadow was a break with Rolls-Royce's past – the company's first monocoque car, its first with independent suspension all round, power hydraulics providing self-levelling ride height and operating disc brakes on all four wheels. It was also to be the most successful model ever produced by Rolls-Royce.

Sales had declined in the 1950s, and late in that decade the V8 Silver Cloud II was introduced, almost to hold the line while design and development work that had been initiated in 1958 was completed. Before it was, and the new model was announced, a Silver Cloud III had been run for two years. The initial response to the new car, the Silver Shadow, was lukewarm – in some aspects, ranging from appearance to performance, it seemed to offer no advances over the 'interim' car.

However, it was soon accepted, and through a long history it was to be the basis for some interesting variants, not least Bentleys as that marque regained some of its identity. There were objections to unitary construction, but the noise and vibration that could result were effectively filtered out by mounting engine and front suspension and the rear suspension on subframes.

The independent suspension was in itself straightforward, with double wishbones and coil springs at the front, semi-trailing arms and coil springs at the rear, but above each shock absorber there was a high-pressure hydraulic ram which automatically compensated for trim changes. By 1969 the front rams had been deleted, as the rear ones could cope with any situation.

Other changes in the 1960s included adding a rear anti-roll bar to balance the stiffer anti-roll bar at the front, to cut out excess understeer and to build in higher-geared steering with more 'feel'. Very large disc brakes were fitted from the start, with high-pressure hydraulic operation on Citroën lines.

An enlarged engine (6750 cc/411.7 cu in) was fitted in 1970, in an effort to 'retrieve' power lost as anti-emission equipment was fitted, and this did nothing to improve fuel consumption, which was to be a cause of great concern to Rolls-Royce engineers through the decade.

A long-wheelbase version had come in 1969, and Mulliner Park Ward had continued to build special versions. These included two-door saloons and convertibles, and in effect led to the Corniche, which from 1980 was offered only as a convertible. The Camargue was a less successful derivative, styled by Pininfarina.

The Silver Shadow II, introduced in 1977, had rack-and-pinion steering, split-level air conditioning and styling changes. In many respects the Silver Spirit was a rebodied and mechanically revised Shadow II, with a long-wheelbase version named Silver Spur. With the Continental, these two models made up the highly successful range which took Rolls-Royce into the late 1980s.

EVOLUTION — ROLLS-ROYCE SILVER SHADOW

1965 Silver Shadow introduced at the London Motor Show

1966 Silver Shadow entered production

1967 Silver Shadow Convertible introduced

1968 GM400 three-speed automatic transmission replaced the Hydramatic on UK cars – it had been standard equipment on US spec cars from 1966. Suspension revised

1969 Long-wheelbase version introduced

1970 Engine displacement increased to 6750 cc (412 cu in)

1971 Corniche convertible introduced

1972 Front suspension redesigned, allowing radial tyres to be fitted. The front track was increased and the front discs ventilated

1975 Pininfarina-styled Camargue introduced

1977 Silver Shadow II introduced, with rack and pinion steering system, revised aerodynamics, front suspension and interior

1980 Silver Shadow was replaced by the Silver Spirit in short- and long-wheelbase versions

1985 100,000th Rolls-Royce, a Silver Spur, completed. Spur was lwb variant of Shadow

1986 Fuel injection fitted to Silver Spirit and Silver Spur (engine power increased by 22 per cent on these models) and Corniche (engine power increased by 14 per cent). Anti-lock braking introduced for European markets. Camargue discontinued

1987 Corniche II convertible introduced

Sunbeam 3 Litre

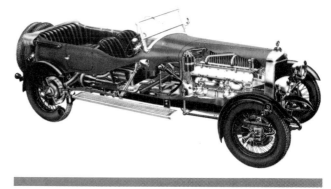

This was a sports car of great promise, a fine design which could have rivalled the Bentleys of the 1920s but which fell victim to muddled management, a result of the very muddled Sunbeam-Talbot-Darracq combine.

STD director Louis Coatalen visualized a comprehensive sports programme for the 1920s, and in part this was carried through successfully. There was for example a Grand Prix victory for a Sunbeam in the 1923 French event, and the Sunbeam name was to feature in record attempts. Sports cars were natural additions to the production list, and the plan for 1922 envisaged a 1.5-litre Darracq to be built in Paris and a 3-litre Sunbeam to be built at Wolverhampton. The Darracq engine was a failure, but the Sunbeam went ahead.

The straight-six engine was planned by Vincent Bertarione, developed by another brilliant engineer, Georges Roesch, and drawn up in detail by George Ward. The curious feature of the first version of this power unit was the skew-gear drive from the crankshaft nose to the twin overhead camshafts.

That was soon abandoned, but time lost meant that plans to run the car at Le Mans in 1924 had to be dropped. The engine reappeared in 1925 with its camshafts driven by conventional gears. It followed the general lines of Sunbeam's 1921 GP straight eight, and initially developed some 90 bhp.

The car gave a long and narrow impression, and looked remarkably light compared with Bentleys and with its Continental counterparts. Before full production got under way, two cars were run at Le Mans. At times both held the lead, one to retire with clutch failure late on the first afternoon, while Jean Chassagne and S.C.H. Davis placed the other second, some 45 miles (72 km) behind the winning la Lorraine. But that was an encouraging showing.

It had also fulfilled a purpose, in showing up weaknesses in the chassis, so this was strengthened for production for the 'F' cars in 1926. These were conventional in the make-up of the chassis and running gear, and a few had special bodies.

In normal form the engine was reported to be remarkably flexible, particularly in top gear. After that Le Mans performance in 1925 the cars were seen surprisingly little in racing. But there was one more direct confrontation with Bentley, in the Essex Six Hours at Brooklands in 1927, which was won by George Duller in one of the Sunbeams (he covered 386 miles/521 km at a speed averaging 64.3 mph/ 103.5 kph).

Sales were never good, and in 1929 Sunbeam followed the quite normal policy of offering a supercharged model, for which a power output increase to 130 bhp was claimed. But that found few buyers, and was seldom seen in racing. Sunbeam's 3-litre sports car line petered out, after only five years, with some 315 cars built.

Talbot 75, 90 and 105

These cars became known as the Roesch Talbots, and were the final sporting fling for the marque while it was part of Sunbeam-Talbot-Darracq. The best-known of these cars actually came into being at the instigation of Fox and Nicholl, motor traders who sought cars to replace the Lagondas they had raced in 1928-29. Their approach gave Georges Roesch an opportunity to develop sporting models on the basis of the 14/45 and 65.

These were straight-six touring cars, but Roesch saw the potential for transformation. His main problem was the Sunbeam management's stipulation that engine and drive train components must remain production items. That left him with little option for engine tuning other than raising the compression ratio. Here he was unwittingly aided as

Pratt's introduced a high-octane fuel, but even so taking compression ratio to 10:1 seemed very risky in 1930. It was done, with domed pistons and cutaway cylinder heads, and for the first Talbot 70 Sports the engine produced 85 bhp.

With light four-seater competitions bodies, the 70 Sports was capable of 100 mph (161 kph), and after an unhappy first race they won their class at Le Mans in the Tourist Trophy, the Irish GP and other races.

With a lower compression ratio, the engine was suited to production cars such as the 75 (because of the car's speed, the 70 Sports had meanwhile become the 90). Roesch felt that there was more to come, and for road and competition cars an engine with bore and stroke increased to give a 2969 cc (181 cu in) capacity was developed. For road use it was rated at 100 bhp and was used in the AM90 chassis, while in competition tune the normal maximum was 120 bhp, although power outputs approaching 140 bhp were obtained.

Dual-purpose designs must have appealed to cost-conscious managements in the early 1930s, but meant that sports versions of the Roesch cars were handicapped once out-and-out sports models such as the Alfa Romeo 8C and MG C arrived, though their stamina helped (for example to three successive third placings at Le Mans and good performances in rallies such as the Alpine Trial).

The road cars seemed set for long runs, with the 3377 cc (206 cu in) Talbot 110 largely identical to the 105 coming in 1934. But the ramshackle Sunbeam-Talbot-Darracq combine collapsed; Rootes took over the British company, and preferred their own range. The last Roesch Talbot was the 110, which survived until 1938.

Talbot-Lago

Antonio – Tony – Lago joined Sunbeam-Talbot-Darracq in 1933, to reorganize the Talbot works at Suresnes in the combine's twilight years. He saw the

potential in one model and its 3-litre engine in the French Talbot range and schemed a new head to marry to the block, and when the STD collapse came the prospect of a new car based on the Talbot-Darracq K78 was a factor which helped Lago attract backing to refloat Automobiles Talbot as an independent company. This coincided with a revival in French sports-car racing.

In the 1920s Lago had marketed LAP overhead valve conversions, and this experience had led him to set designer Walter Becchia working on a new version of the 3-litre straight six, primarily with a cylinder head with cross-over pushrods. It was a 4-litre unit, which was to be rated at 125 bhp in the first Lago Sport Spéciale models, and up to 165 bhp in the competition models of the second half of the 1930s.

Lago laid down a team of competition sports cars for 1936, straightforward machines with box-section side-member chassis frames, transverse leaf spring front suspension and live rear axle with semi-elliptics, initially with friction dampers. Wilson pre-selector gearboxes were fitted. The bodies had a solid look, with cycle wings on the circuit cars.

There were teething troubles through the first season, but in 1937 the blue Talbots won several major races, including the French GP and the Tourist Trophy.

During this time a prestige high-performance road model was launched, the SS (*Sport-Spéciale*). This used the same chassis and running gear and the milder version of the engine, and proved irresistible to French coachbuilders, who produced some splendid *grand routier* bodywork on these Talbot models. The strong engine gave them performance to match, with speeds up to 115 mph (185 kph).

At the other extreme, the competition cars could be stripped and run as single seaters in Grands Prix, before and after World War 2. In this guise there were occasional successes when main-line teams did not enter races, but generally Talbot drivers had to rely on hare-and-tortoise tactics to pick up placings as they ran with fewer fuel stops than their supercharged rivals.

After the war the road cars tended to be known as Lago-Talbots, and in Record and Grand Sport forms had a 4482 cc (274 cu in) version of the engine with twin 'high' camshafts operating inclined overhead valves, and giving up to 190 bhp (240 bhp in competition cars). In racing a high point was outright victory at Le Mans in 1950. That was achieved by Louis and Jean-Louis Rosier, the only father and son team to win the 24-hour classic, in a stripped Grand Prix car rather than one of the heavy production models.

Penal taxation whittled away the French market, a 2.7-litre was not a success, nor were cars with 2.5-litre Maserati and BMW engines, and Simca absorbed Talbot.

Tatra 77, 87 and 97

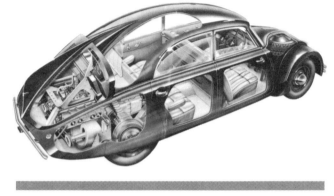

Hans Ledwinka, one of the innovative pioneers of the automobile industry, joined the newly-formed Tatra company in infant Czechoslovakia in 1921, and developed air-cooled engines large and small, petrol and diesel, swing-axle independent suspension, backbone chassis and practical low-drag bodies. Several of these features came together in his rear-engined Tatras of the 1930s, above all in the 2.9-litre V8 Type 87.

Ledwinka developed his theme of vehicles with a central tubular frame and swing axles, coupled with air-cooled opposed-piston engines, through the 1920s, primarily on the Tatra Types 11 and 12. Those were small vehicles, but the same frame and suspension principles were applied to the 6-litre V12 Type 80. At approximately the same time, the first rear-engined Tatra appeared, the little Type 49 528 cc (32 cu in) three wheeler.

As a replacement for the 11/12 a small rear-engined design was progressed to the prototype stage. This did not reach production, but hard on its heels the Type 77 was announced in 1933, in advance of its 1934 launch. It was by no means the first rear-engined streamlined car, but its forerunners in those respects had hardly been production models. This Tatra was, although the numbers were not very large.

It was powered by an air-cooled 3-litre ohv V8, mounted on an easily-detachable subframe behind the rear axle line. It drove forward to a four-speed gearbox. A box-section backbone chassis frame was used, with a wide and long body making for a very spacious interior. It looked aerodynamically effective, with the backbone theme picked up in the styling feature of a prominent spine at the tail (the visual effect of this was partly offset by the engine air intakes behind the quarter light windows), although the claimed drag factor of 0.212 appeared somewhat questionable.

The 77 was followed in 1937 by the 87 and 97, with a 3-litre V8 and a 1.7-litre flat four respectively. The rear suspension was revised, with the transverse spring of the 77 (which must have encouraged odd behaviour) giving way to a set-up with quarter elliptic springs, which gave a softer ride and might also have softened the oversteer characteristics. Bodies were more compact than the 77, though little smoother and still lacking a rear window. The 87 had a maximum speed of 94.5 mph (152 kph).

Because it seemed an obvious competitor to the Volkswagen the smaller model was discontinued on German instructions when Moravia was occupied, but the 87 continued in production until 1941. It was reintroduced after the war, with a 2.5-litre ohv engine, giving way to the similar 603 in 1956, while the Tatraplan deriving from the 97 was built until 1954. The 613, powered by a four-cam 3.5-litre V8, came in the 1970s, made in very small numbers but perpetuating Ledwinka's theme.

Triumph TR2 and TR3

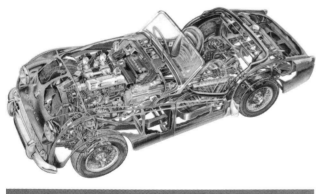

These simple sports cars were produced using many existing components, in response to a clearly-identified demand, and they changed the image of the marque.

The company had been rescued by Standard in 1944, and late in that decade was producing some slightly odd cars in small numbers – the 'knife-edge' Renown and Mayflower saloons and the 1800/2000 Roadsters. Early in the 1950s the US market for small sports cars had been proved and Sir John Black, then Standard-Triumph chairman, decided to take Triumph into it. There were false starts, notably the TRX based on Standard Vanguard components, bulbous and complex, owing too much to the 'roadster' and too little to sports car thinking, and the company's attempt to take over Morgan.

Early in 1952 Black commissioned the development of a low-cost Triumph design, which emerged at the 1952 London Motor Show as the 20TS. After testing this Ken Richardson condemned it, and was invited to join Triumph to help develop the car, which was quickly reworked and 'relaunched' at the 1953 Geneva Motor Show as the TR2.

It was powered by the Standard Vanguard engine, linered down from 2088 cc (127 cu in) to 1911 cc (117 cu in) and mildly tuned with twin SU carburettors to produce 90 bhp, and this drove through a four-speed derivative of the Vanguard gearbox. Other components such as the independent front suspension came from the Triumph Mayflower, while the simple body comprised mainly single-curvature pressings. Top speed was just over 100 mph (161 kph), the car was economical and reliable, and Richardson's development work had resulted in acceptable handling.

Market success did not come instantly, for the car had no pedigree, but publicity came through speed runs, club racing, class successes in major events and, most importantly, through rallies. Within two years Triumph was a sports car marque to be bracketed with MG and Austin-Healey.

The slightly more refined TR3 came in 1955, which had power increased to 95 bhp and became more easily distinguishable in its 1958 form with a wider grille and outside door handles. Meanwhile more significant changes had come in 1956, when cylinder head modifications meant a power increase to 100 bhp, and late in the year it became one of the first production cars to have front-wheel disc brakes as standard fitting. These changes made it a 110 mph

---

EVOLUTION — TRIUMPH TR2 and TR3

1952 Triumph 20TS prototype (retrospectively known as the TR1) introduced at the London Motor Show, an open two-seater fitted with a moderately tuned 75 bhp 2-litre Standard Vanguard engine

1953 TR2 unveiled at the Geneva Motor Show with redesigned and smoother body, a new box-section chassis frame and engine improved to produce 90 bhp

1954 TR2 hard-top version became available; modifications included larger drum brakes at the rear. Total TR2 production was 8628 units

1955 TR3 announced, with its engine further tuned to produce 95 bhp, Girling disc brakes fitted to the front wheels and an egg-box grille

1958 TR3A announced, fitted with full-width grille, and engine power was increased to 100 bhp

1961 TR3B built for the American market, fitted with the forthcoming TR4's all-synchromesh gearbox and a choice of 2- and 2.2-litre engines. TR3-TR3B production reached 83,500

(175 kph) car, while still remaining both rugged and simple.

Those virtues served it well in the rally world, a 1956 high point coming when five TR crews won the Coupes des Alpes for completing that gruelling event without loss of marks.

The works team cars run in that Alpine Rally had engines enlarged to 2138 cc (130 cu in) and producing 105 bhp. This was to become available on TR3As, although few were made with it as it was primarily for the TR4. While that came in Europe, American distributors for a while preferred the old body shape, which was therefore continued as the TR3B in 1961.

TVR Tuscan and M Series

These cars represent the period when TVR was transformed in business terms, changed from a rather uncertain specialist constructor to a manufacturer with a firm niche in the industry and an evolving line of high-performance cars.

The TVR story began in the late 1940s when Trevor Wilkinson built his first 'special' and used the consonants of his Christian name – TreVoR – to name it. By the mid-1950s TVRs were being offered in kit form, basically with a backbone chassis and all-independent suspension. One went to America, where its owner fitted his own body and called it a Jomar; that sparked interest, an exhibit at the 1957 New York Auto Show fanned the spark and the outcome was the car retrospectively named the Grantura, almost a series-production model.

Financing production brought problems and, through to the mid-1960s, several changes of ownership and name. Eventually Martin Lilley steered TVR towards survival. This period produced the Griffith (the first TVR with the distinctive square-cut tail) and the Tuscan.

The Tuscan SE was a fairly small car, with a neat

glassfibre coupé body on a multi-tubular backbone chassis and wishbone and coil spring/damper independent suspension all round. It was powered by Ford's 4.7-litre (287 cu in) 289 CID V8, in a 270 bhp (SAE) form. That gave it exceptional acceleration, and a top speed of 155 mph (250 kph). In that form the Tuscan was not an instant marketing success, so it was adapted for the British Ford 3-litre V6, or for North America the emissions-controlled Triumph 2500 engine (naming this version the TVR 2500).

That car was the forerunner of the M series, which broadly saw TVR through the 1970s and led into the supercar range of the 1980s. The M series cars were built on a revised chassis, with stronger round- and square-section tubing and easier to produce, and a beefed-up suspension following the proven lines. The bodies were longer, with sleeker nose and tail sections, and also better finished (notably so after a fire closed the Blackpool factory for a while in 1975!). The same engines were listed, and in 1976 the Broadspeed turbocharged V6 was offered (rated at 218 bhp when the Turbo was announced in 1975, later 230 bhp and eventually 265 bhp).

The Taimar, with a three-door body, and the Convertible were the last M series models, in 1976 and 1978 respectively, both available in Turbo form. Open cars were rare in the 1970s — the Convertible combined that rarity with true high performance, its claimed top speed being 145 mph (230 kph).

In 1980 the Tasmin at once extended the continuity of the TVR line and introduced a new generation, which proved to have real stamina.

Vauxhall 30/98

Vauxhall was an independent company in the Edwardian period, when it built some high-class cars and leaned towards motor sport. That led it to contest the Prinz Heinrich competition, a Trial which would be described today as a rally, over a 1200 mile (1931 km) course. The three-car Vauxhall team did well and a production version of the Trial car was introduced, leading to an improved 4-litre version, and that in turn to the 30/98.

L.H. Pomeroy was responsible for designing these cars, starting from the basis of his 1908 engine for the Type A, in the long-stroke form encouraged by the Trial regulations. That was a 3-litre unit, and in the production version it developed 55 bhp. For the 4-litre D-type output was up to 75 bhp, and then the engine was taken out to 4.5 litres, almost by accident.

A hill climb enthusiast, Joseph Higginson, approached Vauxhall for a successor to the French La Buire which he had campaigned (apparently his particular ambition was to break the record for the Shelsley Walsh climb). Pomeroy enlarged the engine to 4525 cc (276 cu in), to give 90 bhp, and mounted this in a relatively light chassis following the 1912 3-litre Vauxhall racing car. Non-independent suspension was the norm, but a Pomeroy refinement was to mount the live rear axle at the extremities of cantilevered semi-elliptic springs. There were no front brakes – again quite in keeping with current practice, even for high-performance cars – but the rear-wheel brakes were large and there was a transmission brake. Bodywork was in aluminium, light and stark.

The first car was wholly successful, in that Mr Higginson handsomely broke that record, and drove it to win on other hills and in speed trials. Vauxhall had the basis of a fine sporting car, and announced the E-type late in 1913, although only 13 were to be built before the war. The engine had a new crankshaft and a stronger block and there were brakes to the rear wheels only. It proved an ideal roadster, and its success in breaking city-to-city records in Australia was such that it opened up a substantial market for the 30/98 when it was revived in 1919.

It was refined, for example with full electrical equipment, before the OE was introduced in 1922. This had a 4.2-litre pushrod ohv engine (signified by the 'O' in the designation), which could develop 112 bhp to more than maintain performance as the car also put on weight.

The OE had four-wheel brakes, and the last few cars before production ended in 1927 had hydraulic front brakes – that overcame one of the shortcomings inherent in the earlier cars – as well as a new gearbox and late cars had engines producing 120 bhp.

These cars were never used in the main-line competitions, but were widely seen in lesser sprints, hill climbs and short races. But although it did not have a distinguished racing career, the 30/98 epitomized the early vintage sporting car.

Volkswagen Beetle

The most familiar shape on the world's roads through a quarter of a century had its origins in the early 1930s, in Porsche Büro designs and in Adolf Hitler's ambitions for a peoples' car to follow up his autobahnen programme. The first experimental prototypes of the new low-cost car were completed in 1936, and the second series prototypes built by Daimler-Benz in 1937 were thought to look like beetles, hence the nickname that was to become a designation. In the late 1930s, however, as a green field factory was built to produce it, it was officially called the KdF-Wagen (Strength through Joy car).

As such it never reached production. That was achieved by the British military authorities, as cars were assembled from parts in 1945, ironically as Rootes in Britain and Henry Ford turned down opportunities to acquire the plant and design, and as the French motor industry united to prevent its government from taking over.

Ferdinand Porsche had anticipated the need for a car on these lines in the early 1930s, producing prototypes for Zundapp and NSU. Neither company went ahead, but the Type 33 design (for NSU) provided the basis for the Type 60, which was to become the Beetle. Various engine configurations were tried, then Frank Reimspiess came up with the over-square air-cooled flat four design that was to serve the Beetle through its long life.

By 1938, with a third series of prototypes, the car had taken on its final shape, with sensible additions such as the rear window (albeit a divided one), running boards, one-piece engine cover and so on. It was to be built down to a very low price, hence simplicity was important. Porsche's patented torsion bar independent suspension was used front and rear, and this could be attached to the platform chassis before the body was bolted on (a detail for which a generation of buggy builders should be

grateful, as it made their vehicles possible).

The four seats were adequate, but in aspects such as interior fittings and luggage accommodation the car was minimal. Handling was peculiar and performance not very good. But, in a triumph of marketing over product, the Beetle caught on, even in the USA where Henry Ford had been so sure that a rear-engined, air-cooled car would be such an abnormality that buyers would shun it. And VW had very positive leadership from Heinz Nordhoff, until his death in 1968.

The Beetle evolved, from a 56 mph (90 kph) car in its 1945 form, to a 62 mph (100 kph) car with the 1192 cc (72.7 cu in) engine in 1954. As the engine was progressively enlarged other improvements were made to keep pace (first and foremost suspension changes, with a MacPherson strut arrangement at the front and a semi-trailing arm arrangement at the rear), while the interior became less spartan. In 1973 the Beetle family surpasssed the production record of the Ford Model T, or maybe that came in 1974, as Ford revised their figures. Then a danger seemed to threaten that, like the T, the Beetle might remain in production too long, as its supposed successors failed to catch on. Eventually the Golf, that had virtually nothing in common with the Beetle, became its successor.

EVOLUTION — VOLKSWAGEN BEETLE

1945 Introduced as the VW 1200, with 985 cc (60 cu in) engine and a four-speed manual gearbox

1949 Export model introduced

1950 Hydraulic brakes introduced

1952 Synchromesh gearbox introduced. Tyre size changed to 5.60 × 15 in and quarter lights added

1953 First overseas assembly, in Brazil. The small, two-part rear window replaced by one large single one

1955 Millionth Beetle completed. New rear light clusters

1957 Windscreen and rear window enlarged. New engine compartment lid introduced

1960 Windscreen washer unit, asymmetric dipped beams and turn signals introduced

1963 Steel sunroof available

1964 Window area enlarged

1965 Annual production topped a million, and ten millionth Beetle produced. VW 1300 introduced

1966 VW 1500 launched, with a wider rear track and other detail modifications

1967 Improved fresh air ventilation and three-point safety belt anchorages for all seats introduced

1968 15 millionth Beetle completed. Rear suspension revised, Fitchel & Sachs semi-automatic transmission available

1970 1600 Super Beetle (1302) replaced 1500 model, with MacPherson strut front suspension and semi-trailing arms at rear, 50 bhp engine, larger luggage compartment and through-flow ventilation

1971 Ventilation further refined

1972 Beetle passed Ford Model T production record of 15 million (in 1973 it passed Ford's revised total of 16.5 million)

1977 VW 1200L version introduced, built in Mexico, featuring chromed bumpers and wheel covers, reversing lights, upgraded equipment with padded dashboard, adjustable front head restraints, three-point inertia reel safety belts, lap belts in the rear, heated rear window and radial tyres

1978 Beetle production in Germany ended, continued in Mexico and Brazil

1987 21 millionth Beetle completed in Brazil

The Cutaway Drawings

BELOW The full convertible Porsche 911 Cabriolet of 1984/5, combining a 231 bhp Carrera engine with more traditional design details

Good looks certainly matter in a car, if only because what looks good in this field very often is good. Here the cutaway drawing comes into its own. Save for those few painstakingly sectioned show exhibits, which few in a jostling crowd have time to study, the cutaway drawing is the best aid to understanding what is under the skin of a car. So here they are, presented with specifications rather than in isolation as an art form, because the aim of this book is to 'get inside' these great cars.

MODEL
AC Cobra 427 (1965)

ENGINE
Location: Front, longitudinal
Type: Water-cooled V8 with cast-iron block and heads
Cubic capacity: 6997 cc/427 cu in
Bore × stroke: 107.4 mm × 96 mm/4.23 in × 3.78 in
Compression ratio: 10.5:1
Valve gear: Two valves per cylinder operated by single block-mounted camshaft in centre of vee
Fuel supply: Single Holley 750 CFM downdraught carburettor
Ignition: Mechanical, with coil and distributor
Maximum power: 410 bhp at 5600 rpm
Maximum torque: 462 lb ft at 2800 rpm

TRANSMISSION
Layout: Clutch and gearbox in unit with engine. Rear-wheel drive
Clutch: Single dry plate
Gearbox: Borg Warner four-speed manual

1st	2.20:1	3rd	1.31:1
2nd	1.66:1	4th	1.00:1

Final drive: Spiral bevel
Ratio: 3.54:1 (options ranged between 4.1:1 and 2.9:1)

SUSPENSION
Front: Independent with unequal-length wishbones with combined coil spring and damper units
Rear: Independent with unequal-length wishbones with combined coil spring and damper units

STEERING
Type: Rack and pinion

BRAKES
Type: Girling discs front and rear with a total swept area of 3742 sq cm (580 sq in). Twin master cylinders

WHEELS AND TYRES
Type: 15-inch wire-wheels with 185 × 15 tyres front, 195 × 15 rear

BODY/CHASSIS
Type: Ladder-frame chassis of two 4 in (102 mm) diameter steel tubes with tubular cross members and aluminium open-top two-seater sports bodyshell

DIMENSIONS AND WEIGHT
Length: 3962 mm (156 in)
Width: 1727 mm (68 in)
Wheelbase: 2286 mm (90 in)
Track – front: 1397 mm (55 in)
 – rear: 1372 mm (54 in)
Weight: 1035 kg (2282 lb)

PERFORMANCE
Maximum speed: 140 mph (225 kph)
Acceleration 0–60 mph: 4.5 seconds

EVOLUTION

1961 AC Ace 2.6 introduced with Rudd-tuned Ford Zephyr six-cylinder engine. It was based on a stengthened Ace frame which became the foundation for the V8 Cobra. First AC Cobra built, with the 4.2-litre (260 cu in) Ford V8. A Salisbury final drive and inboard rear brakes were fitted. Production Cobras reverted to outboard rear discs.

1962 Production of 4.2-litre (260 cu in) Cobras ended

1963 Engine changed to the Ford 4.7-litre (289 cu in) V8, Mk II Cobra introduced

1965 Mk III Cobra introduced, powered by either the 6.9-litre (427 cu in) or the 7-litre (428 cu in) Ford V8. Chassis revisions included larger diameter main chassis members and coil spring rear suspension instead of transverse leaf

1968 Cobra production ceased after around 1000 were built

1987 'Mk-IV' replicar by Autokraft approved by Ford, owners of AC (update of original design, with Ford 302 V8 and T5 gearbox)

Underneath the Cobra's curvaceous bodyshell the mechanical layout was extremely simple and very toughly built. The rearward position of the engine gave good front-rear balance, a vital factor with such staggering power-to-weight ratio

MODEL

Alfa Romeo 8C 2300 (1932)

ENGINE

Location: Front, longitudinal
Type: Water-cooled in-line eight cylinder with two four-cylinder blocks with alloy heads in line.
Cubic capacity: 2336 cc/142.5 cu in
Bore × stroke: 65 mm × 88 mm/2.56 in × 3.46 in
Compression ratio: 5.75 : 1
Valve gear: 2 inclined valves per cylinder operated by two gear-driven overhead camshafts.
Fuel supply: Single Memini carburettor with single Roots type supercharger
Ignition: Mechanical with Bosch coil and distributor
Maximum power: 142 bhp at 5200 rpm (see text)

TRANSMISSION

Layout: Clutch and gearbox in unit with engine driving rear wheels
Clutch: Multiplate, wet
Gearbox: Four speed manual without synchromesh

1st 3.65 : 1	3rd 1.39 : 1
2nd 2.03 : 1	4th 1.06 : 1

Final drive: Spiral bevel
Ratio: 4.25 : 1

SUSPENSION

Front: Non independent with semi-elliptic leaf springs and adjustable friction dampers
Rear: Live rear axle located by torque tube semi-elliptic leaf springs and adjustable friction dampers

STEERING

Type: Worm and wheel

BRAKES

Type: Finned alloy drums front and rear, rod operated

WHEELS AND TYRES

Type: Wire spoked wheels with 5.50 × 19 in tyres

BODY/CHASSIS

Type: Pressed steel channel separate chassis with two outer longitudinal members and cross members. Two or four-seat open sports bodywork by various coachbuilders.

DIMENSIONS AND WEIGHT

Length: 3962 mm (156 in)
Width: 1651 mm (65 in)
Wheelbase: 2768 mm (109 in)
Track – front: 1372 mm (54 in)
– rear: 1372 mm (54 in)
Weight: 1117 kg (2464 lb)

PERFORMANCE

Maximum speed: 112 mph (180 kph)
Acceleration 0–60 mph: 9.4 seconds

EVOLUTION

1931 Introduced with in-line eight cylinder·twin-cam engine developed from that of the 6C range. Chassis design also based on the 6C. Cars were produced in short- and long-chassis form. The two-seater short-chassis cars were known as either Spider Corsa or Mille Miglia models. The long-chassis cars were known as Le Mans models and available with drophead coupé or four-seater bodywork. The Monza Grand Prix car was a development of the short chassis 8C 2300.

1932 Series II and III cars were developed between 1932 and 1934 with the power increased to 180 bhp by 1934.

1934 Production of the 8C 2300 ended after 188 cars were built. The range was replaced by the simpler and cheaper 6C 2300 cars.

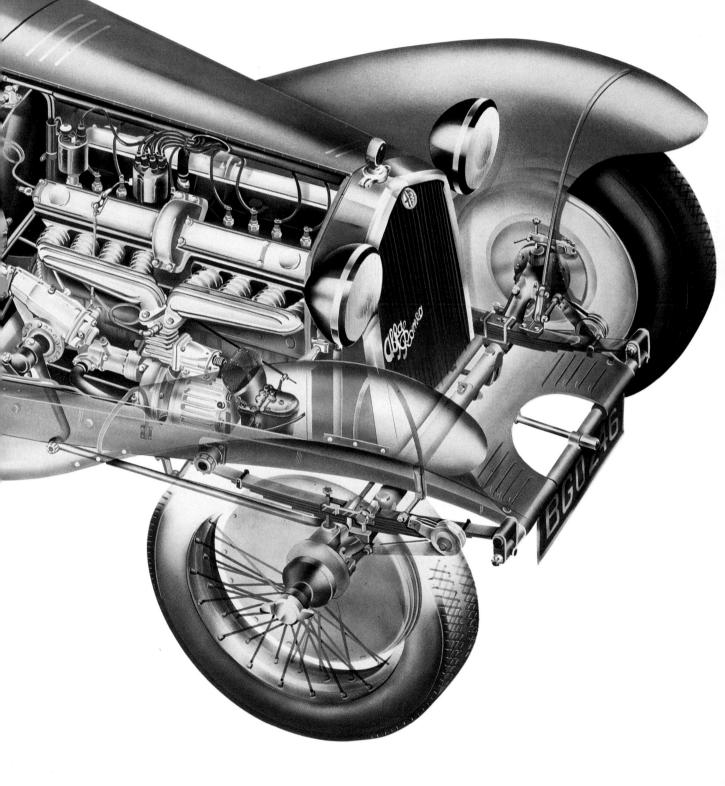

ABOVE The P3s of Shuttleworth, Ralph and Chiron line astern at the 1935 Dieppe GP
BELOW The cutaway shows the central drive for the superchargers, the left-hand Roots-type blower alongside the engine, and the angled propellor shafts running from a differential behind the gearbox to bevels and short shafts to each rear wheel. The cars were run by Scuderia Ferrari, and carried the famous 'prancing horse' badge on either side of the nose
BOTTOM Guy Moll drove this specially streamlined P3 to victory to the top speed Avus GP of 1934. The alterations added 12 mph (19 kph) to the top speed

MODEL
Alfa Romeo Tipo B ('P3')

ENGINE
Location: Front, longitudinal
Type: Water-cooled straight eight, cast in two alloy blocks
Cubic capacity: 2654 cc/161.9 cu in
Bore × stroke: 65 mm × 100 mm/ 2.56 in × 3.94 in
Valve gear: Two valves per cylinder (one inlet, one exhaust), operated by twin gear-driven overhead camshafts
Fuel supply: Twin Memini carburettors
Ignition: Single Marelli high-tension magneto
Maximum power: 215 bhp at 5600 rpm

TRANSMISSION
Layout: Four-speed gearbox in unit with engine. Rear-wheel drive by twin propellor shafts
Gear ratios: 3.52 (3.3 optional), 4.56, 6.54, 11.8
Final drive: Double bevels, short shafts to rear wheels

SUSPENSION
Front: Non-independent, with semi-elliptic springs and friction dampers
Rear: Non-independent, with semi-elliptic springs and friction dampers

BRAKES
Type: Mechanical drum, 40 cm/ 15.75 in diameter, 4.45 cm/1.75 in drum width

WHEELS AND TYRES
Type: Rudge wire wheels, with Dunlop 28 × 5.50 tyres

CHASSIS
Type: Pressed-steel side members, upswept at rear

DIMENSIONS AND WEIGHT
Wheelbase: 264 cm (104 in)
Track – front: 140 cm (55 in)
         – rear: 135 cm (53 in)
Dry weight: 709 kg (1564 lb)

PERFORMANCE
Maximum speed: 140 mph (225 kph)

Major Grand Prix and formula Libre Race Victories

1932
Tazio Nuvolari, Italian GP, Monza
Tazio Nuvolari, Monaco GP, Monte Carlo
Tazio Nuvolari, French GP, Reims
Tazio Nuvolari, Coppa Acerbo, Pescara
Tazio Nuvolari, Coppa Ciano, Montenero
Rudolf Caracciola, Eifelrennen, Nürburgring
Rudolf Caracciola, German GP, Nürburgring
Rudolf Caracciola, Monza GP

1933
Luigi Fagioli, Coppa Acerbo, Pescara
Luigi Fagioli, Italian GP, San Sebastian

1934
Guy Moll, Monaco GP, Monte Carlo
Louis Chiron, French GP, Montlhéry
Louis Chiron, Marne GP
Achille Varzi, Targa Florio
Guy Moll, Avus, Berlin
Achille Varzi, Albo d'Oro, Alessandria

1935
Tazio Nuvolari, German GP, Nürburgring

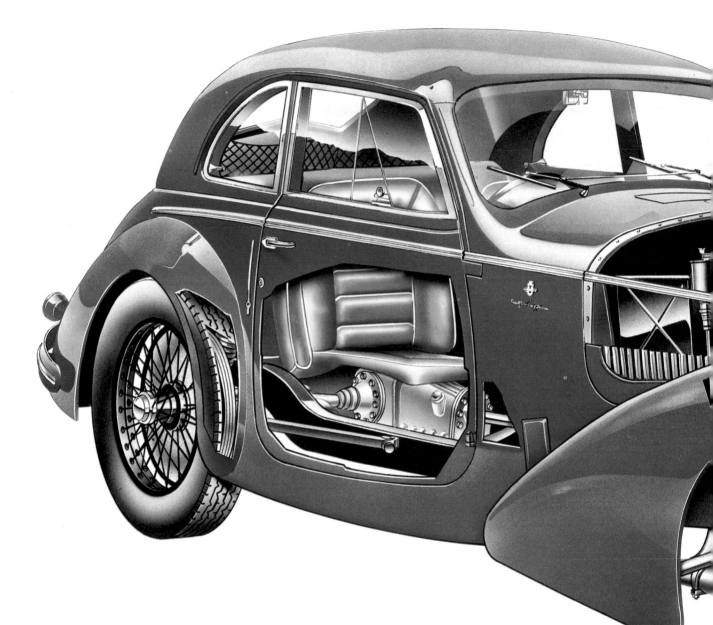

MODEL

Alfa Romeo 8C 2900B Lungo (1937)

ENGINE

Location: Front, longitudinal
Type: In-line, eight cylinder made in two four-cylinder units with central gear drive to twin overhead camshafts
Cubic capacity: 2905 cc/177.2 cu in
Bore × stroke: 68 mm × 100 mm/ 2.7 in × 3.9 in
Compression ratio: 5.75:1
Valve gear: Two valves per cylinder inclined in hemispherical combustion chambers and operated by twin overhead camshafts
Fuel supply: Two downdraught carburettors and two twin-lobe superchargers running at 1.448 times engine speed
Ignition: Mechanical by coil and distributor
Maximum power: 180 bhp at 5200 rpm

TRANSMISSION

Layout: Gearbox in unit with final drive, driving rear wheels
Clutch: Multiple dry plate
Gearbox: Four-speed manual, rear mounted

1st	2.44:1	3rd	1.14:1
2nd	1.50:1	4th	0.88:1

Final drive: Bevel gear
Ratio: 4.54:1

SUSPENSION

Front: Independent, with coil springs, upper wishbones, lower links and hydraulic dampers
Rear: Independent, with swing axles, transverse leaf spring, hydraulic and friction dampers

STEERING

Type: Worm and sector

BRAKES

Type: Hydraulically operated drums all round

WHEELS AND TYRES

Type: 5.50 × 19 tyres on 48 cm (19 in) centre-lock wire wheels

BODY/CHASSIS

Type: Ladder frame, box-section chassis fitted with two-door, four-seat touring body

DIMENSIONS AND WEIGHT

Length: 5000 mm (196.8 in)
Width: 1700 mm (66.9 in)
Wheelbase: 3000 mm (118 in)
Track – front: 1350 mm (53 in)
      – rear: 1350 mm (53 in)
Weight: 1250 kg (2750 lb)

PERFORMANCE

Maximum speed: 110 mph (177 kph)

The 2900 B Coupé revealed, showing the long straight eight and the rear-mounted gearbox. The car was only built because of help from the government, and was designed to increase Italian prestige in the racing world and luxury car markets. This it did, and although only 10 long-wheelbase versions of the 2900 B were made, coachbuilt in open, closed and cabriolet bodies, they have rightly earned classic status

EVOLUTION

1935 The 2900A was introduced with a 220 bhp version of the 2.9-litre straight-eight twin cam. Six were built in all in 1935

1936 A further five sports-racing bodied 2900As were built

1937 The road-going 2900B was introduced in short (Corto) and long (Lungo) wheelbase form. The road cars were, naturally, heavier than the competition cars and the engines were further detuned with the compression ratio lowered to 5.75:1, dropping power to 180 bhp at 5200 rpm. Twenty short-wheelbase models were made between 1937 and 1939 with bodies by Pininfarina and Touring. Ten long-wheelbase cars were built in the same period, again by Pininfarina and Touring, in four-seat convertible and closed coupé styles

MODEL
Alfa Romeo 1750 GTV (1969)

ENGINE
Location: Front, longitudinal
Type: In-line four-cylinder twin-cam with light-alloy block and head, wet cylinder liners and five main bearings
Cubic capacity: 1779 cc/108.5 cu in
Bore × stroke: 80 mm × 88.5 mm/ 3.15 in × 3.48 in
Compression ratio: 9.0:1
Valve gear: 2 valves per cylinder operating in hemispherical combustion chambers by two chain-driven overhead camshafts
Fuel supply: 2 twin-choke sidedraught Weber or Dellorto carburettors. Spica mechanical fuel injection for North American models
Ignition: Mechanical by coil and distributor
Maximum power: 118 bhp (DIN) at 5500 rpm (132 bhp SAE)
Maximum torque: 138 lb ft (SAE) at 3000 rpm

TRANSMISSION
Layout: Gearbox and clutch in-unit behind engine
Clutch: Single dry plate
Gearbox: Five-speed manual
1st 3.30:1   4th 1.00:1
2nd 1.99:1   5th 0.79:1
3rd 1.35:1
Final drive: Hypoid bevel
Ratio: 4.10:1

SUSPENSION
Front: Independent with double wishbones and adjustable lower front link, anti-roll bar, coil springs and telescopic dampers
Rear: Live rear axle located by lower trailing arms and upper torque arm. Coil springs, telescopic dampers and anti-roll bar

STEERING
Type: Recirculating ball or worm and roller. 3.7 turns lock to lock

BRAKES
Type: Discs all round 272 mm (10.71 in) diameter front and 267 mm (10.51 in) rear. Dual circuit, servo assisted

WHEELS AND TYRES
Type: Steel wheels 5½J × 14 with 165 × 14 Michelin or Pirelli steel-belted radial tyres

BODY/CHASSIS
Type: Integral steel chassis/body with two-door 2+2 coupé body

DIMENSIONS AND WEIGHT
Length: 4100 mm (161.42 in)
Width: 1580 mm (62.2 in)
Wheelbase: 2350 mm (92.52 in)
Track – front: 1324 mm (52.13 in)
        – rear: 1274 mm (50.16 in)
Weight: 1040 kg (2293 lb)

PERFORMANCE
Maximum speed: 118 mph (190 kph)
Acceleration 0–60 mph: 9.3 seconds

Under the perfect proportions of Bertone's bodyshell were some quite simple and conventional mechanical components, but although a live rear axle was used it was cleverly located by a T-bar unique to Alfa Romeo. The suspension was also unusual in that the front control arm on the wishbone front suspension was adjustable

EVOLUTION

1955 First Giulietta coupé, the Giulietta Sprint, made its debut at Turin Show, powered by an 80 bhp 1290 cc (78.7 cu in) twin-cam engine

1957 Bertone-designed Giulietta Sprint Special introduced with the 1290 cc engine, with power increased to 100 bhp at 6500 rpm to give a claimed top speed of 124 mph (200 kph)

1962 The twin-cam engine was stretched to 1570 cc (95.8 cu in) and fitted in the new Giulia range. The first Giulia coupé retained the old Giulietta Sprint style bodyshell, with the larger engine

1963 Giulia Sprint Speciale was introduced with the 1570 cc engine, now producing 112 bhp at 6500 rpm. Its bodyshell was the same as the earlier Giulietta SS. Production of both SS versions totalled 2755 between 1957 and 1964. Giulia Sprint GT introduced at the Frankfurt Show with disc brakes all round and the 106 bhp version of the 1570 cc engine

1966 Alfa GTV introduced with 109 bhp version of the 1570 twin-cam. A little later that year the GT junior appeared with the 1290 cc engine

1965 GTA was developed for homologation, 500 being built between 1965 and 1969. It was a lightened version of the GTV with aluminium body panels and a high-compression version of the 1570 twin-cam.

1967 1750 GTV introduced with 1779 cc (108.5 cu in) engine which produced 118 bhp at 5500 rpm. Outwardly distinguished by its four headlights

1970 1750 GTV received the GTA treatment but the engine was enlarged to 1985 cc (121 cu in) to produce the 1750 GTAm

1971 2000 GTV introduced with 1962 cc (119.7 cu in) version of the alloy twin-cam. Power output increased from 118 to 132 bhp at 5500 rpm

1972 A 1600 version of the coupé was reintroduced in the form of the GT Junior

1976 Production of GTVs ceased. In all 40,826 1600 coupés were produced along with 42,040 1750 GTVs and 36,385 2000 GTVs

MODEL

Alpine 110 Berlinette 1600S Tour de France

ENGINE

Location: Rear, longitudinal
Type: Water-cooled four-cylinder, cast iron block and alloy cylinder-head
Cubic capacity: 1565 cc/95.46 cu in
Bore × stroke: 77 mm × 84 mm/ 3.0 in × 3.3 in
Compression ratio: 10.2:1
Valve gear: Two overhead valves per cylinder, pushrod operated by single side-mounted camshaft
Fuel supply: One Weber 45 DCOE horizontal twin-barrel carburettor
Ignition: Ducellier distributor
Maximum power: 138 bhp at 6000 rpm
Maximum torque: 107 lb ft at 5000 rpm

TRANSMISSION

Layout: Clutch and gearbox in unit with engine driving rear wheels
Clutch: Single dry plate
Gearbox: Five-speed all-synchromesh manual

1st 3.61:1	4th 1.29:1
2nd 2.36:1	5th 1.03:1
3rd 1.69:1	

Final drive: Hypoid bevel
Ratio: 3.37:1

SUSPENSION

Front: Independent, with wishbones, coil springs and telescopic dampers
Rear: Independent, with swinging semi-axles, trailing radius arms, coil springs and four dampers

STEERING

Type: Rack and pinion, 3.2 turns lock to lock

BRAKES

Type: Disc brakes all round

WHEELS AND TYRES

Type: Alloy wheels with 145 x 15 in tyres

BODY/CHASSIS

Type: Two-seater glassfibre coupé body on integral steel chassis with central backbone

DIMENSIONS AND WEIGHT

Length: 3850 mm (151.57 in)
Width: 1520 mm (59.84 in)
Wheelbase: 2100 mm (82.68 in)
Track – front: 1296 mm (51.02 in)
 – rear: 1275 mm (50.2 in)
Weight: 635 kg (1400 lb)

PERFORMANCE

Maximum speed: 134 mph (215 kph)
Acceleration 0-60 mph: 8.5 seconds

The Anderson and Stone 1600S Alpine which was victorious in the 1971 Monte Carlo Rally. Its engine was developed from the 138 bhp of the standard car to 160 bhp at 7200 rpm for the rally variant. The engine in this form proved quite torquey which, in conjunction with the car's excellent traction made it very competitive on tarmac and adequate when the going got slippery

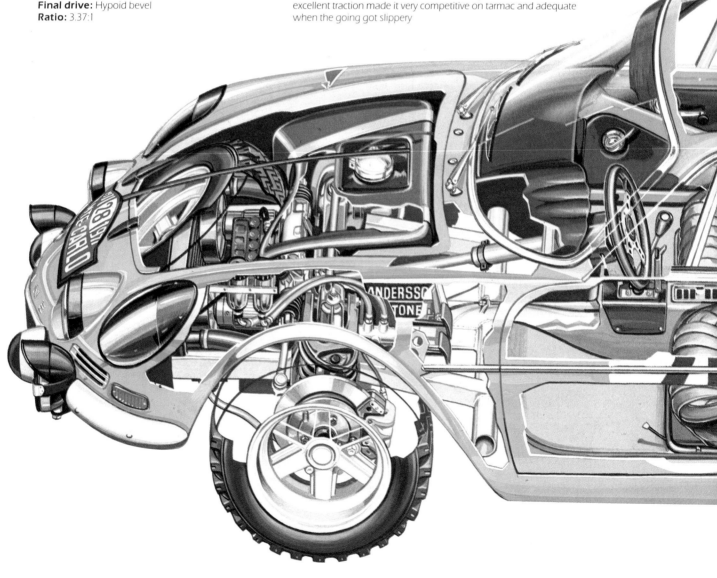

EVOLUTION

1963 Introduced as the Alpine 110 Type 958, a glassfibre-bodied rear-engined coupé with a tubular steel backbone chassis and the 956 cc (58.3 cu in) 44 bhp engine from the Renault R8

1964 Type 1100 '70' introduced, with the 1108 cc (67.6 cu in) 58 bhp engine from the R8 Major

1965 The Type 1100 '100' was introduced, with the 84 bhp 1108 cc Renault Gordini engine

1966 The 1300S was introduced, with a 1296 cc (79 cu in) bored-out version of the Gordini engine, producing 106 bhp

1967 The 1300G model was introduced, fitted with the 1255 cc (76.5 cu in) 95 bhp standard Gordini engine and a five-speed gearbox. The Type 1500 was introduced, fitted with the 62 bhp 1470 cc (89.7 cu in) R16 engine.
Total production (1500): 17

1969 Type 1600 introduced, with 1565 cc (95.5 cu in) R16TS engine, producing 80 bhp

1970 110 '85' introduced, with 1289 cc (78.6 cu in) 72 bhp R12 engine. The 1600S also introduced, with a higher compression ratio, improved breathing and better camshaft, to raise output to 122 bhp

1971 Types 1600 and 1300S discontinued.
Total production: (1600) 77 (1300S) 185

1973 1600 SCC (carburettor) and 1600 SI (injection) models introduced

1974 1600S discontinued. Total production: 1600

1975 1600 SC and SI models discontinued.
Total production: 588

1976 1600 SX introduced, with the R16TX 1647 cc (100.5 cu in) engine, producing 95 bhp, and with A-frame upper and lower wishbone rear suspension

1976 Type '85' discontinued. Total production: 3343

1977 1600SX discontinued. Total production: 385

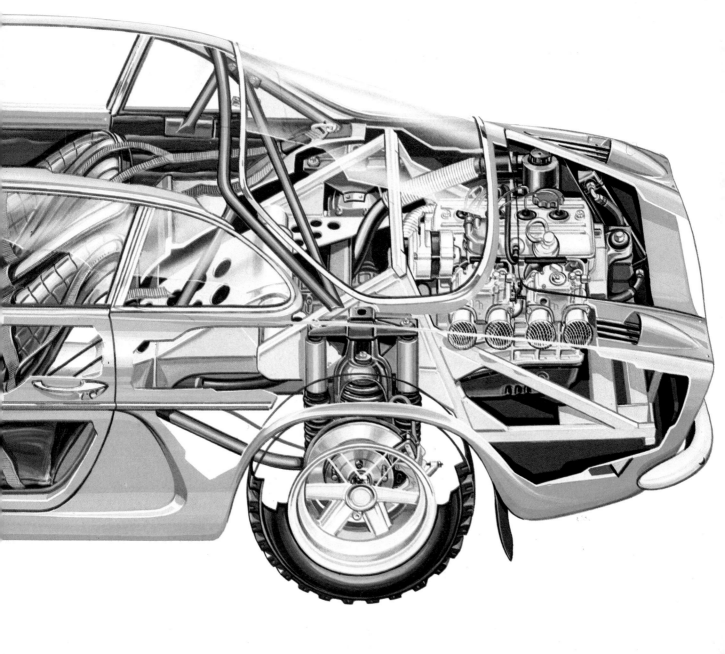

MODEL
Amilcar C6, (1926)

ENGINE
Location: Front, longitudinal
Type: Water-cooled in-line six-cylinder with cast iron block and head. Seven main bearings
Cubic capacity: 1094 cc/66.7 cu in
Bore × stroke: 56 mm × 74 mm/ 2.2 in × 2.9 in
Compression ratio: 5.0:1
Valve gear: 2 valves per cylinder operated by twin overhead camshafts
Fuel supply: Solex 40 carburettor and Roots-type supercharger
Ignition: Coil and magneto
Maximum power: 62 bhp at 5600 rpm

TRANSMISSION
Layout: Gearbox behind engine driving rear wheels
Clutch: Single dry plate
Gearbox: Four-speed manual, non-synchromesh
   1st 2.50:1 3rd 1.31:1
   2nd 1.71.1 4th 1.00:1
Final drive: Spiral bevel
Ratio: 4.5:1 (options ranged between 4.0:1 and 5.5:1)

SUSPENSION
Front: Non-independent, with axle on semi-elliptic leaf springs and friction dampers
Rear: Non-independent, with live rear axle, semi-elliptic leaf springs and friction dampers

STEERING
Type: Worm and wheel

BRAKES
Type: Cable-operated drums front and rear

WHEELS AND TYRES
Type: Rudge Whitworth centre-lock wire wheels with 700 × 90 tyres

BODY/CHASSIS
Type: Steel channel-section chassis with cross members and aluminium single-seat racing body

DIMENSIONS AND WEIGHT
Length: 3400 mm (133.8 in)
Width: 1225 mm (48.2 in)
Wheelbase: 2235 mm (88 in)
Track – front: 1060 mm (41.7 in)
       – rear: 1090 mm (42.9 in)
Weight: 565 kg (1245 lb)

PERFORMANCE
Maximum speed: 102.5 mph (165 kph)
Acceleration 0–60 mph: 12 seconds

The inner workings of Vernon Balls' Amilcar C6, one of the cars which raced in the 200 Miles Race at Brooklands

MODEL
Aston Martin DB2/4

ENGINE
Location: Front, longitudinal
Type: Water-cooled in-line six cylinder. Cast-iron block with removeable liners and cast-iron cylinder head. Four main bearings
Cubic capacity: 2580 cc/157.4 cu in
Bore × stroke: 78 mm × 90 mm/ 3.10 in × 3.54 in
Compression ratio: 8.16:1
Valve gear: 2 valves per cylinder operated by twin direct-acting overhead camshafts
Fuel supply: 2 SU side-draught carburettors. Twin electric fuel pumps
Ignition: Mechanical by coil and distributor with automatic timing advance/retard
Maximum power: 125 bhp at 5000 rpm
Maximum torque: 178 lb ft at 3000 rpm

TRANSMISSION
Layout: Clutch in unit with engine.
Clutch: Single dry plate Borg & Beck
Gearbox: Four-speed manual synchromesh on top three ratios
Standard ratios:

| 1st 2.92:1 | 3rd 1.33:1 |
| 2nd 1.98:1 | 4th 1.00:1 |

Close ratios:

| 1st 2.92:1 | 3rd 1.26:1 |
| 2nd 1.87:1 | 4th 1.00:1 |

Final drive: Hypoid bevel
Ratio: 3.77:1

SUSPENSION
Front: Independent with trailing links, coil springs and double-acting lever arm shock absorbers
Rear: Live rear axle with coil springs, radius arms and Panhard rod

STEERING
Type: Worm and roller

BRAKES
Type: 305 mm (12 in) dia. drums all round

WHEELS AND TYRES
Type: Dunlop centre-lock wire sheels with 5.75 × 16 in tyres

BODY/CHASSIS
Type: Tubular steel chassis with aluminium panelled coupé body

DIMENSIONS AND WEIGHT
Length: 4355 mm (171.5 in)
Width: 1651 mm (65 in)
Wheelbase: 2525 mm (99 in)
Track – front: 1372 mm (54 in)
     – rear: 1372 mm (54 in)
Weight: 1308 kg (2884 lb)

PERFORMANCE
Maximum speed: 125 mph (201 kph)
Acceleration 0–60 mph: 12.6 seconds

EVOLUTION

1950 The DB2 launched, a two-door coupé fitted with the 2.6-litre Aston Martin engine which had been designed by W.O. Bentley for Lagonda. Its chassis was built of square-section tubing and it had trailing independent front suspension and a live rear axle. Just over 400 were built

1952 DB3 introduced. This was a sports racing model campaigned by the factory. It was fitted with the 2.6-litre six

1953 DB2-4 introduced, longer than the DB2 and with two 'occasional' rear seats. The engine output was increased to 125 bhp at 5000 rpm

1954 DB2-4 engine capacity increased to 2922 cc (178 cu in), raising the output to 140 bhp at 5000 rpm

1955 DB2-4 MkII appeared, with a restyled, longer body and revised interior. The car was available in coupé, convertible and 'notchback' form. Approximately 200 were built

1957 DB2-4 MkIII was introduced, with a restyled body and the engine redesigned to give an output of between 162 and 195 bhp with various compression ratios. About 550 were built

The Aston Martin DB2-4, showing its twin-overhead camshaft straight six, independent front suspension and live rear axle. The DB2-4 was the first model in the series to offer seating for four, and thus graduated from being a sports car to a high-

has been the basis of all subsequent models. The car was expensive by the standards of its time, but it was engineered and finished to high standards

MODEL
Aston Martin DB3S

ENGINE
Location: Front-mounted, longitudinal
Type: Water-cooled straight six
Cubic capacity: 2992 cc/182.5 cu in
Bore × stroke: 83 mm × 90 mm/ 3.27 in × 3.54 in
Compression ratio: 8.2:1
Valve gear: Two valves per cylinder, inclined, with twin overhead camshafts driven by chain
Fuel supply: Three twin-choke Weber carburettors
Maximum power: Initially 164 bhp at 5500 rpm (1953, 182 bhp; 1954, 225 bhp)
Maximum torque: Initially 182 lb ft at 3800 rpm

TRANSMISSION
Layout: Clutch and gearbox in unit with engine, driving rear wheels
Clutch: 9 in single dry plate hydraulic
Gearbox: Four-speed manual, overall ratios:
 1st 10.88:1   3rd 4.69:1
 2nd 6.97:1   4th 3.727:1
 (NB final drive rtio 3.727:1)
Final drive: Spiral bevel

SUSPENSION
Front: Independent, by trailing links and torsion bars, anti-roll bar
Rear: De Dion, trailing arms, transverse torsion bar, anti-roll bar

STEERING
Type: Rack and pinion manual, two turns lock to lock

BRAKES
Type: front: 2LS drum, 330 mm (13 in) dia; rear: leading and trailing shoe drum, 304 mm (12 in) dia. Discs fitted in 1954

WHEELS
Type: 6.00 × 16 tyres on 16 in centre-lock wire wheels

BODY/CHASSIS
Type: Tubular chassis, with 102 mm (4 in) dia side members, three cross members. Open two-seater body

DIMENSIONS AND WEIGH
Length: 3905 mm (153.75 in)
Width: 1492 mm (58.75 in)
Track – front: 1244 mm (49 in)
     – rear: 1244 mm (49 in)
Weight: 978 kg (2156 lb), with 35 gal fuel

PERFORMANCE
Maximum speed: Approx 140 mph/225 kph

The DB3S was soundly conventional in its make-up, with a substantial tubular chassis and a lusty twin-cam straight-six engine beneath a well-proportioned sports-racing body. A trailing link front suspension was used, with a De Dion layout at the rear, ahead of that enormous 35-gallon fuel tank. This DB3S has drum brakes outboard front and rear (on the DB3 the rear brakes were mounted inboard), and in 1954 discs were adopted for this car

RIGHT The heart of the DB3S was its classic twin-cam straight-six 2992 cc (182.5 cu in) engine which produced some 160 bhp at 5500 rpm in production form

MODEL
Duesenberg Model J (1928)

ENGINE
Location: Front, longitudinal
Type: Water-cooled in-line eight cylinder with cylinders and crankcase cast integrally. Five main bearings. Alloy sump
Cubic capacity: 6876 cc/418.9 cu in
Bore × stroke: 95.25 mm × 120.65 mm/3.75 in × 4.75 in
Compression ratio: 5.2:1
Valve gear: Four valves per cylinder operated by two chain-driven overhead camshafts. Double valve springs. Intake valves 38 mm (1.5 in) diameter and exhaust valves 47.5 mm (1.87 in) in diameter
Fuel supply: Single 38 mm (1.5 in) duplex updraught carburettor
Ignition: Mechanical by coil and distributor with 6 volt system
Maximum power: 265 bhp at 4200 rpm

TRANSMISSION
Layout: Gearbox behind engine with torque tube to rear axle
Clutch: Twin-plate
Gearbox: Three-speed manual
Final drive: Hypoid bevel
Ratio: 3.0:1 (to special order only, 3.78:1, 4.0:1, 4.3:1, 4.3:1 or 4.7:1)

SUSPENSION
Front: Non-independent with semi-elliptic leaf springs, 104 cm (41 in) long
Rear: Live rear axle with semi-elliptic leaf springs 157 cm (62 in) long

STEERING
Type: Ross cam and lever, 18:1 ratio

BRAKES
Type: Duesenberg hydraulic drums, finned and of 38 cm (15 in) diameter. 21.5 cm (8½ in) hand drum brake on transmission

WHEELS AND TYRES
Type: Chromium plated centre lock wire wheels with 31 in × 7 inch tyres

BODY/CHASSIS
Type: Alloy steel ladder frame with seven cross members. Frame depth of 21.6 cm (8.5 in). Double kickup at rear and single drop at front

DIMENSIONS AND WEIGHT
Wheelbase: 3619 mm (142.5 in)
Track – front: 1425 mm (56 in)
      – rear: 1425 mm (56 in)
Weight: 2390 kg (5270 lb)

PERFORMANCE
Maximum speed: 116 mph (186 kph)

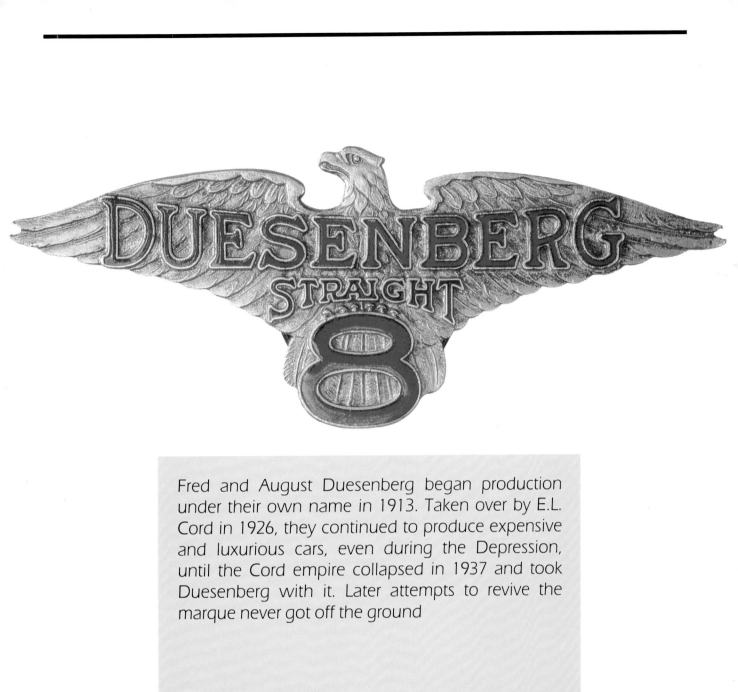

Fred and August Duesenberg began production under their own name in 1913. Taken over by E.L. Cord in 1926, they continued to produce expensive and luxurious cars, even during the Depression, until the Cord empire collapsed in 1937 and took Duesenberg with it. Later attempts to revive the marque never got off the ground

EVOLUTION

1928 Model J Duesenberg introduced at December New York Automobile Salon, powered by a twin-cam straight eight of 6876 cc (419 cu in)

1929 Factory body design department introduced with Gordon Beuhrig as chief designer·

1932 Duesenberg Model SJ introduced with engine supercharged to increase power output from 265 bhp to 320 bhp. 36 built

1935 Long wheelbase JN introduced. Ten built, two as supercharged SJNs

1936 Two short-wheelbase models, the SS and SJ, built on a 317 cm (125 in) wheelbase

1937 Last Duesenberg chassis built at dealers, as factory closed (body for this car eventually completed in 1940)

A Model J Duesenberg Speedster by Figoni. The Model J was a massive construction, quite conventional in its chassis and suspension design but advanced in its use of the superb Lycoming-built straight-eight twin cam and its extraordinarily comprehensive array of instrumentation which set it apart from its competition, as did such niceties as the lower driving lights which turned with the steering

MODEL
Aston Martin DB6 (1966)

ENGINE
Location: Front, longitudinal
Type: Water-cooled in-line six with aluminium block and head. Seven main bearings
Cubic capacity: 3995 cc/243.7 cu in
Bore × stroke: 96 mm × 92 mm/ 3.78 in × 3.62 in
Compression ratio: 8.9:1
Valve gear: 2 valves per cylinder inclined at 80 degrees in hemispherical combustion chambers by 2 chain-driven overhead camshafts
Fuel supply: 3 twin-choke Weber 45DC0E9 carburettors
Ignition: Mechanical with coil and distributor
Maximum power: 325 bhp (DIN) at 5750 rpm
Maximum torque: 290 lb ft (DIN) 4500 rpm

TRANSMISSION
Layout: Clutch and gearbox in unit with engine
Clutch: 10 in diameter diaphragm
Gearbox: Five-speed manual, all synchromesh

1st	2.73:1	4th	1.00:1
2nd	1.76:1	5th	0.83:1
3rd	1.23:1		

Final drive: Hypoid bevel
Ratio: 3.73:1

SUSPENSION
Front: Independent with unequal length wishbones, coil springs, Armstrong telescopic dampers and anti-roll bar
Rear: Live rear axle located by twin parallel trailing arms, Watt linkage and Armstrong Selectaride adjustable lever-arm dampers

STEERING
Type: Rack and pinion

BRAKES
Type: Girling discs all round, 292 mm (11½ in) diameter front and 273 mm (10¾ in) diameter rear, servo-assisted

WHEELS AND TYRES
Type: 15 in dia wire wheels with Avon GT 6.70 × 15 tyres

BODY/CHASSIS
Type: Platform steel chassis with tubular steel superstructure and magnesium alloy 2-door, 4-seat coupé body

DIMENSIONS AND WEIGHT
Length: 4559 mm (179.5 in)
Width: 1721 mm (67.75 in)
Wheelbase: 2591 mm (102.0 in)
Track – front: 1378 mm (54.25 in)
– rear: 1359 mm (53.5 in)
Weight: 1524 kg (3360 lb)

PERFORMANCE
Maximum speed: 148 mph (238 kph)
Acceleration 0–60 mph: 6.1 seconds

ABOVE The imposing lines of a pinnacle of Grand Touring design in the shape of an Aston Martin DB6. At various times Aston Martin toyed with de Dion rear suspension but this DB6 has the ultra-conservative system of live axle and trailing arms

EVOLUTION

1958 DB4 saloon and drophead introduced, with twin-ohc six-cylinder engine of 3670 cc (223.8 cu in)

1959 DB4GT offered, with faired-in headlights and lightened bodywork

1960 Zagato-bodied version of DB4 offered

1961 The last DB4GT built. Total production: 75

1963 DB5 saloon and drophead coupé introduced, with engine bored out to 3995 cc (243.7 cu in). DB4 discontinued. Total production: 1110, plus 19 Zagato versions

1965 DB6 and short-chassis Volante introduced, mechanically similar but the latter with new aerodynamic body. DB5 discontinued. Total production: (saloon) 896, (drophead) 125

1966 DB6 Volante drophead coupé introduced. Short-chassis Volante discontinued. Total production: 37

1969 DB6 Mk II introduced, with restyled interior and optional fuel injection. DB6 discontinued. Total production: 1327 (Volante 140)

1970 DB6 MkII and Volante discontinued

EVOLUTION

1969 Aston Martin DBS V8 introduced in September with a 5.3-litre four-cam V8 and a choice of Chrysler TorqueFlite three-speed automatic or ZF five-speed manual transmission

1972 Front restyled and lengthened and lights improved. Electronic ignition fitted

1973 Fuel injection dispensed with due to emissions problems and Weber carburettors fitted. Power output declined by around 20 bhp

1977 V8 Vantage version introduced along with the Volante convertible

1980 Standard V8 engine was given a higher compression ratio and larger valve area

1983 Vantage's wheel arches flared to accommodate wider wheels and Pirelli P7 tyres

1986 Fuel injection returned to the V8s, except for the Vantage which remained with Weber carburettors. Vantage Zagato introduced

MODEL
Aston Martin V8 Vantage (1986)

ENGINE
Location: Front, longitudinal
Type: Water-cooled V8 with light alloy block and heads, Wet liners and five main bearings
Cubic capacity: 5340 cc/325.7 cu in
Bore × stroke: 100 mm × 85 mm/ 3.94 in × 3.35 in
Compression ratio: 9.3:1
Valve gear: Two valves per cylinder, inclined in hemispherical combustion chambers and operated by two overhead camshafts per bank of cylinders
Fuel supply: Four Weber 481DF carburettors
Maximum power: 360 bhp (DIN)

TRANSMISSION
Layout: Gearbox and clutch in unit with engine
Clutch: Single dry plate
Gearbox: ZF five-speed manual
1st 2.90:1   4th 1.00:1
2nd 1.78:1   5th 0.845:1
3rd 1.22:1
Final drive: Hypoid bevel with limited slip differential
Ratio: 3.540:1

SUSPENSION
Front: Independent with double wishbones, coil springs and anti-roll bar
Rear: De Dion axle, parallel trailing arms, transverse Watt linkage and coil springs

STEERING
Type: Rack and pinion. 2.8 turns lock to lock

BRAKES
Type: Discs front and rear. 29.2 cm (11.5 in) diameter front, 27.4 cm (10.8 in) rear

WHEELS AND TYRES
Type: 20 cm (8 in) wide alloy wheels with 275/55VR × 15 Pirelli P7 tyres

BODY/CHASSIS
Type: Steel sheet box-type platform chassis with two-door 2+2 coupé body

DIMENSIONS AND WEIGHT
Length: 462 cm (182 in)
Width: 183 cm (72 in)
Wheelbase: 261 cm (102.75 in)
Track – front: 150 cm (59 in)
     – rear: 150 cm (59 in)
Weight: 1815 kg (4000 lb)

PERFORMANCE
Maximum speed: 170 mph (273 kph)
Acceleration 0–60 mph: 5.4 seconds

One of the last of the old school of front-engined supercars, the Aston Martin Vantage is as conventional as its traditional layout apart from its use of a de Dion axle and inboard rear disc brakes to save unsprung weight

MODEL
Auburn Speedster 851

ENGINE
Location: Front, longitudinal
Type: Water-cooled in-line flathead side-valve eight cylinder with aluminium alloy cylinder head
Cubic capacity: 4585 cc/280 cu in
Bore × stroke: 77.78 mm × 120.6 mm/3.06 in × 4.75 in
Valve gear: 2 in-line valves per cylinder operated by block mounted camshaft
Fuel supply: Single Stromberg downdraught carburettor with Schweitzer-Cummins centrifugal supercharger
Ignition: Coil and distributor, mechanical
Maximum power: 150 bhp at 4000 rpm

TRANSMISSION
Layout: Clutch and gearbox in unit with engine
Clutch: Single dry plate
Gearbox: Three speed manual with synchromesh on second and third. Ratios in 'high':
 1st 2.86:1
 2nd 1.68:1
 3rd 1.0:1
Final drive: Spiral bevel with epicyclic gear dual ratio axle
Ratios: 3:1 and 4.5:1

SUSPENSION
Front: Non independent with semi-elliptic leaf springs and hydraulic dampers
Rear: Non independent with live axle, semi-elliptic leaf springs and hydraulic dampers

STEERING
Type: Worm and peg

BRAKES
Type: Lockheed drums front and rear; hydraulically operated

WHEELS AND TYRES
Type: Steel pressed wheels with 6.50 x 15 in tyres

BODY/CHASSIS
Type: Steel box section X-braced chassis with steel Speedster body. 2 doors, 2 seats

DIMENSIONS AND WEIGHT
Length: 4938 mm (194.4 in)
Width: 1816 mm (71.5 in)
Wheelbase: 3226 mm (127 in)
Track – front: 1448 mm (57 in)
 – rear: 1575 mm (62 in)
Weight: 1702 kg (3752 lb)

PERFORMANCE
Maximum speed: 103 mph (166 kph)

EVOLUTION

1925 First Auburn eight introduced as the Eight-In-Line

1926 Engine size increased from 4.5 litres (275 cu in) to 4.8 litres (293 cu in) and the model renamed the 8-88

1927 The 8-88 engine uprated to 115 hp and the car renamed the 115. First Speedster version appeared. It used the 115's chassis plus a sleek two-seater, boat-tailed body designed by Count Alexis de Sakhnoffsky

1929 120 development of 115 introduced

1930 125 introduced

1934 The best known Speedster – the 851 – introduced. It used a 4.5-litre supercharged engine, although unblown engines were also available. Although the model designation was changed to 852 in 1936 the basic design remained virtually unchanged

1937 Auburn car production ceased

MODEL
Audi quattro (1985)

ENGINE
Location: Front, longitudinal
Type: Water-cooled in-line five cylinder with six main bearings. Cast-iron block and light-alloy head
Cubic capacity: 2144 cc/130.8 cu in
Bore × stroke: 79.5 mm × 86.4 mm/ 3.13 in × 3.40 in
Compression ratio: 7.0:1
Valve gear: 2 valves per cylinder operated by single belt-driven overhead camshaft and thimble tappets
Fuel supply: Bosch K-Jetronic fuel injection with KKK turbocharger and intercooler
Ignition: Electronic
Maximum power: 200 bhp (DIN) at 5500 rpm
Maximum torque: 211 lb ft (DIN) at 3500 rpm

TRANSMISSION
Layout: Gearbox in unit with engine with integral front differential, lockable inter axle differential and lockable rear differential
Clutch: Single dry plate
Gearbox: Five-speed manual

1st 3.60:1	4th 0.778:1
2nd 2.125:1	5th 0.71:1
3rd 1.458:1	

Final drive: Hypoid bevel
Ratio: 3.889:1 (front and rear)

SUSPENSION
Front: Independent with MacPherson struts, lower wishbones and anti-roll bar
Rear: Independent with MacPherson struts, lower wishbones and anti-roll bar

STEERING
Type: Rack and pinion, servo assisted

BRAKES
Type: Discs front and rear

WHEELS AND TYRES
Type: 15 × 6 inch alloy wheels with 205/60VR × 15 tyres

BODY/CHASSIS
Type: Integral with front auxiliary sub frame. 2-door coupé body

DIMENSIONS AND WEIGHT
Length: 440 cm (173.39 in)
Width: 172 cm (67.83 in)
Wheelbase: 252 cm (99.37 in)
Track – front: 142 cm (55.94 in)
    – rear: 145 cm (57.13 in)
Weight: 1300 kg (2866 lb)

PERFORMANCE
Maximum speed: 132 mph (212.5 kph)
Acceleration 0–60 mph: 7.8 seconds

The quattro succeeded in starting a trend to four-wheel drive for the road where the Jensen FF of the 1960s failed. The permanently engaged four-wheel-drive system is a relatively simple design, inspired by an off-road vehicle, the military VW Iltis

EVOLUTION

1980 Four-wheel drive quattro coupé announced at Geneva Motor Show, with 2144 cc (130.8 cu in) five-cylinder turbocharged engine and permanently engaged four-wheel drive

1981 Lighter Group 4 quattro coupé introduced for rallies, with internal roll cage, enlarged spoiler and flared wheel arches

1982 Quattro was first German car to win world rally championship

1983 Quattro A1 announced with 2145 cc (130.9 cu in) or 2178 cc (132.8 cu in) engines, both producing 340 bhp. Group D quattro A2 announced, with 400 bhp engine. Quattro Sport short-wheelbase model introduced, with 300 bhp engine. US version of coupé appeared, with 160 bhp engine. Rally drivers' championship won by Hannu Mikkola

1984 Coupé modified in detail – larger wheels and arch extensions, coupled with cosmetic changes to give lines that lasted through to 1988. Manufacturers' and drivers' championships won by Audi and Blomqvist

1985 Quattro Sport S1 evolution car appeared

1987 Extensive revisions to sharpen car include 2226 cc (135.8 cu in) engine, with water-cooled turbo and raised compression ratio, giving same max power and torque, but improved mid-range torque to make engine more responsive. 100,000 production mark passed early in year

MODEL
Austin Seven (1925)

ENGINE
Location: Front, longitudinal
Type: Water-cooled in-line four
Cubic capacity: 747.5 cc/45.6 cu in
Bore × stroke: 56 mm × 76.2 mm/
2.2 in × 3.0 in
Compression ratio: 4.9:1
Valve gear: Side valves, two per
cylinder
Fuel supply: Single Zenith updraft
carburettor
Ignition: Magneto
Maximum power: 10.5 bhp at
2400 rpm

TRANSMISSION
Layout: Clutch and gearbox in-unit
Clutch: Single dry plate
Gearbox: Three-speed manual
    1st 3.26:1   3rd 1.0:1
    2nd 1.0:1
Final drive: Spiral bevel
Ratio: 4.9:1

SUSPENSION
Front: Transverse, semi-elliptic leaf
springs
Rear: Semi-floating live axle with
torque tube. Quarter-elliptic leaf
springs.

STEERING
Type: Worm and sector

BRAKES
Type: Drums front and rear,
footbrake on rear, handbrake on
front

WHEELS AND TYRES
Type: Wire wheels, 700 × 80 tyres

BODY/CHASSIS
Type: U-section steel A-frame
chassis with four-seater tourer body

DIMENSIONS AND WEIGHT
Length: 2692 mm (106 in)
Width: 1168 mm (46 in)
Wheelbase: 1905 mm (75 in)
Track – front: 1016 mm (40 in)
Weight: 330 kg (728 lb)

PERFORMANCE
Maximum speed: 35 mph (58 kph)

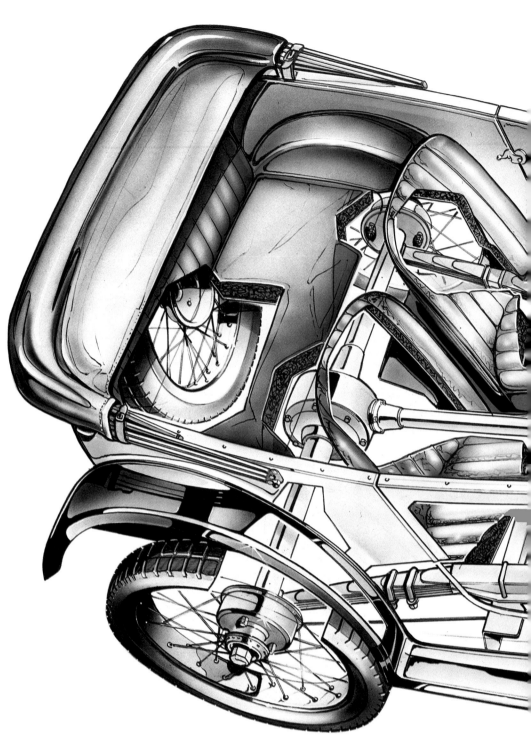

EVOLUTION

1922 Austin Seven announced in July as the car with
the smallest capacity British four-cylinder, with just
696 cc (42.4 cu in)

1923 Engine size was increased from 696 cc to 748 cc
(45.6 cu in). A fan was added to the engine and an
electric starter introduced

1924 Sports Tourer introduced

1926 Seven Saloon introduced

1927 A fabric-bodied version introduced but only built
until 1930

1928 'Top Hat' body style introduced and a nickel-
plated radiator replaced the painted type

1929 The lowered Ulster Seven introduced with
optional Cozette supercharger

1930 The brake system became entirely foot operated

1931 Wheelbase and rear track increased

1933 A four-speed gearbox introduced and the brakes
and tyres uprated. The Opal two-seater introduced,
along with the lowered 65 Seven which had an engine
tuned to produce 23 bhp at 4800 rpm

Simplicity is the key to the Seven's chassis, although in use the poor suspension location gave rise to some rather quirky handling characteriscics. In sharp corners, for example, the outer rear wheel would move backwards in relation to the chassis and the inner one forwards producing quite violent oversteer which was characteristic of the Seven. Additional axle location was later added to alleviate this problem

1934 The 65 renamed the Nippy and the Speedy introduced. Synchromesh appeared on third and fourth gears. Ruby introduced along with the Pearl Cabriolet

1936 A central main bearing was added to the 748 cc engine along with a new cylinder head and different spark plugs. Power output was increased to 17 bhp. A twin-cam single-seater was introduced for competition. Girling hydraulic brakes replaced the cable variety

1939 The final Austin Seven was built on 17 January

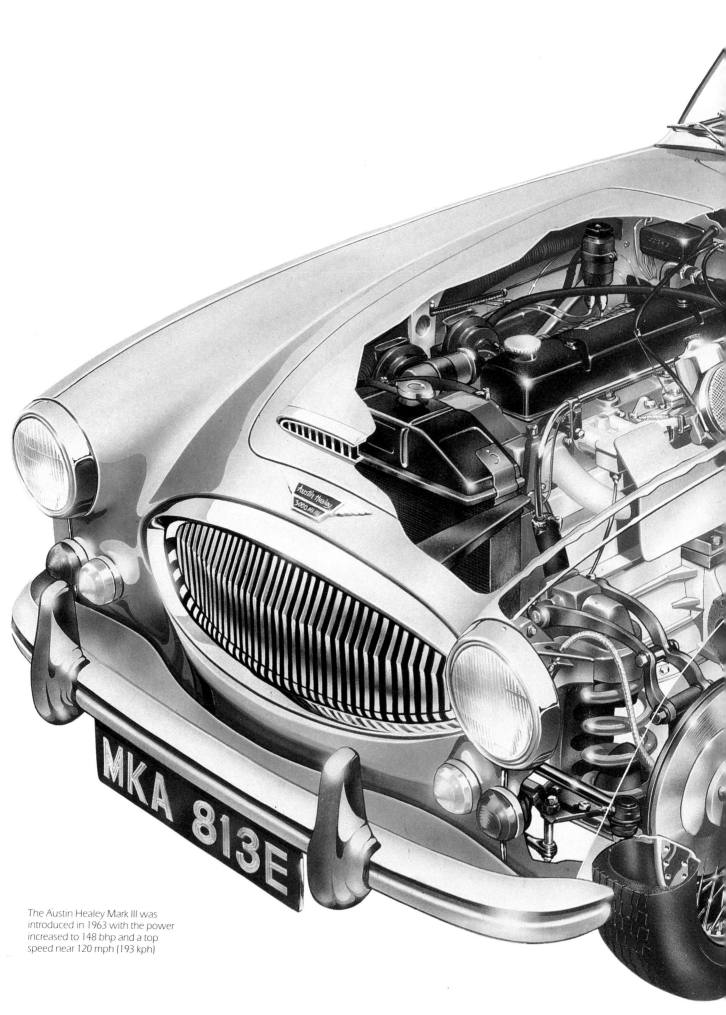

The Austin Healey Mark III was
introduced in 1963 with the power
increased to 148 bhp and a top
speed near 120 mph (193 kph)

SUSPENSION

Front: Independent by double wishbones and coil springs with lever arm dampers and anti-roll bar
Rear: Non independent with live axle, semi-elliptic leaf springs, lever arm dampers and Panhard rod

STEERING

Type: Burman cam and peg, unassisted

BRAKES

Type: Discs front and rear

WHEELS AND TYRES

Type: Wire spoked with 5.90 × 15 in Dunlop Roadspeed

BODY/CHASSIS

Type: Underslung box section ladder chassis with open steel body. 2 doors 2 seats.

DIMENSIONS AND WEIGHT

Length: 4000 mm (157.5 in)
Width: 1537 mm (60.5 in)
Wheelbase: 2337 mm (92.0 in)
Track – front: 1238 mm (48.75 in)
    – rear: 1270 mm (50.0 in)
Weight: 1143 kg (2520 lb)

PERFORMANCE

Maximum speed: 115 mph (185 kph)
Acceleration 0-60 mph:
10.8 seconds

Fuel supply: 44 mm (1¾ in) SU HD carburettors
Ignition: Coil and distributor, mechanical
Maximum power: 124 bhp (DIN) at 4750 rpm
Maximum torque: 162 lb ft (DIN) at 2700 rpm

TRANSMISSION

Layout: Clutch and gearbox in unit with engine driving rear wheels
Clutch: Single dry plate, diaphragm spring, hydraulically operated
Gearbox: Four-speed manual with synchromesh on top three ratios and overdrive on top two ratios

1st 2.93 : 1	4th 1.00 : 1
2nd 2.05 : 1	o/d 0.82 : 1
3rd 1.31 : 1	

Final drive: Hypoid bevel
Ratio: 3.9 : 1

AUSTIN HEALEY 3000 (1959)

ENGINE

Location: Front, longitudinal
Type: Water-cooled in-line six with cast-iron cylinder block and head.
Cubic capacity: 2912 cc/177.6 cu in
Bore × stroke: 83.4 mm × 88.9 mm/ 3.28 in × 3.5 in
Compression ratio: 9.03 : 1
Valve gear: 2 valves per cylinder in line operated via pushrods and rockers by single block-mounted camshaft

EVOLUTION

1921 Bentley 3 Litre introduced in September with choice of three wheelbases and in-line four-cylinder, four-valve-per-cylinder, 3-litre overhead-cam engine. 1619 3 Litres were produced between 1921 and 1929

1923 Four-wheel brakes introduced

1925 Six-cylinder 6½ Litre introduced. 545 6½ Litres built between 1925 and 1930

1927 Four-cylinder 4½ Litre introduced with the longest of the 3 Litre's optional wheelbases. 720 4½ Litres produced between 1927 and 1930

1929 The six-cylinder Speed Six introduced, basically as a Le Mans contender, winning in 1929 and 1930

1930 Production of 50 Blower Bentleys started. The 4½ Litre Supercharged was principally a racing model. Luxury 8 Litre introduced with a larger version of the six-cylinder engine from the 6½ Litre producing 220 bhp. 100 8 Litres built between 1930 and 1931. 'Cut-price' 4 Litre introduced to compete with the 20/25 Rolls-Royce. It featured a 4-litre six-cylinder pushrod engine and was not regarded by Bentley as a true Bentley. 50 were built between 1930 and 1931

1931 Bentley taken over by Rolls-Royce and production of Bentleys at Cricklewood ended: 3034 cars were built

THE BENTLEY LABELS

After World War 2 it became customary in the British motor trade to try to identify special Bentley models as Red, Blue, Black or Green Labels. These colours referred simply to the centre of the winged radiator badge upon which the 'B' was superimposed. The key to them is as follows:

Red Label: All 3 Litre models built up to 1924

Blue Label: Either 6½, 8 or 4 Litre models

Black Label: All 4½ Litre models (and all post-1931 Rolls-Royce-built Bentleys)

Green Label: 3 Litre short chassis Speed Model only (15 examples built)

MODEL Bentley 4½ Litre
Supercharged 1930

ENGINE
Location: Front, longitudinal
Type: water-cooled in-line four
cylinder with cast-iron block and
head
Cubic capacity: 4398 cc/268.28 cu in
Bore × stroke: 100 mm × 140 mm/
3.9 in × 5.5 in

Compression ratio: 5 : 1
Valve gear: 4 inclined valves per
cylinder operated by single
overhead camshaft driven by vertical
shaft from the crankshaft
Fuel supply: 2 SU carburettors and
Amherst Villiers Roots-type
supercharger
Ignition: Twin magneto and coil
Maximum power: 240 bhp at
2400 rpm (racer), 175 bhp at
3500 rpm (production car)

TRANSMISSION
Layout: Gearbox behind engine
driving rear wheels

Clutch: Single dry plate
Gearbox: Four speed manual
  1st 2.66 : 1 3rd 1.35 : 1
  2nd 1.65 : 1 4th 1.00 : 1
Final drive: Shaft
Ratio: 3 : 1

SUSPENSION
Front: Non-independent with 'H'
section steel axle semi-elliptic leaf
springs and friction dampers
Rear: Non-independent with live
rear axle semi-elliptic leaf springs
and friction dampers

STEERING
Type: Worm and wheel

BRAKES
Type: Drums front and rear

WHEELS AND TYRES
Type: Rudge Whitworth centre lock
wire wheels with 6.00 × 15 in
Dunlop tyres

BODY/CHASSIS
Type: Deep section high grade
steel frame with two seater open
sports bodywork

DIMENSIONS AND WEIGHT
Length: 4381 mm (172.5 in)
Width: 1740 mm (68.5 in)
Wheelbase: 3300 mm (130 in)
Track – front: 1384 mm (54.5 in)
      – **rear:** 1384 mm (54.5 in)
Weight: (unladen) 1921 kg
(4236 lb)

PERFORMANCE
Maximum speed: 125 mph
(201 kph)

Although it is regarded as
the classic Bentley in most laymen's
eyes, the supercharged 4½ Litre
Bentley was not approved by W.O.
Bentley. Its maximum power of 182 bhp was
a mere 2 bhp more than that
produced by the Speed Six in Le
Mans trim

MODEL
Bentley R-Type Continental (1952)

ENGINE
Location: Front longitudinal
Type: Water-cooled in-line six cylinder with cast-iron block and head
Cubic capacity: 4566 cc/278.5 cu in
Bore × stroke: 92 mm × 114.3 mm/3.62 in × 4.49 in
Compression ratio: 7.1:1
Valve gear: 2 valves per cylinder, overhead inlet with pushrods, side exhaust
Fuel supply: Twin horizontal SU carburettors
Ignition: 12v coil and 54Ah battery
Maximum power: not quoted

TRANSMISSION
Layout: Gearbox in unit with engine
Clutch: Single dry plate
Gearbox: Four-speed manual (synchromesh on upper three ratios, right-hand change)

1st 1.00:1	3rd 1.54:1
2nd 1.22:1	4th 2.67:1

Final drive: Hypoid bevel
Ratio: 3.077:1

SUSPENSION
Front: Independent with coil springs, wishbones and anti-roll bar
Rear: Live rear axle, semi-elliptic leaf springs with controllable dampers

STEERING
Type: Cam and roller, 3.675 turns lock-to-lock

BRAKES
Type: Drums all round with leading and trailing shoe; front hydraulic, rear mechanical servo

WHEELS AND TYRES
Type: 6.50 × 16 in India Super Silent rayon tyres on pressed steel wheels

BODY/CHASSIS
Type: Pressed steel channel with x-bracing, 2-door 4-seat coupé body

DIMENSIONS AND WEIGHT
Length: 5245 mm (206.5 in)
Width: 1815 mm (71.5 in)
Wheelbase: 3050 mm (120 in)
Track – front: 1440 mm (56.7 in)
    – rear: 1485 mm (58.5 in)
Weight: 1696 kg (3939 lb)

PERFORMANCE
Maximum speed: 116.9 mph (188 kph)
Acceleration 0–60 mph: 13.5 seconds

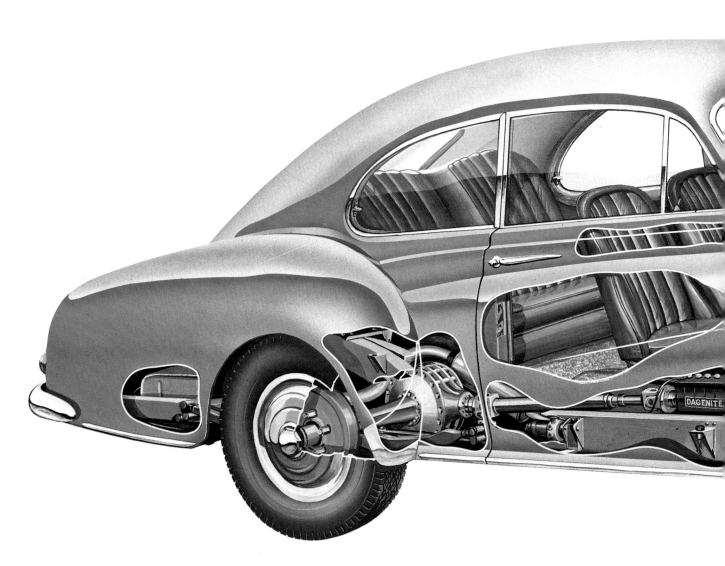

EVOLUTION

1951 Development began on the Bentley Continental in conjunction with coachbuilders Mulliner

1952 The Continental entered production initially for export only

1953 Changes included a one-piece windscreen and a modified wing line. The compression ratio was changed to 7.2:1

1954 The fourth series of Continentals was introduced with the engine bored out to 4887 cc (298 cu in) and the compression ratio increased again, to 7.25:1

1955 The S-type Bentley was introduced to replace the R-type after 207 R types had been built

Apart from the styling and the use of alloy body panelling there was little avant garde about the R-type Continental. It was built along firmly established principles, although naturally engineered to a very high standard, being built by Rolls-Royce. The engine was merely a pushrod six, albeit a large and powerful one tuned to give in the region of 150 bhp from 4½ litres, and the chassis was as heavy and conventional as the suspension was simple. There was one notable feature about the suspension and that was the use of driver-adjustable dampers, controlled via a lever on the steering wheel boss

MODEL

BMW 328 (1937)

ENGINE

Location: Front, longitudinal
Type: Water-cooled in-line six-cylinder with cast-iron block and light-alloy head. Four main bearings
Cubic capacity: 1971 cc/120 cu in
Bore × stroke: 66 mm × 96 mm/ 2.6 in × 3.78 in
Compression ratio: 7.5:1
Valve gear: 2 valves per cylinder operating in hemispherical combustion chambers. Inlet valves operated by pushrods and rockers from single block-mounted camshaft. Exhaust valves operated by horizontal pushrods from inlet side
Fuel supply: 3 Solex downdraught carburettors
Ignition: Mechanical by coil and distributor. Six-volt electrics
Maximum power: 80 bhp at 5000 rpm
Maximum torque: 93 lb ft (approx) at 4000 rpm

TRANSMISSION

Layout: Gearbox and clutch in unit with engine
Clutch: Single dry plate
Gearbox: Four-speed manual with synchromesh on top two gears. Gearboxes were supplied by Hirth or ZF and two sets of ratios were available

1st 3.64:1	3rd 1.487:1
2nd 2.05:1	4th 1.00:1

Final drive: Hypoid bevel
Ratio: 3.90:1

SUSPENSION

Front: Independent with lower wishbones, transverse semi-elliptic leaf spring and lever-arm dampers
Rear: Non independent with live rear axle, semi-elliptic leaf springs and lever arm dampers

STEERING

Type: Rack and pinion

BRAKES

Type: Hydraulically operated drums all round, 28 cm (11 in) in diameter

WHEELS AND TYRES

Type: Steel disc wheels with peg-drive hubs and 5.25 × 16 in low-pressure tyres

BODY/CHASSIS

Type: Tubular steel chassis with cross members in form of a capital 'A' with the apex to the front. Two-seat, two-door convertible sports body

DIMENSIONS AND WEIGHT

Length: 390 cm (153.5 in)
Width: 155 cm (61 in)
Wheelbase: 236 cm (93 in)
Track – front: 115 cm (45.5 in)
– rear: 122 cm (48 in)
Weight: 743 kg (1638 lb)

PERFORMANCE

Maximum speed: 103 mph (166 kph)
Acceleration 0–60 mph: 9.5 seconds

The BMW 328 was one of those rare designs that seemed to be exactly right in every respect, yet there was little completely original in it apart from the stylish semi-streamlined bodywork. Although the front suspension was independent it was a simple system using a transverse semi-elliptic leaf spring. The live axle was also simply located by semi-elliptic leaf springs, but the car still handled extremely well. Its performance matched its handling thanks to the superb straight-six engine which enjoyed the advantages of hemispherical combustion chambers without the need for twin-overhead camshafts. That was made possible by the use of an ingenious cross-over pushrod system (shown right) which was activated by a single block-mounted camshaft

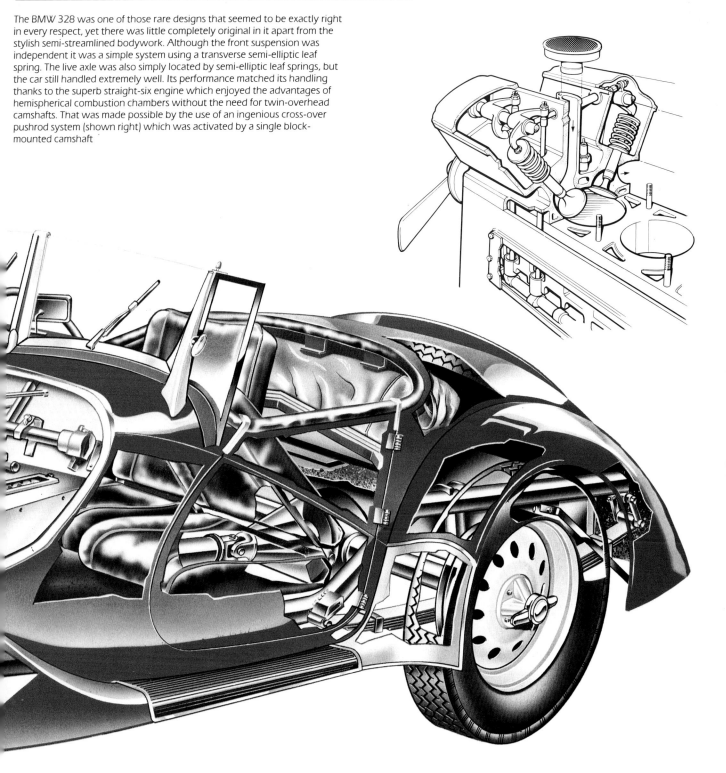

MODEL
BMW M1 (1980)

ENGINE
Location: Mid-mounted, longitudinal
Type: Water-cooled in-line six-cylinder. 7 main bearings. Dry sump lubrication
Cubic capacity: 3453 cc/210.6 cu in
Bore × stroke: 84 mm × 93.4 mm/ 3.3 in × 3.68 in
Compression ratio: 9.0:1
Valve gear: 4 valves per cylinder in inverted vee formation operated by twin chain-driven overhead camshafts
Fuel supply: Kugelfischer-Bosch mechanical fuel injection
Ignition: Marelli electronic contactless timing through flywheel
Maximum power: 277 bhp (DIN) at 6500 rpm
Maximum torque: 239 lb ft (DIN) at 5000 rpm

TRANSMISSION
Layout: Clutch and gearbox in unit with engine
Clutch: Twin plate
Gearbox: ZF five-speed manual synchromesh

1st 2.42:1	4th 0.846:1
2nd 1.61:1	5th 0.704:1
3rd 1.14:1	

Final drive: Hypoid bevel with 40 per cent limited slip differential
Ratio: 4.22:1

SUSPENSION
Front: Independent by double wishbones, gas-filled Bilstein dampers adjustable for height, coil springs and 23 mm (0.9 in) anti-roll bar
Rear: Independent by double wishbones, gas-filled Bilstein dampers adjustable for height, coil springs and 19 mm (0.74 in) anti-roll bar

STEERING
Type: Rack and pinion

BRAKES
Type: 299 mm (11.8 in) ventilated discs front, 297 mm (11.7 in) ventilated discs rear. Servo assisted with split hydraulic system

This Group 4 racing BMW M1 had its 24-valve, twin-cam six-cylinder engine tuned to produce 470 bhp which enabled it to reach speeds approaching 200 mph (332 kph) at Le Mans in 1980

WHEELS AND TYRES
Type: Light alloy wheels, 7 × 16 in front, 8 × 16 in rear with Pirelli P7 205/55VR16 front and 225/50VR16 rear

BODY/CHASSIS
Type: Glassfibre body bonded and rivetted to box section steel frame.

DIMENSIONS AND WEIGHT
Length: 4360 mm (171.6 in)
Width: 1824 mm (71.8 in)
Wheelbase: 2560 mm (100.8 in)
Track – front: 1550 mm (61.0 in)
– rear: 1576 mm (62.0 in)
Weight: 1600 kg (2867 lb)

PERFORMANCE
Maximum speed: 162 mph (262 kph)
Acceleration 0–60 mph: 5.4 seconds

MODEL
Bristol 405 (1956)

ENGINE
Location: Front, longitudinal
Type: In-line six-cylinder, overhead valve with cast-iron block and light alloy head. Four main bearings
Cubic capacity: 1971 cc/120 cu in
Bore × stroke: 66 mm × 96 mm/ 2.6 in × 3.78 in
Compression ratio: 8.5:1
Valve gear: 2 valves per cylinder operated in pentroof combustion chambers at an 80 degree angle via crossover pushrods by single block-mounted camshaft
Fuel supply: Three downdraught Solex carburettors
Ignition: Mechanical by coil and distributor
Maximum power: 105 bhp at 5000 rpm

TRANSMISSION
Layout: Gearbox in unit with engine
Clutch: Single dry plate Borg and Beck
Gearbox: Four-speed manual with overdrive
1st 3.6:1	3rd 1.3:1
2nd 1.83:1	4th 1.00:1
Overdrive top: 0.777:1	
Final drive: Spiral bevel
Ratio: 4.22:1

SUSPENSION
Front: Independent with underslung transverse leaf spring, wishbones and telescopic dampers
Rear: Non-independent with live rear axle, longitudinal torsion bars, A-bracket and telescopic dampers

STEERING
Type: Rack and pinion. 3 turns lock to lock

BRAKES
Type: Lockheed hydraulic with Alfin drums 304 mm × 57 mm (12 in × 2.25 in) front and 279 mm × 44 mm (11 in × 1.75 in) rear

WHEELS AND TYRES
Type: Bolt-on steel perforated wheels with 5.5 in × 16 in tyres

BODY/CHASSIS
Type: Box-section frame with integral floor and propellor shaft tunnel. Two-door, four-seat saloon with bolt-on body panels

DIMENSIONS AND WEIGHT
Length: 4807 mm (189.25 in)
Width: 1727 mm (68 in)
Wheelbase: 2895 mm (114 in)
Track – front: 1333 mm (52.5 in)
    – rear: 1372 mm (54 in)
Weight: 1041 kg (2296 lb)

PERFORMANCE
Maximum speed: 104 mph (167 kph)
Acceleration 0-60 mph: 10.5 seconds

Underneath the aerodynamic shell of the Bristol 405 was a stout box-section steel frame with an integral floor and prop-shaft tunnel to give added rigidity. The suspension design was not particularly adventurous with an underslung transverse leaf spring at the front and a live axle at the rear. The rear suspension, however, is notable in its use of space-efficient longitudinal torsion bars

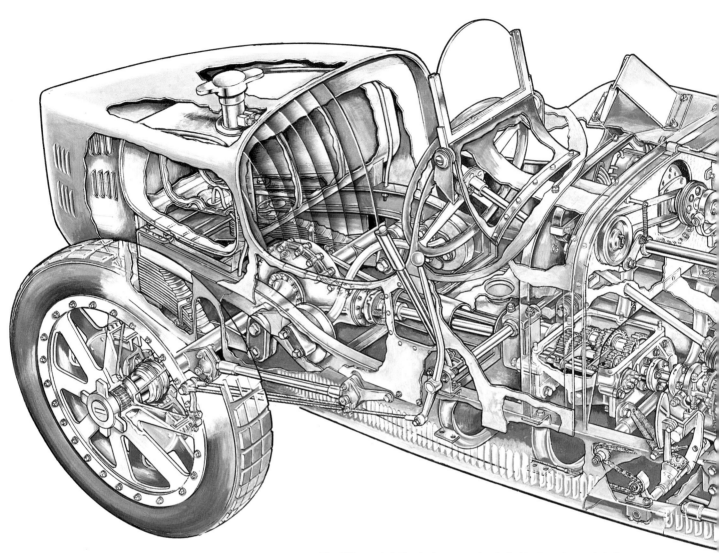

The 35B revealed. Clearly shown are the shaft drive from the crankshaft to the overhead camshaft, the typical Bugatti three-valve-per-cylinder layout and the ribbed housing for the Roots type supercharger. The chain of gears at the bottom of the radiator is the gear drive to the supercharger. Another typical Bugatti feature is the use of reversed quarter elliptic leaf springs at the rear. Bugatti's attention to detail shows in things like the brake pedal with its compensator to ensure that the brake balance was equal on both sides of the car

MODEL

Bugatti Type 35B (1927)

ENGINE

Location: Front longitudinal
Type: Water-cooled straight eight made up from two monobloc fours with roller bearing crankshaft
Cubic capacity: 2262 cc/137.98 cu in
Bore × stroke: 60 mm × 100 mm/ 2.36 in × 3.9 in
Compression ratio:
Valve Gear: 3 vertical valves per cylinder (2 inlet, 1 exhaust) operated by single overhead camshaft
Fuel supply: Zenith or Solex carburettor with three lobe Roots-type supercharger
Ignition: Mechanical, with magneto
Maximum power: 130 to 150 bhp

TRANSMISSION

Layout: Separate gearbox and engine
Clutch: Multi-plate, wet with centrifugal servo assistance
Gearbox: Four-speed manual with straight-cut gears

1st	2.42 : 1	3rd	1.31 : 1
2nd	1.85 : 1	4th	1.00 : 1

Final drive: Spiral bevel
Ratio: Various, ranging from 3.37 : 1 to 4.5 : 1

SUSPENSION

Front: Non-independent with hollow axle and semi-elliptic leaf springs
Rear: Live rear axle with reversed quarter-elliptic leaf springs

STEERING

Type: Worm and wheel with one turn lock to lock

BRAKES

Type: Drums all round, cable operated

WHEELS AND TYRES

Type: Cast alloy wheels with integral brake drum 710 mm × 90 mm (27.9 in × 3.5 in)

BODY/CHASSIS

Type: Tapered channel steel outer longitudinal chassis members with cross members. Two seater racing body.

DIMENSIONS AND WEIGHT

Length: 3683 mm (145 in)
Width: 1321 mm (52 in)
Wheelbase: 2400 mm (94.5 in)
Track – front: 1143 mm (45 in)
  – rear: 1194 mm (47 in)
Weight: 750 kg (1653 lb)

PERFORMANCE

Maximum speed: 120 mph (193 kph)
Acceleration 0-60 mph: 7 seconds (approx)

EVOLUTION

1924 Introduced at French Grand Prix at Lyon with normally aspirated straight eight featuring a ball and roller-bearing crankshaft and displacement of 1995 cc (121.7 cu in). Type 35A introduced, visually similar to the Type 35 but with the same engine as the Type 38 and wire wheels

1925 Unblown version of the 35 appeared in limited numbers for the 1.5-litre Grand Prix formula

1926 Three special 1100 cc (91.5 cu in) cars built for the Alsace Grand Prix. 35T introduced in Targa Florio, hence the 'T' for Targa. It was normally aspirated but with stroke lengthened to 100 mm (3.9 in) to give displacement of 2262 cc (137.9 cu in). The 35B was a supercharged derivative of the 35T with a larger radiator mounted further forward. Type 35C, a 1995 cc (122 cu in) version of the 35B, and Type 39 also introduced (a rare variant of the 35 with a virtually 'square' engine of 60 mm/ 2.36 in bore and 66 mm/2.6 in stroke and a displacement of 1493 cc/91 cu in. It was also produced in supercharged form as the Type 39A

The Royales were built to impress, which they certainly did (and still
do) by virtue of their extravagant dimensions and superb craftsmanship.
With a price equal to that of three Rolls-Royces, the Royale was intended
only for the most wealthy connoisseurs, and those few who bought them
were assured of a mode of transport with few (if any) peers. Some extremely
elegant body designs were fitted to the gargantuan chassis, itself necessarily
strong to support the length, and weight of the car and cope with the
tremendous torque exerted by the 12.7-litre, and in the case of the
prototype, 14.7-litre engines. The engine, some 142 cm (4 ft 8 in) long, was
lubricated with five gallons (23 litres) of oil, cooled with 15 gallons (68 litres)
of water and fed from a petrol tank of 42 gallons (191 litres) capacity. The
'Royales were originally made with the gearbox in unit with the rear axle, but
the example shown has been modified, and an automatic gearbox fitted

MODEL
Bugatti Royale Type 41 (1930)

ENGINE
Type: Water-cooled in-line straight-eight monobloc. Nine main bearings. Dry sump lubrication
Cubic capacity: 12,763 cc/778.5 cu in
Bore × stroke: 125 mm × 130 mm/ 4.92 in × 5.12 in

Valve gear: 3 valves per cylinder (2 inlet, 1 exhaust) operated by single gear-driven overhead camshaft
Fuel supply: Single double-choke Shebler carburettor
Ignition: Mechanical by both coil and magneto. 2 spark plugs per cylinder
Maximum power: 275 bhp at 3000 rpm (approx)

TRANSMISSION
Layout: Shaft drive from engine to clutch and from clutch to gearbox in unit with final drive

Clutch: Multi-plate, dry
Type: Three-speed manual
    1st 2.08:1   3rd 0.727.1
    2nd 1.00:1
Final drive: Spiral bevel
Ratio: 3.66:1

SUSPENSION
Front: Non-independent with hollow axle and semi-elliptic leaf springs passing through axle forging. Friction dampers
Rear: Live rear axle with reversed quarter elliptic leaf springs and friction damper

STEERING
Type: Worm and nut. 3½ turns lock to lock

BRAKES
Type: Cable operated drums all round, 46 cm (18 in) diameter

WHEELS AND TYRES
Type: 24 in diameter cast alloy wheels with 6.75 × 36 Rapson tyres

BODY/CHASSIS
Type: Pressed steel channel section chassis with two main longitudinal outer chassis members and cross members

DIMENSIONS AND WEIGHT
Wheelbase: 432.0 cm (170 in)
Track – front: 160 cm (63 in)
   – rear: 160 cm (63 in)
Weight: 3175 kg (7000 lb)

PERFORMANCE
Maximum speed: 100 mph (160 kph) (approx)

MODEL
Ferrari 365 GTB 4 Berlinetta
(Daytona) (1970)

ENGINE
Location: Front, longitudinal
Type: Water-cooled 60-degree V12
with light-alloy cylinder heads and
block. Seven main bearings
Cubic capacity: 4390 cc/267.8 cu in
Bore × stroke: 81 mm × 71 mm/
3.19 in × 2.79 in
Compression ratio: 8.8:1
Valve gear: Two valves per
cylinder inclined at 46 degrees
operating in hemispherical
combustion chambers via bucket
tappets by two chain-driven
overhead camshafts per bank of
cylinders
Fuel supply: Six Weber 40 DCN-20
downdraught twin-barrel
carburettors
Ignition: Mechanical with twin
coils and distributors
Maximum power: 353 bhp (DIN)
at 7500 rpm
Maximum torque: 319 lb ft (DIN)
at 5000 rpm

TRANSMISSION
Layout: Gearbox in unit with final
drive in rear of chassis
Clutch: Borg and Beck single dry
plate
Gearbox: Five speed manual
  1st 3.075:1   4th 1.250:1
  2nd 2.120:1 5th 0.964:1
  3rd 1.572:1
Final drive: Spiral bevel
Ratio: 3.300:1

SUSPENSION
Front: Independent with double
wishbones, coil springs, telescopic
dampers and anti-roll bar
Rear: Independent with double
wishbones, coil springs and
telescopic dampers and anti-roll bar

STEERING
Type: ZF worm and roller. 3.5 turns
lock to lock

BRAKES
Type: Discs front and rear.
126 sq cm (28.8 sq in) rear

WHEELS AND TYRES
Type: Alloy wheels 7.5 in with 215/
70 × 15 radial tyres

BODY/CHASSIS
Type: Tubular chassis with two-
door coupé body

DIMENSIONS AND WEIGHT
Length: 442 cm (174.21 in)
Width: 176 cm (69.29 in)
Wheelbase: 240 cm (94.49 in)
Track – front: 144 cm (56.69 in)
      – rear: 142 cm (56.1 in)
Weight: 1200 kg (2641 lb)

PERFORMANCE
Maximum speed: 174 mph
(280 kph)
Acceleration 0–60 mph:
5.4 seconds

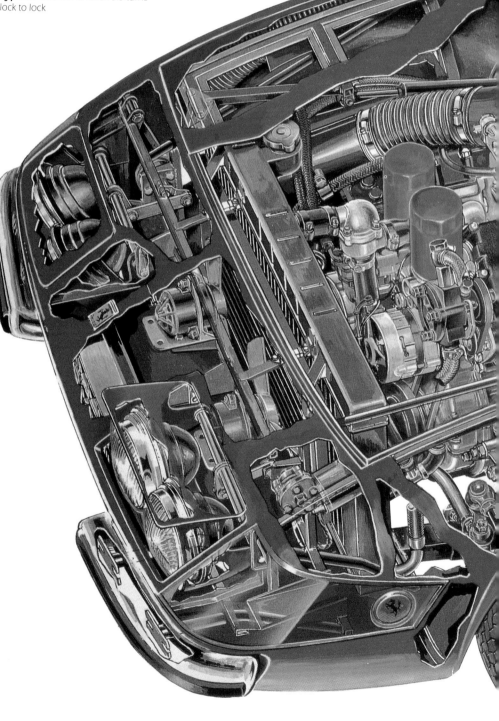

Enzo Ferrari made his name as a racing driver, and eventually began producing cars bearing his own name during World War 2. The famous *Cavallino Rampante* prancing horse badge was presented to him in 1923 by the Contessa Paolina Baracca, whose son, a World War 1 flying ace, had carried it on the fuselage of his fighter plane.

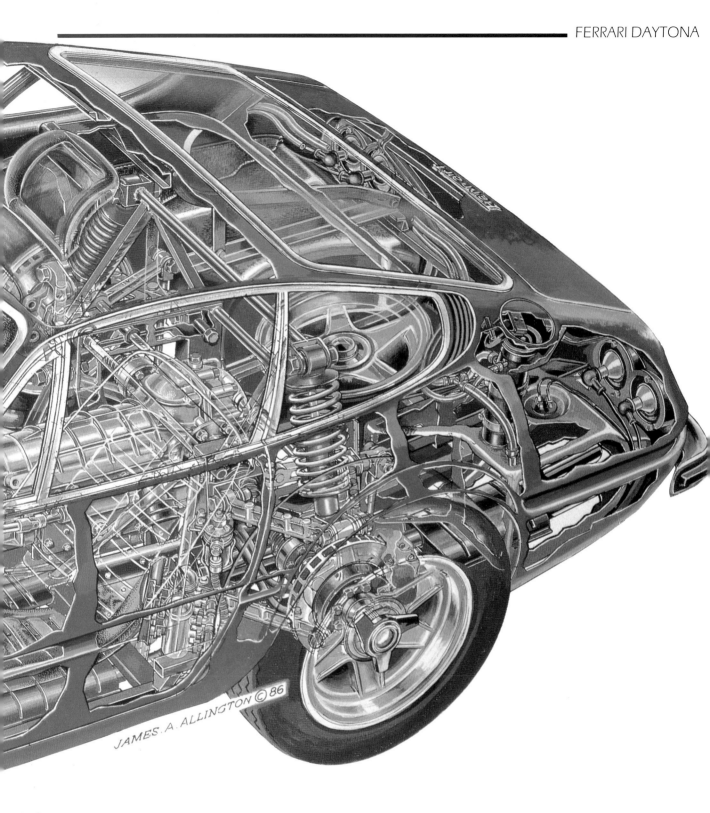

JAMES. A. ALLINGTON © 86

The fact that the 365GTB/4 Daytona had its engine located at the front rather than behind the driver originally seemed a little odd. The chosen layout proved its worth though and the rear mounted gearbox/final drive assembly helped to balance the overall weight distribution. The Daytona had predictable handling, but the masses at each end made for greater inertia than in a mid-mounted arrangement. As a result, oversteer could be difficult to contain. The Daytona was renowned for its throttle sensitivity and this was one good reason

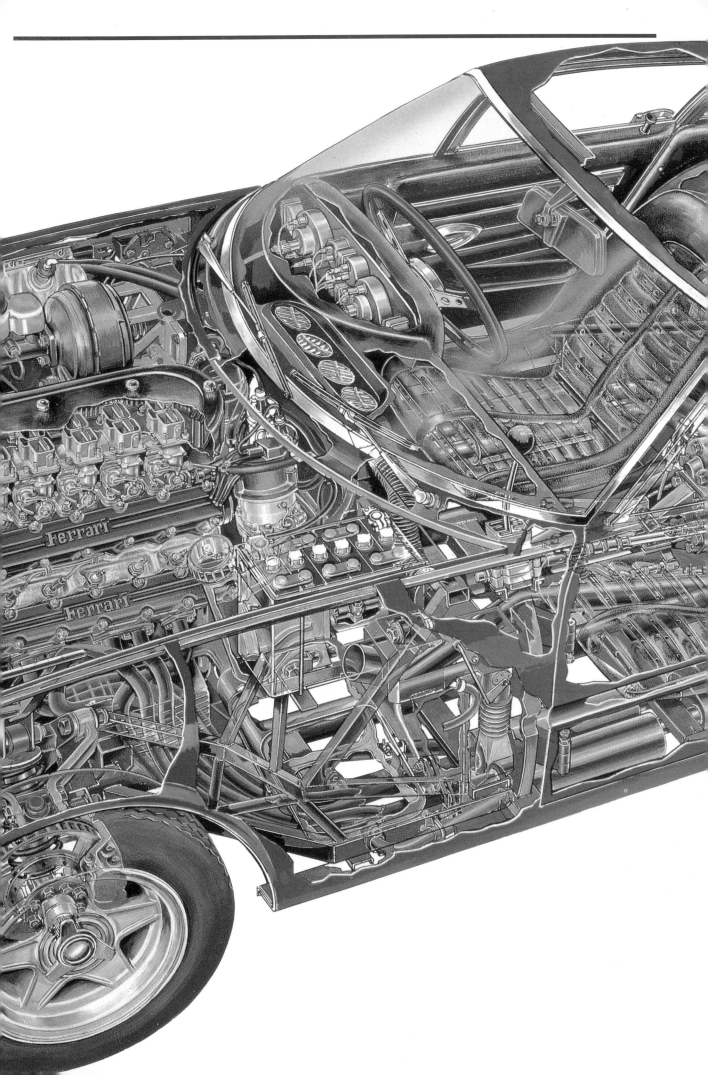

MODEL
Bugatti Type 57

ENGINE
Location: Front-longitudinal
Type: Water-cooled in-line eight cylinder with block and head in-unit. Five main bearings
Cubic capacity: 3257 cc/198.67 cu in
Bore × stroke: 72 mm × 100 mm/ 2.83 in × 3.94 in
Compression ratio: 6:1
Valve gear: 2 valves per cylinder operated in hemispherical combustion chambers by twin overhead, gear-driven camshafts
Fuel supply: Stromberg or Bugatti carburettor; supercharger on 57C and 57SC
Ignition: Coil (57/57C); Scintilla Vertex magneto (57S/57SC)
Maximum power: 135 bhp(57); 160 bhp(57C); 170 bhp(57S); 200 bhp(57SC)

TRANSMISSION
Layout: Gearbox in unit with engine
Clutch: Single dry plate
Gearbox: Four-speed manual
  1st 2.79:1   3rd 1.29:1
  2nd 1.80:1   4th 1.00:1
Final drive: Spiral bevel
Ratio: 4.18:1

SUSPENSION
Front: Non-independent with rigid axle, semi-elliptic leaf springs and Hartford friction dampers
Rear: Non-independent with live rear axle, reversed quarter elliptic leaf springs and Hartford friction dampers

STEERING
Type: Worm and wheel

BRAKES
Type: Cable-operated drum (hydraulic drum from 1938)

WHEELS AND TYRES
Type: Rudge wire wheels, 18 × 5.50 tyres

BODY/CHASSIS
Type: Ladder-type chassis with coachbuilt body

DIMENSIONS AND WEIGHT
Length: 4190 mm (165 in)
Width: 1625 mm (64 in)
Wheelbase: 3300 mm (130 in)
Track – front: 1350 mm (53 in)
     – rear:** 1350 mm (53 in)
Weight: 950 kg (2094 lb) (chassis only)

PERFORMANCE
Maximum speed: 112 mph (180 kph)(57C)

EVOLUTION

1933 Bugatti Type 57 launched at the Paris Salon. The prototype engine displaced 2866 cc (175 cu in), but the production unit had a displacement of 3257 cc (198.67 cu in)

1936 The engine mounted on four rubber blocks rather than being bolted direct to the chassis, which was strengthened and given an extra cross member. The compression ratio was raised from 6.0:1 to 6.2:1, increasing power to 135 bhp. Hartford friction dampers replaced with De Ram hydraulic/friction dampers. The first 57C supercharged model produced, with a power output of 160 bhp. The 57S sports version introduced with a split front axle, shortened chassis and magneto ignition

1937 The 57SC introduced (supercharged version of the 57S); around 30 were built

1938 Allinquant telescopic dampers adopted, along with hydraulic brakes

1940 Type 57 production ceased after approximately 75 chassis had been built

Although strongly influenced by the more advanced ideas of Jean Bugatti, the Type 57 appeared with the traditional Bugatti front axle and reversed quarter elliptic springs for the live rear axle due to the restraining hand of Ettore Bugatti. The first 200 chassis were flexible affairs, again traditionally Bugatti, with the engine mounted directly to the frame. Later it was decided to mount the engine on rubber mountings and switch to a stiffer, cross-braced chassis

MODEL:
Cadillac Series 452 V16 (1930)

ENGINE
Location: Front longitudinal
Type: 45 degree V16

Cubic capacity: 7412 cc/452.6 cu in
Bore × stroke: 76.2 mm × 101.6 mm/
3.0 in × 4.0 in
Compression ratio: 5.5:1
Valve Gear: 2 in-line valves per
cylinder, operated by single block-
mounted camshaft
Fuel supply: updraught Cadillac
carburettor to each bank, fed by
vacuum pump
Ignition: dual 6V coils, mounted in
radiator header to stabilise
temperature
Maximum power: 165 bhp at 3400
rpm

TRANSMISSION
Layout: Unit gearbox, torque tube
final drive
Clutch: Double dry plate
Gearbox: Three-speed
synchromesh in unit with engine
  1st: 3.47:1   3rd: 1:1
  2nd: 1.48:1
Final drive: Hypoid bevel
Ratio: 3.47 (to 1/6/30), 4.07, 4.39,
4.75:1

SUSPENSION
Front: Non independent with
semi-elliptic leaf springs and
hydraulic dampers
Rear: Non independent with live
rear axle, semi-elliptic leaf springs
and hydraulic dampers

STEERING
Type: worm and sector

BRAKES
Type: Mechanical vacuum-servo,
footbrake, internal-expanding on
front, external contracting on rear;
handbrake internal expanding on
rear

WHEELS AND TYRES
Type: Wire wheels, 750/19 tyres

BODY/CHASSIS
Type: 15 body styles available;
pressed steel channel section frame
with wide top flange

DIMENSIONS AND WEIGHT
Wheelbase: 3759 mm (148 in)
Weight: 2812 kg (6200 lb)

PERFORMANCE
Maximum speed: 84-100 mph
(135-160 kph)
Acceleration: 10-60 mph: 21.1
seconds

The Maharaja of Tikari's V16 exposed. Note the arm connecting the lower driving lights to the steering, enabling the driver to see around corners. The use of updraught carburettors explains the unusual manifold configuration

The 1984 Corvette is notable
for its use of plastic monofilament
transverse leaf springs for both
front and rear suspension and for
its superbly forged aluminium alloy
suspension arms

MODEL
Chevrolet Corvette (1984)

ENGINE
Location: Front, longitudinal
Type: Water cooled V8 with cast
iron block and heads
Cubic capacity: 5736 cc/350 cu in
Bore × stroke: 101.6 mm ×
88.4 mm/4.0 in × 3.48 in
Valve gear: 2 valves per cylinder in
line operated via single block-
mounted camshaft, pushrods and
hydraulic tappets
Fuel supply: 'Cross Fire' throttle
body fuel injection
Ignition: Delco Remy high energy
electronic with engine
management control
Maximum power: 205 bhp at
4200 rpm (SAE net)
Maximum torque: 290 lb ft at
2800 rpm (SAE net)

TRANSMISSION
Layout: Clutch and gearbox in unit
with engine
Clutch: Single dry plate
Gearbox: Four-speed manual with
computer-controlled overdrive on
top three ratios or Turbo-Hydramatic
four-speed automatic with
following ratios
  1st 3.060:1   3rd 1.00:1
  2nd 1.630:1   4th 0.70:1
Final drive: Hypoid bevel with
limited slip differential
Ratio: 2.730:1

SUSPENSION
Front: Independent with
wishbones, anti-roll bar and
transverse monofilament plastic leaf
spring
Rear: Independent with five links –
upper and lower control arms per
side with lateral Panhard rod,
transverse monofilament leaf spring

STEERING
Type: Rack and pinion, servo
assisted with 2.36 turns lock to lock

BRAKES
Type: Discs front and rear with
2128 sq cm (329.9 sq in) swept area

WHEELS AND TYRES
Type: Alloy 16 in × 8 in with
Goodyear 225/50VR16 radial tyres

BODY/CHASSIS
Type: High-strength steel perimeter
frame with glassfibre and SMC 2-
door, 2-seat coupé body

DIMENSIONS AND WEIGHT
Length: 4480 mm (176.5 in)
Width: 1800 mm (71 in)
Wheelbase: 2440 mm (96 in)
Track – front: 1510 mm (59.6 in)
   – rear: 1530 mm (60.4 in)
Weight: 1414 kg (3110 lb)

PERFORMANCE
Maximum speed: 136 mph
(219 kph)
0–60 mph: 6.8 seconds

EVOLUTION

1953 Introduced at GM Motorama Show in January as a two-door, two-seat convertible with glassfibre body on separate chassis

1955 V8 engine became available with three-speed manual transmission

1956 Second generation Corvette introduced with restyled body

1957 Four-speed manual Borg-Warner transmission introduced. Rochester-built fuel injection available, along with Positraction limited slip diff

1960 Aluminium cylinder heads and radiator introduced

1962 5.3-litre (327 cu in) V8 introduced

1963 Third generation Corvette introduced as Sting Ray with new ladder frame, lighter body and independent rear suspension with transverse leaf spring introduced. Coupé available for the first time

1965 Four-wheel disc brakes introduced as standard equipment. Close-ratio four-speed transmission optional

1966 425 bhp 7-litre (427 cu in) V8 available

1967 Sting Ray discontinued and longer fourth-generation Corvette introduced

1969 5.6-litre (350 cu in) V8 introduced and Corvette known as the Sting Ray

1970 Turbo jet 7.4-litre (454 cu in) introduced along with 5.6-litre (350 cu in) 'small block' V8

1972 Power outputs appeared to decrease as SAE net standard replaced SAE gross

1975 Catalytic converters introduced and maximum power fell to 205 bhp. Roadster discontinued

1979 Low profile tyres became available

1981 Glassfibre monoleaf rear spring introduced

1982 Throttle body fuel injection introduced along with four-speed automatic transmission. Manual gearbox no longer available

1983 Fifth generation Corvette introduced as a 1984 model with glassfibre springs front and rear and completely new chassis and body. 5.7-litre (350 cu in) V8 continued with power output of 205 bhp

1986 Standard 5.7-litre V8 rated at 230 bhp. Convertible available. Z packages included anti-lock brakes

1987 Uprated brakes, Goodyear tyres with Z rating, cleared for 155 mph (248 kph)

1988 Standard 5.7-litre V8 rated at 245 bhp. Detail changes to suspension

MODEL
Chevrolet Camaro Z28 (1984)

ENGINE
Location: Front, longitudinal
Type: V8 with cast-iron block and heads
Cubic capacity: 5001 cc/305 cu in
Bore × stroke: 94.9 mm × 88.4 mm/3.74 in × 3.48 in
Compression ratio: 9.5:1
Valve gear: 2 valves per cylinder operated by single camshaft mounted in centre of vee, pushrods and rockers
Fuel supply: Single Rochester E4MC downdraught four-barrel carburettor
Ignition: Delco-Remy electronic
Maximum power: 190 bhp (SAE) at 4800 rpm
Maximum torque: 240 lb ft (SAE) at 3200 rpm

TRANSMISSION
Layout: Gearbox in unit with engine
Clutch: Single dry plate
Gearbox: Five-speed manual or four speed automatic (ratios in brackets)

1st	2.950:1	4th	1.00:1
	(3.080:1)		(0.700:1)
2nd	1.940:1	5th	0.730:1
	(1.630:1)		
3rd	1.340:1		
	(1.00:1)		

Final drive: Hypoid bevel
Ratio: 2.760:1 (3.420:1)

SUSPENSION
Front: Independent with MacPherson struts, lower wishbones, coil springs, telescopic dampers and anti-roll bar
Rear: Non-independent with live rear axle, located by two swinging lower longitudinal leading arms, torque tube, anti-roll bar, coil springs and telescopic dampers

STEERING
Type: Recirculating ball

BRAKES
Type: Discs front and drums rear

WHEELS AND TYRES
Type: Five-spoke alloy wheels with 215/65HR × 15 tyres

BODY/CHASSIS
Type: Integral chassis with two-door, four-seat coupé body

DIMENSIONS AND WEIGHT
Length: 477 cm (187.8 in)
Width: 185 cm (72.8 in)
Wheelbase: 257 cm (101.0 in)
Track – front: 154 cm (60.63 in)
– rear: 156 cm (61.41 in)
Weight: 1450 kg (3197 lb)

PERFORMANCE
Maximum speed: 128 mph (205 kph)
Acceleration 0–60 mph: 7 seconds

The 1984 third-generation Camaro was a sleek, high-performance cruiser. Although smaller than the classic Camaro/Firebird, it nevertheless retained the traditional roadholding and handling qualities which made them famous

EVOLUTION

1966 Chevrolet Camaro introduced in both coupé and convertible forms, based on the Chevy II chassis. Standard equipment was a 3.8-litre (231 cu in) straight six with a three-speed manual transmission. Top Camaro performance option was a 6.5-litre (396 cu in) V8 with a four-speed manual transmission

1967 Pontiac Firebird was introduced with a 'twin nostril' front grille and different rear end treatment. Top Firebird engine option was a 6.6-litre (400 cu in) V8 producing 335 bhp. Power-assisted front disc brakes were an option on both Camaro and Firebird

1968 Z28 performance package became available on Camaros; it included a 4.9-litre (298 cu in) V8, heavy duty suspension, four-speed gearbox and power-assisted front disc brakes

1969 Camaro and Firebird were restyled and enlarged and an 'egg crate'-style grille introduced on the Camaro. Pontiac introduced the Firebird TransAm with the 6.6-litre V8

1970 The definitive Camaro and Firebird shape was introduced, in coupé form only

1974 Camaro and Firebird facelifted with more prominent nose sections

1975 Wrap-around rear window added to Camaro and Firebird

1977 Another restyling saw the Firebird receive four rectangular headlights

1978 Camaro further face-lifted

1980 Pontiac introduced a 4.9-litre turbocharged V8 to the range

1982 Third-generation Firebird and Camaro introduced, smaller and lighter. A four-cylinder engine was standard with V6 and V8 options. Z28 and TransAm performance options were still available, using a 155 bhp 5-litre (305 cu in) V8. Performance of the V8 engine was increased steadily over the next few years, reaching 205 bhp by 1987

1984 IROC Camaro Z28 introduced with high-output fuel-injected V8

1986 Emphasis on Pontiac, with Firebird Formula 5.0 for 1987 – effectively a TransAm retaining 'performance' components but stripped of cosmetic items, with tuned 5.0- and 5.7-litre (305 cu in and 350 cu in) V8s as listed options. Although GM F-body common, this standard not listed for Camaro

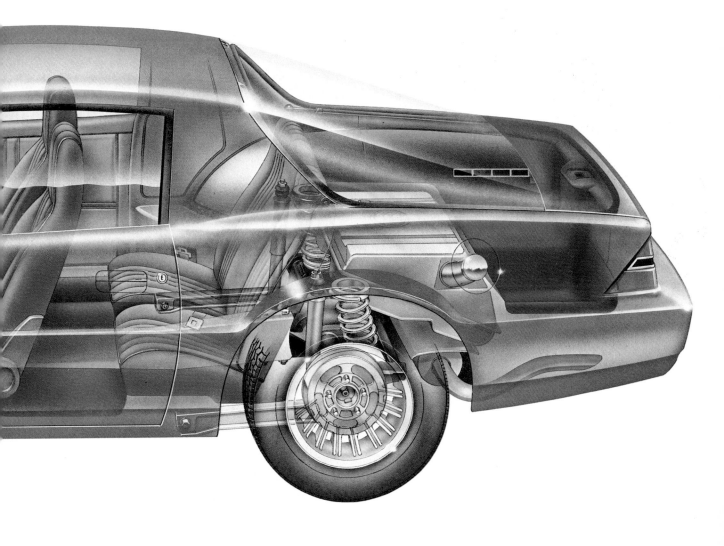

MODEL

Citroën DS (1961)

ENGINE

Location: Front longitudinal
Type: Water-cooled in-line four cylinder with aluminium head and cast iron block
Cubic capacity: 1911 cc 116 57 cu in
Bore × stroke: 78 mm × 100 mm/3.1 in × 3.9 in
Compression ratio: 8 5 : 1
Valve Gear: 2 valves per cylinder operated by single block-mounted camshaft, pushrods and rockers
Fuel supply: Single double choke Weber 24-32 DDC carburettor
Ignition: Coil and distributor, mechanical
Maximum power: 83 bhp (DIN) at 4500 rpm
Maximum torque: 104.88 lb ft (DIN) at 3500 rpm

TRANSMISSION

Layout: Gearbox and transmission ahead of and in unit with engine
Clutch: Single dry plate, hydraulically operated
Gearbox: Four speed manual with synchromesh on top three ratios
  1st 4.16 : 1   3rd 1.44 : 1
  2nd 2.10 : 1 4th 1.00 : 1
Final drive: Spiral bevel
Ratio: 3.31 : 1

SUSPENSION

Front: Independent with upper and lower control arms, pneumatic 'spring' and anti-roll bar
Rear: Independent by trailing arm and pneumatic 'spring'

STEERING

Type: Rack and pinion, hydraulic assistance

BRAKES

Type: Citroën inboard discs front with drums rear, hydraulically operated

WHEELS AND TYRES

Type: Pressed steel wheels with 165 × 400 mm Michelin X radials

BODY/CHASSIS

Type: Steel unitary chassis with four seat saloon body

DIMENSIONS AND WEIGHT

Length: 4801 mm (189.0 in)
Width: 1791 mm (70.5 in)
Wheelbase: 3124 mm (123.0 in)
Track – front: 1449 mm (57.06 in)
    – rear: 1302 mm (51.25 in)
Weight: 1168 kg (2576 lb)

PERFORMANCE

Maximum speed: 95 mph (153 kph)
Acceleration 0–60 mph: 18.4 seconds

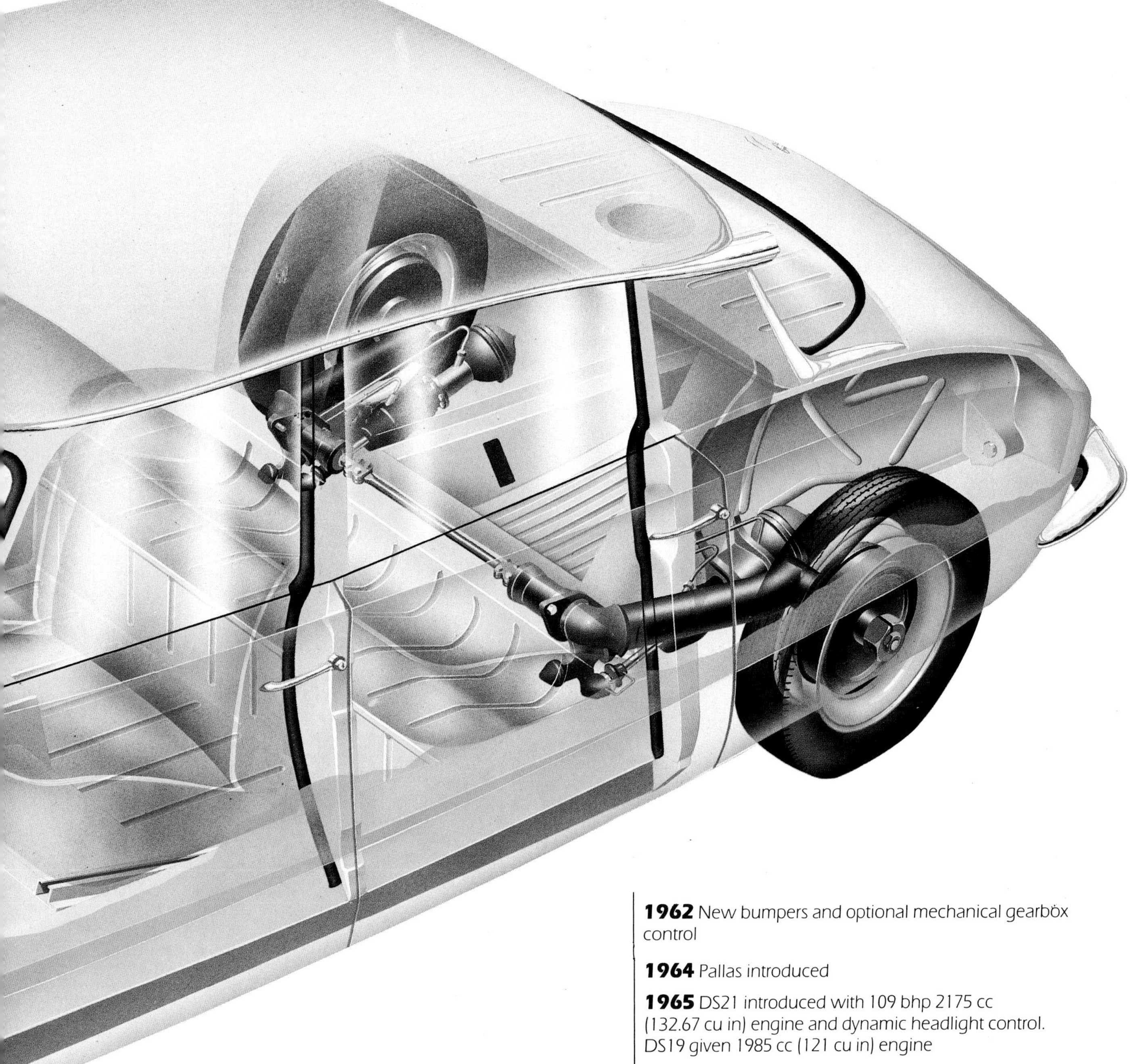

EVOLUTION

1955 Introduced at Paris Motor Show with 1911 cc (116.57 cu in) four-cylinder engine, hydropneumatic suspension and powered clutch and steering

1957 ID introduced with same engine but less power. ID was quickly followed by the Confort

1958 DS Prestige, ID Estate and Ambulance versions appeared

1960 DS Drophead introduced

1961 Power output of DS19 increaed to 83 bhp and top speed to 93 mph (150 kph)

1962 New bumpers and optional mechanical gearbox control

1964 Pallas introduced

1965 DS21 introduced with 109 bhp 2175 cc (132.67 cu in) engine and dynamic headlight control. DS19 given 1985 cc (121 cu in) engine

1966 ID19 receives 1985 cc engine

1968 DS20 replaces DS19

1969 Electronic fuel injection fitted to DS21 to bring power up to 125 bhp. DS production reaches one million

1971 5-speed gearbox introduced on DS21 and D Super. Borg-Warner automatic gearbox available

1972 DS23 introduced with 115 bhp 2347 cc (143.17 cu in) engine (130 bhp with fuel injection). D Super 5 appeared with 2175 cc engine and 5-speed gearboxes

1975 DS range replaced by CX

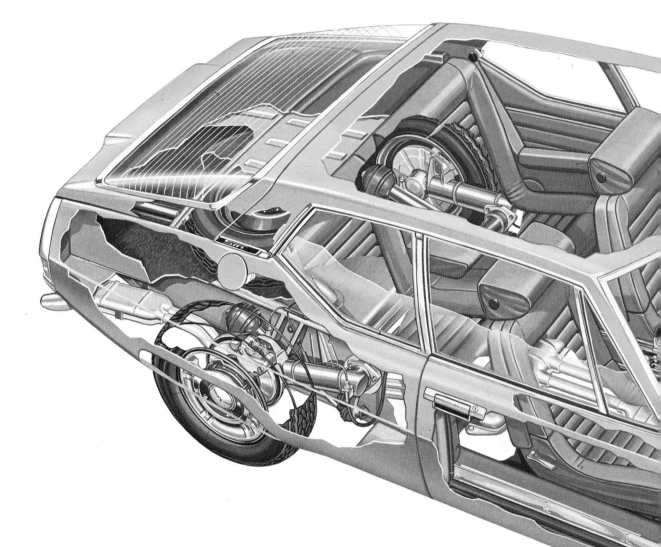

MODEL
Citroën SM (1973)

ENGINE
Location: Front, longitudinal
Type: Water-cooled 90-degree V6 with light-alloy cylinder heads and block. Four main bearings
Cubic capacity: 2670 cc/162.8 cu in
Bore × stroke: 87 mm × 75 mm/ 3.4 in × 2.95 in
Compression ratio: 9.0:1
Valve gear: Two valves per cylinder operated by two chain-driven overhead camshafts per bank of cylinders
Fuel supply: Bosch electronic fuel injection
Ignition: Mechanical by coil and distributor
Maximum power: 178 bhp (DIN) at 5500 rpm
Maximumn torque: 171 lb ft (DIN) at 4000 rpm

TRANSMISSION
Layout: Gearbox in unit with and ahead of engine. Front-wheel drive
Gearbox: Five-speed manual

1st 2.92:1	4th 0.97:1
2nd 1.94:1	5th 0.75:1
3rd 1.32:1	

Final drive: Hypoid bevel
Ratio: 4.375:1

SUSPENSION
Front: Independent with transverse arms, anti-roll bar and hydropneumatic springing with self-levelling
Rear: Independent with trailing arms, anti-roll bar and hydropneumatic springing with self levelling

STEERING
Type: Rack and pinion with variable assistance

BRAKES
Type: Discs front and rear, in-board at front

WHEELS AND TYRES
Type: Steel wheels 6J × 15 in with 205/VR15 Michelin XWX tyres

BODY/CHASSIS
Type: Steel monocoque chassis with bolt-on panels. Steel two-door coupé body

DIMENSIONS AND WEIGHT
Length: 4889 mm (192.5 in)
Width: 1840 mm (72.44 in)
Wheelbase: 2956 mm (116.14 in)
Track – front: 1526 mm (60.08 in)
     – rear: 1326 mm (52.2 in)
Weight: 1450 kg (3197 lb)

PERFORMANCE
Maximum speed: 142 mph (228 kph)
Acceleration 0–60 mph: 8.0 seconds

The SM's sophisticated and unusual layout is immediately apparent in this cutaway. The shortness of the Maserati engine allowed a longitudinal installation and the gearbox could be placed in front of it, thus improving weight distribution (most front-wheel-drive cars have transverse engines). The only springing in the self-levelling hydropneumatic suspension is the use of a pump (driven by the shaft coming from the top of the engine, and sited next to the alternator and air-conditioning compressor) and four high-pressure spheres, the latter visible in each of the wheel-linkage assemblies. The headlamps, as on the Citroën DS series, turned with the front wheels, and the variable-assistance rack can be seen lying across the gearbox. The SM clearly influenced much in Citroën's subsequent CX series saloons

MODEL
Cord 810 (1936)

ENGINE
Location: Front, longitudinal
Type: Water-cooled 90deg V8 built by Lycoming
Cubic capacity: 4729 cc/288.6 cu in
Bore × stroke: 88.9 mm × 92.25 mm/3.5 in × 3.75 in
Compression ratio: 6.5:1
Valve Gear: L-head side-valves, operated by cam and roller mechanism
Fuel supply: 1 in duplex downdraught carburettor
Ignition: Single breaker Autolite
Maximum power: 125 bhp at 3500 rpm

TRANSMISSION
Layout: Front-wheel drive
Clutch: Semi-automatic single dry plate
Gearbox: Electro-vacuum finger-tip controlled four-speed
   1st 2.11:1 3rd 0.90:1
   2nd 1.36:1 4th 0.64:1
Final drive: Spiral bevel
Ratio: 4.3:1

SUSPENSION
Front: Independent, with trailing arms, semi-elliptic leaf springs and friction dampers
Rear: Non-independent, with tubular dead axle, semi-elliptic leaf springs and friction dampers

STEERING
Type: Gemmer centre-point

BRAKES
Type: Hydraulic 304 mm (12 in) drums all round

WHEELS AND TYRES
Type: 6.50 × 16 disc wheels with six-ply tyres

BODY/CHASSIS
Type: Steel boxed channel chassis with separate four-door sedan body

A 1936 Cord 810 Beverly Sedan. The Cord was an advanced front-wheel-drive design and was all the more impressive given the extremely short time allowed for its design and the limited resources. The doors, for example, were made symmetrical to save on tooling; dies were needed only for one front and the opposite rear door

DIMENSIONS AND WEIGHT

Length: 4800 mm (189 in)
Width: 1956 mm (77 in)
Wheelbase: 3175 mm (125 in)
Track – front: 1422 mm (56 in)
   – rear: 1549 mm (61 in)
Weight: 1656 kg (3650 lb)

PERFORMANCE

Maximum speed: 93 mph
(150 kph)
Acceleration 0–60 mph: 20.1
seconds

EVOLUTION

1935 Cord 810 introduced at New York Motor Show, but the first 100 prototypes were not fitted with front-wheel drive. Many orders were attracted but development problems with the transmission and engine delayed the commencement of production

1936 Production began of 810, available as Westchester and Beverly sedans, and four-seat Phaeton and two-seat Sportsman convertibles

1937 Production began of Cord 812, similar to 810 series but with Schweitzer-Cummins supercharger fitted to the Lycoming V8, which raised output to 195 bhp. Production also began of Custom Series Cords, with larger, longer bodies, intended for the top end of the market

1938 Production ended when the receiver sold off the Auburn-Cord-Duesenberg group. In all, 2320 Cord 810 and 812s were produced. The body dies were sold to Hupmobile and used as the basis for the unsuccessful Skylark

The Daimler Double-Six shown was extensively modified to order in 1930 by Thomson & Taylor of Brooklands. Its chassis was redesigned by Reid Railton, the main changes consisting of fitting underslung suspension front and rear to allow a much lower body, and mildy tuning the engine. It was also possibly the first Daimler to be fitted with the Wilson Preselector gearbox, which, with its fluid flywheel coupling and simple quadrant control, allowed an ease of gearchanging far removed from the arcane skills needed to cope with conventional 'crash' boxes. This car was originally a closed, two-door coupé, but after an accident it was put into its present form by Corsica, a British firm which specialised in rebodying cars. It was originally commissioned by a Mr. Hutchings, a wealthy shoe manufacturer, and must have cost considerably more than the £2800 then asked for a Double-Six limousine. It is known that Thomson & Taylor built two such low chassis cars, but the other is no longer believed to be extant. This car was rediscovered in a scrapyard in the early '60s, restored and returned to running order, and purchased by the present owner for £550. It still runs perfectly and is a uniquely beautiful example of the sports styling of the '30s, with a bonnet length of 216 cm (7ft 1 in) and a distance of 274 cm (9 ft) – exactly half the length of the car – between the end of the front dumb irons and the windscreen. Whereas the Double-Six limousines were extraordinarily tall and imposing, this example is so low that the radiator is no higher than the helmet wings

EVOLUTION

1926 First Daimler Double-Six appeared, using two of the six-cylinder blocks to form a 60-degree 7136 cc (435 cu in) V12

1928 Scaled-down '30HP' version of the Double-Six introduced with 3744 cc (228 cu in) V12

1931 Double-Six range improved when a fluid flywheel and a four-speed epicyclic gearbox were offered. Two new V12s of 6511 cc (398 cu in) and 5296 cc (323 cu in) were introduced for the 40-50 and 30-40 models

1934 Sleeve-valve Double-Six production ceased but a conventional overhead (poppet)-valve V12 was built in 50 hp, 6511 cc form. Its body and chassis were slightly smaller than those of the original 50

MODEL
Daimler Double-Six 50, low chassis (1931)

ENGINE
Location: Front, longitudinal
Type: Water-cooled 60-degree V12 with aluminium crankcase, four cylinder heads and aluminium pistons
Cubic capacity: 7136 cc/435.29 cu in
Bore × stroke: 81.5 mm × 114 mm/3.21 in × 4.49 in
Compression ratio: 6:1
Valve gear: Knight double-skin sleeve valves, chain driven by eccentric shafts and 36 con rods
Fuel supply: Two updraught Daimler carburettors, four jets to each cylinder bank
Ignition: Mechanical, with twin coils and magnetos
Maximum power: 150 bhp at 2480 rpm

TRANSMISSION
Layout: Gearbox behind engine, connected by short prop shaft
Clutch: Single dry plate, fabric-lined
Gearbox: Four-speed, non-synchromesh manual (although the car shown is fitted with a four-speed Wilson preselector unit with a fluid coupling)

1st 3.23:1	3rd 1.56:1
2nd 2.08:1	4th 1.00:1

Final drive: Worm and sector
Ratio: 4.86:1 (other ratios were available)

SUSPENSION
Front: Non-independent, with underslung semi-elliptic leaf springs and Hartford friction dampers
Rear: Non-independent, with underslung semi-elliptic leaf springs and Hartford friction dampers

STEERING
Type: Worm and peg unit on bulkhead, with vertical coupling lever to bell-crank on chassis side-member

BRAKES
Type: 38 cm (15 in) drums all round with Dewandre vacuum servo, and expanding brake on prop-shaft

WHEELS AND TYRES
Type: 58 cm (23 in) Daimler wire wheels with 23 × 7.50 crossply tyres

BODY/CHASSIS
Type: Pressed steel channel ladder frame with tubular cross-members, supporting an aluminium, two-door, drop-head body built by Corsica

DIMENSIONS AND WEIGHT
Length: 549 cm (216 in)
Width: 198 cm (78 in)
Wheelbase: 381 cm (150 in)
Track – front: 154 cm (60.5 in)
– rear: 154 cm (60.6 in)
Weight: 2641 kg (5824 lb)

PERFORMANCE
Maximum speed: 100 mph (161 kph)

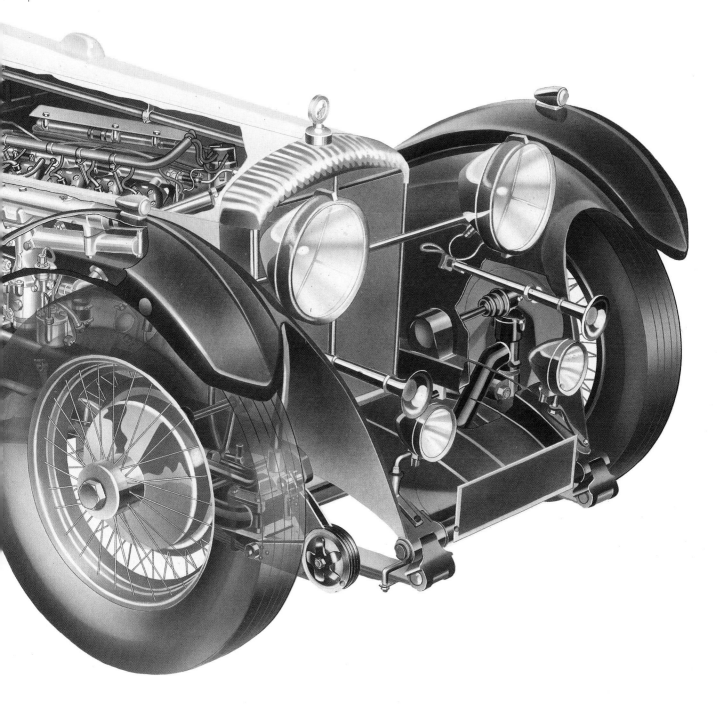

MODEL
Datsun 240Z (1973)

ENGINE
Location: Front, longitudinal
Type: Water-cooled in-line straight six with cast-iron block and aluminium alloy head. Seven main bearings
Cubic capacity: 2393 cc/145.97 cu in
Bore × stroke: 83 mm × 73.7 mm/ 3.26 in × 2.90 in
Compression ratio: 9.0:1
Valve gear: 2 valves per cylinder operated by single chain-driven overhead cam
Fuel supply: 2 Hitachi SU HJG 46W carburettors
Ignition: Mechanical by coil and distributor
Maximum power: 151 bhp (SAE gross) at 5600 rpm
Maximum torque: 146 lb ft (SAE gross) at 4400 rpm

TRANSMISSION
Layout: Clutch and gearbox in unit with engine. Rear-wheel drive
Clutch: Single dry plate
Gearbox: Five speed manual
1st 2.95:1   4th 1.00:1
2nd: 1.86:1   5th 0.85:1
3rd 1.307:1
Final drive: Hypoid bevel
Ratio: 3.9:1

SUSPENSION
Front: Independent with MacPherson struts, lower links torque arms and anti-roll bar
Rear: Independent with struts and lower wishbones

STEERING
Type: Rack and pinion. 2.7 turns lock to lock

BRAKES
Type: Girling/Sumitomo 272 mm (10.7 in) dia discs front with 228 mm (9 in) dia finned drums rear

WHEELS AND TYRES
Type: Pressed steel 4½J × 14 in wheels with 175SR × 14 Bridgestone Speed 20 radials or Dunlop SP Sport CB73 radials

BODY/CHASSIS
Type: Integral steel body with subframes and 2-door, 2+2 coupé body

DIMENSIONS AND WEIGHT
Length: 413 cm (162.8 in)
Width: 163 cm (64.1 in)
Wheelbase: 230 cm (90.7 in)
Track – front: 135 cm (53.35 in)
  – rear: 134 cm (52.95 in)
Weight: 1043 kg (2300 lb)

PERFORMANCE
Maximum speed: 125mph (201 kph)
Acceleration 0–60 mph: 8.0 seconds

The Datsun 240Z owed its great success to the combination of its attractively aggressive looks (partly due to German-born American designer Albrecht Goertz) and rugged mechanical components, such as the immensely strong overhead-cam straight six. This car features the revised rear suspension layout with the drive shaft leaving the differential carrier at 90 degrees rather than trailing back from the diff. The change, introduced for the 1972 model-year cars, prolonged the life of the rear universal joints and made for a smoother transmission

EVOLUTION

1969 Nissan Fairlady 240Z introduced at Tokyo Motor Show with a 2393 cc (146 cu in) straight-six ohc engine

1971 240Z introduced to UK market

1972 Rear suspension and driveshaft geometry improved

1973 260Z introduced with longer stroke 2565 cc (156.5 cu in) version of the six cylinder. In SAE (gross) terms the larger engine produced 11 bhp more than the 240Z

1974 260Z 2+2 introduced with 302 mm (11.9 in) added to wheelbase. Overall the 2+2 was longer, wider, taller and heavier

1975 280Z introduced for North America. Bosch L-Jetronic fuel injection replaced carburettors for emission control reasons. Its performance was similar to that of the first 240

1978 Datsun 280ZX appeared in Europe at the Paris Motor Show. Bodyshell wider and longer with a wider track. Semi-trailing arm rear suspension replaced the previous wishbone and struts

1981 280ZX Turbo introduced with Garrett AiResearch turbocharger on the straight-six engine. Power output was 180 bhp at 5600 rpm

1982 280ZX 2+2 introduced

1983 300ZX and ZX Turbo introduced with 2960 cc (180.5 cu in) V6 engine producing 160 bhp normally aspirated and 227 bhp turbocharged

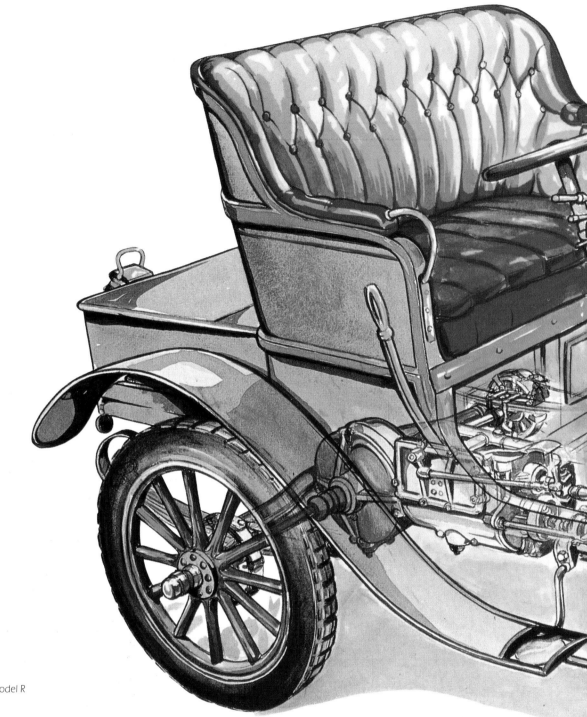

MODEL
De Dion Bouton 8 hp Model R

ENGINE
Location: Front-mounted, vertical
Type: Water-cooled single cylinder with cast-iron block
Cubic capacity: 943 cc/57.5 cu in
Bore × stroke: 100 mm × 120 mm/3.9 in × 4.7 in
Valve gear: Atmospheric inlet valve over camshaft-operated exhaust valve
Fuel supply: De Dion carburettor
Maximum power: Approx 6 hp at 1500 rpm

TRANSMISSION
Layout: Gearbox at rear, separate expanding clutches, rear wheels driven
Gearbox: Two or three speeds and reverse
Final drive: Bevel gears

SUSPENSION
Front: Beam axle, semi-elliptic leaf springs
Rear: De Dion, with tube connecting the wheels behind the differential, three-quarter elliptic leaf springs

BRAKES
Type: Contracting shoes on transmission, hand brake to rear wheel drums

WHEELS
Type: Wood-spoked artillery wheels (wire-spoked in French market) with 710 mm × 90 mm (27.9 in × 3.5 in) tyres

BODY/CHASSIS
Type: Tubular chassis, various two- three- and four-seater body styles

DIMENSIONS
Length: 234 cm (92 in)
Wheelbase: 156 cm (61 in)
Track – front: 112 cm (44 in)
– **rear:** 112 cm (44 in)

PERFORMANCE
Maximum speed: Approx 25 mph/ 40 kph

The 'Populaire' De Dions stood out among the many light cars of the early 1900s, for they were soundly designed, well built and practical. The bonnet was hinged at the rear (hence 'alligator') to give all-round access to the engine. The bulb horn and large brass lamps are essential accessories for a veteran but the De Dion rear suspension was far from commonplace – the right drive shaft and De Dion tube running behind the final drive can be seen in this drawing

MODEL
Delage D8 (1929)

ENGINE
Location: Front, longitundinal
Type: Water-cooled straight eight, cast iron, with detachable block and cylinder head and five main bearings
Cubic capacity: 4050 cc/247 cu in
Bore × stroke: 77 mm × 109 mm/3.0 in × 4.29 in
Compression ratio: 6.8:1
Valve gear: Two valves per cylinder operated by single block-mounted camshaft, pushrods and rockers
Fuel supply: Single Smith-Barriquand five-jet carburettor
Ignition: Delco-Remy coil and distributor
Maximum power: 102 bhp at 3500 rpm

TRANSMISSION
Layout: Gearbox and clutch in unit with engine, driving rear wheels
Clutch: Single dry plate
Gearbox: Four-speed manual
   1st 3.5:1   3rd 1.36:1
   2nd 2.1:1   4th 1.00:1
Final drive: Spiral bevel
Ratio: 3.6:1

SUSPENSION
Front: Non-independent, with beam axle, semi-elliptic leaf springs and friction dampers
Rear: Non-independent, with live axle, semi-elliptic leaf springs and friction dampers

STEERING
Type: Worm and nut

BRAKES
Type: Finned drum brakes all round, cable-operated and assisted by Dewandre vacuum servo

WHEELS AND TYRES
Type: 46 cm (18 in) wire wheels fitted with 7.00/18 crossply tyres

BODY/CHASSIS
Type: Ladder-frame pressed steel chassis with cross members, supporting coachbuilt fabric-covered four-seat tourer

DIMENSIONS AND WEIGHT
Length: 4876 mm (192 in)
Width: 1776 mm (66 in)
Wheelbase: 3098 mm (122 in)
Track – front: 1422 mm (56 in)
   – rear: 1422 mm (56 in)
Weight: 1524 kg (3360 lb)

PERFORMANCE
Maximum speed: 80 mph (129 kph)
Acceleration 0-60 mph: 23 seconds

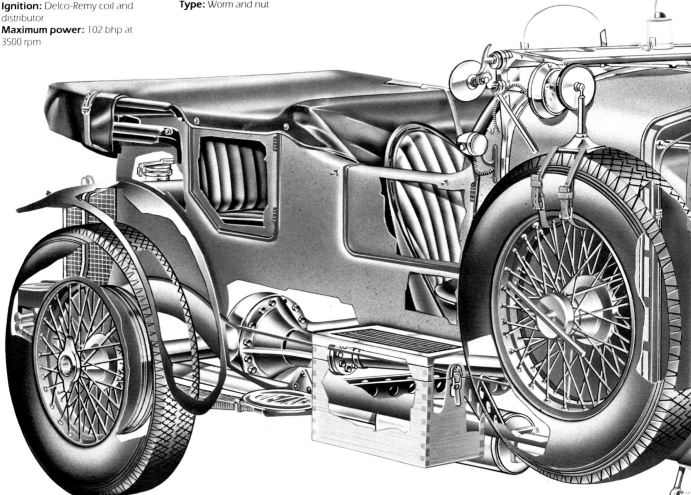

EVOLUTION

1929 D8 Delage introduced with 4050 cc (247 cu in) straight-eight engine, available in three different chassis lengths

1931 D8S sports version introduced with an increased power output of 118 bhp at 3800 rpm

1932 Grand Sport version of the D8 introduced

1934 D8 15 introduced with a 2668 cc (162.7 cu in) engine and transverse leaf and wishbones independent front suspension

1935 D8 85 introduced with a 3591 cc (219 cu in) straight eight. Synchromesh gearboxes and hydraulic brakes were introduced on the six-cylinder D8s

1936 D8 100 introduced with a 4300 cc (262 cu in) engine

1937 Super Sports D8 100 announced

1939 Last of the D8s, the D8 120, introduced with a 4743 cc (289 cu in) straight eight and Cotal electro-magnetic gearbox

The cutaway reveals the mechanical simplicity of the D8's drive train, suspension and chassis. The tall, cast-iron engine featured an unusual valve arrangement wherein the valve spring actually acted directly on the rocker rather than the valve. The engine's weight was partly responsible for the fitting of twin friction dampers to the front beam axle, for the suspension on these cars had been designed with comfort very much in mind, so that the springs were not particularly stiff. The straight-eight had a high torque output and the D8 series cars were all admired for their acceleration and ability to be driven practically everywhere in third and top gears, despite their high ratios. The car shown is a D8 from the first year of production, and its coachwork is far more a workable '20s creation than some of the more flamboyant saloons, coupés, roadsters and Continental tourers which were later featured on D8 chassis and which made the marque so popular with motoring journalists, the nouveaux riches, show people and all who aspired to buy class with style

MODEL
Delahaye 135 (1936)

ENGINE
Location: Front, longitudinal
Type: Water-cooled in-line six-cylinder with cast-iron block and head
Cubic capacity: 3557 cc/216.97 cu in
Bore × stroke: 80 mm × 107 mm/3.15 in × 4.13 in
Compression ratio: 8.2:1
Valve gear: 2 pushrod-operated overhead valves per cylinder
Fuel supply: 3 sidedraught Solex carburettors
Ignition: Mechanical with coil and distributor
Maximum power: 160 bhp at 4200 rpm

TRANSMISSION
Layout: Gearbox behind engine driving rear wheels
Clutch: Single dry plate
Gearbox: Four speed Cotal preselector
  1st 3.456:1   3rd 1.64:1
  2nd 2.22:1   4th 1.00:1
Final drive: Spiral bevel
Ratio: 3.42:1

SUSPENSION
Front: Independent, with under-slung transverse semi-elliptic leaf spring attached to vertical links and friction dampers, the former attached by swinging arms to the chassis, and by radius rods to the side members
Rear: Non-independent with live axle, semi-elliptic leaf springs and friction dampers

STEERING
Type: Worm and nut

BRAKES
Type: Drums front and rear, hydraulically operated and servo assisted

WHEELS AND TYRES
Type: 6.00 × 17 in tyres with wire spoke knock-off wheels

BODY/CHASSIS
Type: Box section steel chassis

DIMENSIONS AND WEIGHT
Length: 4050 mm (159.4 in)
Width: 1700 mm (66.9 in)
Wheelbase: 2946 mm (116 in)
Track – front: 1397 mm (55 in)
    – rear: 1473 mm (58 in)
Weight: 1270 kg (2800 lb)

PERFORMANCE
Maximum speed: 125 mph (201 kph)
Acceleration 0–60 mph: 8.5 seconds

EVOLUTION

1934 Type 135 announced, with 3227 cc (197 cu in) and 3558 cc (217 cu in) straight-six engines, and manual or Cotal electro-magnetic gearbox

1936 Type 135 Compétition and Compétition Spéciale versions introduced, with sparse two-seater sports bodies and engines rated at up to 160 bhp

1946 Production resumed, as Type 135MS with standard engine rated at 130 bhp and factory bodywork

1948 Type 175 derivative introduced

1951 Production of 135/175 ended

A sports racing Delahaye 135 revealed. This particular car was driven with great success by Thailand's Prince Bira in the late 1930s. The cutaway reveals the rather simple and sturdy construction with a live rear axle located by semi-elliptic leaf springs. The independent front suspension features a transverse leaf spring and adjustable friction dampers

MODEL
Delaunay-Belleville F6 (1908)

ENGINE
Location: Front, longitudinal
Type: Individually cast six cylinder, water-cooled
Cubic capacity: 5521 cc/336.8 cu in
Bore × stroke: 98 mm × 122 mm/ 3.86 in × 4.80 in
Valve-gear: Side valve
Fuel supply: Single up-draught Claudel-Hobson carburettor
Ignition: Magneto
Maximum power: 35 hp

TRANSMISSION
Layout: Gearbox in unit with engine driving rear wheels
Gearbox: Four-speed non-synchromesh manual
Final drive: Crown wheel and pinion

SUSPENSION
Front: Non-independent with semi-elliptic leaf springs
Rear: Non-independent, with live axle, semi-elliptic leaf springs and transverse leaf spring

STEERING
Type: Worm and nut

BRAKES
Type: Internal-expanding metal-to-metal drum brakes on rear wheels

WHEELS AND TYRES
Type: Rudge-Whitworth detachable wooden artillery wheels, with metal rims and 880 × 120 beaded-edge tyres

BODY/CHASSIS
Type: Steel U-section ladder-frame chassis with wooden body

DIMENSIONS AND WEIGHT
Length: 4800 mm (189 in)
Width: 1676 mm (66 in)
Wheelbase: 3530 mm (139 in)
Track – front: 1422 mm (56 in)
     – rear: 1447 mm (57 in)
Weight: 2032 kg (4480 lb)

PERFORMANCE
Maximum speed: 65-70 mph (105-113 kph)

The Delaunay-Belleville was built for the pillars of society, clearly intimated in the solidity and sobriety of the styling and engineering. Mechanically it was not a particularly adventurous design, but the Delaunay-Belleville was renowned for the quality of its construction, for they were built in such small numbers as to be made almost entirely by hand. The six-cylinder engine had a single carburettor mounted on the right, the inlet manifold pipe (shown in brown) crossing the engine and entering the block next to the exhaust manifold

EVOLUTION

1908 Type H Delaunay-Belleville introduced with 4-litre six-cylinder engine. In total some 2227 Type H Delaunays were produced between 1908 and 1914, including Type HH, HF and HB variants with a 4426 cc (270 cu in) engine. Type C also introduced with an 8-litre six. The CA featured a 9.3-litre engine and 83 Type C and CA Delaunays were built between 1908 and 1913. The Grand SMT appeared, with an 11,846 cc (722.6 cu in) engine. Type F and Type I were also introduced; 814 Type Fs were built up to 1916 and 185 Type Is up to 1912

1913 The Type K was introduced with a 4-litre engine and 231 were produced up to 1916. The Type M was introduced that year with 4.9 or 5.7-litre engines. 156 were built up to 1916

1914 The 8-litre Type O was introduced and 55 were produced up to 1916

MODEL
De Tomaso Pantera GT5 (1985)

ENGINE
Location: Mid-mounted, longitudinal
Type: Water-cooled Ford V8, cast-iron block and head with five main bearings
Cubic capacity: 5763 cc/351.5 cu in
Bore × stroke: 101.6 mm × 89 mm/4.0 in × 3.5 in
Compression ratio: 8.5:1
Valve gear: Two inclined valves per cylinder operated by pushrods and rockers, hydraulic tappets and single camshaft mounted in centre of vee
Fuel supply: Single Holley 650 CFM downdraught four-barrel carburettor
Ignition: Mechanical by coil and distributor
Maximum power: 350 bhp (DIN) at 6000 rpm
Maximum torque: 333 lb ft (DIN) at 3800 rpm

TRANSMISSION
Layout: Gearbox and clutch in unit with engine, driving rear wheels
Clutch: Single dry plate
Gearbox: ZF five-speed manual, all-synchromesh

1st 2.230:1	3rd 1.040:1
2nd 1.475	4th 0.846:1
	5th 0.705:1

Final drive: Spiral bevel, limited-slip differential
Ratio: 4.22:1, or 'Le Mans' option of 3.77:1

SUSPENSION
Front: Independent, with wishbones, coil springs, telescopic dampers and anti-roll bar
Rear: Independent, with wishbones, coil springs, telescopic dampers and anti-roll bar

STEERING
Type: Rack and pinion

BRAKES
Type: Dual circuit servo assisted, radial-finned discs all round, 28 cm (11 in) diameter

WHEELS AND TYRES
Type: 38.1 cm (15 in) wheels with 25.4 cm (10 in) rims front and 33 cm (13 in) rims rear, fitted respectively with 285/40 and 345/35 VR tyres

BODY/CHASSIS
Type: Steel two-door, two-seat coupé built with integral steel chassis

DIMENSIONS AND WEIGHT
Length: 4267 mm (168 in)
Width: 1970 mm (77.5 in)
Wheelbase: 2510 mm (99 in)
Track – front: 1510 mm (59.5 in)
  – rear: 1580 mm (62 in)
Weight: 1420 kg (3131 lb)

PERFORMANCE
Maximum speed: 162 mph (260 kph)
Acceleration 0-60 mph: 5.4 seconds

EVOLUTION

1970 Pantera launched. Design followed similar lines to 1969 Mangusta, with two-seater sports body styled by Tom Tjaarda of Ghia. The Pantera was powered by Ford's 5763 cc (351 cu in) V8 with a ZF five-speed gearbox, and was available in two forms, the L and the GTS. The engine of the standard Pantera L produced 330 bhp; in the GTS form the engine power output was raised to 350 bhp. The Pantera GTS could be distinguished from the L by the addition of front and rear spoilers

1982 Pantera GT5 announced, with same mechanical specification as GTS but fitted with wider wheels. Claimed maximum speed was 162 mph (261 kph)

1984 Pantera GT5S introduced, with minor styling changes and GT5 mechanical specification, continued through record half of 1980s

The cutaway reveals that although the Pantera was first shown in 1970, the design did not date significantly in the next dozen years in terms of race and performance-car construction

MODEL
Facel Vega HK500 (1960)

ENGINE
Location: Front, longitudinal
Type: Water-cooled Chrysler V8 with cast-iron block and head
Cubic capacity: 6286 cc/383.45 cu in
Bore × stroke: 107.95 mm × 85.5 mm/4.25 in × 3.37 in
Compression ratio: 10.1
Valve gear: 2 valves per cylinder operated by pushrods and hydraulic tappets
Fuel supply: 2 four-choke (48 mm/ 1.8 in bore) Carter downdraught carburettors
Ignition: Coil and distributor, mechanical
Maximum power: 360 bhp (SAE) at 5200 rpm
Maximum torque: 425 lb ft (SAE)

TRANSMISSION
Layout: Gearbox and clutch in unit, behind engine, driving rear wheels
Clutch: Borg and Beck single dry plate
Gearbox: Four-speed all-synchromesh manual
   1st 3.45:1   3rd 1.37:1
   2nd 1.96:1 4th 1:1
or Chrysler epicyclic three-speed automatic gearbox
Final drive: Hypoid bevel
Ratio: 2.93:1

SUSPENSION
Front: Independent, with coil springs, wishbones and anti-roll torsion bar
Rear: Live rear axle with semi-elliptic leaf springs

STEERING
Type: Gemmer cam and roller

BRAKES
Type: Discs front and rear

WHEELS AND TYRES
Type: Ventilated light-alloy wheels with centre-lock hubs, and 6.70-15 Michelin X radial tyres

BODY/CHASSIS
Type: Tubular steel chassis and all-steel body

DIMENSIONS AND WEIGHT
Length: 4797 mm (181 in)
Width: 1803 mm (71 in)
Wheelbase: 2867 mm (105 in)
Track – front: 1410 mm (55.5 in)
   – **rear:** 1460 mm (57.5 in)
Weight: (unladen) 1829 kg (4032 lb)

PERFORMANCE
Maximum speed: 140 mph (225.3 kph)
Acceleration: 0-60 mph (96.5 kph) 8.4 seconds

EVOLUTION

1954 Facel Vega introduced at Paris Motor Show, with a 4.5-litre (274.5 cu in) Chrysler V8, three-speed Torqueflite or four-speed Pont-a-Mousson manual gearbox

1955 Facel Vega put into limited production

1956 4.8-litre (293 cu in) Chrysler V8 fitted. Excellence four-door pillarles saloon introduced

1957 5.4-litre (329.5 cu in) Chrysler V8 fitted, suspension improved and Hydrosteer power steering and right-hand drive offered as optional extras

1958 HK500 introduced with longer wheelbase, wider track and 5.9-litre (360 cu in) Chrysler V8

1960 Disc brakes fitted as standard to the HK500 and to the last of the Excellences. Facellia offered as a 2+2 coupé, four-seater or convertible, with a new Facel Vega 1.6-litre engine

1961 Facel Vega II introduced, with a 6.3-litre (384 cu in) Chrysler V8 and restyled, cleaner body shape. Facellia engine improved and model renamed Facel III and fitted with a Volvo 1.8-litre engine and gearbox

1962 The receiver was called in and SFERMA took over. The Facel III was renamed the Facel 6 and fitted with a 2.8-litre BMC six-cylinder engine. Only 46 were built, and total Facellia production was 1200 cars. The Facel II was still selling in small numbers

1964 Facel Le Mans project abandoned. In September the last Facels were built before the factory closed

MODEL
Ferrari 250 GTO (1962)

ENGINE
Location: Front, longitudinal
Type: Water-cooled, 60-degree V12, all alloy, with seven-bearing crankshaft
Cubic capacity: 2953 cc/180 cu in
Bore × stroke: 73 mm × 58.8 mm/2.87 in × 2.31 in
Compression ratio: 9.6:1
Valve gear: Two valves per cylinder operated by single overhead camshafts
Fuel supply: Six Weber twin-choke 38 DCN carburettors
Ignition: Mechanical, with twin Marelli distributors
Maximum power: 295 bhp at 7500 rpm
Maximum torque: 203 lb ft at 5500 rpm

TRANSMISSION
Layout: Clutch and gearbox in unit with engine
Clutch: Fitchel & Sachs, single dry plate
Gearbox: Five-speed manual with Porsche-patented synchromesh

1st	3.11:1	3rd	1.50:1
2nd	2.05:1	4th	1.21:1
		5th	1.03:1

Final drive: Limited-slip differential
Ratio: 4.85:1, 4.57:1, 4.25:1, 4.0:1, 3.89:1, 3.77:1, 3.66:1, 3.55:1

SUSPENSION
Front: Independent, with double wishbones, coil springs and telescopic dampers
Rear: Non-independent, with rigid axle and semi-elliptic leaf springs

STEERING
Type: ZF worm and sector

BRAKES
Type: Dunlop discs all round

WHEELS AND TYRES
Type: Rudge hubs (42 mm/1.6 in) with 38 cm (15 in) Borrani wire-spoke wheels with Dunlop racing tyres, 600 × 15 RW3711 front and 700 × 15 RW3808 rear

BODY/CHASSIS
Type: Two-door, two-seat aluminium sports coupé built over tubular steel spaceframe

DIMENSIONS AND WEIGHT
Length: 4445 mm (175 in)
Width: 1600 mm (63 in)
Wheelbase: 2590 mm (102 in)
Track – front: 1346 mm (53 in)
          – rear: 1354 mm (53.3 in)
Weight: 1270 kg (2800 lb)

PERFORMANCE
Maximum speed: 165 mph (266 kph)
Acceleration 0-60 mph: 6 seconds

The Ferrari GTO exposed, revealing its tubular spaceframe and aluminium bodywork (the latter was built by Scaglietti), main chassis members and suspension design

EVOLUTION

1952 Vignale-bodied prototype 250 Sport first tested, the earliest Ferrari fitted with a 3-litre version of Colombo's V12. 250MM, based on the Sport, also shown. In all, 17 Pininfarina coupés, 13 Vignale spyders and one coupé were built

1953 250 Europa introduced, with a 3-litre version of Lampredi's 4.5-litre V12. Approximately 20 were built

1954 Second Series 250 GT Europa announced, with the short Colombo engine and styled by Pininfarina; about 32 were made

1956 250 GT Boano 'low-roof' coupé announced, of which 70-80 were made, along with the 250 GT long-wheelbase Tour de France Berlinetta Coupé, of which 74 were made

1957 250 GT Pininfarina Cabriolet launched (about 45 were built). The 250 GT 'high-roof' Ellena coupé introduced (50 were made), as was the sports-racing 250 Testa Rossa, designed for the 1958 World Sports Car Championship (34 were built). Also introduced was the long-wheelbase Pininfarina-styled 250 GT California Spyder (46 made)

1958 250 GT Pininfarina Coupé launched. 350 were built

1959 Short-wheelbase GT Berlinetta launched for racing. 162 were made

1960 Short-wheelbase 250 GT California Spyder launched. 55 were built

1962 250 GT 2+2 introduced, styled by Pininfarina; about 900 were made. 250 GT Berlinetta Lusso, styled by Pininfarina, also announced (400 were made) and the 250 GTO of which 39 were built

1964 250 GTO modified in detail, this variant sometimes dubbed GTO 64

MODEL
Ferrari 275GTB/4 (1967)

ENGINE
Location: Front, longitudinal
Type: V12, water cooled with light-alloy block and heads. Seven main bearings
Cubic capacity: 3286 cc/200 cu in
Bore × stroke: 77 mm × 58.8 mm/ 3.0 in × 2.3 in
Compression ratio: 9.8:1
Valve gear: 2 valves per cylinder inclined at 54 degrees operated by two chain-driven overhead camshafts per bank of cylinder
Fuel supply: 6 Weber twin-choke 40 DCN carburettors
Ignition: Mechanical by coil and distributor
Maximum power: 300 bhp (DIN) at 8000 rpm
Maximum torque: 217 lb ft (DIN) at 6000 rpm

TRANSMISSION
Layout: Clutch mounted at front with engine. Final drive and gearbox mounted at rear connected to clutch housing by torque tube
Clutch: Single dry plate
Gearbox: Five speed manual with Porsche-type synchromesh
1st 3.076:1	4th 1.250:1
2nd 2.119:1	5th 1.038:1
3rd 1.572:1	
Final drive: Hypoid bevel with limited-slip differential
Ratio: 3.555:1

SUSPENSION
Front: Independent with double wishbones and coaxial coil spring/ Koni dampers
Rear: Independent with double wishbones, coil springs and Koni dampers mounted above top wishbone

STEERING
Type: Recirculating ball

BRAKES
Type: Dunlop disc brakes, 27.9 cm (10.9 in) dia front and 27.4 cm (10.7 in) dia rear

WHEELS AND TYRES
Type: Cast alloy 650 × 14 wheels with 205VR14 Pirelli Cinturato tyres

BODY/CHASSIS
Type: Ladder chassis in oval section tube with tubular outrigger side-members and diagonal bracing. Two-door two-seat coupé body welded and bolted to chassis

DIMENSIONS AND WEIGHT
Length: 441 cm (173.6 in)
Width: 172.5 cm (67.9 in)
Wheelbase: 240 cm (94.5 in)
Track – front: 140 cm (55.1 in)
    – rear: 142 cm (55.9 in)
Weight: 1100 kg (2425 lb)

PERFORMANCE
Maximum speed: 161 mph (260 kph)
Acceleration 0–60 mph: 6.2 seconds

EVOLUTION

1964 Introduced in GTB (Berlinetta coupé) and GTS (spyder convertible) forms, both styled by Pininfarina. The engine, Colombo-designed V12, had a capacity of 3286 cc (200 cu in) and in standard form produced a claimed 280 bhp at 7600 rpm; with the option of six twin-choke Webers, power rose to 300 bhp at 7500 rpm

1965 Nose re-shaped to provide extra downforce at high speeds. Transmission modified, with a torque tube installed between the engine and gearbox/final drive

1966 275 GTB/4 introduced, with a four-cam version of the V12 engine and fitted with six Weber carburettors. The engine produced 300 bhp at 8000 rpm. Other changes included the adoption of a ZF limited-slip differential and wider wheels

1968 Ferrari 275 discontinued. Total production: 950 (approx)

The complexity of the 1967 275 GTB/4 revealed. In the quest for equal weight distribution the engine was mounted at the front and the transmission in the rear. To begin with the thin propellor shaft between the two was supported by a single centre steady-bearing but as the car was developed a torque tube was introduced, rigidly joining engine and transmission, and the prop shaft ran within that. The oval section spaceframe was not as torsionally rigid as it should have been, and it was also difficult to repair, being made of a special grade of steel

MODEL
Ferrari Dino 246 GT (1971)

ENGINE
Location: Mid, transverse
Type: Water-cooled 65-degree V6 with cast-iron block and alloy heads
Cubic capacity: 2418 cc/147.5 cu in
Bore × stroke: 92.5 mm × 60 mm/ 3.64 in × 2.36 in
Compression ratio: 9.0:1
Valve gear: 2 46-degree inclined valves per cylinder operated by twin gear- and chain-driven overhead camshafts per cylinder bank
Fuel supply: 3 Weber 40 DCF twin-choke downdraught carburettors
Ignition: Marelli transistorised
Maximum power: 195 bhp (DIN) at 7600 rpm
Maximum torque: 166 lb ft (DIN) at 5500 rpm

TRANSMISSION
Layout: Gearbox mounted beneath engine
Clutch: Single dry plate
Gearbox: Five-speed manual synchromesh

1st 3.07:1	4th 1.25:1
2nd 2.12:1	5th 0.86:1
3rd 1.52:1	

Final drive: Helical
Ratio: 3.62:1

SUSPENSION
Front: Independent with unequal length wishbones, coil springs and dampers and anti-roll bar
Rear: Independent by unequal length wishbones, coil springs and dampers and anti-roll bar

STEERING
Type: Rack and pinion. 3.2 turns lock to lock

BRAKES
Type: Discs all round. 27 cm (10.6 in) diameter front. 25.4 cm (10 in) diameter rear. Vacuum servo-assisted

WHEELS AND TYRES
Type: Light alloy wheels with Michelin 205/70VR14 tyres

BODY/CHASSIS
Type: Multitubular steel frame with square-section tubing and steel coupé body

DIMENSIONS AND WEIGHT
Length: 4343 mm (171 in)
Width: 1702 mm (67 in)
Wheelbase: 2375 mm (93.5 in)
Track – front: 1448 mm (57 in)
– rear: 1454 mm (57.25 in)

PERFORMANCE
Maximum speed: 151 mph (243 kph)
Acceleration 0–60 mph: 6.8 seconds
Fuel consumption: 16–20 mpg

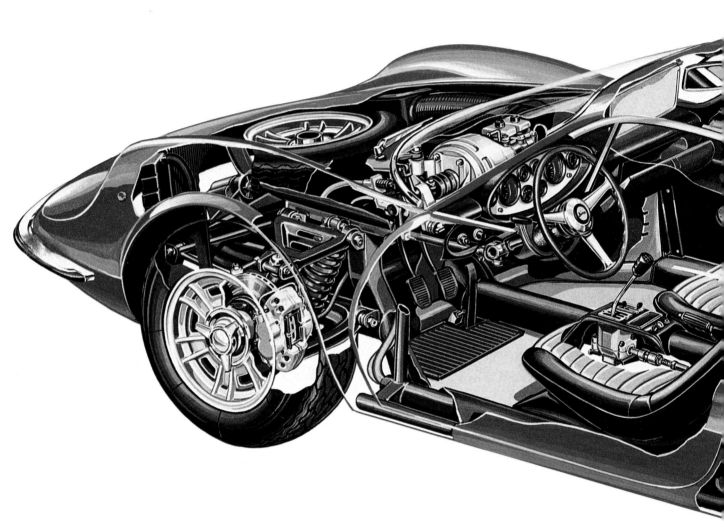

A cutaway of the rare 206GT Dino; it differed from the 246 in having an alloy body and the 2-litre version of the V6. Visually it was virtually impossible to distinguish the 206 from the 246. When Fiat undertook production of the Dino V6 engine they used cast iron rather than alloy for the castings. The engine is from a Fiat Dino

EVOLUTION

1965 Prototype shown by Pininfarina at Paris show with longitudinally-mounted V6

1966 Second prototype introduced at Turin Show. It was higher than the first car and featured revised headlight design and smaller side airscoops

1968 Dino 206GT entered production with 2-litre V6 mounted transversely

1969 Dino 246GT replaced 206GT, with larger version of the V6 with bore and stroke increased to give 2418 cc (147.5 cu in). The block was now in cast iron and produced by Fiat. The 246GT was longer overall and in the wheelbase than the 206GT

1972 GTS Cabriolet introduced with Targa top

1974 Dino production ceased. Total production was 2700 coupés and nearly 1200 cabriolets

ABOVE When Fiat took over production of the Dino V6 engine they used cast iron rather than alloy for the castings. The engine is from a Fiat Dino

MODEL
Ferrari 308 quattrovalvole (1983)

ENGINE
Location: Mid/rear, transverse
Type: Water-cooled V8 with light-alloy block and heads, wet cylinder liners. Five main bearings
Cubic capacity: 2927 cc/178.55 cu in
Bore × stroke: 81 mm × 71 mm/3.19 in × 2.79 in
Compression ratio: 9.2:1
Valve gear: 4 valves per cylinder operated via thimble tappets by two belt-driven overhead camshafts per bank of cylinders
Fuel supply: Bosch K-Jetronic fuel injection
Ignition: Electronic
Maximum power: 240 bhp at 7000 rpm
Maximum torque: 192 lb ft at 5000 rpm

TRANSMISSION
Layout: Transmission below and behind engine, housed in same casing as the engine sump
Clutch: Single dry plate
Gearbox: Five-speed manual
1st 3.390:1   4th 1.244:1
2nd 2.353:1   5th 0.919:1
3rd 1.693:1
Final drive: Helical spur with limited slip differential
Ratio: 3.824:1

SUSPENSION
Front: Independent with double wishbones, coil springs, telescopic dampers and anti-roll bar
Rear: Independent with double wishbones, coil springs, telescopic dampers and anti-roll bar

STEERING
Type: Rack and pinion. 3.28:1 turns lock to lock

BRAKES
Type: Discs front and rear. 1489 sq cm (230.8 sq in) swept area front, 1242 sq cm (192.5 sq in) rear

WHEELS AND TYRES
Type: Alloy wheels with Michelin TRX 240/55 VR415 radials

BODY/CHASSIS
Type: Tubular with 2-door, 2-seat steel coupé body

DIMENSIONS AND WEIGHT
Length: 423 cm (166.5 in)
Width: 172 cm (67.72 in)
Wheelbase: 234 cm (92.13 in)
Track – front: 146 cm (57.48 in)
**   – rear:** 146 cm (57.48 in)
Weight: 1275 kg (2811 lb)

PERFORMANCE
Maximum speed: 158 mph (255 kph)
Acceleration 0–60 mph: 6.8 seconds

EVOLUTION

1974 Bertone-styled 308 introduced, with dohc, V8 with a displacement of 2927 cc (178.5 cu in) and, in its original version, four Weber carburettors. The Bertone body had an additional rear seat, hence the full designation of 308 GT4 2+2. 2-litre version (208 GT4) produced for Italian market only

1975 Pininfarina-bodied 308GTB introduced with only two seats and bearing a close resemblance to the Dino 246. The GTB's body was of glassfibre

1977 The GTB was re-skinned in pressed steel. Open-top (Targa) 308 GTS released

1981 Bosch K-Jetronic fuel injection and Marelli Digiplex electronic ignition were introduced in order to meet more stringent emission regulations. New model designations were 308 GTBi and GTSi. 308 GT4 gave way to Mondial 8

1982 Re-designed cylinder head introduced on 308 and Mondial featuring four valves per cylinder (known as 'quattrovalvole')

1985 Capacity of the V8 engine raised from 3 to 3.2 litres

1986 Subtle styling update plus 3.2-litre engine led to 328 GTB designation superseding 308 QV

The 308GTB quattrovalvole is still on traditional Ferrari lines with a square-section tubular chassis and separate body. Although early GTB bodies were of glassfibre the later cars were all steel

The Ferrari 365/BB was introduced in 1973 and soon became known as the Boxer. Its flat-twelve engine, pictured below left, followed the style of the company's 3-litre Formula One engines with the opposing con rods working on a single crank. The gearbox had to be fitted underneath the engine which led to the whole unit sitting high in the car, as can be seen above

EVOLUTION

1971 Introduced at Turin Show as mid-engined 4.4-litre coupé

1973 365GT4BB in production, with 4390 cc (267 cu in) flat 12 engine. Discontinued in 1976, when almost 400 had been built

1976 Berlinetta Boxer 512 introduced with 4942 cc (296.5 cu in) engine

1981 Weber carburettors replaced by Bosch K-Jetronic fuel injection to form the 512BBi. Both maximum power and torque produced at lower rpm and fuel and emission standards improved. Suspension revised to suit Michelin TRX tyres

1984 Berlinetta Boxer 512i discontinued after over 2500 Boxers built, to be replaced by four valve per cylinder Testa Rossa

FERRARI BERLINETTA BOXER
BB512i (1984)

ENGINE
Location: Mid, longitudinal
Type: Flat 12 with light-alloy block and heads, cast-iron cylinder liners and seven main bearings
Cubic capacity: 4942 cc/296.5 cu in
Bore × stroke: 82 mm × 78 mm/ 3.23 in × 3.07 in
Compression ratio: 9.2:1
Valve gear: 2 inclined valves per cylinder operated by twin belt-driven overhead camshafts per cylinder bank
Fuel supply: Bosch K-Jetronic fuel injection

Ignition: Marelli electronic
Maximum power: 340 bhp (DIN) at 6000 rpm
Maximum torque: 333 lb ft (DIN) at 4200 rpm

TRANSMISSION
Layout: Gearbox in unit with differential, mounted below engine
Clutch: Double dry plate
Gearbox: Five speed manual

1st 2.937:1	4th 1.200:1
2nd 2.099:1	5th 0.913:1
3rd 1.587:1	

Final drive: Hypoid bevel with limited slip differential
Ratio: 3.214:1

SUSPENSION
Front: Independent by double wishbones, coil springs and anti-roll bar.
Rear: Independent by double wishbones, coil springs and 2 telescopic dampers per wheel

STEERING
Type: Rack and pinion

BRAKES
Type: Discs front and rear

WHEELS AND TYRES
Type: Alloy 7.5 in × 415 mm front and 9.0 in × 415 mm with Michelin TRX tyres 180TR × 415 front and 210TR × 415 rear.

BODY/CHASSIS
Type: Tubular steel chassis with steel two-door, two-seat coupé bodywork.

DIMENSIONS AND WEIGHT
Length: 440 cm (173.2 in)
Width: 183 cm (72.05 in)
Wheelbase: 250 cm (98.43 in)
Track – front: 150 cm (59.06 in)
– rear: 157 cm (61.89 in)
Weight: 1499 kg (3305 lb)

PERFORMANCE
Maximum speed: 170 mph (274 kph)
Acceleration 0–60 mph: 5.6 seconds

MODEL
Ford Thunderbird (1983)

ENGINE
Location: Front, longitudinal
Type: Water-cooled 60-degree V6 with cast-iron block and light alloy heads
Cubic capacity: 3797 cc/231.6 cu in
Bore × stroke: 96.8 mm × 86 mm/ 3.81 in × 3.38 in
Compression ratio: 8.6:1
Valve gear: Two overhead valves per cylinder operated by pushrods, rockers and single camshaft at centre of vee, belt-driven from crankshaft
Fuel supply: Single 4-K 700 DR downdraught double-barrel carburettor, mechanical fuel pump
Ignition: Motorcraft transistorised
Maximum power: 120 bhp at 3600 rpm
Maximum torque: 205 lb ft at 1600 rpm

TRANSMISSION
Layout: Gearbox in unit with engine, driving rear wheels
Clutch: Torque convertor
Gearbox: Select-Shift three-speed automatic
   1st   2.46:1 3rd   1.00:1
   2nd 1.46:1
Final drive: Hypoid bevel
Ratio: 2.73:1

SUSPENSION
Front: Independent, with McPherson struts, coil springs, telescopic dampers and anti-roll bar
Rear: Non-independent, with rigid axle, lower trailing radius arms, upper oblique arms, coil springs and telescopic dampers

STEERING
Type: Rack and pinion, servo-assisted

BRAKES
Type: Discs front, 25.5 cm (10 in) diameter, drums rear, 23 cm (9 in) diameter, servo-assisted

WHEELS AND TYRES
Type: Pressed steel, 36 cm (14 in) wheels with 13 cm (5 in) rims, fitted with P215/70R14 BSW radial tyres

BODY/CHASSIS
Type: Chassis integral with steel two-door, five-seat coupé body

DIMENSIONS AND WEIGH
Length: 502 cm (197.6 in)
Wheelbase: 264 cm (104 in)
Track – front: 147 cm (58 in)
     – rear:** 149 cm (58.5 in)
Weight: 1392 kg (3069 lb)

PERFORMANCE
Maximum speed: 116 mph (187 kph)
Acceleration 0-60 mph: 13.5 seconds

EVOLUTION

1954 Introduced in September with a 4785 cc (292 cu in) V8

1956 5112 cc (312 cu in) V8 offered as an option

1957 Restyled, and tailfins added

1958 Four-seat Thunderbird appeared

1961 The car was restyled, and offered with a 6390 cc (390 cu in) V8 with outputs of 300, 375 and 401 bhp and Cruise-O-Matic transmission

1962 A two-seat roadster was reintroduced, and a 6653 cc (406 cu in) V8 was offered

1965 Disc brakes fitted at the front. Engines ranged between 6390 cc (390 cu in) and 6997 cc (427 cu in) V8s

1966 The last convertible model was offered

1967 A four-door model was offered, and the range made with body-on-frame construction

1970 Restyled, powered by a 7030 cc (429 cu in) V8 and Cruise-O-Matic transmission

1972 A new, two-door range was offered. The millionth Thunderbird was sold

1975 Similar in appearance, the new models were longer and heavier, powered by a 7538 cc (460 cu in) V8

1977 Smaller, Thunderbird range offered, fitted with a 4949 cc (302 cu in) V8

1980 Smaller still, the Thunderbird was fitted with a 3277 cc (200 cu in) in-line six

1983 Restyled, the Thunderbird became an aerodynamic two-door coupé with engine options of the 3277 cc six, a 4950 cc (302 cu in) V8 and a turbocharged 2300 cc (140 cu in) in-line four

1985 Interior restyled

1987 Restyled, slightly larger and heavier, with ABS brakes and automatic ride control. Power output of turbo engine incresed to 190 bhp

1988 Limited functional changes pending all-new 1989 range

With comfort as a priority, automatic transmission and seating for five, the modern Thunderbird has little in common with its now-classic forebears of the 1950s other than its name, compact size and above-average performance. This is the 3.8-litre V6 version of 1983

1972 Mustang Mach 1, one of the last muscle cars

MODEL
Mustang Mach I (1972)

ENGINE
Location: Front, longitudinal
Type: Water-cooled V8 with cast-iron block and heads, known as Super Cobra-Jet Ram-Air
Cubic capacity: 7030 cc/429 cu in
Bore × stroke: 110.7 mm × 91.2 mm/4.36 in × 3.59 in
Compression ratio: 11.3:1
Valve gear: 2 valves per cylinder operated by single camshaft mounted in centre of vee, pushrods, rockers and solid tappets
Fuel supply: Single Holley 9510 D00F downdraught 4-barrel carburettor
Ignition: Mechanical with coil and distributor
Maximum power: 375 bhp (SAE gross) at 5600 rpm
Maximum torque: 450 lb ft at 5600 rpm

TRANSMISSION
Layout: Clutch and gearbox in unit behind engine
Clutch: Single dry plate with manual gearbox
Gearbox: Four-speed manual all-synchromesh gearbox or Select Shift Cruise-o-Matic three-speed automatic with torque convertor (automatic ratios in brackets)

1st	2.32:1	3rd	1.29:1
	(2.46:1)		(1.00:1)
2nd	1.69:1	4th	1.00:1
	(1.46:1)		

Final drive: Hypoid bevel
Ratio: 3.50:1

SUSPENSION
Front: Independent with wishbones, lower trailing links, coil springs, telescopic dampers and anti-roll bar
Rear: Live axle with semi-elliptic leaf springs and inclined telescopic dampers one each side of axle

STEERING
Type: Recirculating ball

BRAKES
Type: Discs front and drums rear, with 1824 sq cm (282.8 sq in) rubbed area

WHEELS AND TYRES
Type: Steel wheels 14 in × 6 in with E-200 Firestone crossply tyres

BODY/CHASSIS
Type: Integral steel chassis with two-door coupé body

DIMENSIONS AND WEIGHT
Length: 4722 mm (185.9 in)
Width: 1882 mm (74.1 in)
Wheelbase: 2768 mm (109.0 in)
Track – front: 1562 mm (61.5 in)
– rear: 1549 mm (61.0 in)
Weight: 1460 kg (3220 lb)

PERFORMANCE
Maximum speed: 130 mph (209 kph)
Acceleration 0–60 mph: 5.7 seconds

ABOVE Although it shared the same front-engine, live-rear-axle layout as the muscle-car era Mach 1 shown in the main cutaway, the 1984 SVO Mustang was a far more advanced machine, boasting electronic fuel injection and engine management to complement the intercooled turbocharged engine. The SVO's coil-sprung rear axle was rather better located than the simple cart-sprung affair of the Mach 1, using a variety of links and gas-filled Koni dampers to improve its handling

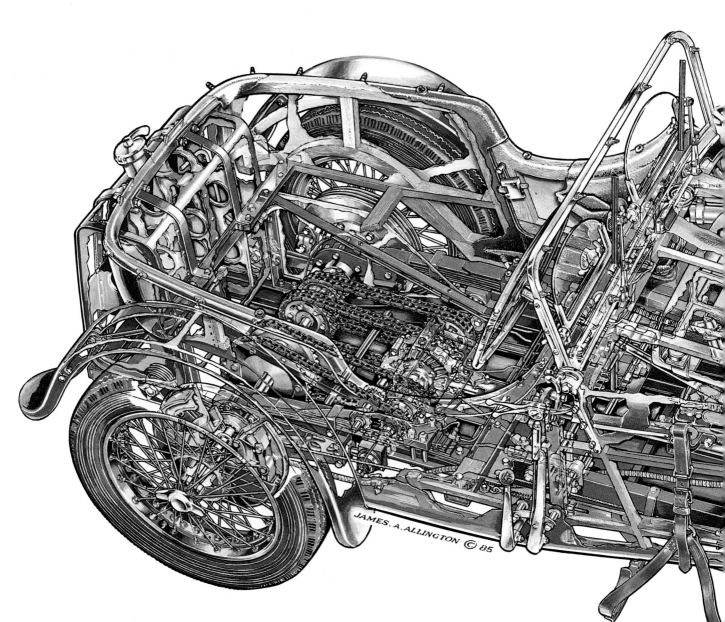

JAMES. A. ALLINGTON © 85

The Frazer Nash Shelsey (named after the famous Shelsey Walsh hillclimbs) shows the curious duplex chain-drive system used by Frazer Nash long after every other manufacturer had changed to the more conventional shaft drive. The overhead-camshaft engine was Frazer Nash's own, known as the 'Gough' after its designer Albert Gough

MODEL
Frazer Nash Shelsley

ENGINE
Location: Front longitudinal
Type: In-line water-cooled four-cylinder
Cubic capacity: 1496 cc/91.26 cu in
Bore × stroke: 69 mm × 100 mm/ 2.72 in × 3.94 in
Compression ratio: 8.5:1
Valve gear: 2 overhead valves per cylinder operated by a single chain-driven overhead camshaft
Fuel supply: Two SU carburettors, mounted on two single rotor Centric superchargers, feeding a common inlet manifold
Ignition: Dual system with magneto and distributor, each switchable from the dashboard. Magneto advance/retard controlled by a lever inside the cockpit
Maximum power: 105 bhp at 5600 rpm

TRANSMISSION
Layout: Clutch and propellor shaft behind engine to transverse cross shaft in front of rear axle, with four chain sprockets on each, continuously engaged
Clutch: Single dry plate
Gearbox: Four forward speeds and reverse selected by engaging, with dog clutches, a sprocket on the cross shaft
3rd and 4th gears have double chains
1st 3.56:1   3rd 1.33:1
2nd 2:1   4th 1.08:1
Final drive: Bevel gears between propellor shaft and cross shaft
Ratio: 3.5:1

SUSPENSION
Front: Live axle supported by semi-elliptic cantilever springs, with radius rods to absorb brake torque in compression, and friction dampers
Rear: Live axle supported by quarter-elliptic cantilever springs with radius arms to maintain chain tension, and friction dampers

STEERING
Type: Worm and peg

BRAKES
Type: 35.5 cm (14 in) finned drums on all wheels, cable operated

WHEELS AND TYRES
Type: Rudge-Whitworth wire wheels, with 450 × 19 in tyres

BODY/CHASSIS
Type: Hand-built aluminium open-top two-seater supported on ladder-type U-section steel chassis

DIMENSIONS AND WEIGHT
Length: 3327 mm (131 in)
Width: 1498 mm (59 in)
Wheelbase: 2565 mm (101 in)
Track – front: 1250 mm (49.25 in)
           – rear: 1041 mm (41 in)
Weight: 838 kg (1848 lb)

PERFORMANCE
Maximum speed: 105 mph
(169 kph)
Acceleration 0–60 mph: 9
seconds

MODEL
Hispano-Suiza 15T Alfonso XIII

ENGINE
Location: Front longitudinal
Type: Water-cooled in-line four-cylinder monobloc in cast iron with alloy crankcase. Three main bearings
Cubic capacity: 3619 cc/220.76 cu in
Bore × stroke: 80 mm × 180 mm/3.15 in × 7.09 in
Valve gear: 2 per cylinder, either side of cylinder in T-head side-valve formation
Fuel supply: Hispano-Suiza three-jet automatic carburettor pressure-fed from rear-mounted fuel tank
Ignition: Bosch HT magneto
Maximum power: 63 bhp at 2300 rpm

TRANSMISSION
Layout: In unit with engine
Clutch: 42-plate dry metallic disc
Gearbox: Three-speed manual
Final drive: Straight-cut bevels, live axle
Ratio: 3.0:1 or 3.25:1

WHEELS AND TYRES
Type: Rudge-Whitworth detachable 885 × 105 beaded edge wire wheels

BODY/CHASSIS
Type: Pressed steel perimeter chassis with cross members. Bodywork to order

STEERING
Type: Worm and sector. 1.25 turns lock-to-lock

BRAKES
Type: Drums on rear wheels (hand) and transmission (foot)

SUSPENSION
Front: Non independent with semi-elliptic leaf springs
Rear: Non independent, live axle with semi-elliptic leaf springs

DIMENSIONS AND WEIGHT
Wheelbase: 2650 mm (104 in) or 3000 mm (118 in)
Track – front: 1220 mm (48 in)
   – rear: 1295 mm (51 in)
Chassis weight: 660 kg (1450 lb) or 710 kg (1570 lb)

PERFORMANCE
Maximum speed: 78 mph (125 kph)

The Hispano-Suiza Alfonso mirrored the American raceabouts in being basically a chassis with very skimpy bodywork, giving excellent performance for a relatively low power output. The Alfonso was in fact based on a successful racing voiturette. Despite the apparent crudity of a simple leaf-sprung front axle, ride and steering feel were both good thanks to the low unsprung weight, helped by the absence of front brakes

MODEL
Hispano-Suiza Type 68 V12 (1931)

ENGINE
Location: Front, longitudinal
Type: V12 with aluminium block and cylinder heads. 7 main bearings
Cubic capacity: 9425 cc/574.9 cu in
Bore × stroke: 100 mm × 100 mm/3.94 in × 3.94 in
Compression ratio: 6.0:1
Valve gear: 2 overhead valves per cylinder operated by single camshaft mounted in centre of the vee block, pushrods and rockers
Fuel supply: 2 Hispano-Suiza twin-choke carburettors
Ignition: Mechanical with 4 coils and 2 distributors (later replaced by twin Scintilla magnetos)
Maximum power: 220 bhp at 3000 rpm

TRANSMISSION
Layout: Clutch and gearbox in unit with engine
Clutch: Dry multi-plate clutch
Gearbox: Three-speed manual with synchromesh on top two gears
   1st 2.0:1   3rd 1.0:1
   2nd 1.50:1
Final drive: Helical spur
Ratio: 2.72:1

SUSPENSION
Front: Non-independent with semi-elliptic leaf springs and Duplex adjustable friction dampers (this car was later fitted with hydraulic dampers)
Rear: Non-independent, live rear axle with semi-elliptic leaf springs and Duplex adjustable dampers

STEERING
Type: Screw and nut

BRAKES
Type: Cable-operated drums front and rear with Hispano mechanical servo

WHEELS AND TYRES
Type: Rudge Whitworth centre lock wire wheels with 17 × 45 Michelin tyres

BODY/CHASSIS
Type: Pressed steel ladder frame with three cross-members using engine as stressed member

DIMENSIONS AND WEIGHT
Length: 4949 mm (194.8 in)
Wheelbase: 3810 mm (150 in)
Track – front: 1500 mm (59 in)
      – **rear:** 1500 mm (59 in)
Weight: 1570 kg (3454 lb)

PERFORMANCE
Maximum speed: 108 mph (174 kph)
Acceleration 0–60 mph: 12 seconds

The coachbuilder of this two-seater coupé on the 'normal' chassis is unknown. The extremely neat engine is set low down and bolted rigidly to the chassis, but the number of cylinders resulted in almost vibration-free running. The spare wheel is mounted inside at the rear, where there is also plenty of luggage space

MODEL
Model T Ford (1908)

ENGINE
Location: Front, longitudinal
Type: In line four-cylinder
Cubic capacity: 2895 cc/176.6 cu in
Bore × stroke: 95.25 mm ×
101 mm/3.75 in × 3.97 in
Compression ratio: 4.5:1
Valve gear: Two side valves per
cylinder
Fuel supply: Updraught Holley
carburettor
Ignition: Mechanical by flywheel
magneto and trembler coils
Maximum power: 20 bhp at
1800 rpm

TRANSMISSION
Layout: Clutch and gearbox in unit
with engine
Clutch: Multiple steel disc
Gearbox: Manually-controlled
two-speed epicyclic
    1st 2.74:1
    2nd 1.00:1
Final drive: Bevel gear
Ratio: 3.64:1

SUSPENSION
Front: Non-independent with
beam axle and transverse semi-
elliptic leaf springs
Rear: Non-independent with live
axle and transverse semi-elliptic leaf
springs

STEERING
Type: Epicyclic (1.25 turns lock to
lock)

BRAKES
Type: Foot-operated enclosed
band-brake on transmission, and
hand-operated internal expanding
brake on rear wheels

WHEELS AND TYRES
Type: Fixed wooden wheels with
76 cm × 8 cm (30 in × 3½ in)
beaded-edge tyres

BODY/CHASSIS
Type: Vanadium steel channel with
cross members at front and rear, and
separate, bolted-on coachbuilt body

DIMENSIONS AND WEIGHT
Length: 3556 mm (140 in)
Width: 1676 mm (66 in)
Wheelbase: 2553 mm (100.5 in)
Track – front: 1448 mm (57 in)
    – rear: 1461 mm (57.5 in)
Weight: 698.5 kg (1540 lb)

PERFORMANCE
Maximum speed: 42 mph
(67.5 kph)
Acceleration 10–30 mph: 12.8
seconds

Farmer's son Henry Ford decided at an early age that he would invent a machine to 'take the drudgery out of the farm.' After a couple of unsuccessful attempts to establish car companies – the 1902 Henry Ford Company became Cadillac after he left – Ford founded the Ford Motor Company on 24 June, 1903

EVOLUTION

1908 Model T introduced on 1 October; 305 cars built that year

1909 Cars to No. 1000 had only two pedals and a separate lever for reverse gear; cars to No. 2500 had a centrifugal water pump, shorter engine block and camshaft

1910 Torpedo Roadster introduced

1911 Engine and transmission accessibility improved, sheet metal bodies standardised

1912 Engine compression was lowered and a four-door touring model was announced

1913 The last year in which models were offered with a choice of colours and lined-out panels

1914 Model T only available in 'any colour you like so long as it's black'

1915 Millionth car built and detail changes made

1916 A steel bonnet replaced the old aluminium type

1917 The square brass radiator shell was replaced by one of rounded black steel. An electric horn standardised

1918 Coupelet and Town Car discontinued

1919 Electric starter and detachable rims available as optional equipment

1922 Centre-door sedan discontinued

1923 Model T lower and more streamlined, and a one-man hood was fitted

1924 The 10 millionth Model T was built

1925 Balloon tyres and hand-operated windscreen wipers introduced

1926 Model T available in a choice of colours. Nickel radiator shell, lowered chassis and lightweight cast-iron pistons introduced

1927 15 millionth Model T built; wire wheels were standardised and the range of colours increased. Production ended

The Model T Ford, or 'Tin Lizzie' as it was widely and affectionately known, was an extremely elementary design even in 1908. Unusual, however, was the simple transverse-leaf front and rear suspension, which attached the axles to the chassis above their centres. This was an inexpensive and rapidly-assembled system which provided a straight-line ride little different from that obtained with the more common arrangement of semi-elliptic leaf springs at each end of the axle, but offered considerably less resistance to side-roll and twisting when the car was negotiating corners. The car's engine was very unsophisticated and inefficient, with a tiny carburettor and a restricted exhaust manifold, but being so unstressed was consequently very reliable. Today it may look a crude, spindly design, but the functional excellence, reliability and appeal of the Model T have proved it to be one of the most sensible applications of 20th century technology

The Horch V12 was the epitome of teutonic orderliness, constructed throughout with great concern for durability and longevity, and it is ironic that of the 54 made only four have survived. The drive train in particular was engineered to extremely fine tolerances and beautifully finished, and much effort was put into making it as silent as possible. The engine was separate from the chassis, supported on oil-filled hydraulic dampers, and even the fuel pump was specially designed to be noiseless. The engine had full pressure lubrication, though before starting the driver would pump oil by hand (from the dashboard) through the oil ways. A gauge on the dashboard showed the oil level, and when it was low, more could be pumped in from a reserve tank. Nevertheless, the Horch V12 was conservative in design and appearance, and its high price and lack of performance (the latter due both to its enormous weight and relatively inefficient engine) meant that it did not offer much competition to the other V12s then available in Europe

MODEL
Horch V12 Cabriolet 670 (1932)

ENGINE
Location: Front, longitudinal
Type: Water-cooled 60-degree V12 with cast iron block and heads and seven-bearing crankshaft
Cubic capacity: 6031 cc/367.9 cu in
Bore × stroke: 80 mm × 100 mm/ 3.15 in × 3.94 in
Compression ratio: 6:1
Valve gear: Two side valves per cylinder operated by pushrods. Camshaft in centre of vee
Fuel supply: Single downdraught Solex carburettor
Ignition: Mechanical by magneto and distributor
Maximum power: 120 bhp at 300 rpm

TRANSMISSION
Layout: Clutch and gearbox in unit with engine, driving rear wheels
Clutch: Single dry plate
Gearbox: Horch four-speed manual
   1st 2.43:1 3rd 1.45:1
   2nd 1.89:1 4th 1.00:1
Final drive: Spiral bevel
Ratio: 3.8:1

SUSPENSION
Front: Non-independent, with beam axle, semi-elliptic leaf springs and friction dampers
Rear: Non-independent, with live axle, semi-elliptic leaf springs and friction dampers

STEERING
Type: Worm and peg

BRAKES
Type: Hydraulic drums all round, servo-assisted, mechanical hand-brake on rear wheels

WHEELS AND TYRES
Type: 19 in diameter wire wheels fitted with 19 × 6.00 crossply tyres

BODY/CHASSIS
Type: Heavy-duty box-section ladder-frame chassis supporting coachbuilt sports cabriolet or limousine body

DIMENSIONS AND WEIGHT
Length: 5400 mm (213 in)
Width: 1800 mm (71 in)
Wheelbase: 3450 mm (136 in)
Track – front: 1436 mm (56.5 in)
       – rear: 1490 mm (58.7 in)
Weight: 3000 kg (6614 lb)

PERFORMANCE
Maximum speed: 81 mph (130 kph)

MODEL
Isotta-Fraschini Tipo 8

ENGINE
Location: Front longitudinal
Type: Eight cylinders in line
Cubic capacity: 5902 cc/360 cu in
Bore × stroke: 85 mm × 130 mm/
3.35 in × 5.12 in
Compression ratio: 5:1
Valve gear: Overhead pushrod
Fuel supply: Twin Zenith
sidedraught triple-diffuser
carburettors
Ignition: Bosch HT magneto
Maximum power: 85 bhp

TRANSMISSION
Layout: Sliding-pinion gearbox in
unit with engine
Clutch: Multiple disc
Gearbox: Three-speed manual
   1st 3.37:1
   2nd 1.91:1
   3rd 1.00:1
Final drive: Helical bevel
Ratio: 3.75:1

SUSPENSION
Front: Non-independent with
semi-elliptic leaf springs
Rear: Non-independent with semi-
elliptic leaf springs

STEERING
Type: Worm and sector

BRAKES
Type: Four wheel mechanical drum
with mechanical servo assistance

WHEELS AND TYRES
Type: Detachable wire or steel disc
beaded-edge, 895 × 135 tyres

BODY/CHASSIS
Type: Pressed steel channel chassis
with separate coachbuilt body

DIMENSIONS AND WEIGHT
Length: 4980 mm (196 in)
Width: 1575 mm (62 in)
Wheelbase: 3700 mm (145 in)
Track – front: 1410 mm (56 in)
    – rear: 1410 mm (56 in)
Weight (chassis only): 1575 kg
(3472 lb)

PERFORMANCE
Maximum speed: 80 mph
(130 kph)

EVOLUTION

1919 Tipo 8 Isotta announced but its introduction was delayed due to labour troubles. Nevertheless it became the world's first production straight eight

1922 Tipo 8 was launched in the USA

1924 Tipo 8 introduced with a larger engine of 7372 cc (449.7 cu in) and output increased to 120 bhp. The brakes and tyres were uprated to match the extra performance and the final drive ratio was also changed

1926 A sports version of the 8A was introduced, the 8ASS. Its engine featured power output increased to 135 bhp

1931 Tipo 8B was introduced; it was a totally revised version of the 8A with a redesigned chassis and engine. A four-speed Wilson preselector gearbox was available as an option

1932 Car production ceased after around 400 Tipo 8s, 950 Tipo 8As and 30 Tipo 8Bs had been built

The Type 8 Isotta Fraschini of Rudolf Valentino revealed in rather more detail than he would have seen it. The coupé de ville body is by Fleetwood and as formal as the Isotta's chassis engineering was conservative. The engine was interesting as the world's first production straight eight although in some respects it was more like two four-cylinder units in a tandem. Although Isotta had considerable experience of aero engine engineering they still opted for the simplicity (and silence) of overhead valves operated by pushrods rather than a chain-driven overhead cam

MODEL
Itala Grand Prix (1908)

ENGINE
Location: Front, longitudinal
Type: In-line four-cylinder, pair-cast
Cubic capacity: 12,045 cc/734.7 cu in
Bore × stroke: 154.8 mm × 160 mm/6.1 in × 6.3 in
Compression ratio: 3.8:1
Valve gear: Two valves per cylinder, 4 in (10 cm) diameter, inlet over-exhaust, operated by single camshaft
Fuel supply: Single Itala updraught carburettor, fed from rear-mounted fuel tank pressurised by hand pump
Ignition: Low-tension magneto
Maximum power: 100 bhp

TRANSMISSION
Layout: Separate gearbox with open propellor shaft
Clutch: Hele-Shaw multi-plate, 8.25 in (21 cm) diameter
Gearbox: Four-speed manual, non-synchromesh
  1st 3.20:1   3rd 1.39:1
  2nd 2.06:1   4th 1.00:1
Final drive: Straight-cut bevel gears
Ratio: 1.65:1

STEERING
Type: Worm and wheel, ⅞ turn lock to lock

BRAKES
Type: Footbrake, 28 cm (11 in) band brake on transmission; handbrake 37 cm (14.5 in) internal-expanding drums on rear wheels

WHEELS AND TYRES
Type: Fixed wooden wheels with Michelin detachable beaded-edge rims, fitted with 915 mm × 105 mm tyres front, 895 mm × 135 mm tyres rear (but the car is presently fitted with detachable wire wheels)

BODY/CHASSIS
Type: Racing two-seater

DIMENSIONS AND WEIGHT
Length: 4144 mm (163 in)
Width: 1730 mm (68 in)
Wheelbase: 3023 mm (119 in)
Track – front: 1520 mm (60 in)
        – rear: 1520 mm (60 in)
Weight: 1400 kg (3086 lb)

PERFORMANCE
Maximum speed: 106 mph (170 kph)
Acceleration 0–60 mph: 12 seconds

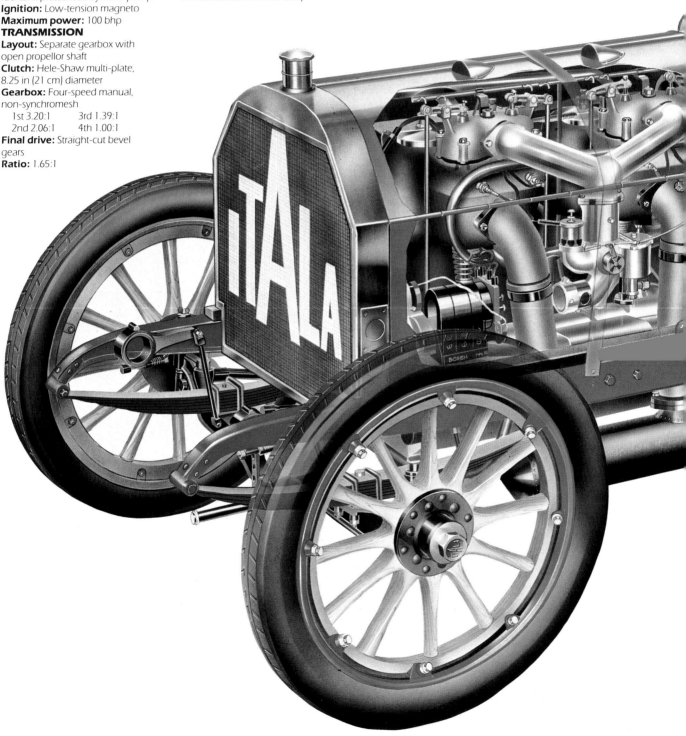

The Itala was built at a time when increased power could only be obtained by making the engine larger, which necessitated increasing the size of the chassis, suspension, fuel tank and practically all the moving parts. The cavernous cylinders were fed by what seems today an absurdly small carburettor, and although the power output was low and engine speed limited (particularly the long-stroke models), the torque produced by four pistons each the size of a top hat was considerable. It was that which gave these vehicles such good top-gear flexibility. Entirely functional in construction and styling, the car is simply a strong platform supporting the engine, seats and petrol tank. The suspension was rudimentary, its design showing little understanding of the science of roadholding and cornering; in any case its turning circle was vast. The main desire was for sustainable straight-line (or near-straight) speed

MODEL
SS 100 (3½-litre)

ENGINE

Location: Front, longitudinal
Type: Water-cooled in-line six cylinder with cast-iron cylinder block. Seven main bearings
Cubic capacity: 3485.5 cc/212.6 cu in
Bore × stroke: 82 mm × 110 mm/ 3.23 in × 4.33 in
Compression ratio: 7.0:1
Valve gear: 2 in-line valves per cylinder operated by single block-mounted camshaft, pushrods and rockers
Fuel supply: 2 SU carburettors with twin electric fuel pumps
Ignition: Mechanical with Lucas coil and distributor
Maximum power: 125 bhp at 4500 rpm

STEERING

Type: Burman Douglas worm and nut with Bluemel adjustable steering wheel

BRAKES

Type: Girling rod-operated with finned Millenite drums 126 sq cm (19.5 sq in) swept area. Hand brake operates on front and rear wheels

WHEELS AND TYRES

Type: Dunlop centre-lock wire wheels, 45.7 cm (18 in) diameter. Dunlop 5.25 × 18 Sports type tyres

BODY/CHASSIS

Type: Pressed steel underslung chassis with box-section main members fore and aft of cruciform centre section. 2-door, 2-seat open sports body

TRANSMISSION

Layout: Gearbox and clutch in unit with engine
Clutch: Single dry plate, 24.4 cm (10 in) in diameter
Gearbox: Four-speed manual with synchromesh on top three gears
  1st 3.59:1   3rd 1.37:1
  2nd 2.11:1   4th 1.00:1
Final drive: Spiral bevel
Ratio: 3.78:1

SUSPENSION

Front: Non-independent with semi-elliptic leaf springs in sliding trunnion bearings. Adjustable hydraulic Luvax CMP dampers plus Hartford friction dampers
Rear: Live axle with semi-elliptic leaf springs with Luvax hydraulic adjustable CMP dampers

DIMENSIONS AND WEIGHT

Length: 3672 mm (153 in)
Width: 1575 mm (62 in)
Wheelbase: 2642 mm (104 in)
Track – front: 1372 mm (54 in)
    – rear: 1372 mm (54 in)
Weight: 1168 kg (2576 lb)

PERFORMANCE

Maximum speed: 102 mph (164 kph)
Acceleration 0–60 mph: 10.9 seconds

The cutaway reveals the low underslung frame with the cruciform cross members. The aluminium body was built over an ash frame, and its lightness contributed greatly to the car's performance and effortless cruising speeds. The Luvax hydraulic dampers were adjustable from the dashboard and together with the long leaf springs formed an 'excellent combination', according to a contemporary road test by *Motor*, which greatly praised the car's cornering power

EVOLUTION

1935 SS90 introduced in March. SS100 announced in September with 2.7-litre overhead-valve engine rather than the side-valve unit of the SS90. No SS100s were sold in 1935 but SS90 production totalled 23

1936 Production of SS100s totalled 31 in 1936, along with just one SS90

1937 Chassis updated and 3.5-litre engine offered along with the 2.7-litre. Production totalled 91 2.7-litre SS100s

1938 One-off SS100 coupé shown at the London Motor Show at Earls Court. 55 2.7-litre and 69 3.5-litre SS100s built that year

1939 SS production ceases although sales continued into 1940 and amounted to 21 2.7-litre and 116 3.5-litre cars. Total production was 24 SS90 and 308 SS100, 49 of which were exported

MODEL
Jaguar XK120 (1948)

ENGINE
Location: Front, longitudinal
Type: In-line six-cylinder twin cam with cast-iron block and light-alloy head. 7 main bearings
Cubic capacity: 3442 cc/210 cu in
Bore × stroke: 83 mm × 106 mm/ 3.27 in × 4.17 in
Compression ratio: 7, 8 or 9:1
Valve gear: Two 70-degree overhead valves per cylinder operated in hemispherical combustion chambers by twin overhead chain-driven camshafts
Fuel supply: Two SU H6 carburettors
Ignition: Mechanical by coil and distributor
Maximum power: 160 bhp at 5000 rpm
Maximum torque: 195 lb ft

TRANSMISSION
Layout: Clutch and gearbox in unit with engine. Rear wheel drive
Clutch: Single dry plate
Gearbox: Four-speed manual
| 1st 3.37:1 | 3rd 1.37:1 |
| 2nd 1.98:1 | 4th 1.00:1 |
Final drive: Hypoid bevel
Ratio: 3.64:1

SUSPENSION
Front: Independent with double wishbones and longitudinal torsion bars and telescopic dampers
Rear: Live rear axle with semi-elliptic leaf springs and lever arm dampers

STEERING
Type: Burman worm and nut

BRAKES
Type: Drums front and rear

WHEELS AND TYRES
Type: Pressed steel wheels 16 in diameter with Dunlop Road Speed 600 x 16 crossply tyres

BODY/CHASSIS
Type: Pressed steel ladder chassis with cross bracing. 2-seat, 2-door roadster body

DIMENSIONS AND WEIGHT
Length: 4419 mm (174 in)
Width: 1562 mm (61.5 in)
Wheelbase: 2591 mm (102 in)
Track – front: 1295 mm (51 in)
– rear: 1270 mm (50 in)
Weight: 1321 kg (2912 lb)

PERFORMANCE
Maximum speed: 124 mph (199 kph)
Acceleration 0–60 mph: 11 seconds

EVOLUTION

1948 Prototype XK120 introduced at British Motor Show with aluminium body and 3.4-litre twin-cam six-cylinder engine

1949 First production XK completed in July

1950 Steel replaced aluminium for the bodies after 238 cars had been built

1951 XK120 fixed-head coupé was introduced

1953 Drophead coupé version of the XK120 introduced

1954 XK140 announced in the same three versions as the 120 but with occasional rear seats. Rack and pinion steering replaced the Burman box and telescopic dampers replaced the lever arm type on the rear

1957 XK150 introduced. Disc brakes front and rear were standard

1958 Weslake-designed cylinder head available which produced an extra 30 bhp. The 150 was also available with the larger, 3.8-litre, version of the twin-cam to form the 150S

1961 XK range discontinued. XK120 production reached 12,078 and 140 production reached 8884. 9395 XK150s were built and total XK production 1948-1961 was 30,357

The Jaguar XK120 offered unrivalled power, performance and elegance for the price. It was originally intended for low volume production but conventional mass-production techniques had to be used to meet the demand. Apart from that splendid twin-cam engine and the stylish body there was little sophisticated about the XK, and the brakes were barely adequate for the performance

MODEL

E-type Series One, 1961

ENGINE

Location: Front, longitudinal
Type: Water-cooled in-line six with cast-iron block and aluminium alloy head.
Cubic capacity: 3781 cc/230.6 cu in
Bore × stroke: 87 mm × 106 mm/ 3.42 in × 4.17 in
Compression ratio: 9.0:1
Valve gear: 2 inclined valves per cylinder, operated in hemispherical combustion chambers by twin chain-driven overhead camshafts.
Fuel supply: 3 SU HD8 carburettors
Ignition: Coil and distributor, mechanical
Maximum power: 265 bhp (gross) at 5500 rpm
Maximum torque: 260 lb ft (gross) at 4000 rpm

TRANSMISSION

Layout: Clutch and gearbox in unit with engine driving rear wheels
Clutch: Single plate, diaphragm spring
Gearbox: Four-speed manual with synchromesh on top three ratios

1st 3.377:1	3rd 1.283:1
2nd 1.86:1	4th 1.00:1

Final drive: Hypoid bevel with limited slip differential
Ratio: 3.31:1 or 3.07:1

SUSPENSION

Front: Independent by double wishbones, longitudinal torsion bars, telescopic dampers and anti-roll bar
Rear: Independent with one lower lateral link and one lower radius arm per side with the drive shaft acting as the upper lateral link. 2 telescopic spring/damper units per side.

STEERING

Type: Rack and pinion, manual

BRAKES

Type: Discs front and rear, inboard at rear. Hydraulic with servo assistance

WHEELS AND TYRES

Type: 5½J × 15in wire spoked with Dunlop 6.40 × 15in RS5 cross-ply tyres

BODY/CHASSIS

Type: Steel monocoque centre section with square-tube front sub frame and pressed steel rear sub frame. Convertible or coupé bodywork, 2 doors 2 seats

DIMENSIONS AND WEIGHT

Length: 4457 mm (175.5 in)
Width: 1658 mm (65.3 in)
Wheelbase: 2438 mm (96 in)
Track – front: 1270 mm (50 in)
     – rear: 1270 mm (50 in)
Weight: (dry) 1117 kg (2464 lb) roadster, 1143 kg (2520 lb) coupé

PERFORMANCE

Maximum speed: 149 mph (240 kph)
Acceleration 0-60 mph: 7.1 seconds

EVOLUTION

1961 Introduced at Geneva Motor Show in March in both roadster and coupé forms with in-line 3.8-litre six-cylinder engine

1964 Engine enlarged to 4.2 litres. New all synchromesh gearbox fitted along with new diaphragm clutch

1966 2+2 introduced, available with Borg-Warner three-speed automatic transmission

1971 Series Three cars introduced in long wheelbase roadster and 2+2 coupé forms only. In theory the Series Three cars were available with the 4.2-litre engine but in reality all cars were produced with the alloy 5.3-litre V12. Anti-dive front suspension and ventilated front discs added

1973 Series Three 2+2 production ceased after 7300 V12 2+2s built

1975 E-type production ceased after 72,520 cars built. Series One accounted for 15,490 cars, Series Two for 41,740 and Series Three for 15,290. Over half (33,990) the production consisted of roadsters

The sophisticated engineering of the XJS was largely shared with the XJ6 range. The effortless power of the 5.3-litre V12, which completely fills the large under-bonnet area, required extremely efficient suspension and braking, and the wishbone front suspension incorporates anti-dive geometry to maintain the car's stability under heavy braking. The body has a very strong passenger compartment, and although its styling was somewhat controversial when first introduced, its aerodynamic efficiency was notably better than the E-type's

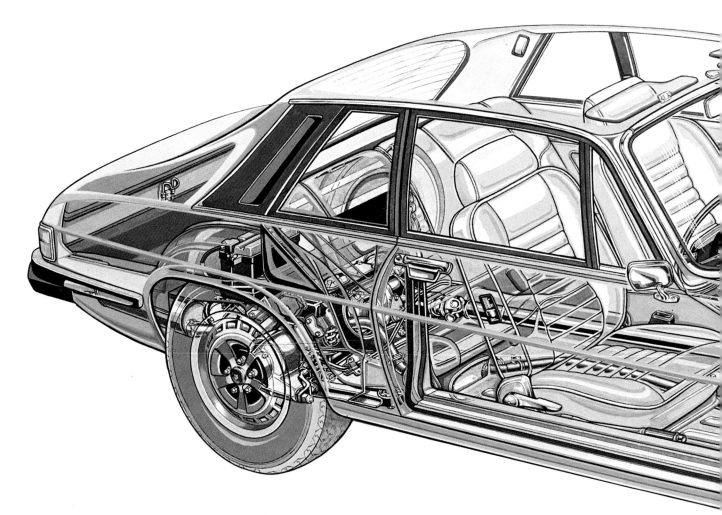

MODEL
Jaguar XJS (1975)

ENGINE
Location: Front, longitudinal
Type: Water-cooled V12 with cast alloy block and heads and seven-bearing crankshaft
Cubic capacity: 5343 cc/325.9 cu in
Bore × stroke: 90 mm × 70 mm/ 3.54 in × 2.75 in
Compression ratio: 9:1
Valve gear: Two overhead, in-line valves per cylinder operated by single overhead camshafts
Fuel supply: Lucas Opus Mk II electronic fuel injection
Ignition: Lucas Opus comtactless electronic ignition
Maximum power: 285 bhp at 5500 rpm
Maximum torque: 294 lb ft at 3500 rpm

TRANSMISSION
Layout: Gearbox in unit with engine
Clutch: Hydraulic torque converter
Gearbox: Three-speed Borg-Warner Model 12 automatic transmission
1st 1.44:1   3rd 1.0:1
2nd 2.39:1
Final drive: Hypoid bevel limited-slip differential
Ratio: 3.07:1

SUSPENSION
Front: Independent, with wishbones, coil springs, hydraulic dampers and anti-roll bar
Rear: Independent, with lower wishbones, drive shafts acting as upper links, trailing lower radius arms, twin coil springs, twin hydraulic dampers and anti-roll bar

STEERING
Type: Power-assisted rack and pinion

BRAKES
Type: Discs front and rear, servo-assisted

WHEELS AND TYRES
Type: Cast alloy 38 cm (15 in) wheels fitted with 205/70VR 15 steel-belted radial tyres

BODY/CHASSIS

DIMENSIONS AND WEIGHT
Length: 4749 mm (187.6 in)
Width: 1793 mm (70.6 in)
Wheelbase: 2591 mm (102 in)
Track – front: 1488 mm (58.6 in)
    – rear: 1504 mm (59.2 in)
Weight: 1755 kg (8370 lb)

PERFORMANCE
Maximum speed: 152 mph (245 kph)
Acceleration 0-60 mph: 6.75 seconds

EVOLUTION

1975 Jaguar XJS two-door coupé introduced at British Motor Show, with 5.3-litre V12 and fitted with automatic transmission as standard

1976 Four-speed manual transmission was offered as an option and the Borg-Warner automatic transmission was replaced by GM THM400 unit

1981 XJS HE was introduced, with the engine heads modified to give improved fuel consumption and a power output of 300 bhp

1983 XJS 3.6 announced, with the 3.6-litre straight six and available in coupé and convertible forms

1985 XJSC-HE introduced, the cabriolet version fitted with the 5.3-litre V12

1987 Suspension uprated, engine management system from new XJ6 adopted, trim enhanced

MODEL
Jensen Interceptor

ENGINE
Location: Front, longitudinal
Type: Water-cooled V8 with cast-iron block and heads
Cubic capacity: 6276 cc/382.8 cu in
Bore × stroke: 108 mm × 86 mm/4.25 in × 3.38 in
Compression ratio: 10.0:1
Valve gear: 2 parallel valves per cylinder operated by single block-mounted camshaft in centre of vee. Hydraulic tappets
Fuel supply: Single Carter four-barrel carburettor
Ignition: Mechanical with coil and distributor
Maximum power: 325 bhp at 4600 rpm (SAE gross)
Maximum torque: 425 lb ft at 2800 rpm (SAE gross)

TRANSMISSION
Layout: Gearbox in unit with engine. Rear-wheel drive
Gearbox: Chrysler Torqueflite three-speed automatic
   1st 2.45:1   3rd 1.00:1
   2nd 1.45:1
Final drive: Hypoid bevel with 'Power-lok' limited slip differential
Ratio: 3.07:1

SUSPENSION
Front: Independent with twin wishbones and coil springs
Rear: Non-independent with live rear axle located by semi-elliptic leaf springs and Panhard rod

STEERING
Type: Cam Gears rack and pinion

BRAKES
Type: Dunlop discs front and rear, servo assisted with divided hydraulic circuit. 1606 sq cm (249 sq in) swept area front and rear

WHEELS AND TYRES
Type: 5J steel wheels with Dunlop RS5 6.70 × 15 in tubeless crossply tyres

BODY/CHASSIS
Type: Tubular steel chassis with unitary steel coupé body. 2 doors, 4 seats

DIMENSIONS AND WEIGHT
Length: 4775 mm (188 in)
Width: 1778 mm (70 in)
Wheelbase: 2667 mm (105 in)
Track – front: 1422 mm (56 in)
   – rear: 1448 mm (57 in)
Weight: 1676 kg (3696 lb)

EVOLUTION

1966 Jensen Interceptor Saloon introduced at British Motor Show in October, with 6276 cc (382.8 cu in) Chrysler V8 and three-speed Torqueflite automatic transmission. The chassis and suspension were derived from the earlier CV8, and the body styled by Touring of Milan

1968 Jensen FF introduced fitted with Ferguson Formula four-wheel drive and a Dunlop-Maxaret anti-lock braking system

1969 Interceptor Director announced

1970 Interceptor Series I discontinued. Total production: 1033. Interceptor Mk II introduced with minor styling changes

1971 Interceptor SP introduced with 7.2-litre (439 cu in) Chrysler V8, with power steering and air conditioning as standard. The last FF was made. Total production: 320

1972 Interceptor II discontinued. Total production: 693. Interceptor III introduced fitted with detuned 7.2-litre Chrysler V8

1973 Interceptor SP discontinued. Total production: 208

1974 Interceptor Convertible introduced

1976 Interceptor Coupé introduced, and 54 were built before production of all Interceptors stopped. Total production of saloons: 5358; convertibles: 267

1982 Jensen show a newly-built Interceptor III at British Motor Show

1984 New Interceptor Saloon and Convertible Series IV shown, fitted with 5.9-litre (360 cu in) small-block Chrysler V8. Largely built by hand, a production of 12 a year was planned initially

ERFORMANCE

Maximum speed: 140 mph 25 kph)

Acceleration 0–60 mph: 7.3 econds

The engine was mounted quite far back into the car, and the overall weight ratio of 50/50 gave safe handling despite the rather simple rear suspension by live axle and semi-elliptic leaf springs

In most respects the Lagonda's layout followed the accepted practices of the time, but the independent front suspension by means of longitudinal bars (seen running from the bulkhead to the front of the car) was a departure in such a car. The cross-braced chassis was extremely strong, an important factor in a fast and heavy car with a high-torque engine. The assembly shown in the dummy spare wheel cover is a hand-opeated hydraulic pump to lower the built-in jacks, which are visible at the ends of the rear axle and at the front between the wishbones

MODEL
Lagonda 4½-litre 12-cylinder (1938)

ENGINE
Location: Front, longitudinal
Type: Water-cooled 60-degree V12, cast iron block
Cubic capacity: 4480 cc/273.3 cu in
Bore × stroke: 75 mm × 84.5 mm/ 2.95 in × 3.33 in
Compression ratio: 7.5:1
Valve gear: Two overhead valves per cylinder operated by single overhead camshaft on each bank of cylinders
Fuel supply: Two downdraught SU carburettors
Ignition: Coil and twin Delco distributors
Maximum power: 156 bhp at 5000 rpm
Maximum torque: 208 lb ft at 2000 rpm

TRANSMISSION
Layout: Gearbox behind engine driving rear wheels
Clutch: Single dry plate
Gearbox: Four-speed manual
  1st 3.25:1   3rd 1.25:1
  2nd 1.67:1   4th 1.00:1
Final drive: Salisbury hypoid bevel unit
Ratio: 4.45:1 (five options were available)

SUSPENSION
Front: Independent, with equal-length wishbones and torsion bar springs
Rear: Non-independent, with live rear axle and semi-elliptic leaf springs

STEERING
Type: Mahle worm and peg

BRAKES
Type: Hydraulically operated drums all round, with twin master cylinders

WHEELS AND TYRES
Type: Detachable 46 cm (18 in) wire wheels with 6.5 × 18 crossply tyres

BODY/CHASSIS
Type: Steel U-section chassis with two longitudinal members and diagonal cross-beams. Separate coachbuilt body

DIMENSIONS AND WEIGHT
Length: 5232 mm (206 in)
Width: 1829 mm (72 in)
Wheelbase: 3353 mm (132 in)
Track – front: 1524 mm (60 in)
    – rear: 1524 mm (60 in)
Weight: 1981 kg (4368 lb)

PERFORMANCE
Maximum speed: 101 mph (163 kph)
Acceleration 0–60 mph: 13.4 seconds

EVOLUTION

1933 M45 Lagonda introduced with 4493 cc (274 cu in) six-cylinder Meadows engine and Lagonda's own four-speed gearbox; the Meadows unit was thereafter adopted

1934 M45R Rapide announced, with a shorter wheelbase, Girling brakes and modified engine

1936 LG45 announced, a slightly detuned Rapide clothed in new streamlined bodies. It also featured synchromesh on third and top gears, hydraulic dampers and design improvements to the engine

1937 LG45 Rapide announced, an open four-seater with helmet wings, external exhaust pipes and rounded tail

1938 LG6 Lagonda V12 announced, with an engine designed by W. O. Bentley

1940 Production halted by the War

MODEL
Lamborghini Miura, 1967

ENGINE
Location: Mid, transverse
Type: Water-cooled 60 degree V12 with aluminium alloy cylinder heads and block
Cubic capacity: 3929 cc/239.67 cu in
Bore × stroke: 82 mm × 62 mm/ 3.23 in × 2.44 in
Compression ratio: 9.8:1
Valve gear: 2 inclined valves per cylinder operated in hemispherical chambers by twin chain-driven overhead camshafts per bank of cylinders
Fuel supply: 4 Weber 40 IDL3Cs downdraught triple choke carburettors

Ignition: Twin coil and distributor, mechanical
Maximum power: 350bhp (net DIN) at 7000rpm
Maximum torque: 271lb ft (net DIN) at 5100rpm

TRANSMISSION
Layout: Clutch and gearbox transversely mounted behind and in unit with the engine with direct gear drive
Clutch: Single plate, diaphragm spring, hydraulically operated
Gearbox: Five-speed manual, synchromesh on all forward and reverse gear

1st 2.520:1		4th 1.00:1	
2nd 1.735:1		5th 0.815:1	
3rd 1.225:1			

Final drive: Helical spur with limited slip differential
Ratio: 4.08:1

SUSPENSION
Front: Independent by double wishbones, coil springs and concentric telescopic dampers and anti-roll bar
Rear: Independent by double unequal wishbones, coil springs and concentric telescopic dampers and top-mounted anti-roll bar

STEERING
Type: Rack and pinion, manual

BRAKES
Type: Girling discs front and rear

WHEELS AND TYRES
Type: 7 x 15in Atesia alloy with radial-ply Pirelli Cinturato 210HS 15

BODY/CHASSIS
Type: Steel spaceframe chassis with alloy body. Coupé body, 2 doors, 2 seats

DIMENSIONS AND WEIGHT
Length: 4360 mm (171.6 in)
Width: 1760 mm (69.3 in)
Wheelbase: 2500 mm (98.4 in)
Track – front: 1412 mm (55.6 in)
     – rear: 1412 mm (55.6 in)
Weight: (kerb) 1292 kg (2850 lb)

PERFORMANCE
Maximum speed: 172mph (277kph)
Acceleration 0-60mph: 6.7 seconds

EVOLUTION

1965 Introduced in chassis form at Turin Motor Show and available in 1967 as a two-seater 4-litre coupé

1968 P400S Miura introduced with power up to 370 bhp at 7700 rpm, electrically operated windows and rocker switches to replace the 'unsafe' toggle variety. Later the Miura S received ventilated disc brakes and reinforced rear suspension

1971 Miura SV introduced at Geneva Show with revised and wider bodywork and engine uprated to produce a claimed 385 bhp at 7850 rpm. Chassis reinforced further and rear suspension changed as a new quadrilateral link replaced the lower wishbones. Some SVs built with limited slip differentials and some with dry-sump lubrication

1971 Miura Jota appeared as a one-off prospective sports racer with narrower chassis, fabricated wishbone suspension, different subframes, a more aerodynamically efficient body and 440 bhp engine

1973 Miura production ended in January. 750 cars built

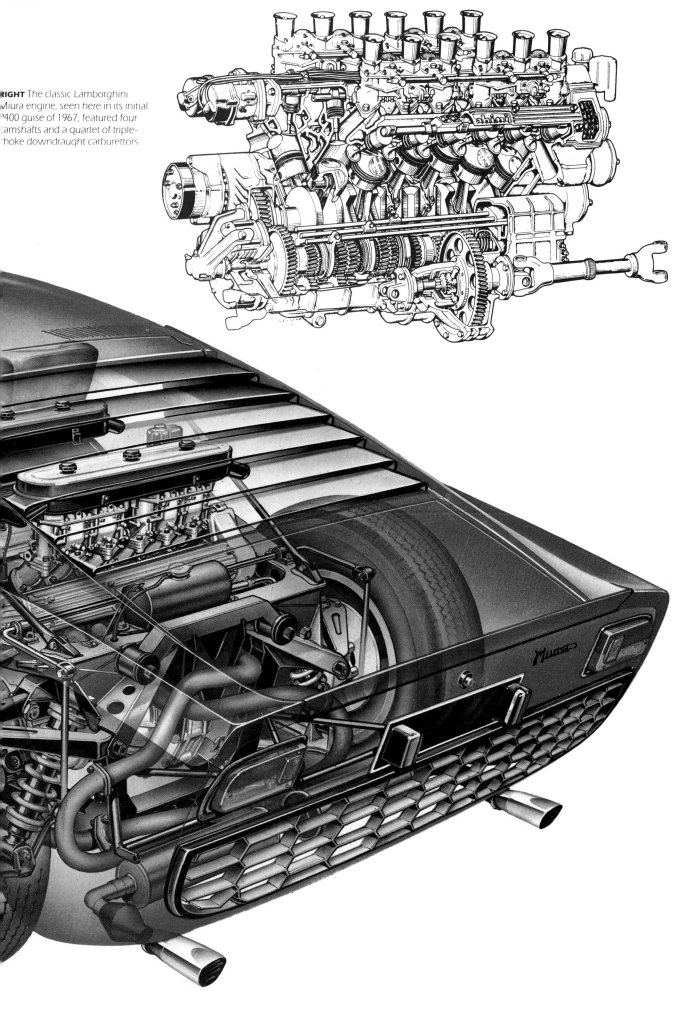

RIGHT The classic Lamborghini
Miura engine, seen here in its initial
P400 guise of 1967, featured four
camshafts and a quartet of triple-
choke downdraught carburettors

MODEL
Lamborghini Urraco P300 (1975)

ENGINE
Location: Mid-mounted, transverse
Type: Water-cooled V8 with light alloy block and heads. 5 main bearings
Cubic capacity: 2996 cc/182.75 cu in
Bore × stroke: 86 mm × 64.5 mm/ 3.4 in × 2.54 in
Compression ratio: 9.2.1
Valve gear: 2 valves per cylinder operated in hemispherical combustion chambers by 2 belt-driven overhead camshafts per bank of cylinders
Fuel supply: 4 Weber 40 DCNF downdraught carburettors
Ignition: Mechanical by coil and distributor
Maximum power: 265 bhp (DIN) at 6500 rpm
Maximum torque: 302 lb ft (DIN) at 2800 rpm

TRANSMISSION
Layout: Gearbox and clutch on end of engine, driving rear wheels
Clutch: Single dry plate
Gearbox: Five-speed all synchromesh manual

1st	2.933:1	4th	1.185:1
2nd	2.105:1	5th	0.903:1
3rd	1.565		

Final drive: Helical spur
Ratio: 4.350:1

SUSPENSION
Front: Independent with MacPherson struts, lower wishbones and anti-roll bar
Rear: Independent with MacPherson struts, wishbones and anti-roll bar

STEERING
Type: Rack and pinion

BRAKES
Type: Discs front and rear with internal fins. 251 sq cm (38.9 sq in) swept area front, 182 sq cm (28.2 sq in) rear

WHEELS AND TYRES
Type: 35.56 cm (14 in) alloy wheels with 195/70 × 14 radial tyres

BODY/CHASSIS
Type: Integral with sub frame for engine and transmission. 2 door 2 seat coupé body

DIMENSIONS AND WEIGHT
Length: 4249 mm (167.32 in)
Width: 1759 mm (69.29 in)
Wheelbase: 2448 mm (96.4 in)
Track – front: 1450 mm (57.09 in)
– rear: 1419 mm (55.87 in)
Weight: 1300 kg (2685 lb)

PERFORMANCE
Maximum speed: 165 mph (265 kph)
Acceleration 0–60 mph: 6.5 seconds

The layout of the Lamborghini Urraco P300 demonstrates some of the advantages of a V8 engine compact enough to allow Lamborghini to squeeze it in across the car even when the gearbox is mounted on the end of the crankshaft in the conventional manner for a longitudinally mounted engine

EVOLUTION

1970 Lamborghini Urraco introduced at Turin Motor Show with a body by Bertone, powered by a 2.5-litre light-alloy V8

1972 Urraco production started, but only 35 cars were built that year

1974 Urraco sales in USA began and the 3-litre 250 bhp Urraco introduced at Turin Show

1975 Smaller 2-litre, 182 bhp, engine developed for the Italian market and the Urraco S introduced with better trim. Only 66 2-litre cars were built

1976 Silhouette introduced at the Geneva Show. It was inspired by the Bravo project car and used Urraco mechanicals. With few orders from the all-important American market only 56 were built and by the end of 1976 only 130 of the 3-litre Urracos had been produced

1978 The Urraco ceased production

MODEL
Lamborghini Countach
Quattrovalvole (1985)

ENGINE
Location: Centre-rear, longitudinal
Type: Water-cooled 60 degree V12
with light-alloy block and heads,
wet cylinder liners and seven main
bearings
Cubic capacity: 5167 cc/315.2 cu in
Bore × stroke: 85.5 mm × 75 mm/
3.37 in × 2.95 in
Compression ratio: 9.5.1
Valve gear: Four inclined valves
per cylinder operated by two chain-
driven overhead camshafts per bank
of cylinders
Fuel supply: Six Weber twin-choke
44DCNF carburettors
Ignition: Electronic
Maximum power: 455 bhp (DIN)
at 7000 rpm
Maximum torque: 370 lb ft (DIN)
at 5200 rpm

TRANSMISSION
Layout: Gearbox mounted ahead
of engine
Clutch: Single dry plate
Gearbox: Five-speed manual
  1st 2.232:1   4th 0.858:1
  2nd 1.625:1   5th 0.707:1
  3rd 1.088:1
Final drive: Hypoid bevel with
limited-slip differential
Ratio: 4.09:1

SUSPENSION
Front: Independent with
wishbones, coil springs, telescopic
dampers and anti-roll bar
Rear: Independent with
wishbones, coil springs, trailing links,
anti-roll bar and two telescopic
dampers per side

STEERING
Type: Rack and pinion. Three turns
lock to lock

BRAKES
Type: Discs all round. 30 cm
(11.81 in) dia front and 28 cm
(11.02 in) dia rear. Dual circuit,
servo-assisted

WHEELS AND TYRES
Type: Alloy wheels: 21.6 cm ×
38 cm (8.5 in × 15 in) front and
30.5 cm × 38 cm (12 in × 15 in) rear
with Pirelli P7 radials: 225/50VR 15
front and 345/35VR 15 rear

BODY/CHASSIS
Type: Tubular steel frame with
aluminium two-seater coupé body
with glassfibre floor

DIMENSIONS AND WEIGHT
Length: 4140 mm (162.99 in)
Width: 2000 mm (78.74 in)
Wheelbase: 2500 mm (98.4 in)
Track – front: 1536 mm (60.5 in)
      – rear: 1606 mm (63.2 in)
Weight: 1480 kg (3263 lb)

In view of the Countach's massively
engineered chassis it is hardly
surprising the car weighs as much
as 1480 kg (3263 lb)

PERFORMANCE
Maximum speed: 183 mph
(295 kph)
Acceleration 0–60 mph: 5.0
seconds

EVOLUTION

1971 Introduced at Geneva Show on the Bertone
stand with 5-litre 440 bhp V12 engine

1974 Countach entered production with changes
such as the 4-litre V12 from the Miura and vertical rather
than horizontal radiators

1978 Revised LP400S introduced with wider Pirelli P7
tyres, wider wheel arches, a deeper nose spoiler and a
boot-lid wing

1981 LP500S introduced with '5-litre' engine (actually
4754 cc/290 cu in). Power and torque increased by
seven and 14 per cent respectively. Absolute top speed
was not affected

1985 Countach Quattrovalvole introduced with four-
valves-per-cylinder 5167 cc (315 cu in) V12. Power
increased from 375 bhp to 455 bhp. Top speed
increased to 183 mph (295 kph)

1988 Suspension uprated, side skirts subtly changed
body lines

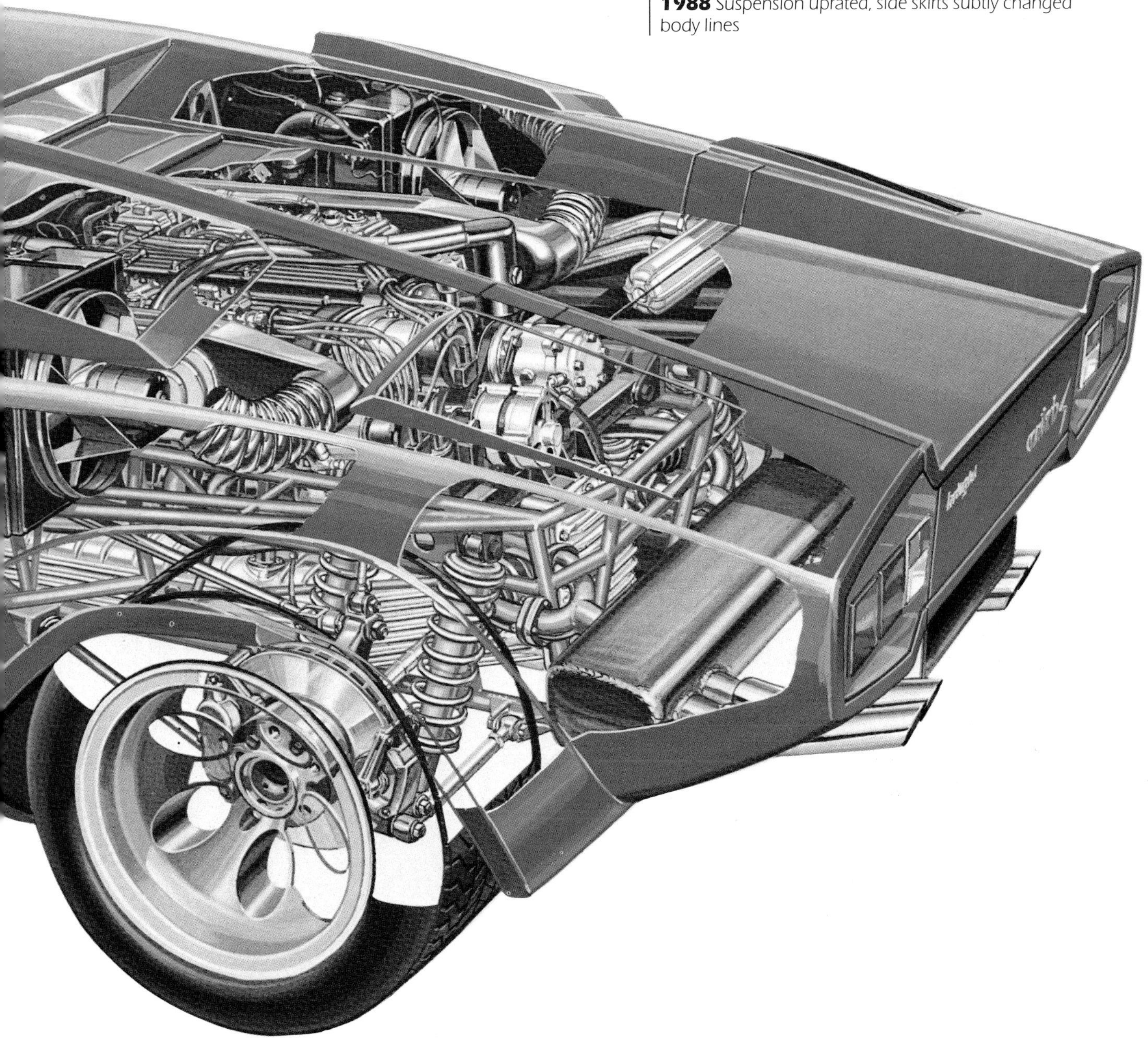

MODEL
Lancia Lambda (8th series) 1928

ENGINE
Location: Front, longitudinal
Type: (Tipo 79) Water-cooled narrow-angle V4 with light-alloy block, cast-iron heads and cast-iron cylinder liners
Cubic capacity: 2570 cc/156.77 cu in
Bore × stroke: 82.57 mm × 120 mm/3.25 in × 4.72 in
Compression ratio: 5.15:1
Maximum power: 69 bhp at 3500 rpm

TRANSMISSION
Layout: Clutch and gearbox mounted behind, and separate from, engine
Clutch: Multiple dry plate
Gearbox: Four-speed manual
  1st 3.19:1   3rd 1.44:1
  2nd 1.89:1   4th 1.00:1
Final drive: Spiral bevel
Ratio: 4.45:1

SUSPENSION
Front: Independent with Lancia sliding pillar, combining coil springs and telescopic dampers
Rear: Live axle with semi-elliptic leaf springs and Hartford friction dampers

STEERING
Type: Worm and wheel

BRAKES
Type: Steel-disc brake drums with shrunk-on cooling fins

WHEELS AND TYRES
Type: Wire wheels with Michelin Bibendum 14 × 50 tyres

BODY/CHASSIS
Type: Steel platform chassis with various body styles available

DIMENSIONS AND WEIGHT
Length: 4572 mm (189.0 in)
Width: 1661 mm (65.4 in)
Wheelbase: 3419 mm (134.6 in)
Track – front: 1417 mm (55.0 in)
     – rear: 1417 mm (55.0 in)
Weight: 1117 kg (2464 lb)

PERFORMANCE
Maximum speed: 75 mph (121 kph)
Fuel consumption: 19–20 mpg

This cutaway drawing shows an Eighth Series Lambda, while **BELOW** is shown its body pressing, which contributes to a very stiff monocoque chassis

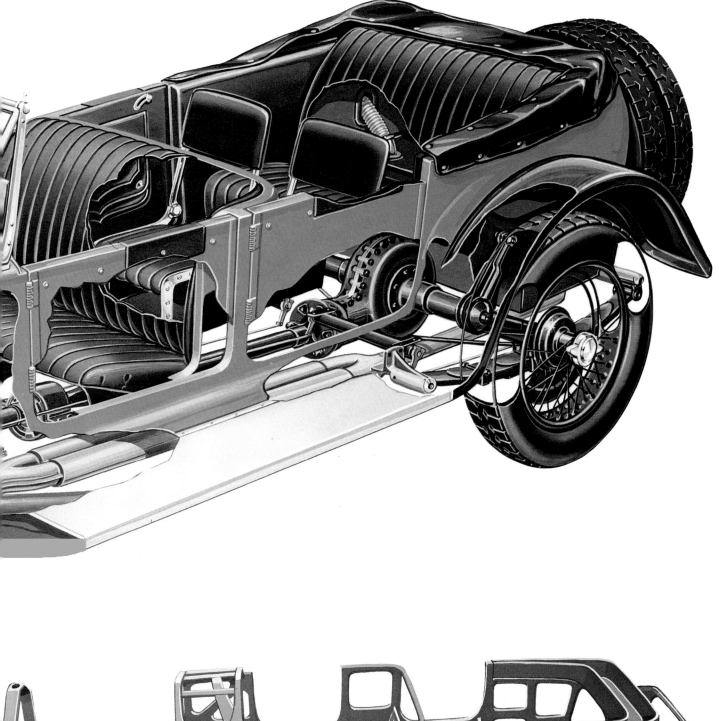

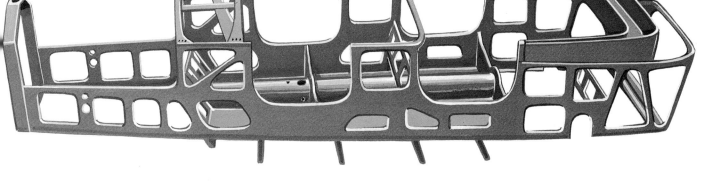

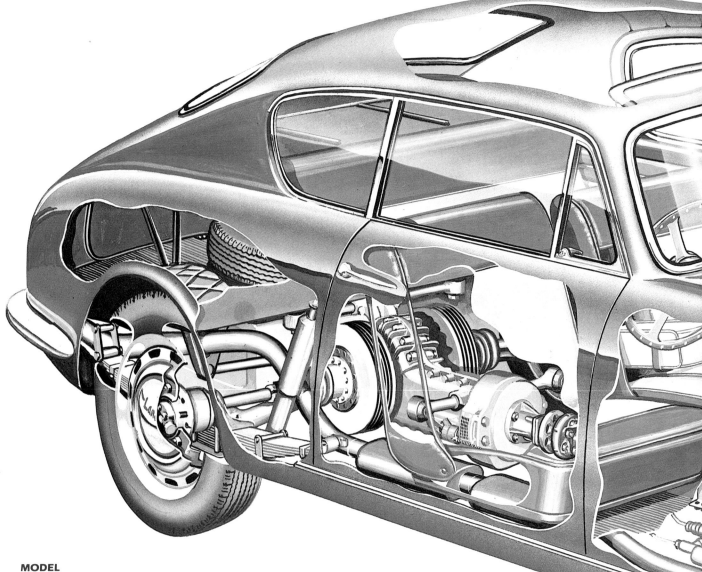

MODEL
Lancia Aurelia GT2500 (1954)

ENGINE
Location: Front, longitudinal
Type: V6, water-cooled with light-alloy block and heads. Four main bearings
Cubic capacity: 2451 cc/149.5 cu in
Bore × stroke: 78 mm × 85.5 mm/ 3.1 in × 3.36 in
Compression ratio: 8.4:1
Valve gear: 2 inclined valves per cylinder operated by single camshaft
Fuel supply: Single Solex twin-choke
Ignition: Mechanical by coil and distributor
Maximum power: 118 bhp (gross) at 5000 rpm
Maximum torque: 126.5 lb ft at 3500 rpm

TRANSMISSION
Layout: Clutch and transmission in-unit at rear
Clutch: Single dry plate
Gearbox:

1st 3.09:1	3rd 1.41:1
2nd 2.06:1	4th 1.00:1

Final drive: Hypoid bevel
Ratio: 3.69:1

SUSPENSION
Front: Independent with sliding pillars and coil springs
Rear: Non-independent with de Dion axle, swinging axle shafts and semi-elliptic leaf springs

STEERING
Type: Worm and sector

BODY/CHASSIS
Type: Integral chassis with two-door, four-seat coupé body

BRAKES
Type: Sabif hydraulically operated drums front and rear. Rear mounted inboard. 539 sq cm (83.6 sq in) lining area front, 819 sq cm (127 sq in) rear

WHEELS AND TYRES
Type: Steel wheels with 165–400 mm (15.7 in) tyres

DIMENSIONS AND WEIGHT
Length: 437 cm (172 in)
Width: 155 cm (61 in)
Wheelbase: 265 cm (104.5 in)
Track – front: 128 cm (50.4 in)
 – rear: 130 cm (51.2 in)
Weight: 1292 kg (2849 lb)

PERFORMANCE
Maximum speed: 111 mph (178 kph)
Acceleration 0–60 mph: 14.0 seconds

EVOLUTION

1950 Aurelia introduced at Turin Show, powered by a 1754 cc (107 cu in) V6 producing 56 bhp

1951 Aurelia B21 and B21S introduced with engine displacement increased to 1991 cc (121.4 cu in). Power increased to 70 bhp at 4800 rpm. Same engine also used in the B20 Aurelia GT but with slightly more power (80 bhp at 5000 rpm). the GT was a 2+2 coupé with a shorter wheelbase, styled by Pininfarina

1952 Aurelia B15 and B15S introduced with larger body, wider track and longer wheelbase, along with a 64 bhp version of the 2-litre. The B22 and B22S were also introduced with the normal wheelbase and track and a 90 bhp version of the 2-litre engine

1953 B20 Aurelia GT2500 appeared with engine displacement increased to 2451 cc (149.5 cu in) and power increased to 116 bhp

1954 Second series Aurelia B12 and B12S introduced with a displacement of 2266 cc (138.2 cu in) and a power output of 85 bhp

1955 The Aurelia Spider (B24, B24S) was introduced with the same 2.5-litre V6 as the GT2500

1956 Aurelia Spider's power output declined, to 110 bhp at 5300 rpm

1957 Power output of the Spider recovered, to 112 bhp at 5300 rpm

The sporty Lancia Aurelia GT2500 Coupé (codenamed B20) was innovative in many ways: the new V6 engine had unconventional 60-degree cyclinder spacing and separate cylinder heads for each bank. The GT also had a de Dion tube rear suspension rather than the semi-trailing arm type of its saloon counterpart. The rear-mounted transmission gave even weight distribution, as did the use of in-board mounted rear brakes and the de Dion rear suspension

The Stratos was an homologation special, hence the built-in roll-over protection. Note how mounting the 2.5-litre Ferrari V6 transversely meant an awkward route for the exhaust pipes on the inner cylinder bank, running under the engine. In its early days the Stratos had wishbone and coil suspension all round but that was soon changed to MacPherson struts at the rear, as on this example

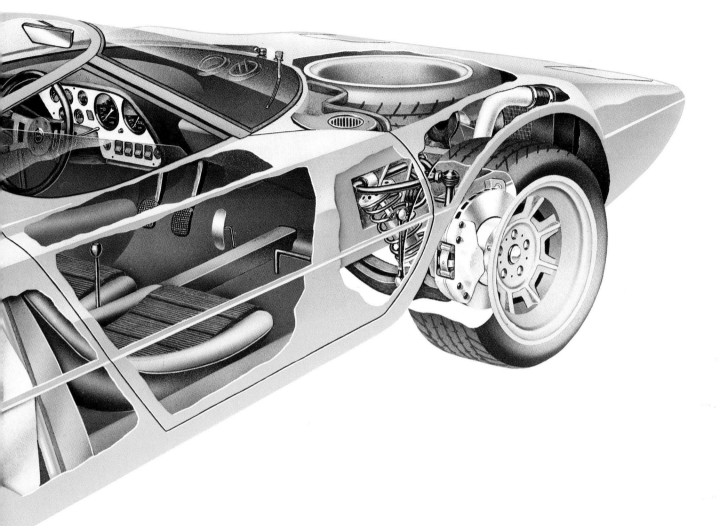

MODEL
Lancia Stratos (1974)

Engine
Location: Rear/mid transverse
Type: Water-cooled V6 with light-alloy cylinder heads and cast-iron block
Cubic capacity: 2418 cc/147.5 cu in
Bore × stroke: 92.5 mm × 60 mm/3.64 in × 2.36 in
Compression ratio: 9.0:1
Valve gear: 2 46-degree inclined valves per cylinder operated by twin gear and chain-driven overhead camshafts per cylinder bank
Fuel supply: 3 Weber 40DCF twin-choke downdraught carburettors
Ignition: Marelli transistorised
Maximum power: 190 bhp (DIN) at 7000 rpm
Maximum torque: 166 lb ft (DIN) at 5500 rpm

TRANSMISSION
Layout: Gearbox mounted below engine
Clutch: Single dry plate
Gearbox: Five-speed manual

1st 3.07:1	4th 1.25:1
2nd 2.12:1	5th 0.86:1
3rd 1.52:1	

Final drive: Helical
Ratio: 4.7:1

SUSPENSION
Front: Independent with wishbones, coil springs, telescopic dampers and anti-roll bar
Rear: Independent with struts, lower wishbones and anti-roll bar

STEERING
Type: Rack and pinion

BRAKES
Type: Girling ventilated discs all round, 28 cm (11 in) diameter

WHEELS AND TYRES
Type: Campagnolo cast alloy wheels with 205/70VR × 14 Michelin XWX or Pirelli Cinturato CN36 tyres

BODY/CHASSIS
Type: Monocoque centre section with welded on subframes. Two-door coupe body in steel and glassfibre

DIMENSIONS AND WEIGHT
Length: 371 cm (146.1 in)
Wheelbase: 218 cm (85.5 in)
Track – front: 143 cm (56.4 in)
– rear: 146 cm (57.4 in)
Weight: 979 kg (2160 lb)

PERFORMANCE
Maximum speed: 140 mph (225 kph)
Acceleration 0–60 mph: 6.8 seconds

MODEL
Lotus Elite Series II (1962)

ENGINE
Location: Front, longitudinal
Type: In-line four-cylinder, water cooled
Cubic capacity: 1216 cc/74.17 cu in
Bore × stroke: 76.2 mm × 66.6 mm/3.0 in × 2.6 in
Compression ratio: 10.0:1
Valve gear: 2 inclined parallel valves per cylinder operated by single chain driven overhead camshaft
Fuel supply: 2SU HS4 381 mm (1.5 in) carburettors
Ignition: Mechanical, coil and distributor
Maximum power: 80 bhp (SAE) at 6100 rpm
Maximum torque: 75 lb ft (SAE) at 4750 rpm

TRANSMISSION
Layout: Clutch and gearbox in unit with engine
Clutch: Single dry plate
Gearbox: Four-speed manual with synchromesh on top three ratios
  1st 2.53:1   3rd 1.23:1
  2nd 1.71:1   4th 1.00:1
Final drive: Hypoid bevel
Ratio: 4.23:1

SUSPENSION
Front: Independent with double wishbones, the anti-roll bar forming one half of the top wishbones. Concentric coil spring/damper units
Rear: Independent with Chapman struts with narrow angle lower wishbone

STEERING
Type: Rack and pinion, manual

BRAKES
Type: Discs front and rear, inboard at rear

WHEELS AND TYRES
Type: Wire spoked wheels and 155 × 15 Michelin X or Pirelli Cintura radial tyres

BODY/CHASSIS
Type: Monocoque glassfibre body/chassis with steel front suspension sub-frame bonded into body. 2-door coupé body

DIMENSIONS AND WEIGHT
Length: 3733 mm (147.0 in)
Width: 1486 mm (58.5 in)
Wheelbase: 2240 mm (88.2 in)
Track – front: 1194 mm (47.0 in)
    – rear: 1224 mm (48.2 in)
Weight: 644 kg (1420 lb)

PERFORMANCE
Maximum speed: 115 mph (185 kph)
Acceleration 0–60 mph: 11.8 seconds

A Series II Elite. Note the steel reinforcing for the front suspension mounting points and the windscreen support. They were the only metal parts used in the body

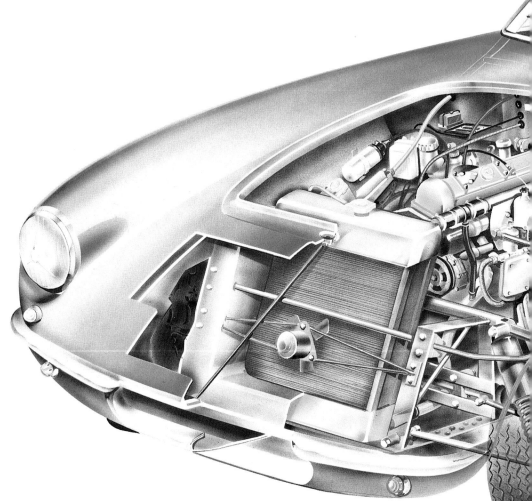

EVOLUTION

1957 Introduced at British Motor Show in October, featuring revolutionary glassfibre monocoque body, independent supension all round and Coventry Climax 1200 cc (74 cu in) engine

1958 First production car sold

1960 Series II Elite introduced, coinciding with production switch of chassis/body units from Maximar Company to Bristol. Series II differed from Series I in having revised rear suspension. SE (special equipment) version introduced at the 1960 Motor Show in October with 85 bhp engine and ZF gearbox

1961 Elite available as a kit from October

1962 Super 95 model introduced in May. Later that year the single SU was replaced by twin SUs

1963 Production ceased after 1030 body/chassis units built

RIGHT The Lotus Elite's revolutionary glassfibre monocoque was made up from various preformed units

MODEL
Lotus Elan S3 (1966)

ENGINE
Location: Front, longitudinal
Type: Water-cooled in-line four cylinder with cast-iron block and aluminium head. Five main bearings
Cubic capacity: 1558 cc/95 cu in
Bore × stroke: 82.55 mm × 72.75 mm/3.25 in × 2.86 in
Compression ratio: 9.5:1
Valve gear: Two inclined valves per cylinder operated by twin chain-driven overhead camshafts. Hemispherical combustion chambers
Fuel supply: Two Weber 40DCOE side-draught carburettors fed by AC mechanical fuel pump and 45 litre (10 gallon) fuel tank
Ignition: Mechanical, by coil and distributor
Maximum power: 93 bhp at 6000 rpm
Maximum torque: 108 lb ft at 4000 rpm

STEERING
Type: Rack and pinion, with telescopic steering column

BRAKES
Type: Discs all round, 24 cm (9½ in) diameter front, 25 cm (10 in) rear

WHEELS AND TYRES
Type: 4½J × 13 in (33 cm) centre-lock steel wheels fitted with 145 × 13 in radial tyres

BODY/CHASSIS
Type: Glassfibre two-seat two-door fixed-head coupé bolted to pressed-steel box-section backbone chassis with forks at each end to support engine, transmission and suspension. Front cross member served as headlamp vacuum reservoir

TRANSMISSION
Layout: Gearbox behind engine driving rear wheels
Clutch: Single dry plate, 20 cm (8 in) in diameter
Gearbox: Four-speed manual, all-synchromesh
  1st 2.972:1   3rd 1.396:1
  2nd 2.009:1 4th 1.000:1
Final drive: Hypoid bevel unit
Ratio: 3.90:1 on early S3s; later models had 3.777:1, and 3.555:1 was optional

SUSPENSION
Front: Independent, with upper and lower pressed-steel wishbones, coil spring/damper units and anti-roll bar
Rear: Independent, with coil spring/damper struts and lower transverse A-frames

DIMENSIONS AND WEIGHT
Length: 3683 mm (145 in)
Width: 1422 mm (56 in)
Wheelbase: 2134 mm (84 in)
Track – front: 1193 mm (47 in)
      – rear:** 1193 mm (47 in)
Weight: 694 kg (1530 lb)

PERFORMANCE
Maximum speed: 115 mph (185 kph)
Acceleration 0–60 mph: 9 seconds

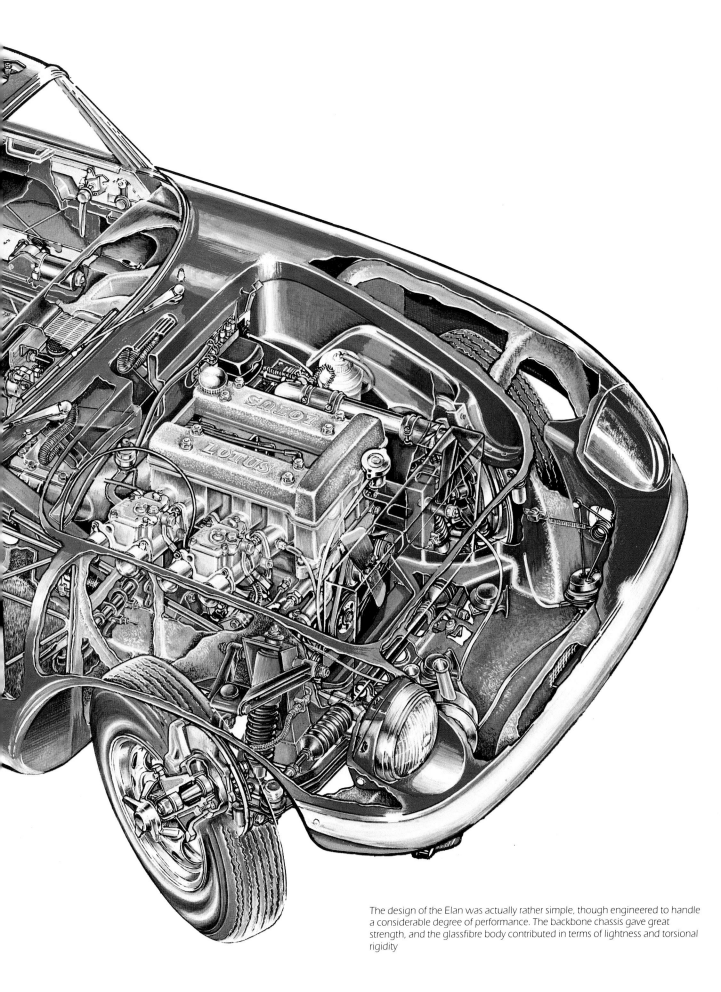

The design of the Elan was actually rather simple, though engineered to handle a considerable degree of performance. The backbone chassis gave great strength, and the glassfibre body contributed in terms of lightness and torsional rigidity

MODEL

Lotus Turbo Esprit (1985)

ENGINE

Location: Rear, longitudinal
Type: Water-cooled all-aluminium in-line four cylinder, five main bearings
Cubic Capacity: 2174 cc/ 132.6 cu in
Bore × stroke: 95.25 mm × 76.20 mm/3.75 in × 2.99 in
Compression ratio: 7.5:1
Valve gear: Four valves per cylinder operated by belt-driven twin overhead camshafts. Exhaust valves sodium cooled
Fuel supply: Two twin-choke Dellorto 40 DHLA H carburettors and Garrett AiResearch T3 turbocharger, set at boost-pressure limit of 8 lb per square inch
Ignition: Electronic
Maximum power: 210 bhp (DIN) at 6000 rpm
Maximum torque: 200 lb ft (DIN) at 4000 rpm

TRANSMISSION

Layout: Clutch and gearbox in unit with engine
Clutch: Single dry plate, 24 cm (9.5 in) dia, hydraulically operated

Gearbox: Five-speed all-synchromesh manual
  1st 2.92:1 3rd 1.32:1
  2nd 1.94:1   4th 0.97:1
             5th 0.76:1
Final drive: Hypoid bevel
Ratio: 4.375:1

SUSPENSION

Front: Independent with unequal-length upper and lower wishbones, separate anti-roll bar, coil springs and telescopic dampers (pre-1985 models had upper wishbone and single lower link assembly)
Rear: Independent with double unequal non-parallel transverse links with radius arms. Plunging drive shafts with aluminium hub carriers

STEERING

Type: Rack and pinion

BRAKES

Type: Discs all round, inboard at rear

WHEELS AND TYRES

Type: 15 in alloy wheels with 195/ 60 tyres at the front and 235/60 tyres at the rear

BODY/CHASSIS

Type: Galvanised steel backbone chassis with aerodynamic two-seat glassfibre sports body

DIMENSIONS AND WEIGHT

Length: 4191 mm (165 in)
Width: 1854 mm (73 in)
Wheelbase: 2438 mm (96 in)
Track – front: 1537 mm (60.5 in)
  – rear: 1554 mm (61.2 in)
Weight: 1220 kg (2690 lb)

PERFORMANCE

Maximum speed: 152 mph (245 kph)
Acceleration 0–60 mph: 5.5 seconds

EVOLUTION

1975 Introduced at Paris and London Motor Shows, the Esprit was a mid-engined two-seater with the 2-litre 16-valve Lotus 907 engine which developed 140 bhp

1978 Limited edition Esprit S2 launched. The engine of the S2 Esprits was improved and there were minor body and trim changes

1980 Lotus Turbo Esprit launched. Engine size was increased to 2.2 litres, which in normally aspirated form produced 160 bhp and 160 lb ft of torque and in turbo form delivered 210 bhp and 200 lb ft. The bodyshell was competition-modified to improve the aerodynamics. Esprit S2.2 launched with the normally-aspirated 2.2-litre engine

This cutaway is of an American spec Turbo Esprit, hence the left-hand drive. Early Turbos like this one had single-link lower front suspension

1981 Launch of 'normal' Turbo Esprit and Esprit Series 3, the latter incorporating the chassis and suspension modifications of the Turbo model

1983 Esprit Turbo was given larger boot and offered with option of removable glass roof

1985 Suspension modifications to Esprit range, including ventilated discs fitted at the front, larger rear disc calipers, and front anti-roll bar separated from front suspension

1987 Turbo HC with 215 bhp high-compression 912S engine introduced in Spring. Restyled versions launched at London Motorfair in Autumn

MODEL
Marcos 1800 (1965)

ENGINE
Location: Front longitudinal
Type: Water-cooled in-line Volvo B18 four cylinder with cast-iron block and head. Five main bearings
Cubic capacity: 1778 cc/108.46 cu in
Bore × stroke: 84.1 mm × 80 mm/ 3.31 in × 3.15 in
Compression ratio: 10:1
Valve gear: 2 parallel valves per cylinder operated by single block-mounted camshaft, pushrods and rockers
Fuel supply: 2 Stromberg CD 175 carburettors
Ignition: Mechanical by coil and distributor
Maximum power: 114 bhp at 5800 rpm
Maximum torque: 110 lb ft at 4200 rpm

TRANSMISSION
Layout: Gearbox in unit with engine, Rear-wheel drive. Laycock de Normanville Type D overdrive
Gearbox: Four-speed manual (overdrive optional extra)
1st 3.12:1	3rd 1.36:1
2nd 1.99:1	4th 1.00:1
Final drive: Hypoid bevel
Ratio: 3.91:1

SUSPENSION
Front: Independent with wishbones, coil springs and telescopic dampers
Rear: Live rear axle located by twin leading arms, with coil spring damper units

STEERING
Type: Rack and pinion

BRAKES
Type: Discs front and drums rear

WHEELS AND TYRES
Type: 175/13 Pirelli Cinturato tyres on 13 in 5½ J steel wheels (magnesium-alloy wheels optional)

BODY/CHASSIS
Type: Monocoque chassis of exterior grade Sitka spruce plywood, with 2-door glassfibre 2+2 coupé bodyshell

DIMENSIONS AND WEIGHT
Length: 4077 mm (160.5 in)
Width: 1587 mm (62.5 in)
Wheelbase: 2273 mm (89.5 in)
Track – front: 1238 mm (48.75 in)
– **rear:** 1295 mm (51 in)
Weight: 772 kg (1702 lb)

PERFORMANCE
Maximum speed: 116 mph (187 kph)
Acceleration 0–60 mph: 8.2 seconds

A 1965 Marcos 1800 with the Volvo engine. Although it did, of course, have a wooden chassis, note how the front suspension is located by a tubular steel subframe. This particular car has Weber carburettors but twin Strombergs were standard wear. The wooden chassis gave way to a tubular steel frame, with GRP bodywork, but externally the lines were little changed more than 20 years later, when the fuel-injected Rover V8 was the normal power unit

EVOLUTION

1963 Marcos 1800 introduced in October with wooden chassis and glassfibre body, powered by B18 Volvo four-cylinder pushrod engine

1966 A new version introduced with 85 bhp Ford 1.5-litre (91.5 cu in) four-cylinder engine

1967 Volvo engine replaced by bored-out Ford unit which grew to 1650 cc (100.6 cu in), producing 120 bhp. The crossflow Ford 1600-engined version also introduced. 99 Volvo 1800-engined cars were built while production of Ford 1500 and 1600-engined cars reached 300

1969 Ford 2-litre (122 cu in) V4 and 3-litre (183 cu in) V6 engines offered. Production of V4s reached 87 and 100 V6-engined cars were built with the wooden chassis before the steel chassis was introduced

1970 3-litre straight-six Volvo engine offered, along with overdrive. 200 cars with the Volvo 3-litre were built

1971 Production ceased after around 1000 of the 1800-style Marcos were built. That total included 11 with the 2.5-litre Triumph engine

1981 Marcos reintroduced in kit form with a choice of engine which included the 1.6-litre (97.6 cu in) crossflow Ford, the 3-litre Ford V6 and the 3-litre Volvo straight six

1984 Marcos Mantula introduced with 3.5-litre Rover V8

1986 Mantula Spyder introduced, coupé uprated (eg with air conditioning)

MODEL
Maserati Mistral 3500GTI (1964)

ENGINE
Location: Front, longitudinal
Type: Water-cooled all alloy in-line six-cylinder twin cam
Cubic capacity: 3692 cc/225.2 cu in
Bore × stroke: 86 mm × 106 mm/3.38 in × 4.17 in
Compression ratio: 8.8:1
Valve gear: Two inclined valves per cylinder operated by two gear and chain-driven overhead camshafts
Fuel supply: Lucas mechanical fuel injection
Ignition: Mechanical with coil and distributor. Double-contact Marelli distributor and two plugs per cylinder
Maximum power: 245 bhp (SAE gross) at 5500 rpm
Maximum torque: 253 lb ft (SAE gross) at 4000 rpm

TRANSMISSION
Layout: Gearbox and clutch in unit behind engine. Rear-wheel drive
Clutch: Single dry plate
Gearbox: Four or five-speed ZF manual

1st	3.00:1	4th	1.00:1
2nd	1.705:1	5th	0.85:1
3rd	1.240:1		

Final drive: Hypoid bevel
Ratio: Various, from 3.31:1 to 4.09:1. 3.77:1 typical

SUSPENSION
Front: Independent with wishbones, coil springs, telescopic dampers and anti-roll bar
Rear: Live rear axle with cantilever semi-elliptic leaf springs, flexible trailing radius arms, transverse linkage bar and anti-roll bar

STEERING
Type: Recirculating ball

BRAKES
Type: Discs front and rear, 306 mm (12.06 in) dia front and 291 mm (11.46 in) dia rear. Dual circuit, servo-assisted

WHEELS AND TYRES
Type: 165 mm (6.5 in) wide wire or steel wheels with 205 × 15 Pirelli radial tyres

BODY/CHASSIS
Type: Separate steel tubular chassis with coupé or convertible body

DIMENSIONS AND WEIGHT
Length: 450 cm (177.17 in)
Width: 165 cm (64.96 in)
Wheelbase: 240 cm (94.49 in)
Track – front: 139 cm (54.72 in)
– **rear:** 136 cm (53.54 in)
Weight: 1300 kg (2867 lb)

PERFORMANCE
Maximum speed: 144 mph (232 kph)
Acceleration 0–60 mph: 7.6 seconds

A 1964 3500GTI Mistral Coupé. Note in particular its crude rear suspension of live axle and semi-elliptic leaf springs

EVOLUTION

1957 3500GT introduced at Geneva Motor Show with 3485 cc (212.6 cu in) straight-six twin-cam engine

1959 Engine redesigned and power output increased to 260 bhp

1960 Front disc brakes introduced

1962 Rear disc brakes introduced. 3500GTI introduced with Lucas mechanical fuel injection giving an extra 15 bhp. Five-speed ZF gearbox made available. Vignale-bodied Sebring introduced on same short wheelbase as the 3500GT Spider

1963 Frua-styled Mistral introduced in both coupé and spider form

1966 Sebring production ended after nearly 450 cars were built

1968 Engine stretched to 4012 cc (244.7 cu in) and power increased to 255 bhp

1970 Production ended after 800 coupés and 120 spiders had been produced

MODEL
Maserati Bora (1972)

ENGINE
Location: Mid, longitudinal
Type: Water-cooled V8 with light-alloy block and heads. Five main bearings
Cubic capacity: 4719 cc/287.86 cu in
Bore × stroke: 93.9 mm × 85 mm/ 3.69 in × 3.35 in
Compression ratio: 8.5.1
Valve gear: 2 valves per cylinder operated by twin chain-driven overhead camshafts per bank of cylinders
Fuel supply: 4 Weber 42 DCNF carburettors
Ignition: Mechanical by coil and distributor
Maximum power: 290 bhp (SAE) at 6000 rpm
Maximum torque: 341 lb ft (SAE) at 4200 rpm

TRANSMISSION
Layout: Gearbox behind engine driving rear wheels
Clutch: Single dry plate
Gearbox: Five-speed ZF manual
  1st 2.580:1   4th 0.850:1
  2nd 1.520:1   5th 0.740:1
  3rd 1.040:1
Final drive: Hypoid bevel
Ratio: 3.770:1

SUSPENSION
Front: Independent with double wishbones, coil springs, telescopic dampers and anti-roll bar
Rear: Independent with double wishbones, coil springs, telescopic dampers and anti-roll bar

STEERING
Type: Rack and pinion. 3 turns lock to lock

BRAKES
Type: Discs all round. Servo assisted

WHEELS AND TYRES
Type: 7.5 × 15 in alloy wheels with 215/70 × 15 Michelin radial tyres

BODY/CHASSIS
Type: Integral with square-section steel tube subframe for engine and transmission 2-door 2-seat sports coupé body

DIMENSIONS AND WEIGHT
Length: 2735 mm (170.67 in)
Width: 1768 mm (69.61 in)
Wheelbase: 2599 mm (102.36 in)
Track – front: 1474 mm (58.03 in)
       – rear: 1474 mm (58.03 in)
Weight: 1400 kg (3087 lb)

PERFORMANCE
Maximum speed: 165 mph (265 kph)
Acceleration 0-60 mph: 6.5 seconds

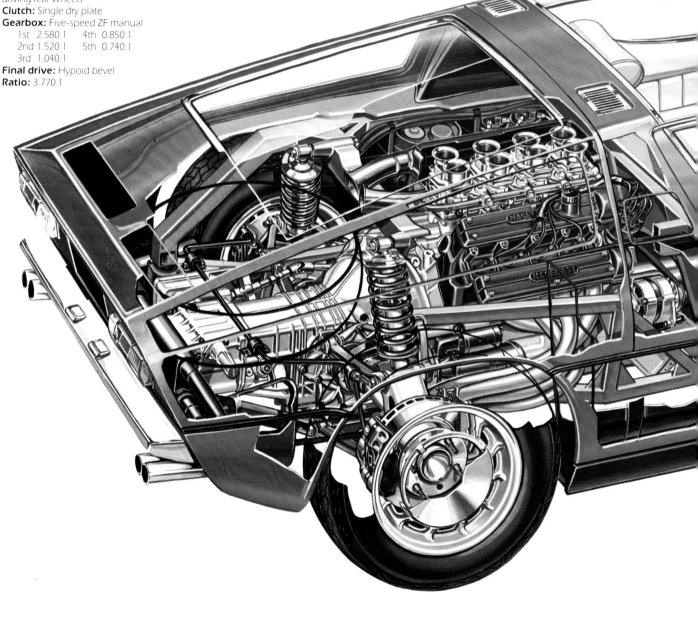

EVOLUTION

1971 The Maserati Bora was introduced at Geneva Show, powered by a short-stroke V8

1973 Merak introduced. It was powered by a 2.7-litre V6 derived from Maserati's existing V8 and developed for Citroën and the SM. The Merak's dimensions were identical to those of the Bora but it was some 227 kg (500 lb) lighter. The Merak could be distinguished from the Bora by its 'flying buttress' rear and flat engine cover

1974 Merak SS was introduced with the larger, 2965 cc (180.8 cu in), V6. A 159 bhp 2-litre version of the Merak was produced for the Italian market

1980 The Bora was discontinued

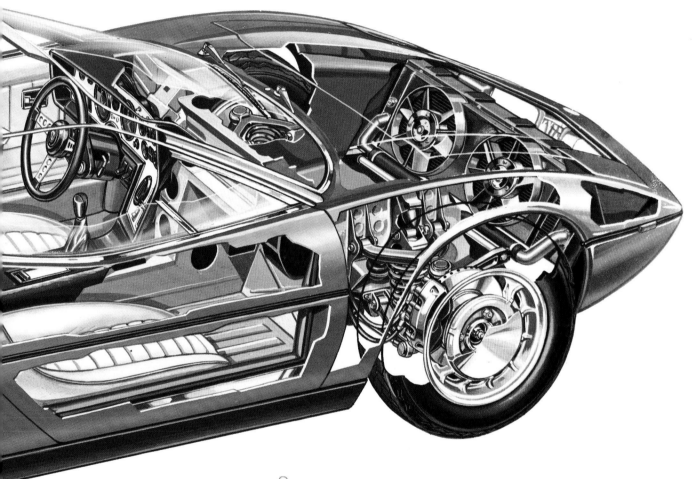

BRUNO BETTI

The Maserati Bora was one of Guigiaro's finest mid-engined designs, elegant and with very clean aerodynamics (the drag coefficient was particularly good for its era). It was also a very space-efficient design, far roomier than its rivals. Although it had a monocoque shell the Bora featured a very substantial engine and transmission subframe and the car weighed more than 1400 kg (3000 lb)

MODEL
Maybach Zeppelin V12 Cabriolet
(1934)

ENGINE
Location: Front longitudinal
Type: 60-degree V12 overhead
valve with aluminium cylinder block
and cast-iron liners. Eight main
bearings
Cubic capacity: 7922 cc/483.2 cu in
Bore × stroke: 92 mm × 100 mm/
3.62 in × 3.94 in
Compression ratio: 5.6:1
Valve gear: Two overhead valves
per cylinder operated by single
central camshaft via pushrods
Fuel supply: Two twin-choke Solex
carburettors
Ignition: Battery and coil with
automatic timing adjustment
Maximum power: 200 bhp at
2800 rpm

TRANSMISSION
Layout: Clutch and gearbox in unit
with engine
Clutch: Single dry plate
Gearbox: Four-speed manual with
pre-selection and low ratio option
Final drive: Helical bevel
Ratio: 3.58:1 or 5.66:1

SUSPENSION
Front: Non-independent with rigid
axle, semi-elliptic leaf springs and
double-acting dampers
Rear: Non-independent with live
axle, semi-elliptic leaf springs and
double-acting dampers

STEERING
Type: Worm

BRAKES
Type: Drums front and rear with
servo-assistance

WHEELS AND TYRES
Type: Wire wheels 20 in diameter
with 7.0/7.5 × 20 truck-type tyres

DIMENSIONS AND WEIGHT
Length: 5486 mm (216 in) approx
Width: 1753 mm (69 in) approx
Wheelbase: 3734 mm (147 in)
Track – front: 1473 mm (58 in)
   – rear: 1473 mm (58 in)
Weight: 3545 kg (7800 lb)

PERFORMANCE
Maximum speed: 110-115 mph
(177-185 kph)

A 1934 Maybach Zeppelin V12 Cabriolet with coachwork by Graber. These majestic cars were built on a massive 1905 mm (12 ft 3 in) wheelbase chassis. The vacuum-controlled transmission offered eight forward speeds; the driver simply selected the gear he wanted, which was automatically engaged as soon as he lifted his throttle foot; there were also two reverse gears. Before long this model carried a tiny model Zeppelin on the badge bar to recall its designer's association with airships

MODEL
Mazda RX-7 (1978)

ENGINE
Location: Front, longitudinal
Type: Twin rotor Wankel
Cubic capacity: 2292 cc/139.8 cu in
Compression ratio: 9.4:1
Valve gear: Side inlet, circumferential exhaust
Fuel supply: Downdraught two-stage, four-choke Nippon
Ignition: Electronic breakerless
Maximum power: 105 bhp (DIN) at 6000 rpm
Maximum torque: 106 lb ft (SAE) at 4000 rpm

TRANSMISSION
Layout: Gearbox in unit with engine
Clutch: Single dry plate
Gearbox: Five-speed manual
1st 3.674:1	4th 1.000:1
2nd 2.217:1	5th 0.825:1
3rd 1.432:1	
Final drive: Hypoid bevel
Ratio: 3.909:1

SUSPENSION
Front: Independent with MacPherson struts and anti-roll bar
Rear: Live axle with Watts linkage, upper and lower trailing links, coil springs telescopic dampers and anti-roll bar

STEERING
Type: Recirculating ball, variable ratio with 4.3 turns lock to lock

BRAKES
Type: Discs front and drums rear, 22.7 cm (8.94 in) diameter front and 22.8 cm (9.0 in) diameter rear

WHEELS AND TYRES
Type: 5½J alloy wheels with 185/70HR13 Pirelli Cinturato CN36 radial tyres

BODY/CHASSIS
Type: Integral steel chassis with two-door 2+2 coupé body

DIMENSIONS AND WEIGHT
Length: 4285 mm (168.7 in)
Width: 1675 mm (65.9 in)
Wheelbase: 2420 mm (95.3 in)
Track – front: 1420 mm (55.9 in)
      – rear: 1400 mm (55.1 in)
Weight: 1024 kg (2258 lb)

PERFORMANCE
Maximum speed: 115 mph (185 kph)
Acceleration 0–60 mph: 9.5 seconds

Engine apart the RX-7 was a very simple design without even independent rear suspension. The live rear axle was, however, well located with trailing arms and featured a distorted form of Watts linkage with unequal length arms for lateral location. The original RX-7 featured drum brakes at the rear, slightly surprisingly in view of its performance; the switch to rear discs was made in 1981

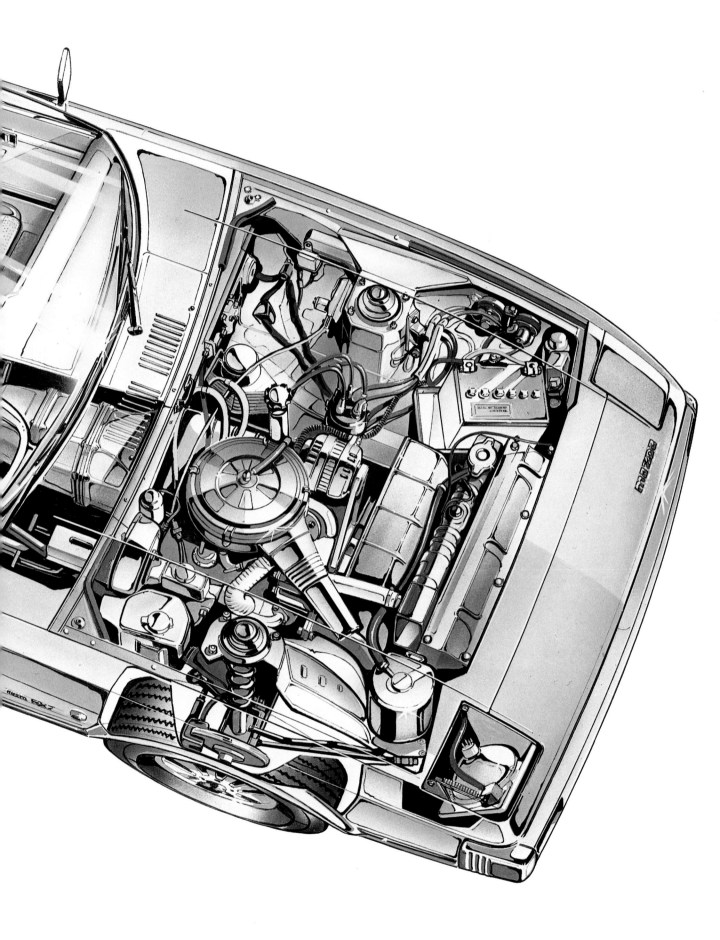

MODEL

Mercedes-Benz 38/250 SS TT (1929)

ENGINE

Location: Front, longitudinal
Type: Water-cooled straight six with cast light-alloy crankcase and block. Four main bearings
Cubic capacity: 7069 cc/431.2 cu in
Bore × stroke: 100 mm × 150 mm/3.9 in × 5.9 in
Valve gear: 2 valves per cylinder operated by single gear-driven overhead camshaft
Fuel supply: Twin Mercedes-Benz carburettors with Roots-type supercharger
Ignition: Coil and magneto
Maximum power: 220 bhp at 3000 rpm

TRANSMISSION

Location: Clutch and gearbox behind engine with torque tube location to rear axle
Clutch: Multi-disc type with central spring

Gearbox: Three-speed manual
 1st 3.15:1   3rd 1.36:1
 2nd 1.81:1
Final drive: Spiral bevel
Ratio: 2.76:1
(2.50:1, 3.09:1 optional)

SUSPENSION

Front: Non-independent with solid axle, semi-elliptic leaf springs and friction dampers
Rear: Live axle with semi-elliptic leaf springs and friction dampers

STEERING

Type: Screw and nut

BRAKES

Type: Internal-expanding drums all round

WHEELS AND TYRES

Type: Knock-on wire wheels or wooden artillery-type, with 20 × 6.5 in tyres

BODY/CHASSIS

Type: Pressed steel channel chassis with two side rails and five cross members. Open four-seater tourer body

DIMENSIONS AND WEIGHT

Length: 5080 mm (200 in)
Width: 1727 mm (68 in)
Wheelbase: 3403 mm (134 in)
Track – front: 1422 mm (56 in)
      – rear: 1422 mm (56 in)
Weight: 2134 kg (4704 lb)

PERFORMANCE

Maximum speed: 115 mph (187 kph)
Acceleration 0–60 mph: 8 seconds

The Mercedes S series cars were essentially simple; note, for example, the non-independent suspension by semi-elliptic leaf springs and friction dampers. The underslung rear springs, however, contributed to the car's handling and road holding. The S series was surprisingly good in both respects considering the weight and upright stance of the cars. Later SSKL models had the chassis side rails drilled for lightness

EVOLUTION

1926 Mercedes K introducéd, then the world's fastest production tourer

1927 Mercedes S introduced with engine enlarged to 6789 cc (414 cu in) and power output increased to 180 bhp

1928 Engine displacement increased to 7069 cc (431.2 cu in) to form the SS with power output of 200 bhp supercharged. SSK introduced on the 295 cm (116 inch) wheelbase with tuned version of the 7-litre engine producing maximum power of 225 bhp

1930 SSKL introduced. It was the same size as the SSK but had a much lighter chassis and a larger supercharger to boost power output to 300 bhp

1931 Production of S models ended

MODEL
Mercedes-Benz 540K (1937)

ENGINE
Location: Front, longitudinal
Type: Water-cooled in-line straight eight. Nine main bearings
Cubic capacity: 5401 cc/329.59 cu in
Bore × stroke: 88 mm × 111 mm/ 3.46 in × 4.37 in
Compression ratio: 6.13:1
Valve gear: 2 valves per cylinder operated by single block-mounted camshaft, pushrods and rockers
Fuel supply: Single Mercedes-Benz updraught carburettor with Roots type supercharger
Ignition: Mechanical with coil and magneto
Maximum power: 115 bhp nomally aspirated, 180 bhp with supercharger engaged

TRANSMISSION
Layout: Gearbox behind engine
Clutch: Multi-plate
Gearbox: Four-speed manual with preselector change on third and fourth
1st 3.89:1   3rd 1.419:1
2nd 2.27:1   4th 1.00:1
Final drive: Spiral bevel
Ratio: 3.03:1

SUSPENSION
Front: Independent with double wishbones and coil springs
Rear: Independent with swinging axles and two coil springs per side either side of drive shaft

STEERING
Type: Screw and nut

BRAKES
Type: Lockheed hydraulic, drums front and rear. Servo assisted

WHEELS AND TYRES
Type: Wire spoke wheels with Dunlop Fort 7 × 17 in tyres

BODY/CHASSIS
Type: Pressed steel chassis with two side rails and five cross members. Two-door, two-seater convertible body

DIMENSIONS AND WEIGHT
Length: 5258 mm (207 in)
Width: 1905 mm (75 in)
Wheelbase: 3289 mm (129.5 in)
Track – front: 1511 mm (59.5 in)
    – rear: 1492 mm (58.75 in)
Weight: 2502 kg (5516 lb)

PERFORMANCE
Maximum speed: 106 mph (171 kph)
Acceleration 0–60 mph: 13.8 seconds

This cutaway of a two-seater cabriolet reveals the innovative coil spring and double-wishbone front suspension first seen on the 380 models and subsequently widely imitated. Note the use of twin coil springs at each side of the rear swinging axle shafts to support the 540K's imposing mass. The total weight of nearly 2.5 tons handicapped fuel economy but endowed the speedster with an exemplary ride quality

When the Coventry-based SS Car Company decided its name must be changed after World War 2, Jaguar came into being. Since 1945 it has acquired Daimler, Guy Motors and Coventry Climax Motors, and merged with the British Motor Corporation – returning spectacularly to private ownership in 1984

MODEL
Jaguar D-type (production version)

ENGINE
Location: Front-mounted, longitudinal
Type: Water cooled straight-six, with cast-iron cylinder block
Cubic capacity: 3442 cc/210 cu in
Bore × stroke: 83 mm × 106 mm 3.27 in × 4.12 in
Valve gear: two valves per cylinder, with twin overhead camshafts driven by two-stage chain
Fuel supply: three twin-choke Weber DC03 carburettors
Ignition: coil and distributor
Maximum power: 246 bhp at 5500 rpm
Maximum torque: 242 lb ft at 4500 rpm

TRANSMISSION
Layout: Clutch and gearbox in unit with engine, driving rear wheels
Clutch: Triple-plate Borg & Beck hydraulic
Gearbox: Four-speed all-synchromesh manual
1st 2.144:1   3rd 1.28:1
2nd 1.645:1   4th 1:1
Final drive: Hypoid bevel
Ratio: 3.54:1 (normal)

SUSPENSION
Front: independent by wishbones and torsion bars, with hydraulic dampers
Rear: non-independent axle with radious arms, transverse torsion bar and hydraulic dampers

STEERING
Type: rack and pinion, manual

BRAKES
Type: Dunlop discs front and rear

WHEELS AND TYRES
Type: Dunlop 16 × 5½ K light alloy centrelock, with Dunlop 6.50 × 16 in racing tyres

BODY/CHASSIS
Type: central monocoque structure with fore and aft subframes. Open, nominal two-seater

DIMENSIONS AND WEIGHT
Length: 3911 mm (154 in)
Width: 1658 mm (65.3 in)
Wheelbase: 2300 mm (90.5 in)
Track – front: 1270 mm (50 in)
     – rear: 1219 mm (48 in)
Weight (dry): 861.8 kg (1900 lb)

PERFORMANCE
Maximum speed: approx 160 mph/257 kph (depending on ratios – with 2.79:1 axle ratio a speed of 164.136 mph/264.095 kph was timed at Daytona in 1955)

Tony Matthews '86

BELOW If you wish to combine a true space-frame chassis with a roof, the only possible solution is to use gullwing doors, as the chassis relies heavily on the stressed side sections for its strength

EVOLUTION

1952 Introduced as a sports-racing car at the Mille Miglia

1954 Pre-production prototype shown at New York Auto Show in February with production following later that year. Visual differences between the race car and road model included a restyled nose and the addition of side cooling vents. Fuel injected engine rated at 215 bhp (DIN) (240 bhp SAE)

1957 Production of the 300SL gullwing ended after 1400 built. 300SL Roadster introduced with revised chassis, no gullwing doors and single-low-pivot rear suspension

1958 Hardtop became available as an option

1961 Brakes changed from drums to discs all round

1963 Production of 300SL Roadster ended

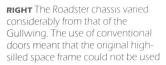

RIGHT The Roadster chassis varied considerably from that of the Gullwing. The use of conventional doors meant that the original high-silled space frame could not be used

MODEL
Mercedes-Benz 300SL Coupé, 1955

ENGINE
Location: Front, longitudinal
Type: Water-cooled in-line six
Cubic capacity: 2996 cc/182.75 cu in
Bore × stroke: 85 mm × 88 mm/ 3.35 in × 3.46 in
Compression ratio: 8.55:1
Valve gear: 2 valves per cylinder in line operated via rocker arms by chain-driven overhead camshaft
Fuel supply: Bosch injection
Ignition: Coil and distributor
Maximum power: 240bhp (SAE) at 6100rpm
Maximum torque: 2171b ft (SAE) at 4800rpm

TRANSMISSION
Layout: Clutch and gearbox in unit
Clutch: Single dry plate
Gearbox: Four-speed manual
   1st 3.14:1   3rd 1.305:1
   2nd 1.85:1   4th 1.0:1
Final drive: Hypoid bevel with limited slip differential
Ratio: 3.64:1

SUSPENSION
Front: Independent by double wishbones with concentric coil springs and telescopic dampers
Rear: Independent by swinging half axles

STEERING
Type: Recirculating ball, manual

BRAKES
Type: Drums front and rear, servo

WHEELS AND TYRES
Type: Pressed steel 5K x 15in with 6.70 x 15 tyres

BODY/CHASSIS
Type: Tubular steel space-frame chassis with coupé bodywork

DIMENSIONS AND WEIGHT
Length: 4217 mm (175.7 in)
Width: 1778 mm (70 in)
Wheelbase: 2387 mm (94 in)
Track – front: 1384 mm (54.5 in)
       – rear: 1435 mm (56.5 in)
Weight: 1293 kg (2850 lb)

PERFORMANCE
Maximum speed: 135mph (217kph)
Acceleration 0-60mph: 8.8 seconds

MODEL
MG TD (1950)

ENGINE
Location: Front, longitudinal
Type: Water-cooled in-line four-cylinder. Cast-iron block and head and three main bearings
Cubic capacity: 1250 cc/76.25 cu in
Bore × stroke: 66.5 mm × 90 mm/ 2.62 in × 3.54 in
Compression ratio: 7.25:1
Valve gear: 2 valves per cylinder operated via pushrods and rockers by single block-mounted camshaft
Fuel supply: 2 SU semi-downdraught carburettors. SU electric fuel pump
Ignition: Mechanical by coil and distributor
Maximum power: 54.4 bhp at 5200 rpm

TRANSMISSION
Layout: Clutch in unit with engine. Rear-wheel drive
Clutch: Single dry plate Borg and Beck
Gearbox: Four-speed manual with synchromesh on top three ratios
　　1st 3.50:1　　　3rd 1.38:1
　　2nd 2.07:1　　　4th 1.00:1
Final drive: Hypoid bevel
Ratio: 5.125:1

SUSPENSION
Front: Independent with wishbones coil springs and Girling piston-type dampers
Rear: Live rear axle with semi-elliptic leaf springs and Girling piston-type dampers

STEERING
Type: Rack and pinion

BRAKES
Type: 22.8 cm (9 in) dia Lockheed drums all round with twin leading shoes

WHEELS AND TYRES
Type: Bolt-on steel disc wheels with Dunlop 5.50 × 15 in tyres

BODY/CHASSIS
Type: Ladder type steel chassis with steel two-door two-seat open sports body

DIMENSIONS AND WEIGHT
Length: 3683 mm (145 in)
Width: 1489 mm (58.6 in)
Wheelbase: 2388 mm (94 in)
Track – front: 1203 mm (47.3 in)
　　　– rear: 1270 mm (50 in)
Weight: 914 kg (2016 lb) (unladen)

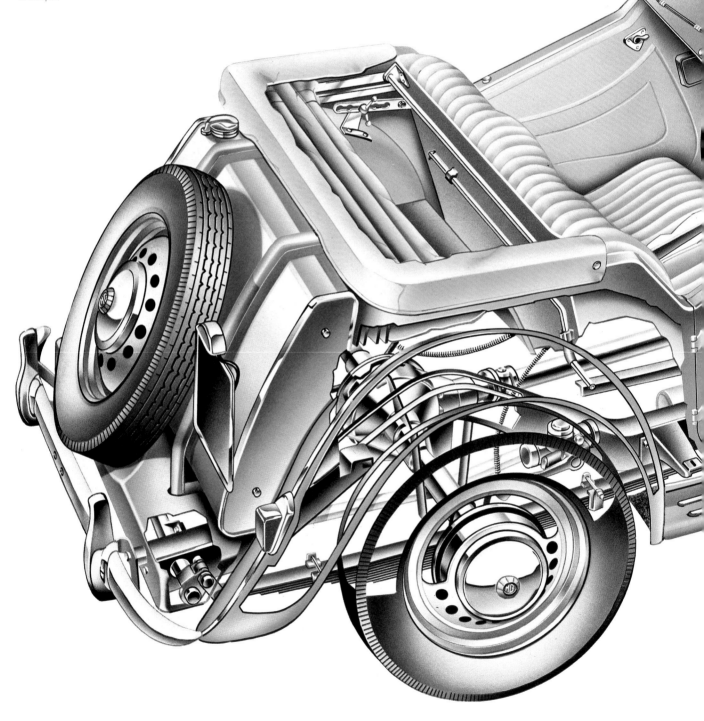

PERFORMANCE
Maximum speed: 83 mph
(134 kph)
Acceleration 0–60 mph: 21.3
seconds

The MG TD was mechanically a very orthodox design and the body design was firmly rooted in the 1930s, for as the company well knew, MG buyers were not particularly keen on change

EVOLUTION

1936 MG TA introduced, replacing the P-series Midgets, with a 1292 cc (79 cu in) overhead-valve engine. It was available as an Airline coupé and drophead coupé as well as the normal two-seater open sports body. 3003 TAs were built

1939 MG TB introduced, essentially the same as the TA except for its Morris-based 1250 cc (76 cu in) engine and a dry clutch. TB production totalled 379

1945 MG TC introduced. The 1250 cc engine was retained, its body was slightly wider. 10,000 TCs were built and two-thirds of them were exported

1949 MG TD introduced, loosely based on the Y-type saloon with the 1250 cc engine. The TD was the first MG Midget that could be built with left-hand drive and consequently the vast majority of the 29,664 TDs built were exported

1953 MG TF introduced. It was basically a face-lifted version of the TD with more rakish bodywork

1954 The 1466 cc (89 cu in) engine was made available in the TF from July. 6200 1250 cc TFs were built, along with 3400 of the 1500 version

1955 MG T series discontinued in favour of the MGA

MODEL
MGA 1600 (1959)

ENGINE
Location: Front longitudinal
Type: Water-cooled in-line four-cylinder with cast iron block and head
Cubic capacity: 1588 cc/96.87 cu in
Bore × stroke: 75.4 mm × 88.9 mm/2.97 in × 3.5 in
Compression ratio: 8.3:1
Valve gear: 2 valves per cylinder operated by pushrods and rockers, activated by single block-mounted camshaft
Fuel supply: 2 SU H4 carburettors
Ignition: Mechanical by coil and distributor
Maximum power: 79.5 bhp (gross) at 5600 rpm
Maximum torque: 87 lb ft (gross) at 3800 rpm

TRANSMISSION
Layout: Gearbox and clutch in unit with engine. Rear wheel drive
Clutch: Single dry plate
Gearbox: Four-speed manual
1st 3.64:1   3rd 1.37:1
2nd 2.21:1   4th 1.00:1
Final drive: Hypoid bevel
Ratio: 4.3:1

SUSPENSION
Front: Independent with wishbones, coil springs and Armstrong lever arm hydraulic dampers incorporated in top wishbones
Rear: Live rear axle located by semi-elliptic leaf springs and lever arm Armstrong hydraulic dampers

STEERING
Type: Rack and pinion

BRAKES
Type: Lockheed discs front and drums rear

WHEELS AND TYRES
Type: Centre-lock wire wheels with Dunlop 5.60 × 15 in crossply tyres

BODY/CHASSIS
Type: Cross-braced steel box-section perimeter chassis with two-door body

DIMENSIONS AND WEIGHT
Length: 396 cm (156 in)
Width: 147 cm (58 in)
Wheelbase: 238 cm (94 in)
Track – front: 120 cm (47.5 in)
      – rear: 122.5 cm (48.25 in)
Weight: 940 kg (2072 lb)

PERFORMANCE
Maximum speed: 98.5 mph (158.5 kph)
Acceleration 0–60 mph: 16.5 seconds

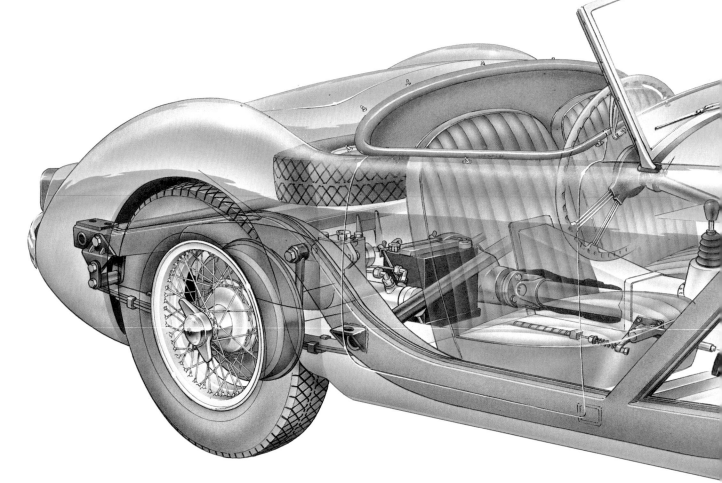

The MGA shown here is the early 1588 cc (97 cu in) model; when the engine was enlarged to 1600 cc (98 cu in) the front drum brakes were replaced by discs. Whilst the car was certainly a dramatic leap forward in terms of styling for MG, its mechanical design was not particularly advanced for its day. The MGA offered lively performance and good touring capabilities, and has today become a much sought-after classic car

EVOLUTION

1955 MGA introduced in convertible form with the 1489 cc (91 cu in) B-series engine producing 68 bhp (soon increased to 72 bhp)

1956 Fixed head coupé introduced with winding windows and larger windscreen

1958 MGA Twin Cam introduced with 1588 cc (97 cu in) twin-cam engine producing 108 bhp at 6700 rpm. Lockheed disc brakes replaced the drum brakes at the front

1959 Displacement of the overhead-valve engine increased to 1588 cc (97 cu in), giving more power (80 bhp). Front disc brakes introduced on MGA

1960 Twin Cam discontinued and its bodyshells used for 'De Luxe' versions of the pushrod cars

1961 MGA Mk II introduced in April with new 1622 cc (99 cu in) engine which produced 93 bhp

1962 MGA production discontinued in June

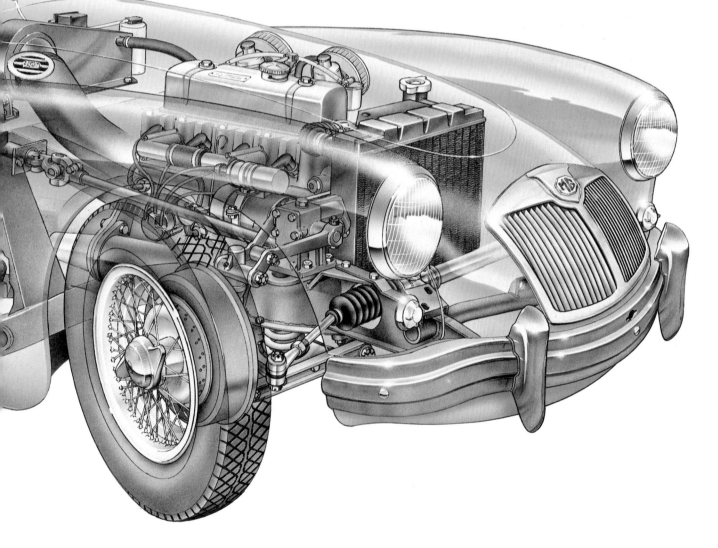

The Cooper S of 1970 was essentially the same as the very first Mini of 1959 and, with its 76 bhp, proved just how conservative the original management had been in giving the first car the small 850 cc (52 cu in) 37 bhp version of the famous A-series engine. This particular model has the Hydrolastic suspension rather than the 'dry' rubber cone system of the first cars. The Mini was a superb piece of packaging, with the gearbox housed actually in the engine sump and the rear suspension so designed that it did not encroach on the passenger compartment

MODEL
Morris Mini Cooper S (1970)

ENGINE
Location: Front, transverse
Type: In-line water-cooled four-cylinder with cast-iron block and head. Three main bearings
Cubic capacity: 1275 cc/77.77 cu in
Bore × stroke: 70.7 mm × 81.4 mm/ 2.78 in × 3.20 in
Compression ratio: 9.7:1
Valve gear: Two valves per cylinder operated by single block-mounted camshaft, pushrods and rockers
Fuel supply: Two SU HS 2 carburettors
Ignition: Mechanical by coil and distributor
Maximum power: 76 bhp (DIN) at 6000 rpm
Maximum torque: 79 lb ft at 3000 rpm

TRANSMISSION
Layout: Gearbox mounted below engine in sump with clutch on end of engine
Clutch: Single dry plate
Gearbox: Four-speed manual
   1st 3.200:1   3rd 1.357:1
   2nd 1.916:1   4th 1.000:1
Final drive: Helical spur
Ratio: 3.440:1

SUSPENSION
Front: Independent with wishbones and Hydrolastic rubber cone springs. Hydraulic connecting pipe to rear wheels
Rear: Independent with swinging longitudinal trailing arms, Hydrolastic rubber-cone springs, connecting pipe to front wheels and pitch control tension springs

STEERING
Type: Rack and pinion. 2.33 turns lock to lock

BRAKES
Type: Discs front (190 mm/7.48 in dia) and drums rear, servo-assisted

WHEELS AND TYRES
Type: Steel wheels with 5.2 in × 10 in radial tyres

BODY/CHASSIS
Type: Integral steel with auxiliary subframes front and rear. Two-door four-seat saloon body

DIMENSIONS AND WEIGHT
Length: 3054 mm (120.24 in)
Width: 1410 mm (55.51 in)
Wheelbase: 2036 mm (80.16 in)
Track – front: 1207 mm (47.53 in)
      – rear: 1176 mm (46.31 in)
Weight: 661 kg (1458 lb)

PERFORMANCE
Maximum speed: 98 mph (157 kph)
Acceleration 0–60 mph: 10.9 seconds

MODEL
Morgan Super Aero (1930)

ENGINE
Location: Front
Type: Water-cooled vee-twin JAP
Cubic capacity: 1096 cc/66.8 cu in
Bore × stroke: 85.7 mm × 95 mm/3.37 in × 3.74 in
Compression ratio: 6 : 1
Valve gear: Two inclined valves per cylinder, operated by push rods
Fuel supply: Gravity feed to a single Amal carburettor
Ignition: Magneto
Maximum power: 45 bhp
Maximum torque: Not known

TRANSMISSION
Layout: Enclosed prop shaft from engine to rear mounted gearbox
Clutch: Fabric-lined cone
Gearbox: Two-speed
1st 3.166 : 1
2nd 1.833 : 1
Final drive: Bevel gears with chain drive to rear wheel
Ratio: 2.583 : 1 (Overall ratios: 1st 8 : 1, 2nd 4 : 1)

SUSPENSION
Front: Morgan sliding pillar and coil springs
Rear: Quarter-elliptic leaf springs and forks

STEERING
Type: Geared

BRAKES
Type: Foot brake to 20 cm (8 in) drum on rear wheel, handbrake via cables to 17.8 cm (7 in) drums on front wheels

WHEELS AND TYRES
Type: 482.6 mm (19 in) wire-spoked wheels with 400-section tyres

BODY/CHASSIS
Type: Tubular steel chassis with steel two-seat open body

DIMENSIONS AND WEIGHT
Length: 3048 mm (124 in)
Width: 1498.6 mm (59 in)
Wheelbase: 2209.8 mm (87 in)
Track – front: 1270 mm (50 in)
Weight: 406.4 kg (896 lb)

PERFORMANCE
Maximum speed: 75 mph (120 kph)

A 1930 Morgan Super Aero M type with water-cooled JAP vee twin – the archetypal Morgan three-wheeler with its distinctive vee engine, sliding pillar front and quarter elliptic rear suspension and tubular chassis. The two-speed transmission's ratios were determined by the diameter of the chain sprockets

MODEL
Morgan Plus 8 (1984)

ENGINE
Location: Front, longitudinal
Type: V8 with light-alloy block and heads. Five main bearings
Cubic capacity: 3528 cc/215.21 cu in
Bore × stroke: 89 mm × 71 mm/ 3.5 in × 2.8 in
Compression ratio: 9.3:1
Valve gear: 2 valves per cylinder operated by pushrods rockers and hydraulic tappets by single camshaft mounted in centre of vee
Fuel supply: Lucas electronic fuel injection
Ignition: Lucas Constant-Energy electronic
Maximum power: 190 bhp at 5280 rpm
Maximum torque: 220 lb ft at 4000 rpm

TRANSMISSION
Layout: Gearbox and clutch in unit with engine
Clutch: Single dry plate
Gearbox: Five-speed manual

1st 3.320:1	4th 1.00:1
2nd 2.080:1	5th 0.792:1
3rd 1.390:1	

Final drive: Hypoid bevel with limited-slip differential
Ratio: 3.310:1

SUSPENSION
Front: Independent with vertical sliding pillars, coil springs and telescopic dampers
Rear: Live rear axle with semi-elliptic leaf springs and lever arm dampers

STEERING
Type: Rack and pinion. 3.25 turns lock to lock.

BRAKES
Type: Discs front, drums rear. Total swept area 2097 sq cm (325 sq in)

WHEELS AND TYRES
Type: Alloy wheels 6.5 in wide with 205 × 15 radial tyres

BODY/CHASSIS
Type: Ladder frame with Z-section longitudinal members, tubular and box-section cross members. 2-door, 2-seat roadster body built on ash frame

DIMENSIONS AND WEIGHT
Length: 373 cm (147 in)
Width: 158 cm (62 in)
Wheelbase: 249 cm (98 in)
Track – front: 132 cm (52 in)
 – rear: 135 cm (53 in)
Weight: 889 kg (1956 lb)

PERFORMANCE
Maximum speed: 130 mph (209 kph)
Acceleration 0–60 mph: 6.3 seconds

This drawing of a fuel-injected Plus 8 shows the pressed-steel chassis and the use of wood frames around the cockpit and in the doors. Morgan's traditional front suspension gives positive control, while the old-fashioned rear suspension contributes to a firm ride

EVOLUTION

1935 Prototype Morgan four wheeler appeared, powered by a 933 cc (60 cu in) side-valve Ford engine

1936 Production 4/4s introduced with a 1222 cc (74 cu in) Coventry Climax engine

1938 Le Mans and TT replicas introduced

1939 Engine changed to the 40 bhp 1267 cc (77 cu in) Standard four and Morgan production was almost standardized until 1950

1950 2.1-litre Standard engine fitted, which entailed lengthening the wheelbase, forming the Plus 4. Girling telescopic dampers replaced the antiquated Newton and André type. Hydraulic brakes also introduced

1953 Plus 4 with 1991 cc (121 cu in) Triumph TR2 engine introduced. Series 2 4/4 introduced with the side-valve 1172 cc (72 cu in) Ford engine

1957 Triumph TR3 engine was fitted to the Plus 4

1960 Front disc brakes became standard equipment on the Plus 4. Series 3 4/4 introduced with the overhead-valve 997 cc (61 cu in) Ford engine. A four-speed gearbox replaced the three-speed

1961 Triumph 2138 cc (130 cu in) engine introduced on Plus 4. Series 4 4/4 appeared with 1340 cc (82 cu in) Ford engine

1962 Series 5 4/4 introduced with the 1498 cc (91 cu in) Ford engine

1963 The glassfibre-bodied Plus 4 Plus coupé introduced

1968 Rover V8 engine installed in a longer and wider chassis to form the Plus 8 and the 4/4 was uprated to take the 1600 cc (98 cu in) Ford unit

1972 The Plus 8 was given the Rover four-speed gearbox

1976 The five-speed Rover gearbox was fitted to the Plus 8

1980 The 4/4 was fitted with a 1600 cc Fiat engine and then Ford's CVH 1600 unit

1983 The Plus 8 became available with its V8 in Rover Vitesse tune. Rack and pinion steering was introduced to the Plus 8

1985 The 4/4 made available with the 2-litre Fiat twin-cam

1987 Fiat-engined version of 4/4 discontinued

1988 Plus Four fitted with Rover M16 1994 cc (122 cu in) engine, in place of 1.6-litre (98 cu in) Ford CVH

MODEL
NSU Ro80 (1968)

ENGINE
Location: Front
Type: Twin rotor Wankel, water cooled with alloy rotor housing and two spark plugs per rotor
Cubic capacity: 994 cc/60.6 cu in
Bore × stroke: N/A
Compression ratio: 9.0:1
Valve Gear: Single inlet and exhaust port per rotor
Fuel supply: 2 Solex twin-choke 18/32 HHD carburettors
Ignition: Electronic thyristor capacitor discharge
Maximum power: 113.5 bhp (DIN) at 5500 rpm
Maximum torque: 117 lb ft (DIN) at 4500 rpm

TRANSMISSION
Layout: Transaxle in unit with engine
Clutch: Single dry plate with torque converter. Servo assisted
Gearbox: Three-speed semi automatic
  1st 2.06 : 1   3rd 0.791 : 1
  2nd 1.21 : 1
Final drive: Hypoid bevel
Ratio: 4.86 : 1

SUSPENSION
Front: Independent with MacPherson struts and anti-roll bar
Rear: Independent with MacPherson struts and tubular trailing arms

STEERING
Type: Rack and pinion, power assisted

BRAKES
Type: Discs front and rear with rear drums for handbrake

WHEELS AND TYRES
Type: 5J pressed steel wheels with Michelin XAS 175 SR14 tyres

BODY/CHASSIS
Type: Steel, integral with four door saloon bodywork

DIMENSIONS AND WEIGHT
Length: 4826 mm (190.0 in)
Width: 1765 mm (69.5 in)
Wheelbase: 2863 mm (112.7 in)
Track – front: 1486 mm (58.5 in)
    – rear: 1435 mm (56.5 in)
Weight: 1210 kg (2668 lb)

PERFORMANCE
Maximum speed: 107 mph
(172 kph)
Acceleration 0-60 mph: 13.9
seconds

The compact engine/transaxle unit of this very advanced car, showing
both the complexity of the twin-rotor engine and its compact
dimensions (bottom), the MacPherson strut suspension and the inboard
disc brakes at the front

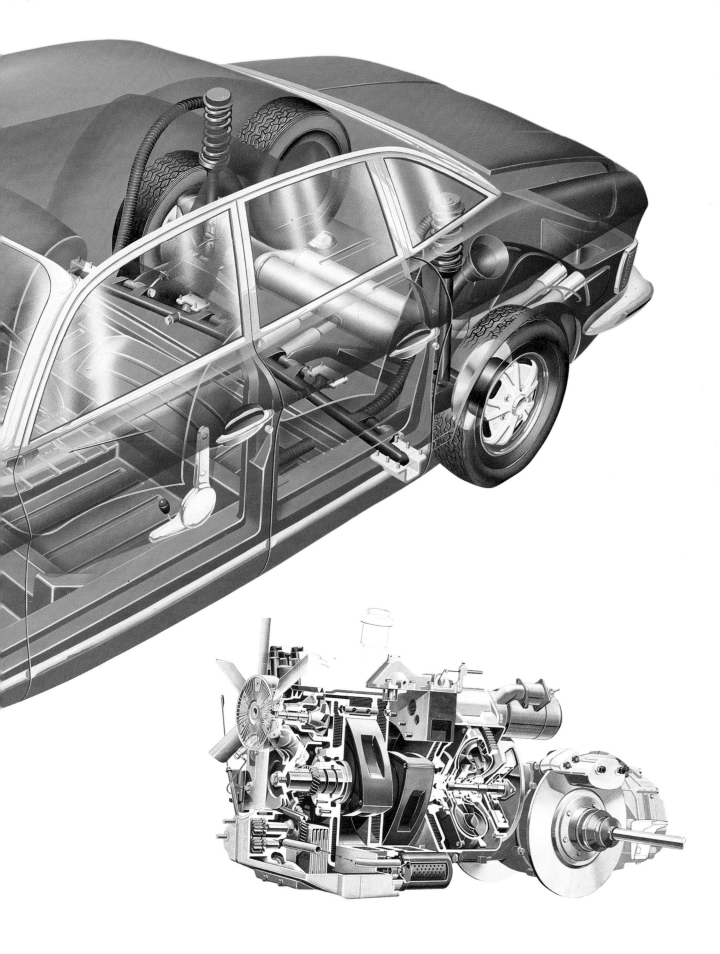

The Packard Twin Six was built to the highest possible standards of the day, and was built for only the wealthiest of clients. Silence, comfort and ease of driving were extremely important selling points at the top end of the market, and with its very smooth-running and understressed engine, all synchromesh gearbox and cushioned ride (aided in no small measure by the inertia of such a heavy car), the Packard satisfied many customers during its several series. The car's straight-line performance was excellent, for the V12 would have had a prodigious torque output (although this was not often measured in the 1930s). In all its mechanical, body and trim parts, the Packard was made to last a lifetime, and today the Twin Six is among the most valuable classic cars in the world

MODEL
Packard Twin Six V12, Tenth Series (1934)

ENGINE
Location: Front, longitudinal
Type: Four-bearing, 76-degree V12
Cubic capacity: 7297 cc/445 cu in
Bore × stroke: 87.3 mm × 101.5 mm/ 3.44 in × 3.99 in
Compression ratio: 6.0:1
Valve gear: Two valves per cylinder, L-head and hydraulic valve-lifters
Fuel supply: Dual down-draught Stromberg EE3 carburettor; mechanical fuel pump driven from camshaft
Ignition: Dual coil and battery
Maximum power: 175 bhp at 3200 rpm

TRANSMISSION
Layout: Clutch and gearbox in unit with engine
Clutch: Single dry plate, vacuum-servo assisted
Gearbox: Three-speed manual, all-synchromesh

1st 2.45:1	3rd 1.00:1
2nd 1.52:1	

Final drive: Angleset hypoid gearing
Ratio: 4.41:1

SUSPENSION
Front: Non-independent, with semi-elliptic leaf springs and dashboard-adjustable hydraulic dampers
Rear: Non-independent, with semi-elliptic leaf springs and dashboard-adjustable hydraulic dampers

STEERING
Type: Worm and roller

BRAKES
Type: Four-wheel vacuum-boosted Bendix mechanical drums

WHEELS AND TYRES
Type: 43 cm (17 in) wire wheels with 7.50 × 17 crossply white-wall tyres

CHASSISS/BODY
Type: Separate pressed steel channel ladder-frame chassis with central X-shaped cross-members, supporting two-door convertible Victoria body built by Dietrich

DIMENSIONS AND WEIGHT
Length: 5461 mm (215 in)
Width: 1880 mm (74 in)
Wheelbase: 3530/3658 mm (139/ 144 in)
Track – front: 1524 mm (60 in)
– rear: 1549 mm (61 in)
Weight: 2794 kg (6160 lb)

PERFORMANCE
Maximum speed: 93 mph (150 kph)
Acceleration 0–60 mph: 17 seconds

MODEL
Pegaso Z102B (1953)

ENGINE
Location: Front, longitudinal
Type: Water-cooled V8 with light-alloy block and heads
Cubic capacity: 2816 cc/171.77 cu in
Bore × stroke: 80 mm × 70 mm/ 3.15 in × 2.75 in
Compression ratio: 8.8:1
Valve gear: 2 inclined valves per cylinder operated by twin overhead camshafts per bank of cylinders.
Fuel supply: 4 Weber 36 DCF3 carburettors
Ignition: Mechanical by coil and distributor, or magneto
Maximum power: 170 bhp at 6300 rpm
Maximum torque: 160 lb ft at 3600 rpm

TRANSMISSION
Layout: Clutch in unit with engine, gearbox in unit with rear axle
Clutch: Single dry plate
Gearbox: Five-speed manual with synchromesh on top four gears

1st 3.00:1	4th 1.00:1
2nd 1.80:1	5th 0.86:1
3rd 1.24:1	

Final drive: Spiral bevel
Ratio: Various, from 5.2:1 to 4.18:1

SUSPENSION
Front: Independent by unequal length wishbones, torsion bars and telescopic dampers
Rear: De Dion axle located by radius rods to the rear

STEERING
Type: Worm and screw

BRAKES
Type: Drums all round

WHEELS AND TYRES
Type: Rudge type wire wheels with 6.0 × 16 tyres. 17 in wheels optional

BODY/CHASSIS
Type: Platform frame of square section members with welded pressings of chrome-moly steels. Alloy two-door coupé body by Touring. Other bodies by Saoutchik

DIMENSIONS AND WEIGHT
Length: 410 cm (129.2 in)
Wheelbase: 234 cm (92.0 in)
Track – front: 132 cm (52.0 in)
     – rear: 129 cm (50.8 in)
Weight: 990 kg (2200 lb)

PERFORMANCE
Maximum speed: 140 mph (225 kph)
Acceleration 0–60 mph: 8.5 seconds

The sophisticated Z102B comes to life in this cutaway. The space-saving
torsion bar front suspension is clearly evident and other notable features
are the de Dion rear suspension with the de Dion tube running ahead of
the final drive and the massive inboard rear brake drums. Such careful
and particular design was only possible in extremely expensive
low-volume cars like the Pegaso

MODEL
Pierce-Arrow Silver Arrow (1933)

ENGINE
Location: Front longitudinal
Type: Water-cooled 80 degree V12 with cast iron block and heads
Cubic capacity: 7566 cc/461.5 cu in
Bore × stroke: 88.9 mm × 101.6 mm/3.50 in × 4.00 in
Compression ratio: 6:1
Valve gear: Side valve. 2 valves per cylinder operated by single central camshaft and hydraulic tappets. Nickel-steel inlet valves, silchrome exhaust valves
Fuel supply: Twin Stromberg Ex 32 single-barrel downdraught carburettors
Ignition: Mechanical with coil and distributor, 6V, Delco-Remy or Owen Dyneto
Maximum power: 175 bhp
Maximum torque: 175 lb ft

TRANSMISSION
Layout: In-unit with engine, freewheel housed at rear of gearbox
Clutch: Double-plate dry disc
Gearbox: Three-speed manual
  1st 2.83:1   3rd 1.00:1
  2nd 1.70:1
Final drive: Hypoid bevel
Ratio: 4.21:1

SUSPENSION
Front: Non-independent, with semi-elliptic leaf springs 96 cm (38 in) long, with 12 leaves
Rear: Live rear axle with semi-elliptic leaf springs 60 inches long with ten leaves. Delco-Lovejoy hydraulic double-acting shock-absorbers front and rear

STEERING
Type: Ross cam and roller, 3.7 turns lock to lock

BRAKES
Type: Stewart-Warner mechanical servo-assisted 40.6 cm (16 in) drums

WHEELS AND TYRES
Type: 14-spoke steel artillery, five-stud mounting, 7.50 × 17 in tyres

BODY/CHASSIS
Type: Fastback sedan body, electrically-welded box-section ladder frame

DIMENSIONS AND WEIGHT
Wheelbase: 3530 mm (139 in)
Track – front: 1500 mm (59 in)
  – rear: 1560 mm (61.5 in)
Weight: 2314 kg (5100 lb)

PERFORMANCE
Maximum speed: 115 mph (185 kph)

The Pierce-Arrow Silver Arrow was produced in 1933 as a special show car of which only five examples were made in all, costing around $10,000. This handsome vehicle foreshadowed automobile styling in the 1940s; it was also a very successful exercise in aerodynamics. Note the wide included angle of the V12 engine – this allowed for better access to the central camshaft and also afforded a small height saving

EVOLUTION

1932 First Pierce-Arrow V12 range introduced. Three different models were offered, the 51, 52 and 53, with a choice of two engine displacements, 6524 cc (398 cu in) and 7035 cc (430 cu in), and three wheelbase lengths

1933 The V12 engine was modified to include hydraulic tappets, a US first, and the smaller V12 discontinued while a larger, 7566 cc (462 cu in) unit was added. The Silver Arrow was introduced at the Chicago Exposition on the 7.5-litre (458 cu in) chassis

1934 Five 'production' Silver Arrows were built

1936 The Model 1602 and 1603 V12s were introduced with new X-braced chassis and extremely efficient servo-assisted brakes. Overdrive and automatic restart were standard features and the V12's output was boosted to 185 bhp with the introduction of alloy cylinder heads

1938 All production ceased after just 17 1938 models had been built

MODEL
Porsche 356C (1965)

ENGINE
Location: Rear, longitudinal
Type: Air-cooled flat-four with plain bearings. Cast-iron block and alloy cylinder heads
Cubic capacity: 1582 cc/96.5 cu in
Bore × stroke: 82.5 mm × 74 mm/ 3.25 in × 2.91 in
Compression ratio: 8.5:1
Valve gear: Two valves per cylinder operated by pushrods and single central camshaft
Fuel supply: Two Zenith 32 ND1X carburettors
Ignition: Mechanical by coil and distributor
Maximum power: 75 bhp at 5200 rpm
Maximum torque: 90.4 lb ft at 4200 rpm

TRANSMISSION
Layout: Gearbox ahead of engine
Clutch: Single dry plate
Gearbox: Four-speed manual
1st 1.765:1	3rd 1.130:1
2nd 1.309:1	4th 0.815:1
Final drive: Spiral bevel
Ratio: 4.428:1

SUSPENSION
Front: Independent with trailing arms, transverse torsion bars, anti-roll bar and telescopic dampers
Rear: Independent with swinging half axles, swinging longitudinal trailing arms, transverse torsion bars, telescopic dampers and optional transverse leaf spring fixed to differential

STEERING
Type: Worm and roller

BRAKES
Type: Ate discs front and rear

WHEELS AND TYRES
Type: 5.60 × 15 steel sport wheels with 165/15 crossply tyres

BODY/CHASSIS
Type: Integral with steel two-door coupé body welded to steel floor pan

DIMENSIONS AND WEIGHT
Length: 4011 mm (157.9 in)
Width: 1671 mm (65.8 in)
Wheelbase: 2101 mm (82.7 in)
Track – front: 1305 mm (51.4 in)
   – rear: 1273 mm (50.1 in)
Weight: 925 kg (2040 lb)

PERFORMANCE
Maximum speed: 106.6 mph (172 kph)
Acceleration 0-60 mph: 13.5 seconds

The layout of the last of the 356s, the 356C, still owed an obvious debt to the VW Beetle on whch the original 356 was based. The 356 maintained the VW's torsion bar suspension front and rear along with a rear-mounted flat four engine

EVOLUTION

1948 Prototype open two-seater sports 356 built

1949 356 unveiled at the Geneva Motor Show, powered by an 1100 cc (67 cu in) engine

1950 Production commenced with 1300 cc (79 cu in) flat-four engine producing 44 bhp

1951 60 bhp 1488 cc (90 cu in) engine introduced

1952 1500 Normal (N) introduced with plain rather than roller bearings. The 1500 Super (S) continued with roller bearings, producing 70 bhp

1954 356 Speedster introduced in 1300 and 1500 N and S form. Front anti-roll bar added

1955 Engine bored out to 1582 cc (97 cu in). 1600 N produced 60 bhp and 1600 S 75 bhp, giving a top speed of 100 mph (161 kph). 7627 cars built before the 356A was introduced with revised body and chassis details. First 356 Carrera introduced with 1498 cc (91 cu in) twin-cam engine and top speed of 125 mph (201 kph)

1958 Carreras given the 1600 engine. Speedster discontinued in favour of Convertible D. 21,045 356As were built in all

1959 365B introduced at the Frankfurt Show

1960 356 Super 90 introduced with the plain-bearing 1582 cc (97 cu in) engine and transverse leaf spring attachment to improve rear suspension

1962 356 Carrera 2 introduced with 130 bhp engine and disc brakes all round. 30,963 356Bs were built

1963 356C introduced in Coupé and Cabriolet form, both with the 1582 cc engine. 356SC introduced with 95 bhp

1965 Porsche 356 range discontinued. 356C production totalled 16,668 and in total 76,303 356s were built

MODEL
Porsche 911 Carrera Coupé (1984)

ENGINE
Location: Rear, longitudinal
Type: Horizontally opposed six cylinder, air cooled
Cubic capacity: 3164 cc/193 cu in
Bore × stroke: 95 mm × 74.4 mm/ 3.74 in × 2.93 in
Compression ratio: 10.3 : 1
Valve gear: 2 inclined valves per cylinder operated by single belt-driven overhead camshaft per bank of cylinders
Fuel supply: Bosch L-Jetronic fuel injection
Ignition: Electronic with DME (digital motor electronics)
Maximum power: 231 bhp (DIN) at 5900 rpm
Maximum torque: 207 lb ft (DIN) at 4800 rpm

TRANSMISSION
Layout: Clutch and gearbox in unit with, and ahead of, engine
Clutch: Single dry plate
Gearbox: Five speed manual with synchromesh on all forward gears

1st 3.182 : 1	4th 0.966 : 1
2nd 1.833 : 1	5th 0.763 : 1
3rd 1.261 : 1	

Final drive: Spiral bevel
Ratio: 3.875 : 1

SUSPENSION
Front: Independent with MacPherson struts, lower wishbones, longitudinal torsion bars and anti-roll bar
Rear: Independent with semi-trailing arms, transverse torsion bars and anti-roll bar

STEERING
Type: Rack and pinion

BRAKES
Type: 23.4 cm (9.25 in) diameter discs front and 24.4 cm (9.61 in) discs rear, dual circuit, servo assisted

WHEELS AND TYRES
Type: Steel 6 in × 15 in front and 7 in × 15 in rear with 185/70VR15 tyres front and 215/60VR15 rear

BODY/CHASSIS
Type: Integral steel chassis with 2-door coupé body and 2+2 seating

DIMENSIONS AND WEIGHT
Length: 4290 mm (168.9 in)
Width: 1649 mm (64.96 in)
Wheelbase: 2271 mm (89.41 in)
Track – front: 1372 mm (54.02 in)
  – rear: 1379 mm (54.33 in)
Weight: 1160 kg (2558 lb)

PERFORMANCE
Maximum speed: 152 mph (245 kph)
Acceleration 0–60 mph: 6.1 seconds

MODEL
Porsche 928 S (1986)

ENGINE
Location: Front, longitudinal
Type: Water-cooled, all alloy V8 with linerless cylinder bores and five main bearings
Cubic capacity: 4664 cc/284.5 cu in
Bore × stroke: 97 mm × 78.9 mm/ 3.82 in × 3.11 in
Compression ratio: 10.4:1
Valve gear: Two valves per cylinder mounted in-line operated via hydraulic tappets by single belt-driven overhead cam per bank of cylinders
Fuel supply: Bosch LH Jetronic fuel injection
Ignition: Electronic
Maximum power: 310 bhp at 5900 rpm
Maximum torque: 295 lb ft at 4100 rpm

TRANSMISSION
Layout: Transmission in rear, with clutch in-unit with engine
Clutch: Single dry plate
Gearbox: Five speed manual or four-speed automatic

1st 3.765:1	4th 1.354:1
2nd 2.512:1	5th 1.00:1
3rd 1.790:1	

Final drive: Hypoid bevel
Ratio: 2.727:1

SUSPENSION
Front: Independent with wishbones, coil springs telescopic dampers and anti-roll bar
Rear: Independent with Weissach axle consisting of wishbones, semi-trailing arms, transverse torsion bars, coil springs and telescopic dampers

STEERING
Type: Rack and pinion. 3.13 turns lock to lock

BRAKES
Type: Discs front and rear. 28.2 cm (11.1 in) dia front, 28.9 cm (11.38 in) dia rear

WHEELS AND TYRES
Type: Alloy wheels with 7 in rims. 225/50VR16 tyres

BODY/CHASSIS
Type: Integral with two door 2+2 coupé body in steel and alloy

DIMENSIONS AND WEIGHT
Length: 445 cm (175.2 in)
Width: 184 cm (72.44 in)
Wheelbase: 250 cm (98.43 in)
Track – front: 155 cm (60.98 in)
– rear: 152 cm (59.88 in)
Weight: 1500 kg (3307 lb)

PERFORMANCE
Maximum speed: 158 mph (255 kph)
Acceleration 0–60 mph: 6.2 seconds

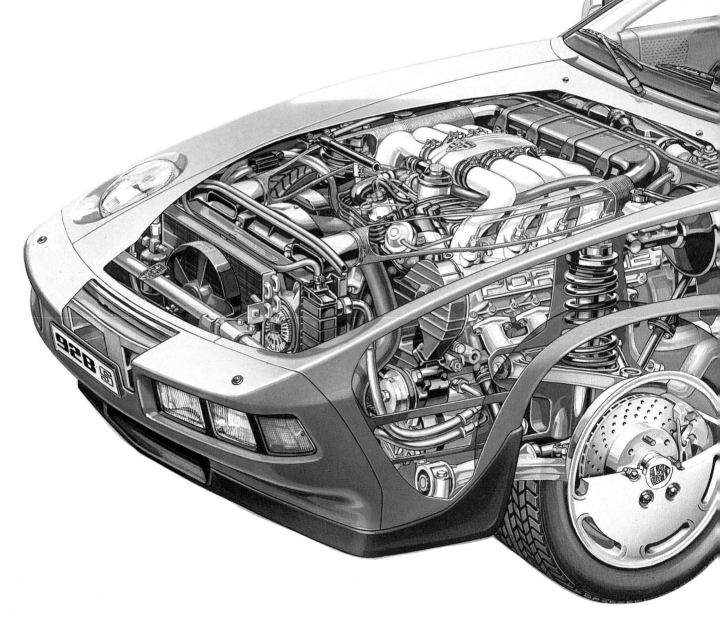

EVOLUTION

1977 Porsche 928 introduced at the Geneva Show with a 4.5-litre alloy V8 producing 240 bhp

1979 928S introduced alongside the 928. Engine bore increased to give a displacement of 4664 cc (285 cu in) and power increased to 300 bhp

1982 4.5-litre 928 discontinued

1983 928S Series 2 introduced with increase in power to 310 bhp. Mercedes-derived four-speed automatic transmission introduced. Anti-lock braking made standard equipment for some markets

1985 Anti-lock brakes became standard equipment worldwide. Series 3 introduced for US market, with quad-cam 32-valve version of 4664 cc (285 cu in) engine, with catalytic converter

1986 Series 4 introduced with quad-cam 32-valve 4957 cc (302 cu in) engine rated at 320 bhp. Nose and tail refined to improve drag figures

Locating the gearbox and final drive in unit at the rear of the car allowed the V8 to be set well back in the engine compartment to give the ideal equal weight distribution. While the front suspension is thoroughly conventional with double wishbones (albeit massive ones) the rear suspension is the 928's most interesting technical feature with links designed to decrease oversteer in high-speed corners by controlling the toe angle of the rear wheels

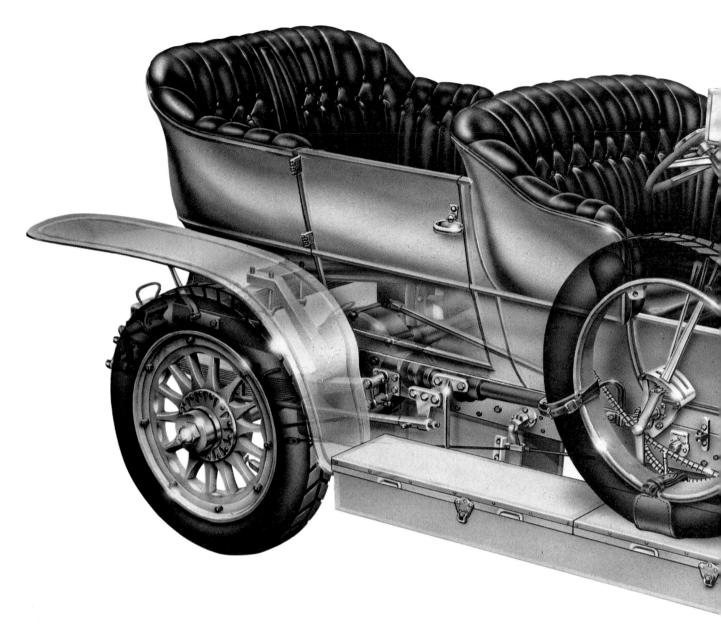

MODEL
Rolls-Royce Silver Ghost, 1907

ENGINE
Location: Front, longitudinal
Type: Water cooled straight six, in two groups of three cylinders
Cubic capacity: 7046 cc/430 cu in
Bore × stroke: 114 mm × 114 mm/ 4.49 in × 4.49 in
Compression ratio: 3.2:1
Valve gear: One two-jet Royce carburettor
Ignition: Coil and magneto, two sparking plugs per cylinder
Maximum power: 50 bhp at 1500 rpm

TRANSMISSION
Layout: Clutch and gearbox in unit with engine driving rear wheels
Clutch: Four speed manual with reverse

1st 2.83:1	3rd 1:1
2nd 1.66:1	4th 0.8:1

Final drive: Spiral bevel drive
Ratio: 2.708:1

SUSPENSION
Front: Forged axle on semi-elliptic leaf springs
Rear: Live axle supported on semi-elliptic leaf springs and transverse leaf spring

STEERING
Type: Worm and nut

BRAKES
Type: Rod-operated drums at rear

WHEELS AND TYRES
Type: Wooden spoked, with 875 mm × 105 mm (34.4 in × 4.1 in) tyres at the front, 880 mm × 120 mm (34.6 in × 4.7 in) tyres at the rear

BODY/CHASSIS
Type: Ladder type U-section steel chassis with six cross members. Special Roi-des-Belges touring style body built by Barker & Co.

DIMENSIONS AND WEIGHT
Length: 457 cm (180 in)
Width: 159 cm (62.5 in)
Wheelbase: 344 cm (132.5 in)
Track – front: 142 cm (56 in)
      – rear: 142 cm (56 in)
Weight: 1671 kg (3685 lb)

PERFORMANCE
Maximum speed: 55 mph (88.5 kph)

The bare bones of the original Silver Ghost The six-cylinder side-valve engine was made up of two three-cylinder monobloc units. Note the rear suspension which featured a transverse leaf spring along with the more conventional longitudinal semi-elliptic leaf springs. The high armchair-style seats were the distinctive feature of Roi-des-Belges coachwork

MODEL
Rolls-Royce Phantom III

ENGINE
Location: Front longitudinal
Type: Water-cooled V12 with light-alloy block and heads with cast-iron wet cylinder liners and seven main bearings
Cubic capacity: 7340 cc/447.7 cu in
Bore × stroke: 82.55 mm × 114.3 mm/ 3.25 in × 4.5 in
Compression ratio: 6.0:1
Valve gear: Two valves per cylinder operated via pushrods, rockers and hydraulic tappets by single camshaft mounted in centre of vee
Fuel supply: Single down-draught dual-choke Stromberg, fed by compound electric pump from 33 gallon fuel tank
Ignition: Dual Rolls-Royce battery ignition through two independent coils, twin contact breakers in each distributor, two spark plugs per cylinder
Maximum power: 165 bhp

SUSPENSION
Front: Independent wishbone with coil springs in oil-filled casing
Rear: Non independent with live axle, semi-elliptic springs and transverse anti-roll torsion bar

STEERING
Type: Marles cam and roller, three turns lock-to-lock

BRAKES
Type: Drums all round with gearbox-driven servo-assistance

WHEELS AND TYRES
Type: Wire wheels with 7.00 × 18 tyres (7.50 × 18 tyres to special order)

BODY/CHASSIS
Type: Separate X-braced pressed steel box-section chassis with built-in DWS hydraulic jacks; separate coachbuilt body

TRANSMISSION
Layout: Gearbox separate from engine
Clutch: Single dry plate
Gearbox: Four-speed manual
1st 3.00:1   3rd 1.32:1
2nd 1.98:1   4th 1.00:1
Final drive: Hypoid bevel gears
Ratio: 4.25:1

DIMENSIONS AND WEIGHT
Length: 4850 mm (191 in)
Width: 1955 mm (77 in)
Wheelbase: 3605 mm (142 in)
Track – front: 1535 mm (60.5 in)
        – rear: 1585 mm (62.5 in)
Weight (chassis only): 1835 kg (4050 lb)

PERFORMANCE
Maximum speed: 96 mph (155 kph)
Acceleration 0–60 mph: 16.8 seconds

The Phantom III was blessed with the very advanced V12 engine developed by Rolls-Royce as a determined break away from the dated side-valve unit used in the Silver Ghost. With a single alloy casting for the cylinder block, encompassing both banks of the vee, wet liners of cast iron and alloy cylinder heads, this flexible and refined engine truly reflected state-of-the-art development and helped change Rolls-Royce's somewhat conservative image where engineering was concerned. The clever independent front suspension incorporated spring and shock absorber in one unit

MODEL
Rolls-Royce Silver Shadow (1966)

ENGINE
Location: Front, longitudinal
Type: All-alloy V8 with wet liners.
Five main bearings
Cubic capacity: 6230 cc/380 cu in
Bore × stroke: 104.1 mm × 91.4 mm/
4.1 in × 3.6 in
Compression ratio: 9.0:1
Valve gear: Two valves per
cylinder operated via pushrods,
rockers and hydraulic tappets by
single camshaft mounted in centre
of vee
Fuel supply: Twin SU HD8
carburettors with twin electric fuel
pumps
Ignition: Mechanical by coil and
distributor
Maximum power: Approximately
200 bhp

TRANSMISSION
Layout: Transmission in unit with
engine, driving rear wheels
Gearbox: Four-speed Hydramatic
automatic
  1st 3.820:1   3rd 1.450:1
  2nd 2.630:1   4th 1.000:1
Final drive: Hypoid bevel
Ratio: 3.080:1

SUSPENSION
Front: Independent with
wishbones coil springs telescopic
dampers and automatic self
levelling
Rear: Independent with semi-
trailing arms, coil springs telescopic
dampers and automatic self
levelling

STEERING
Type: Recirculating ball. 3.5 turns
lock to lock

BRAKES
Type: Discs all round, 27.9 cm
(11 in) diameter with twin calipers,
three independent circuits and servo

WHEELS AND TYRES
Type: Steel wheels 8J × 15 in with
8.45 × 15 in crossply tyres

BODY/CHASSIS
Type: Integral steel monocoque
with subframes front and rear. Four-
door, five seat saloon body

DIMENSIONS AND WEIGHT
Length: 5169 mm (203.5 in)
Width: 1829 mm (72 in)
Wheelbase: 3035 mm (119.5 in)
Track – front: 1460 mm (57.5 in)
        – rear: 1460 mm (57.5 in)
Weight: 2067 kg (4556 lb)

PERFORMANCE
Maximum speed: 120 mph
(193 kph)
Acceleration 0–60 mph:
10.9 seconds

This cutaway of the Rolls-Royce Silver Shadow shows all the car's major components. The body/chassis is an integral unit, but the engine and suspension are mounted on separate front and rear subframes. The Silver Shadow's engine is a 6750 cc (412 cu in) V8, which produces 'adequate' power. The Series 1 Shadow was capable of 120 mph (183 kph) and could accelerate to 60 mph (86 kph) in little more than ten seconds

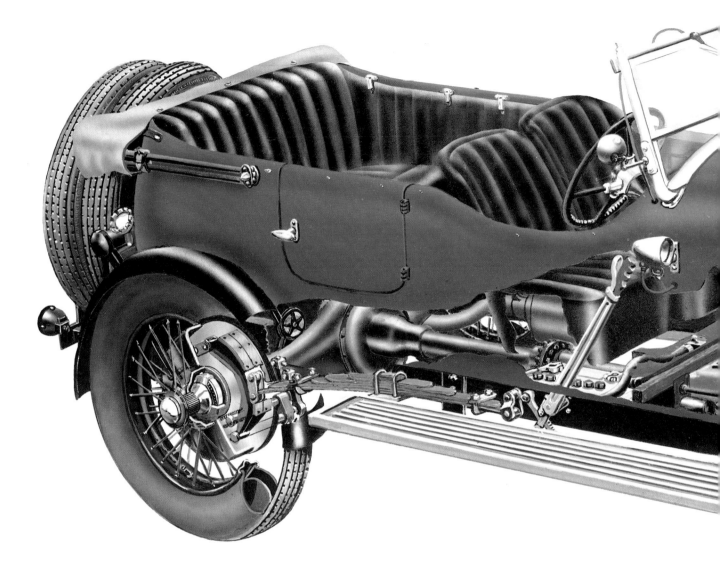

MODEL
3-litre Super Sports Sunbeam

ENGINE
Location: Front longitudinal
Type: Six fixed-head cylinders in line with dry sump lubrication
Cubic capacity: 2916 cc/177.9 cu in
Bore × stroke: 75 mm × 110 mm/2.95 in × 4.33 in
Compression ratio: 6.4:1
Valve gear: Twin overhead camshafts driven by helical gear trains, two valves per cylinder inclined at 110 degrees
Fuel supply: Two Claudel Hobson H42A carburettors fed by Autovac from rear-mounted 18 gallon fuel tank
Ignition: BTH CE6 magneto
Maximum power: 90 bhp at 3800 rpm

TRANSMISSION
Layout: Gearbox in unit with crankcase. Rear wheel drive
Clutch: Single dry plate, 11.85 in (301 mm)
Gearbox: Four-speed manual
1st 3.17:1	3rd 1.44:1
2nd 2.04:1	4th 1.00:1
Final drive: Spiral bevel
Ratio: 4.5:1

SUSPENSION
Front: Non-independent with semi-elliptic leaf springs (eight leaves 5 cm (2 in) wide)
Rear: Live rear axle with cantilever springs (six leaves 5.7 cm (2.25 in) wide)

STEERING
Type: Screw and nut

BRAKES
Type: Four wheel vacuum-servo assisted drums, 400 mm (15.75 in) diameter

WHEELS AND TYRES
Type: Detachable wire wheels 5.25 × 21 (originally 820 mm × 120 mm/32.2 in × 4.7 in beaded edge

BODY/CHASSIS
Type: Pressed steel channel chassis with four-seat tourer, Weymann body

DIMENSIONS AND WEIGHT
Length: 4475 mm (188 in)
Width: 1702 mm (67 in)
Wheelbase: 8315 mm (130.5 in)
Track – front: 1397 mm (55 in)
– rear: 1397 mm (55 in)
Weight (chassis only): 1340 kg (2954 lb)

PERFORMANCE
Maximum speed: 95 mph (153 kph)
Acceleration 0–75 mph: 35 seconds

The simple lines of the 3-litre Sunbeam. Although the Sunbeam rivalled the more famous Bentley 3 Litre in some respects, performance for example, it was certainly nowhere near as robust as the car described by Bugatti as 'the fastest lorry in Europe'. Its spindly construction is obvious and in fact one of the long chassis cars for Le Mans 1925 broke a chassis side member on the drive down to the race. That weakness was soon remedied, however, and the Sunbeam earned a reputation for its light controls and precise handling

EVOLUTION

1924 Prototype Sunbeam 3 litre built with a six-cylinder twin-cam engine. It was intended for the Le Mans 24 Hours but did not race

1925 The 3-litre Sunbeam introduced

1926 Revisions with the introduction of the F-sanction cars included a strengthened chassis and a redesigned front chassis cross member. Cylinder head also modified and cooling improved. 250 cars were built in 1926, making it the high point of 3-litre production

1929 Supercharged version of the 3 litre introduced, boosting power output by 50 per cent. 3 litre production ended after just 315 cars had been built

MODEL
Roesch Talbot 75 (1930)

ENGINE
Location: Front, longitudinal
Type: Water-cooled in-line six cylinder, cast-iron block and head and seven-bearing, counter-balanced crankshaft
Cubic capacity: 2276 cc/138.8 cu in
Bore × stroke: 69.5 mm × 100 mm/ 2.74 in × 3.94 in
Compression ratio: 6.5:1
Valve gear: Two overhead valves per cylinder, pushrod-operated, single gear-driven camshaft
Fuel supply: Single updraught Zenith carburettor
Ignition: Coil and Delco Remy double contact-breaker distributor
Maximum power: 74 bhp at 9500 rpm

TRANSMISSION
Layout: Gearbox in unit with engine, driving rear wheels
Clutch: single dry plate
Gearbox: Four-speed manual
1st 3.6:1   3rd 1.3:1
2nd 2.0:1   4th 1.0:1
Final drive: Crown wheel and pinion
Ratio: 4.9:1

SUSPENSION
Front: Non-independent, with beam axle, quarter-elliptic leaf springs and friction dampers
Rear: Non-independent, with live axle, quarter-elliptic leaf springs and friction dampers

STEERING
Type: Worm and nut

BRAKES
Type: Drums all round, rod and cable-operated

WHEELS AND TYRES
Type: Talbot bolt-on, 41 cm (16 in) wire wheels fitted with 600 × 16 crossply tyres

BODY/CHASSIS
Type: Steel U and I-section ladder-frame chassis supporting steel four-door, four-seat saloon body

DIMENSIONS AND WEIGHT
Length: 4343 mm (171 in)
Width: 1727 mm (68 in)
Wheelbase: 8048 mm (120 in)
Track – front: 1410 mm (55.5 in)
    – rear: 1410 mm (55.5 in)
Weight: 1575 kg (3472 lb)

PERFORMANCE
Maximum speed: 75 mph (121 kph)
Acceleration 0–60 mph: 28 secon

EVOLUTION

1927 The first Roesch Talbot vehicles were the 14/45 and 65 models, powered by a six-cylinder engine of 1665 cc (102 cu in)

1928 Type AG introduced with strengthened chassis and brakes and 46 bhp engine

1930 New 70 and 75 models with 2276 cc (139 cu in) 60 bhp engine and 305 cm (10 ft) chassis. AM90 introduced as short-chassis version of 70/75 with 123 bhp engine. Twelve sports versions of the 105 were produced, and the BA 105 model, a 3-litre version of the BA75, was introduced

1931 Six-cylinder 2969 cc (181 cu in) 105 introduced with engine producing between 100 and 138 bhp

1932 AU65 and AX65 introduced with 48 bhp engine. AX had preselector gearbox and cable front brakes. AW75 version introduced with 290 cm (9 ft 6 in) chassis of 90 and 105 models, fitted with preselector gearbox. AW90 had AM90 engine on AW75 short chassis. Low compression 305 cm (10 ft) chassis, high radiator version of 105 made available and known as the 95. Preselector gearbox available on the 105

1934 BA75 model appeared with new, low 305 cm (10 ft) chassis and softer suspension. 110 introduced identical to 105 but with increased bore giving 3377 cc (206 cu in) and 120 bhp. Improved and strengthened 305 cm (10 ft) dropped chassis on 110 made the BG 3½-litre version with 123 bhp

1935 Roesch Talbot production ended

The Talbot 75 was introduced in 1930 and quickly proved to be a successful model. Mechanically the 75 was not particularly adventurous, but it was the foundation for Roesch's development work which led to the very advanced 90 and 105 models. The radiator was high on the earlier 75s, leaving a large space over the engine, but the bonnet line was lowered in 1932. In its day the 75 was a fast saloon, known for its quality, moderate price and reliability

MODEL

Talbot Lago Record (1946)

ENGINE

Location: Front, longitudinal
Type: Water-cooled straight six with cast-iron block and heads, seven main bearings and Lanchester counter-balance shafts.
Cubic capacity: 4482 cc/273.4 cu in
Bore × stroke: 93 mm × 110 mm/ 3.66 in × 4.33 in
Compression ratio: 6.5:1
Valve gear: 2 inclined valves per cylinder in hemispherical combustion chambers operated via short cross pushrods by twin block-mounted camshafts
Fuel supply: 3 Zenith Stromberg carburettors
Ignition: Mechanical by coil and distributor
Maximum power: 170 bhp at 4000 rpm

TRANSMISSION

Layout: Gearbox and clutch in unit with engine
Clutch: Single dry plate
Gearbox: Wilson preselector four-speed epicyclic
    1st 3.0:1   3rd: 1.29:1
    2nd 1.8:1   4th: 1.00:1
Final drive: Hypoid bevel
Ratio: 3.58:1

SUSPENSION

Front: Independent with double wishbones and coil springs
Rear: Live rear axle with semi-elliptic leaf springs. 2 hydraulic and 2 friction dampers

STEERING

Type: Worm and nut

BRAKES

Type: Lockheed hydraulic drums all round, 38 cm (14.9 in) diameter

WHEELS AND TYRES

Type: Rudge Whitworth 3.62 × 18 in wire wheels with 6.00 × 18 in tyres

BODY/CHASSIS

Type: Separate cruciform chassis underslung at rear with 2-door coachbuilt saloon body

DIMENSIONS AND WEIGHT

Length: Varied according to body style
Width: Varied according to body style
Wheelbase: 3125 mm (123.0 in)
Track front: 1420 mm (55.9 in)
    – rear: 1485 mm (58.4 in)
Weight (approx): 1700 kg (3740 lb)

PERFORMANCE

Maximum speed: 111 mph (178 kph)

This 1946 Talbot Lago Record features the optional triple-carburettor 4.5-litre engine from the Grand Sport

1947 Grand Sport and Record models introduced with the 4.5-litre straight six in what was basically the pre-war chassis. Cheaper Quinze Luxe models were produced with the 2.7-litre four cylinder or the 4.5-litre six with disc wheels

1950 Talbot Lago Bébé introduced with the 2.7-litre, three-bearing, four-cylinder engine from the Quinze Luxe tuned to produce 118 bhp. 1950 production of all cars totalled 433

1951 Total output for 1951 was 80 cars

1952 Talbot Lago range restyled

1955 2.5-litre GT introduced with the last new Talbot Lago engine. That was a 2.5-litre, five-bearing twin cam

1957 GT bodyshell powered by 2.8-litre BMW V8 in the Lago America built in very small numbers

1959 Talbot Lago taken over by Simca and the 2.5-litre GT was re-engined with Simca V8

1960 Antonio Lago died and Talbot Lago production ceased

EVOLUTION

1935 Antonio Lago took over Automobiles Talbot, producing new 2.7-litre and 3-litre tourers

1936 New 4-litre Lago Special introduced. This was popular with coachbuilders

MODEL
Tatra 77 (1934)

ENGINE
Location: Rear, longitudinal
Type: Air-cooled 90-degree V8 with alloy block and detachable cylinder heads
Cubic capacity: 2969 cc/181 cu in
Bore × stroke: 75 mm × 84 mm/ 2.95 in × 3.31 in
Compression ratio: 5.6:1
Valve gear: 2 overhead valves per cylinder operated by single overhead camshaft per bank of cylinders
Fuel supply: Single downdraught Solex carburettor. 12-gallon fuel tank at front of car
Ignition: Coil and distributor
Maximum power: 75 bhp at 3500 rpm
Maximum torque: 98 lb ft at 2400 rpm

TRANSMISSION
Layout: Gearbox and clutch in-unit with engine and rear axle
Clutch: Single dry plate
Gearbox: Four-speed manual with dog-clutch engagement of 2nd and synchromesh on 3rd and 4th
1st 4.70:1	3rd 1.56:1
2nd 2.95:1	4th 1.04:1

Final drive: Jointless drive by means of spur-wheel differential driving two concentric pinion shafts
Ratio: 3.15:1

SUSPENSION
Front: Independent with transverse leaf spring and twin-wishbone assemblies plus hydraulic dampers
Rear: Independent, with swinging half axles and transverse semi-elliptic leaf spring

STEERING
Type: Rack and pinion

WHEELS AND TYRES
Type: Pressed-steel 40.6 cm (16 in) wheels with 650 × 16 cross-ply tyres

BODY/CHASSIS
Type: Box-section steel chassis frame with central single tube backbone, with fork at rear to support engine and gearbox. Aerodynamic four-door six-seat saloon body

DIMENSIONS AND WEIGHT
Length: 540 cm (212.6 in)
Width: 167 cm (66 in)
Wheelbase: 315 cm (124 in)
Track – front: 125 cm (49 in)
– rear: 125 cm (49 in)
Weight: 1799 kg (3968 lb)

PERFORMANCE
Maximum speed: 90 mph (145 kph)
Acceleration 0–60 mph: 14 seconds

The truly cavernous interior of a Type 77 Tatra. Its huge wheelbase, coupled with the rear-mounted V8, meant that there was more than ample room for the passengers. Note the central spine chassis, one of the Tatra's main features, as is the swing-axle rear suspension with the upper transverse semi-elliptic leaf spring

EVOLUTION

1931 First rear-engined Tatra introduced

1933 Type 77 announced and introduced (in 1934) with a 3.4-litre overhead-valve V8 and independent suspension

1935 Type 77A introduced with 3.4-litre V8 engine; power output 70 bhp

1937 Types 87 and 97 introduced. The 87 was shorter than the 77 and featured quarter-elliptic springs at the rear rather than the transverse leaf of the 77. It was powered by a 3-litre V8. The 97 was a smaller saloon powered by a 1.7-litre flat four. Total 97 production only reached 500 before it was suppressed by the Germans

1946 Engine displacement of the 87 was reduced to 2.5 litres. Total production of the 77 amounted to just 255 but more than 3000 87s were built

There was nothing in the least pretentious about the TR3. Its simple chassis owed its robustness and rigidity solely to its bulk, the live rear axle was located only by its semi-elliptic leaf springs and the damping was by old-fashioned lever arm units. At least the front suspension, with its double wishbones, coil springs and telescopic dampers was more modern – there were even disc brakes at the front. Triumph had not aimed for sophistication, however, and the engine was a development of a rugged Standard unit as tough as the chassis. The result was a fast and cheap sports car, albeit one that demanded a certain respect from its driver

EVOLUTION

1952 Triumph 20TS prototype (retrospectively known as the TR1) introduced at the London Motor Show, an open two-seater fitted with a moderately tuned 75 bhp 2-litre Standard Vanguard engine

1953 TR2 unveiled at the Geneva Motor Show with redesigned and smoother body, a new box-section chassis frame and engine improved to produce 90 bhp

1954 TR2 hard-top version became available; modifications included larger drum brakes at the rear. Total TR2 production was 8628 units

1955 TR3 announced, with its engine further tuned to produce 95 bhp, Girling disc brakes fitted to the front wheels and an egg-box grille

1958 TR3A announced, fitted with full-width grille, and engine power was increased to 100 bhp

1961 TR3B built for the American market, fitted with the forthcoming TR4's all-synchromesh gearbox and a choice of 2- and 2.2-litre engines. TR3-TR3B production reached 83,500

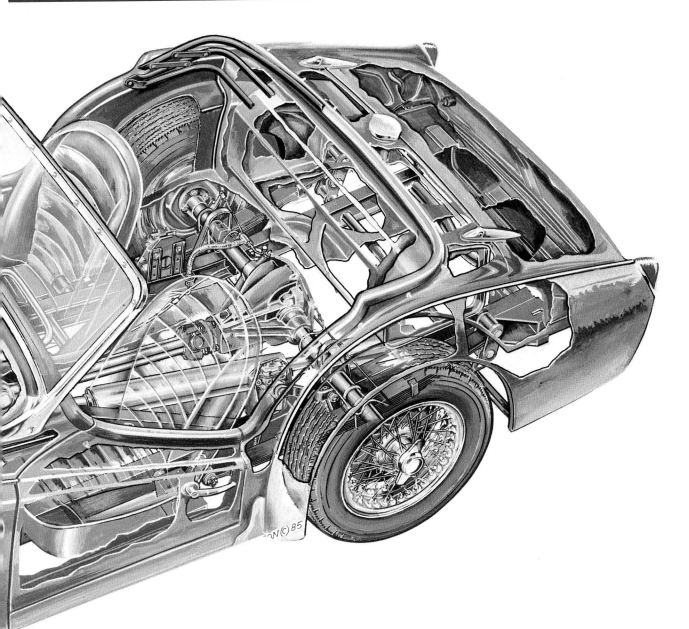

MODEL
Triumph TR3 (1957)

ENGINE
Location: Front, longitudinal
Type: Water-cooled in-line four with cast-iron block and head

Cubic capacity: 1991 cc/121.45 cu in
Bore × stroke: 83 mm × 92 mm/ 3.26 in × 3.62 in
Compression ratio: 8.5:1
Valve gear: Two valves per cylinder operated by single block-mounted camshaft, pushrods and rockers
Fuel supply: Two inclined SU H6 carburettors
Ignition: Coil and distributor, mechanical
Maximum power: 100 bhp at 5000 rpm
Maximum torque: 117 ft lb at 3000 rpm

TRANSMISSION
Layout: Clutch and gearbox in unit with engine, driving rear wheels
Clutch: Single dry plate, 23 cm (9 in) diameter
Gearbox: Four-speed manual gearbox with synchromesh and overdrive (ratios in brackets) on upper three gears

1st 3.38:1	3rd 1.32:1
2nd 2.00:1	(1.08:1)
(1.64:1)	4th 3.70:1
	(0.82:1)

Final drive: Hypoid bevel
Ratio: 3.7:1

SUSPENSION
Front: Independent, with coil and wishbones and telescopic dampers
Rear: Non-independent, with live axle, semi-elliptic leaf springs and piston-type hydraulic damper

STEERING
Type: Cam and lever

BRAKES
Type: Girling discs front, drums rear

WHEELS AND TYRES
Type: 15 in wire wheels and 5.50–15 tyres

BODY/CHASSIS
Type: Steel two-seat sports car (available as hardtop or convertible) built on box-section ladder-frame chassis

DIMENSIONS
Length: 3816 mm (150.25 in)
Width: 1435 mm (56.5 in)
Wheelbase: 2248 mm (88.5 in)
Track – front: 1181 mm (46.5 in)
– rear: 1168 mm (46 in)
Weight: 1003 kg (2212 lb)

PERFORMANCEE
Maximum speed: 110 mph (177 kph)
Acceleration 0–60 mph: 11.4 seconds

EVOLUTION

1954 The first real TVR appeared with Austin A40 running gear

1956 TVR chassis design revised as a steel tube backbone chassis was introduced, a style which became normal TVR practice

1967 Tuscan introduced with 4.7-litre (289 cu in) Ford V8. In standard tune it produced 200 bhp but the SE (Special Equipment) version had 271 bhp on tap. Vixen introduced, a development of the Mk III powered by a Ford Cortina GT engine

1968 Vixen became available with the Tuscan's long-wheelbase chassis

1969 Ford 3-litre (183 cu in) V6 engine was put into the Tuscan to form the Tuscan V6

1970 To meet American emission regulations, the 2.5-litre Triumph straight six was fitted in Tuscan chassis, as 2500

1972 M-series cars introduced with stronger chassis and more robust suspension. The nose of the car was lengthened to accommodate the spare wheel and the cars were available with various engine options – the 1.6-litre (98 cu in) or 3-litre (183 cu in) Fords or the Triumph 2.5-litre

1975 Broadspeed turbo conversion of the V6 introduced offering 218 bhp

1976 TVR's first hatchback design, the Taimar, introduced

1978 TVR Convertible, the last variation on the M-series, was introduced in normally aspirated or turbo V6 guise

MODEL
TVR Tuscan SE

ENGINE
Location: Front, longitudinal
Type: Water-cooled V8 with cast iron block and heads
Cubic capacity: 4727 cc/289 cu in
Bore × stroke: 101.6 mm × 72.9 mm/3.99 in × 2.87 in
Compression ratio: 11:1
Valve gear: 2 valves per cylinder operated via pushrods and rockers by single camshaft mounted in centre of vee
Fuel supply: Single Ford four-barrel carburettor
Ignition: Mechanical by coil and distributor
Maximum power: 271 bhp (SAE gross) at 6000 rpm
Maximum torque: 314 lb ft (SAE gross) at 3400 rpm

TRANSMISSION
Layout: Gearbox in unit with engine
Clutch: 16.9 cm (10.5 in) single dry plate
Gearbox: Four-speed manual
1st 2.36:1	3rd 1.41:1
2nd 1.78:1	4th 1.00:1

Final drive: Hypoid bevel with limited-slip differential
Ratio: 3.07:1

SUSPENSION
Front: Independent with double wishbones, coil springs, telescopic dampers and anti-roll bar
Rear: Independent with double wishbones, four coil springs, four telescopic dampers and anti-roll bar

STEERING
Type: Rack and pinion. 3.5 turns lock to lock

BRAKES
Type: Discs front and drums rear. Servo-assisted. 276 mm (10.85 in) diameter front

WHEELS AND TYRES
Type: Wire spoked wheels 6L × 15 with Dunlop 185 15 SP41 tyres

BODY/CHASSIS
Type: Multi-tubular steel backbone chassis with 2-door glassfibre coupé body bonded in place

DIMENSIONS AND WEIGHT
Length: 3683 mm (145 in)
Width: 1626 mm (64 in)
Wheelbase: 2286 mm (90 in)
Track – front: 1346 mm (53 in)
– rear: 1372 mm (54 in)
Weight: 1219 kg (2688 lb)

PERFORMANCE
Maximum speed: 155 mph (250 kph)
Acceleration 0-60 mph: 5.7 seconds

The Tuscan's construction followed the TVR tradition with a tall, strong central backbone to the tubular chassis: it had to be very rigid in order to cope with the high torque of the 4.7-litre V8. The suspension gave good roadholding characteristics, although in a short-wheelbase car with a very heavy engine the handling could be tricky in the wet. The car's performance was phenomenal by any standards, for the Special Equipment Tuscan could out-accelerate the contemporary E-type Jaguar, Aston Martin DB6, Ford Mustang and Corvette Sting Ray – it was a true supercar, although TVR lacked the cachet of the established makers of exotica

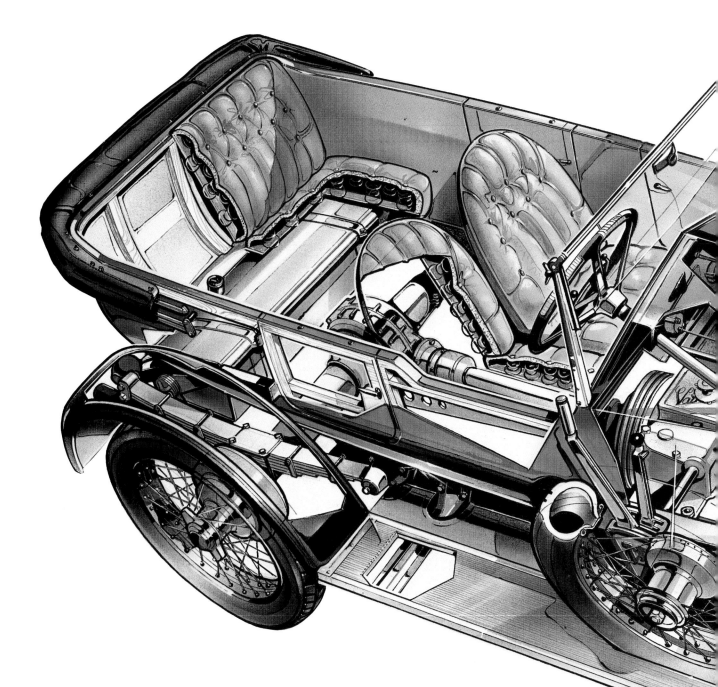

MODEL
Vauxhall 30/98 OE Type (1923)

ENGINE
Location: Front, longitudinal
Type: Water-cooled in-line four-cylinder, monobloc with detachable head and five-bearing crankshaft
Cubic capacity: 4224 cc/257.6 cu in
Bore × stroke: 98 mm × 140 mm/ 3.86 in × 5.51 in
Compression ratio: 5:1
Valve gear: Two overhead valves per cylinder operated by pushrods and three-bearing camshaft
Fuel supply: One Zenith 48RA carburettor. Pressure feed from petrol tank until 1925, and Autovac fitted thereafter
Ignition: Magneto
Maximum power: 115 bhp at 3300 rpm

TRANSMISSION
Layout: Clutch and gearbox in-unit with engine driving rear wheels
Clutch: Vauxhall multi-plate
Gearbox: Four-speed manual without synchromesh

1st 3.69:1	3rd 1.54:1
2nd 2.36:1	4th 1.00:1

Final drive: Spiral bevel
Ratio: 3.3:1

SUSPENSION
Front: Non-independent with beam axle, semi-elliptic leaf springs and Hartford adjustable friction dampers
Rear: Non-independent with live axle, semi-elliptic leaf springs and Hartford adjustable friction dampers

STEERING
Type: Worm and wheel

BRAKES
Type: Cable-operated drums all round plus transmission brake

WHEELS AND TYRES
Type: 820 × 120 BE Rudge-Whitworth centre-lock wire wheels with 81 cm (32 in) diameter tyres

BODY/CHASSIS
Type: Pressed steel separate chassis with two outer longitudinal beams and cross members and subframe to support engine and gearbox. Two- or four-seat coachbuilt bodies; standard fitment was the works-built Velox four-seat open tourer

DIMENSIONS AND WEIGHT
Length: 4165 mm (164 in)
Width: 1676 mm (66 in)
Wheelbase: 2972 mm (117 in)
Track – front: 1372 mm (54 in)
– rear: 1372 mm (54 in)
Weight: 1473 kg (3248 lb)

PERFORMANCE
Maximum speed: 85 mph (137 kph)
Acceleration 0–60 mph: 20 seconds

EVOLUTION

1913 Prototype 30/98 appeared

1919 Vauxhall 30/98 E Type sports tourer introduced with 5425 cc (331 cu in) 90 bhp four-cylinder engine. Top speed with Velox four-seat open tourer body was 85 mph (137 kph). Total production: 274

1923 30/98 OE Type announced with overhead-valve 4224 cc (257.6 cu in) engine. Towards the end of the year four-wheel braking introduced

1925 Engine further improved and power output increased to 120 bhp at 3500 rpm

1926 Hydraulic brakes introduced

1927 30/98 discontinued. Total production (OE Type) 312

As this cutaway shows, the 30/98 OE was quite simple with conventional semi-elliptic leaf spring suspension and an overhead-valve engine; it was its superb engineering that made the car so great

MODEL
Volkswagen Beetle 1300 (1970)

ENGINE
Location: Rear, longitudinal
Type: Air-cooled horizontally-opposed four cylinder with aluminium cylinder blocks, cast-iron liners and alloy cylinder heads. Four main bearings
Cubic capacity: 1285 cc/78.38 cu in
Bore × stroke: 77 mm × 69 mm/ 3.03 in × 2.72 in
Compression ratio: 7.3:1
Valve gear: 2 valves per cylinder operated by pushrods from one central camshaft
Fuel supply: 1 Solex downdraught single-choke carburettor
Ignition: Mechanical by coil and distributor
Maximum power: 44 bhp DIN at 4100 rpm
Maximum torque: 69 lb ft (SAE) at 2600 rpm

TRANSMISSION
Layout: Gearbox in front of engine driving rear wheels
Clutch: Single dry plate
Gearbox: Four-speed manual
1st 3.800:1 3rd 1.260:1
2nd 2.060:1 4th 0.890:
Final drive: Spiral bevel
Ratio: 4.375:1

SUSPENSION
Front: Independent twin trailing arms with transverse laminated torsion bars, anti-roll bar and telescopic dampers.
Rear: Independent swinging semi-axles with trailing arms, transverse torsion bars and telescopic dampers

STEERING
Type: Worm and roller. 2.6 turns lock to lock

BRAKES
Type: Drums all round

WHEELS AND TYRES
Type: Steel perforated wheels with 5,60 × 15 in tyres

BODY/CHASSIS
Type: Backbone platform and integral bodyshell. 2-door, 4-seat saloon

DIMENSIONS AND WEIGHT
Length: 407 cm (160 in)
Width: 155 cm (61 in)
Wheelbase: 240 cm (94.50 in)
Track – front: 131 cm (51.57 in)
– rear: 135 cm (53.15 in)
Weight: 760 kg (1676 lb)

PERFORMANCE
Maximum speed: 75 mph (120 kph)
Acceleration 0-50 mph: 14 seconds

Although the car was much modernised over the years, the basic, distinctive shape and the flat four air-cooled engine of the legendary Beetle always remained. Torsion bar suspension all round allowed separation of chassis and bodyshell without disturbing any of the running gear; the Beetle chassis has proved to be the most widely used base for kit cars for this reason

Picture Credits

James Allington: 94–95, 128–130, 164–165, 176–177, 218–219, 280–281 Audi AG: 108–109 Autocar/Quadrant Picture Library: 198–199 Paul Bambrick: 116–117, 212–213, 246–247, 286–287 Jerry Banks/Ferrari: 170–171 Laurie Caddell: 4–5 J. Crees: 194–195 CW Editorial Ltd: 78–79 Terry Davey: 282–283 Martin Donovan: 104–105, 206–207, 214–215 Roger Farrington: 134–135, 248–249 Ford Motor Company: 172–173, 177 Keith Fretwell: 204–205 Keith Fretwell/Karl Ludvigsen Picture Library: 240–241 General Motors: 136–137 Geoff Goddard: 84 Jeremy Gower: 92–93, 138–139, 148–149, 244–245, 266–267, 278–279 Keith Harmer: 112–113 Roy Haynes: 110–111, 122–123, 202–203, 230–231, 284–285 David Hodges: 6–7 Inkwell Studios: 98–100, 102–103, 118–119, 126–127, 132–133, 144–145, 152–153, 156–157, 178–179, 182–184, 186–187, 188–189, 200–201, 222–223, 228–229, 232–233, 242–243, 254–255, 258–259, 268–269, 276–277 Jaguar: 231 Dave Kennard/CW: 2–3 Caarl Knowles: 180–181, 220–221 John Lawson: 168–169, 256–257 London Art Tech: 84–85 Tony Matthews: 106–107, 114–115, 162–163, 192–193, 236–238 Brian Mayor: 196–197 Danny Mercer: 80–81, 154–155, 160–161 National Motor Museum: 76–77, 86–87, 99, 123 Orbis Publishing: 270–271 Cyril Posthumus: 85 Quadrant Picture Library: 150–151 Quattroruote: 90–91, 140–141, 142–143, 174–175, 208–209, 210–211, 224–225, 226–227, 234–235 Paul Shakespeare: 88–89, 146–147, 158–159, 190–191, 250–251, 274–275 Les Shaw: 272–273 Technical Art: 120–121, 262–263, 264–265 Grose Thurston: 260–261 Tony Townsend: 82–83, 216–217